D1128891

00700

THE POLITICAL AUTHORITY AND THE MARKET SYSTEM

ROBERT A. SOLO

Professor of Economics and Management
Michigan State University

H12

Published by

SOUTH-WESTERN PUBLISHING CO.

CINCINNATI   WEST CHICAGO, ILL.   DALLAS   PELHAM MANOR, N.Y.
PALO ALTO, CALIF.   BRIGHTON, ENGLAND

Copyright © 1974
Philippine Copyright 1974

By South-Western Publishing Co.
Cincinnati, Ohio

ALL RIGHTS RESERVED

The text of this publication, or any part thereof, may not be reproduced
or transmitted in any form or by any means, electronic or mechanical,
including photocopying, recording, storage in an information retrieval
system, or otherwise, without the prior written permission of the
publisher.

ISBN: 0-538-08120-1

Library of Congress Catalog Card Number: 73-75260

1234567D0987654

Printed in the United States of America

PREFACE

This book falls into three parts. First, a theory of social change is proposed. Second, in the light of that theory, the changes in the organization and function of the political authority in the United States, are described and explained from the early days of the Republic until today. Third, having traced the path by which we have come to where we are, the present functions of the political authority are analyzed, current policies are evaluated, and reforms are proposed. This preface, however, has to do only with the first part of the book, the theory of social change.

At the heart of science there is that which is not research but reflection. The theory that will be proposed here is not a product of research but of reflection, the reflections upon the experience of a lifetime. Why not? For social science surely the ultimate laboratory is society where, for the observant eye, every event can be a test, an experiment, a clue, a revelation. I have lived in a time of social disintegration, or at least of a rapid transition toward something other than we know. What undercurrents are dragging us so swiftly? And what is our destination? What should be done? In trying to understand this phenomenon of social change in our time, the conceptual apparatus of economics was no help, nor could I find my answers in the analytic approaches of the other social sciences. So I stood outside the disciplines, and drawing upon the experience, encounters, and learning of a lifetime, tried to think the matter through. There nevertheless remains the obligation to account for the genesis of the theory, and especially to indicate its links to the thought of others. This I will try to do by retracing the path to its formulation.

About the nature of the theory, this much at least must now be said. Its emphasis is on *ideology*; and by ideology is meant any set of ideas as to what is and ought to be with respect to some field of choice and action. Ideology is the complex of images that interface experienced event and observed phenomena on the one side and evaluation, reflection, decision, and choice on the other. It is the cultural heritage, inculcated and learned, that mediates between the self and the world. In it every individual finds his identity and every group its cohesion. It is the rationale of commitment, a source of motivation, criterion, and guide to behavior. Received out of the past and shaped by the experiences of former generations in ages long vanished, eroded, and rendered hollow by time and tide, vaporous, incomplete, and more or less false, these ideologies and the process by which they are formed, deformed, and reformed will be taken as the key to the understanding of social change.

How did I come to this notion? Certainly it would have been rejected by the economist I was, graduating from Harvard in 1938. That young man very soon learned that the hard-nosed positivism, the mechanistic utilitarianism, and the analytic concepts with which he was professionally equipped, served him not at all in his effort to understand or act upon the world of his direct experience: the Europe of Munich, the work with a "brain trust" in New Deal Washington, then with the war government, and finally himself adrift in the tides and currents of war. Demobilized, I rode the GI Bill back to academic life, and it would seem in retrospect that ever since then I have been developing, on the trail and off again, the relationships of ideology to behavior. From 1946 until 1949 I was enrolled at the London School of Economics. During those years I wrote a big novel that mingled fiction and social commentary, and a huge essay intended as a doctoral dissertation. Both the novel and the dissertation were abortive, but both were concerned with the relationship between behavior and ideology. The dissertation argued, among other things, that the methods of physics, i.e., of classical "science" are not appropriate for economics, in part because social behavior is a function of ideologies and images, created out of nothing and vanishing absolutely, hence inherently, outside the domain of scientific law and prediction; and that economic motivation must be understood in relation to the multiplicity of roles played by each individual where every role has a particular ideological content. As for the novel, the only part that was ever published is a translation of a chapter appearing as a small book in French, titled *Essai sur l'Amerique*, which describes the ideology underlying social behavior in the United States.

Occasionally in the years that followed, my thoughts on the matter of ideology and behavior were nurtured by encounters with the works of others. Certainly this was true with Kenneth Boulding's wonderful little book *The Image*, that unrolls with felicity and beauty the skein of imagery to the outer reaches of an individual's universe of contemplation and action. It happened too in a remarkable series of lectures given (I believe) in 1954 by the late Professor Eric Kahler at Princeton. In the study of modern poetry, art, and literature, Professor Kahler found evidence of a basic change in the prevailing image of the universe, or more fundamentally in the way in which man creates that image. No longer was man himself the center or the measure. No longer was the world conceived from the perspective of the individual, in his dimensions and in terms proper to his competence and experience qua individual. Gone was the presumption, born of the Renaissance, that the self-contained and independent man was the natural foci of artistic interest, with the sounds of the world to be heard through his ears, its meanings spoken with his voice, and its visions seen from his eye level. In 1955–56 while I was teaching at McGill University in Montreal, I encountered Herbert Butterfield's extraordinary work, *The Origins of Modern Science*. Butterfield demolishes the classical rationalization of science as a systematic search for objective fact—very much like searching for seashells on the seashore. First the biggest and the most exposed are taken away, since these are the easiest to find. And cumulatively as the beach is emptied, the search becomes more and more difficult. Some of the searchers have more energy and better eyesight than the others, and they bring in shells more quickly than the rest. But according to this view of things, if those searchers hadn't found them first, then others would surely find them later, for with time and diligence all that there is must eventually be found. In opposition to this concept, Butterfield shows that the first modern scientific revolution, culminating with Newton, came not at all through diligent researchers discovering new facts and producing better information, but rather through the abandonment and collapse of a great and once solid image of the universe that had withstood the assaults of experience and had served to explain phenomena for more than a thousand years. It came about because "men changed their thinking caps." In line with Butterfield, Thomas Kuhn's book *The Structure of Scientific Revolutions* decisively refutes the classical concept of scientific endeavor and that image of science associated with the work of Karl Popper as a body of laws unrefuted by observation or experiment. Kuhn contrasts *normal* and *revolutionary* science. In normal science research is done and information is produced within the frame of an ideological complex that Kuhn calls a "paradigm." For each discipline the prevailing paradigm embodies a certain matrix of relationships falling within and consistent with a larger image of physical reality, a set of normative experiments, an accepted form of discourse and approved directions of inquiry. Disregarding the anomalies and contradictions that are always there, nearly all scientists nearly all of the time work contentedly in that framework, and the whole thrust of scientific authority is to preserve and to propagate the paradigm. Very rarely, and always against the bitter resistance of the established scientific authority, the paradigm is shattered and is replaced by another. It is the paradigm-shattering phase that produces the fundamental advances in science. The process of scientific revolution then is conceived as a contestation of ideologies, each with its proper rationale, its imperfections, its inherent contradictions, and its limits.

Kuhn's thesis leaves many questions unanswered. Granted that there are these occasional scientific revolutions, what are the forces that bring them about? Why has academic research in the United States produced vast reams of normal science, but no scientific revolutions? How might scientific policy and the system for the public support of science be redesigned to promote scientific revolution? And why is it that scientific revolutions in the different disciplines of science — and also cultural, artistic, and social revolutions — seem to occur not singly but in tandem, reflecting a common impetus and having fundamentally similar characters? In 1965–66, when we were colleagues at Princeton, I asked Kuhn those questions. At the time he had no answers, and no interest in the questions either.

During 1967–68 the work of Erik Erikson clued me in to the relationships between the needs and drives of the psychic system in its process of development, and ideological change and the transformation of the social system.

In France in the summer of 1970, I gave a seminar to a small group at the Institut de Recherche Economique et Planification at the University of Grenoble. The subject of the seminar was "The Theory of Social Change." One of my audience called me a "structuralist," which led me to try to read some of those associated with that continental school: Jean Piaget, Claude Levi-Straus, Jean Foucault. Foucault demonstrates with an enormous erudition, that revolutionary but fundamentally identical changes have occurred periodically and simultaneously over a range of natural and social sciences. This he attributes to the displacement and replacement of an underlying and universal imagery that he calls an épistime. It is the épistime, i.e., the prevailing way of seeing and knowing, that forms the sciences and defines the period.

There are many others whom I have read about but have not read whose interests and inquiries seem sometimes to have been parallel to mine: Vico in deducing the fundamental imageries, éspistimes of ages past, from the form and structure of the language; Kant in postulating the a priori as an essential constituent of observation and thought; Durkheim in emphasizing the role of myth as a determinant of social behavior; Hegel, for whom the spirit of any people was their Idea (and surely, Idea, hence spirit, may be understood as the prevailing ideology), embodied in their institutions, their law, and the policies of their state. History was understood by him as the confrontation and consequent (dialectical) transformation of ideologies through the confrontation of the societies in whom those ideologies were embodied.

So much for the genesis of the theory and some of its links to the work of others.

Robert A. Solo

CONTENTS

Chapter 1

Ideology
and Social Change:
An Introduction

In great part this book, which is about the relationship between the political authority and the market economy in the United States (i.e., about the relationship between government and business), will deal with concrete and practical matters such as the Supreme Court's interpretations of the Constitution, government policies and practices, and market institutions as these have been formed and changed through the nearly two centuries of American experience. Underlying all this is a theory of social change. This first chapter will try to make the theory explicit.

It is a theory that turns on the notion of "ideology." This is a term that has been variously used with connotations that are not intended here. It is important, therefore, to make its meaning clear from the start.

IDEOLOGY AND THE INDIVIDUAL

Ideology is any set of the individual's ideas concerning what is (what exists, what is there, how things work) and what should be (what should not be, what is better, what is worse) with respect to a field of choice and action. Ideology is the individual's notion of what should be done, framed necessarily within his conception of what is possible. Without an ideology suited to the problem or question at issue, there can be no coherent choice or purposeful action. Without an ideology

1

suited to the problem or question at issue, the individual can only move blindly, act intuitively, imitate, or obey. Nor is the need for *an* ideology singular, no more than there is a single field of choice and action. With respect to home, family, neighbors, and strangers; with respect to career, profession, business, employer, employees, clients, customers, creditors, and competitors; with respect to religion, religions, church, and churches; with respect to nation, nations, government, party, politics, and politicians, the individual may act and react, positively or in imagination. And for any and each of these fields of choice and action, a different and distinct set of ideas and values may be brought to bear. Hence, as a working instrument of the mind, ideology is not singular but plural. Choice and action operate by reference to an ideological complex, or to a cluster of ideologies.

The following might be said, as a constituent of the mind about that ideological cluster:

1. Its scope is always limited, as is the individual's capacity to choose and to act in the light of a clear purpose and a coherent conception.

2. Given their diversity, the ideologies of the cluster need not be harmonious, congruous, or rationally compatible. Implicit values and their logical consequences that overlap spheres of choice and decision may be, and frequently are, wholly in contradiction. Whether and when such contradiction will cause discomfort is a moot point.

3. There is a mechanism, nevertheless, operating slowly and imperfectly withal, for bringing the ideologies of the individual toward a condition of congruence and rational consistency. Contradictions must sometimes be resolved in the specifics of choice. This choosing between opposing values or conceptions that intersect at the margin of decision can bring the fact of contradiction to the surface of consciousness, but that awareness of contradiction neither requires nor will necessarily bring about a reformulation of images — no more than an awareness of anomalies in science requires or necessarily brings about the reformulation of scientific theory. Yet the awareness of contradictions, like the cumulation of anomalies, is presumed to have an effect, for there are some personalities blessed or cursed with a need for intellectual and moral integrity for whom the self-knowledge of anomaly or of ideological contradiction produces a tension and anguish that generates the energy to resolve such contradictions and

incongruities. These are the sort who produce scientific revolutions and ideological transformations.[1]

4. Rather than of an ideological cluster, a more useful image might be of ideological layers, skins of the onion, further from or closer to the reach of direct individual experience. Perhaps no ideology is wholly the product of an individual's experience, nor are any wholly reachable by and, so to speak, subject to the test of direct individual experience. But certainly there are very great differences in the degree to which the diverse images held by the mind are removed from or are within reach of individual sensation, observation, and volition. What am I? In what do I find myself? A thought? A set of hungers, ambitions, and lusts? A creature with stomach, brain, and genitals? An ego floating on the libidinous dark sea of the Id? A satisfaction-maximizing machine? A philosopher, economist, teacher? A husband, a father? An American, a citizen? A link in an infinite system of life and evolution? A child of God? And every one of these images carries with it a complex, even a boundless, universe of ideas and values. One image transcends the other, some nearer, some further from the reach of sensation, observation, and personal volition. Commitment and the sense of identity shift from layer to layer, depending on the matter at issue, on the state of the faith, and on the commitment to, and the acceptability of, authority and that which has been handed down and given from the outside.

5. Perforce we have spoken of ideologies as though they were completed objects, with a beginning and an end, like reference books to be pulled down from the shelves with the answers already inscribed, or like pictures filed in cabinets of memory retrieved as by a mental computer for the occasion. That is not the case at all. Ideology is not an image or a set of images, but an image-forming, judgmental process, a choice-making, problem-solving capability.

Let the mind respond to the signal of a word — war, peace, son, daughter, woman, man, marriage, divorce, conception, abortion, poor, rich, trade union, welfare state,

---

[1]In contrasting scientific theory with ideology and the process of scientific change with the process of ideological change as though these were separate and distinct, I yield to a convention which is, in fact, false. All scientific activity is ideologically based. The scientific commitment, the choice of the problems, and the selection of areas of research in the frame of an accepted conception of the nature of phenomena and of accepted criteria of evaluation are all expressions of an ideology. And the paradigm-shattering changes that Thomas Kuhn called "scientific revolutions" are a species of ideological transformation.

fascism, communism, France, Germany, India. The mind dwelling upon that word, reflecting upon it, rolls out a stream of images that fill imagined space and time in a process that can combine memories, fantasies, conceptions of existential reality, and values; and that can produce judgments, evaluations, questions and answers to questions, and problems and their solutions. Images of an infinite variety and novelty flow into new and unexplored terrain. This process and capability is not unconstrained. It operates from a basis of preconceived relationships and implanted nuclear imageries. It is these, together with certain psychic proclivities, that give a particular character to the flow of thought and to the patterns of choice, and that constitute the elements of the ideological cluster.

IDEOLOGY AND SOCIETY

The ideological cluster is a necessary working instrument of the individual mind, but the ideologies of the cluster are not normally an individual creation. They are the product of society, received by individuals through acculturation, education, indoctrination, and all else that denotes the transmission of ideas and images from person to person and from generation to generation; hence, the perpetuation and propagation of ideas and images. The following might be said about the social function of ideologies.

1. Ideology conveys legitimacy and status. Ideology determines commitment. "Commitment to" and "identification with" are ideological conditions. Priorities, loyalties, and patterns of behavior are functions of the ideological cluster.
2. Prerequisite to the general acceptability and support of institutions—i.e., the congruous behavior of those who participate together in complex endeavors and in the commitments and loyalties necessary for effective collective action—are ideologies that must be held in common. Hence, the effective operation of any complex of systems integrating the activities of numerous individuals in the performance of diverse social functions (i.e., the effective operation of any *society*) requires that ideologies be shared or be congruent. For the survival of a society, it is categorically imperative that ideologies be held in common; and hence, that social institutions protect and propagate

supportive ideologies and, conversely, that they resist ideological deviation and oppose ideological change.

3. A "prevailing ideology" will denote an ideology (or ideological set or cluster) that is generally accepted by those who participate in that complex of functional systems called a *society*. This is not to suppose that all those who accept the prevailing ideology think in the same way, but that their outlooks and values and their reference imageries are commensurable. Differences there will be, as variations on a theme or as deviations from the norm. Such deviations and variations may be important; they are the normal center of political controversy under conditions of social equilibrium. It is not necessary that everyone — or even most of those who participate in the social functions — *believe* in that ideology in order that it continue to prevail, so long as they accept it as the operational basis for choice and interaction. And indeed, once the ideology has been established and embodied in institutions and fixed in behavioral patterns, it is very difficult for any individual (hence, for the sum of individuals qua individuals) to do otherwise than to accept it as the operational basis for choice and interaction. This is true for two reasons.

   a. Faced with an ideology that is fixed in behavioral patterns and established in the organization of institutions, the individual (and hence, the sum of individuals) can either "go along" or "drop out" into solitude and nullity. In dropping out the individual may affect the efficacy of the system, but by that act he does not change it. And in conforming he gives force to and perpetuates an ideological understructure in which he has ceased to believe.

   b. An ideology that once prevails is made manifest in policies, in behavioral patterns, and in institutions — institutions such as the Army, the State Department, the Church, and the University. Such an institution — through the manner and means of renewing itself in recruitment, training, and indoctrination; through the precedents that it accumulates; through the inertia of practice; and through the self-interest of its participants in protecting their status and in preserving the value of their skills — must continue to express the founding image and to act out the ideology around which it was created, long after that ideology has lost its hold on the minds of men and its force in the social system. Thus, ideological strongholds, the temples of old gods and forgotten images, remain. Encased in institutions, old ideologies never die and only very slowly fade away.

4. A given society may be characterized not by a prevailing ideology but by numerous and diverse ideological sets, each established and having an institutional embodiment and finding their modus vivendi in the relationship of domination and subordination, in the demarcation of role and function, or in the counterbalancing of forces.

5. Expectation and self-expectation are functions of ideology. And where ideologies are not congruent, action, inter-action, and expectation cannot mesh. There will be "mis-understanding" and, as a consequence, tension, frustration, and possibly conflict. Such is the case with individuals within a society and also in the relations between societies where different ideologies prevail.

IDEOLOGY AND SOCIAL CHANGE

The ancient philosopher, contemplating a river, saw that everything was perpetually changing and nothing changed. No droplet remained what it had been, where it had been, or as it had been for an instant. Wavelets and currents were perpetually moving in patterns that varied infinitely. Yet the flow was continuous. The course of the river was the same. Its cycle of renewal was unbroken. The *system* did not change. In all this continuous movement in the frame of recurrent forms, the philosopher saw *flux* but no change.

So it may be in a society. Politicians are elected or rejected. One party comes in and another goes out, but the political process remains. Competitors compete; goods are bought and sold. Income generates expenditure and expenditure generates income. X gets rich and Y becomes poor. But the market process remains. Its institutional structure remains. Its distributional mode remains. Its power arrangements remain. There is flux without change.

It is not flux, but change, that concerns us — change in the institutional structure, change in the nature of power, and change in the system and its objectives. What can bring about such change?

If ideology provides the blueprint for individual behavior, for institutional organization, and for social policy, it follows that a change in the ideology that prevails or that dominates can bring about a change in all that constitutes the social system. Question: Can there be social change without the impetus of ideological change? Surely so. Exogenous forces, war and conquest, or technological infiltration can upset all the ideological applecarts. And change may come from within society without ideological forewarning or intent. There is a chain of cause and consequence in social event whose effects go beyond all pre-conceptualization. More and more automobiles are produced and sold and used—and the cities are choked and poisoned. Entrepreneurs compete. Firms produce, make profits, grow, and grow, and grow until their scale transcends the scope of entrepreneurial control; the old role and significance of property disappears and business entities become of another quality and character. The atomic bomb is invented in a war between nations for the purposes of national power and security and, as a consequence, the securities of nationhood and the rationale of the nation-state vanish. Thus, situations are created, beneficent or malignant, that are inexplicable in the frame of prevailing conception. Sometimes the captains encounter perils unmarked on their navigational charts. And then they twist and dodge, acting instinctively, adaptively, escaping threats, yielding to pressures, riding with the wind, seeking inch by inch a path of survival, but always in ignorance of cause and effect and without an idea of destination. Such choice is pragmatic, and though it is outside the scope of ideological intent or of any rational strategy or coherent conceptualization, it may be revolutionary in its consequences.

Policy is often the product of social drift. Expressing no ideological intent, it emerges, it "happens," brought about through a great number of discrete decisions, interests, purposes, and pressures that coalesce and counterbalance. Policy formation of this order will be called here "composite choice." The chapters that follow will have much to say concerning it.

This drift of event and policy can produce problems outside the scope of ideological conceptualization and social change without the intermediary of ideological intent. But if and when ideological change does not produce social change, it surely must follow it. For when the social system changes and ideology lags, then the widened gap between ideology and experience must erode the faith in the prevailing imageries. If the social system changes and ideology lags, then choice stumbles and fails. The inoperability of accepted principles or the seeming incongruities and incertitudes of the policies of pragmatic choice set in train the search for another outlook and a new set of imageries that can make sense of things. And if this brings about an ideological transformation, the ideology that then prevails becomes itself a new and autonomous force. Given the ideological transformation, and only then, can social change be goal-directed as a matter of conscious intent or can institutions find a coherent form.

Thus, ideological change can follow in the wake of social changes that have been brought about through chance and drift. But ideology can as well evolve autonomously and become the initiator, the spearhead of social change. Individuals learn; and through their learning, through the common lessons of experience, and through the ceaseless accumulation of information, societies learn. Learning changes values, criteria of evaluation, intellectual horizons, the sense of the possible, and expectations, all with the effect of making ideas and imageries that were once sufficient and workable no longer so.

Marx's Theory of Social Change

A number of sociologists have written about social change. It usually suffices for them to postulate stages of development — i.e., growth, maturation, and decline — or to claim to have identified some recurring pattern in the panorama of history.[2] But so far as I know, only Karl Marx has developed a coherent theory explaining this phenomenon, understood as a process, with cause and effect specified and the logic of their interaction made explicit.

It is not my intention to refute Marx's great work. He postulates one viable path of social change. It can happen as Marx said it would, and, I will hold, it can happen in other ways as well. I will try to show the Marxian model as one case in a larger genre; and in generalizing beyond Marx, to develop an analysis that is relevant and useful in understanding the course of social change in our time.

---

[2]For a survey of these theories, see Robert A. Nisbet, *Social Change in History: Aspects of the Western Theory of Development* (New York: Oxford University Press, 1969) and Richard Appelbaum, *Theories of Social Change* (Chicago: Markham Publishing Company, 1970).

In the first instance Marx's theory of social change will be briefly restated using the concepts and the terminology already developed in this chapter so that, hopefully, the reader can more easily locate the approach by reference to a set of ideas and concepts with which he is already familiar. Subsequently, referring back to Marxian theory, my arguments will be further developed.

Marx starts with social organization and the prevailing ideology in a state of equilibrium. The social organization is the system for the most effective and efficient exploitation of the existing technological potential and ideology is the blueprint for policy and behavior. Marx then introduces exogenous change in the development of technology, and endogenous social drift, e.g., the growth of the proletariat, the saturation of markets, and the maturation of capitalism. The effect of these is at once to create a new technological potential and to produce problems and crises not to be comprehended within the conceptual framework of the prevailing ideology nor resolvable through the operations of the social system rooted in and rationalized by that ideology.

In the face of unresolved crisis on the one hand and an unexploitable technological potential on the other a new blueprint for social action develops; i.e., an alternative ideology confronts that which once universally prevailed. Society now splits into ideologically-opposed groups. Those most advantaged by the retention of the existing system (the ruling class) hold fast to the once prevailing and now dominant ideology. Those who would benefit most from its installation (the revolutionary class) learn to appreciate the opposing blueprint for social organization, and rally in support of the new, still subordinated ideology. Policy failures and crises, and the evident incapacity to realize upon the technological potential, erode the faith in and the commitment to the dominant ideology, and all the forces of social drift serve to increase the strength of the revolutionary class. Eventually they take control of the political authority and from that position of power, install their own blueprint for social organization.

Marxian theory fairly well describes the sequence that transformed feudal agrarian Europe into the industrial capitalisms of the 19th Century. There has been no repeat of that sequence and, in that sense, the Marxian prognosis has failed. It is certainly very often true that important or fundamental change in the system of social organization has been preceded by a prior change in "material," "objective" circumstances, and that the former was ushered in under the pressure of cataclysmic event. But what has happened most often (I am tempted to say always) is that the effect of exogenous change in objective circumstances and the cataclysmic crisis it produced has been to shatter the cohesive and resistant force of an established ideology and to open the field for pragmatic experiment and maneuver, as well as for ideological reformulations and contestations without a priori limit on the ideological forms that might emerge or on the blueprint for policy and social organization that might eventually be installed. The terrible stress and catastrophic defeat of World War I collapsed the profound commitment to the Tsarist State in Russia. A century of policy failure, defeat in war, and decline dissolved the ideological force that gave form and cohesion to ancient China. Complete defeat in war and the American period of tutelage opened the paths of change in Japan. The Great Depression broke the back of ideological liberalism in the United States and in Western Europe. And in every case the ideological breakdown was followed by pragmatic groping and ideological contestation. Of the ideologies that were eventually installed (and indeed, who can yet say what they are or would have been) — the Communism of Lenin, of Stalin, of Khrushchev, of Tito, and of Mao; the New Catholicism; the Fascism of Hitler, of Petain, of Mussolini, of Salizar, of Franco; the New Dealism; the New Frontierism; the Welfarism; the Planificationism — it can only be said that their variations are very great and that the form in which they emerged cannot be accounted for by any universal law. Nor can it be denied that ideologies themselves — Marxism, Leninism, Maoism, Gandhism, and above all, Nationalism — have exerted and continue to exert a powerful autonomous force in the shaping of event. Ideology has been formed, and thereby policy and practice has changed, through the process of social learning. How else can one account for the transcending of ancient prejudices and institutionalized hatreds toward the economic unification of Europe, or for the radical transformation in the status of the blacks in the United States, or for the collapse of colonialism throughout the world?

The Class War

Central to the Marxist mode of conceptualization is the image of the class war. The classes, defined by their respective status and function in a system of economic organization, are seen as engaged in a remorseless struggle for power and dominance. Class, in this image, is a faceless force. Personalities have no role or relevance. Private self-interest is submerged in an identification with the group and in a conception of the interests of the group. Class is, in fact, an ideology made manifest and class warfare is a struggle between opposing ideologies.

Class, then, has this function. It gives force to an idea. It provides the energy source for ideologies in conflict. And Marx is right. The idea must find its source of force and energy before it can be realized in policy and practice. But is class interest the only or the necessary energy source for ideological replacement and social transformation?

One thing is certain. Ideologies do not emerge full-born, nor does a class, or any other group of individuals united by a common self-image and a shared ideological commitment, step fully armed from Minerva's brow. Ideology is not given, nor is the group that will provide its power and thrust. The formation of both must be accounted for. An explanation of the process of social change must include the breakdown of and alienation from a dominant or prevailing ideology, ideological creation or the formulation of ideological alternatives, the propagation of ideology and its embodiment in the imageries and commitments of a group, and the unfolding of the implications of an ideology for policy and practice.

When Ideology Breaks Down

I know of no coherent ideology that has ever emerged in history to open new avenues of choice and action, and to provide a rational basis for social organization, that has not been preceded by a long period of ideological breakdown and disaffiliation — a period characterized by crises, heresies, and abortive efforts at reform within the established conceptual framework; by the weakening of social ties and the disintegration of institutions; and by pure protest, often violent but purposeless, without ideological alternative or coherent strategy.

Ideological breakdown may be rooted in the incapacity of the established system to cope with changed circumstance, or to satisfy values and expectations learned through the cumulation of social experience. The process of ideological alienation has its syndromes—the dropouts, the solitaries, the escapisms, and the fantasies. It has its function and value as well in the crying out for a new direction. It opens the way for social reconstruction. It readies the eye of society for a new vision and its ear for a new prophecy. The disciples come before the discipline. The stage must be readied.

The process of ideological disaffiliation produces social division, tension, and conflict. The conflict may be between those who are particularly victimized by the operation of the existing system of power or who bear the brunt of policy failure and economic crisis, and those who are entrenched in privilege and secure from the whiplash of events. But inevitably, during this phase of social transformation, society will divide itself on psychic lines. On the one side are those who, when faced with the failure of established belief and the disintegration of institutions, are driven to escape the falsehood, to break away, to wipe the slate clean, to make a new beginning, and for whom utopia must surely be just over that near horizon. Ranged against them are those who when faced with the same failure of established belief and the same disintegration of institutions, see before them the awful dark abyss of the unknown, and shrinking from that, regress to find security in an absolute assertion of the old faith and in a most fervid embrace of its symbols. How else to account for divisions that characterized the "revolutions" in France in 1849 and in 1968? And how else to account for the Yippies, the Weathermen, the hard hats with Old Glory painted on their plastic helmets and clubs in their fists, the Jesus Freaks, or the John Birchers?

The Force for Change

The "material interests" of a "revolutionary class" can provide the force for social transformation. But ideological change can find its power base and its energy source elsewhere as well. Thus, for example, *youth* itself is perpetually a potential source of commitment in energizing the process of ideological change and social transformation. Particularly, this group is important in the phase of ideological breakdown and disaffiliation.

In this light consider Erik H. Erikson's theory of epigenesis.[3] Erikson charts the individual's path of psychic development conceived as a series of steps or stages, each of which has a threshold crisis particular to itself. These crises range from that which determines whether or not the infant will acquire an "ontological source of faith and hope . . . a sense of basic trust," to that of human need, as life draws to a close, to find "meaning" in the face of encroaching age and approaching death. The threshold crisis of specific relevance to ideological transformation and social change occurs in the transition from adolescence to adulthood when the individual leaves the bosom of the family to become (or to try to become) no longer theirs but his own, him*self*, to achieve selfhood—implying settled conviction of where he is, what he is, what he is for, what he is against, what he's worth, and where he intends to go or is going. Then, more than at any other time in life, a "clear comprehension of life in the light of an intelligible theory"—i.e., an *ideology* that is acceptable, that illuminates and captures dedication, and serves to guide choice and action—is needed. Erikson calls the search for such an ideology, and the insecurities, torments, and disorientation that occur in its absence, the crisis of identity.

> . . . it is through their ideology that social systems enter into the fiber of the next generation and attempt to absorb into their lifeblood the rejuvenative power of youth. Adolescence is thus a vital regenerator in the process of social evolution, for youth can offer its loyalties and energies both to the conservation of that which continues to feel true and to the revolutionary correction of that which has lost its regenerative significance.[4]

The crossing over from adolescence into adulthood is above all the time of ideological commitment and the search for that which makes sense, for that which commands fidelity, for that which rings true.

As to youth and the question of what is in the center of its most passionate and most erratic striving, I have concluded that

---

[3]Erik H. Erikson, *Identity: Youth and Crisis* (New York: W. W. Norton & Co., 1968); idem, *Young Man Luther* (New York: W.W. Norton & Co., 1958); idem, *Childhood and Society* (2d ed.; New York: W.W. Norton & Co., 1963); idem, *Insight and Responsibility* (New York: W.W. Norton & Co., 1964).
[4]Erikson, *Identity: Youth and Crisis*, op. cit., p. 134.

fidelity is the vital strength which it needs to have an opportunity to develop, to employ, to evoke — and to die for.[5]

What youth seeks and must have as the ground for a secure
selfhood is an *ideology* to satisfy this craving for fidelity.

We are speaking here not merely of high privileges and lofty
ideals but of psychological necessities. For the social institution which is the guardian of identity *is* what we have called
ideology.[6]

. . . only when fidelity has found its field of manifestation is the
human ready as, say, the nestling in nature when it can rely on
its own wings and take its adult place in the ecological order.[7]

The individual, moreover, must find an identity that gears into
and is supported by the identity choice of others. The individual
striving, hence, is joined to a group striving, requiring a common
commitment and an ideology that is shared.

. . . only when, in our linked orders, we confirm or negate ourselves and each other clearly, is there identity — psychosocial
identity.[8]

Youth seeks to base itself upon and to locate itself with a
coherent body of ideas and values. As the child looked to the
parent for nurture, protection, and guidance, now youth looks
to society and its institutions, beliefs, theories, religions, and
value systems for an ideology that can enlist its faith and its
fidelity.

Thus, it is at this threshold crossing that every new generation
is impelled by its psychic needs to examine afresh the ideology
that society offers, and to ask again: It is true or false? It is
significant or trivial? Is it sufficient or insufficient? Does it
command a passionate and faithful commitment? When the
response is negative, this crisis of identity becomes not only the
pathological state of a few, but a general condition of youth —
and even of the strongest, most courageous, and clear-headed
of the generation.

---

[5]*Ibid.*, p. 233.
[6]*Ibid.*, p. 133.
[7]*Ibid.*, p. 248.
[8]*Ibid.*, p. 220.

Not all youth feels the need for a coherent posture, a clear purpose, or dedication in the face of the world at large. Not everyone of any generation is humanistic, idealistic, in need of ideology, or in search of meaning. Far from it; among those approaching the threshold of adulthood there will always be many satisfied to master a skill, to demonstrate virtuosity, to produce whatever pays off, or to perform whatever is applauded. (Erikson differentiates between "a new dominant class of specialists — those who 'know what they are doing' — and an intense new group of universalists — those who 'mean what they are saying'.") In times of ideological bankruptcy, the technicians become the natural masters of the age.

Thus, at least the Eriksonian path of psychic development suggests that youth, in its peculiar need for coherent purpose and for an outlet for commitment, provides a perennial energy source for ideological change and social transformation. But is this need of youth a genetic necessity or is it itself a function of ideology and, hence, of social organization? It might be supposed that the path of psychic development is culturally determined, and that there are societies where the individual is never pressed or permitted to break out of the shell of authority and take a position, hence, to find an identity of his own. Such generations renew themselves without ever leaving the shelter of traditional (or some other) authority. And it is precisely in those societies where child and adult never break free of authority nor assert the apartness and isolation of the individual — and hence, are never called upon to make an independent ideological commitment and can never, therefore, suffer the crisis of identity — where social organization does not change, where there is no spontaneous development, and where the people live at a very ancient level of poverty. Can it be, with this phase of psychic development aborted, that these societies lack the energy source that has produced the continued transformation of social systems elsewhere?

Controlled and dominated peoples, groups, and classes, as well as those bound into the self-perpetuating traditional cultures, have been denied the capacity for a self-assertive and independent commitment. But everywhere in our time the protective and suppressive forces of domination and tradition have been shattered. And whole peoples, classes, and groups emerging from the broken shells of domination and tradition are in the position of the individual in the Eriksonian model of epigenesis who leaves the parental authority and, in crossing the threshold of adulthood, desperately seeks an outlook and a belief upon which he can stand and take independent root. They suffer *collectively* a crisis like his, but one that is more truly a crisis of *identity*, for they must develop the very image of the self that has the right and the power to choose and who bears the responsibility for that choice.

Ideological Creation

Marxism does not account for Marx himself, and yet he too played a role in the process of social change. The psychology and sociology of ideological creation cannot be ignored and we can say at least the following concerning it.

1. There is no direct and necessary relationship between the facts and the manner of their conceptualization, between the reality and the imagery it evokes, or between the truth and the theory. The same crisis can produce a diversity of workable conceptualizations, as Fascism, Nazism, Socialism, New Dealism were all workable responses to the crisis of depression and the disintegration of ideological liberalism.

2. It is reasonable to suppose with Erik Erikson that while ideological creation is an individual act, it is the act of an individual who shares the dilemmas of his age and who, usually, asks questions that derive from deep personal needs; and in so doing, finds answers that respond to the torments and the uncertitudes of a generation. Such was the case with Luther and probably also with Marx.

3. The acceptability of an ideology, its capacity to capture energy and commitment, depends on its congruence with underlayers of the psyche that determine the space and limit the form of potential change. Nothing could have been further from Marx's conception of the prerequisites of socialist revolution than the conditions that actually prevailed in prerevolutionary Russia and China. But Marxist ideology, as a blueprint for policy, was perhaps uniquely suited to the moral proclivities and organizational aptitudes of those two peoples.

4. Ideological creation and social transformation are society's means of learning, of adapting, of progressing—or conversely, depending on the quality of the ideologies that capture the seats of power, of self-destruction, degradation, and decline.

If ideological creation is a most essential social function, what group, what sector, what class, what part of society can be looked to, to perform it? In the past certainly it has not been the workers or their bosses, or the officials and politicians, or the soldiers and generals, or any of those caught on the treadmills of power and action. Ideological reformulation has been exclusively the function of those who found a dwelling off from the mainstream, immobilized in one of the eddies and havens that permit, to some significant degree, a contemplative life where inner turmoil can overshadow the external turbulence and where the individual is sufficiently removed from the parts to conceive of the whole. The task of ideological creation has been for the rabbis, the monks, the scholars, the jobless intellegentsia, and the leisured aristocrats. Some of those categories have virtually vanished in modern society, and the margin of those who live the contemplative life has greatly diminished. It remains only in academia and, increasingly, the academic too is drawn onto the treadmills of power and action. Yet never has the task of reconceptualizing the immense and immensely variable complex of social activity been so difficult or so critical.

Ideological Confrontation

When ideologies have been formulated and enter into a struggle for power and dominance, then the social division is more likely to follow classical Marxian lines since functional groups can then see on which side their bread is buttered. Very often the outlook at issue wholly eludes any Marxist dichotomy. Who is the ruler and the ruled or the exploiter and the exploited when the issue is nuclear holocaust, or nationalist separatism, or polluted air, or a purposeless life? For such lines of change, another sort of awareness must infiltrate the consciousness and capture the commitment of groups whose will and energy is sufficient to overcome the inertial strength of the established orders.

SUMMARY: A MODEL OF IDEOLOGICAL CHANGE AND SOCIAL TRANSFORMATION

In this final section the arguments that have been made in this chapter will be reviewed, and a general model of ideological change and social transformation will be proposed.

The argument turns on the conception of ideology, and by ideology is meant any coherent idea (or set of ideas) as to what is and what ought to be with respect to some field of choice and action. Ideology is, in effect, the individual's notion of what ought to be, framed in his idea of what exists and of what is possible — an integral set of values embedded in a cognitive structure in terms of which the individual conceives, comprehends, and judges some, indeed any, particular part of existential reality.

Thus understood, the term would include those large, articulated, institutionally propagated ideological systems such as Marxism, Liberalism, and Catholicism. It would include the myriad of smaller, narrowly vectored outlooks such as PTAism, Black Pantherism, Boy Scoutism, Zionism, and all those that have no name or formal articulation, but in whose framework an individual conceives, comprehends, evaluates, and acts with respect to family, friend, foe, home, club, church, business, economy, nation, society, school, university, profession, and all the rest.

Ideologies die. They vanish and are forgotten. But there can be no end to ideology itself, for ideology is a functional necessity. It is the interface of the psychic and the social system; it is man's window on his world.

The ideological apparatus of the individual is multifaceted and perpetually incomplete. The individual, in fact, never has a wholly coherent, wholly viable conception of any aspect of existential reality. Nor has he ever any all-encompassing conceptualization framing the whole universe of choice and action. He operates, rather, through a multiplicity of outlooks shaped to the different dimensions and aspects of experience. He has not an ideology, but always a cluster of ideologies.

The ideologies of the cluster will never be wholly congruous (one in respect to the others), never wholly viable, and never complete. Between and within the parts, there will be lacunas of nonknowledge and nonbelief. Always. We live with such incongruities, inconsistencies, and limitations. To the degree that such incongruities or contradictions exist, uncertainty will befog choice and a sense of guilt will burden behavior. To the degree that ideology malconceives reality, the individual will err in action and the consequence of choice will diverge from expectations.

Ideology, like the head of the god Janus, faces in two directions: outward, responding to the need and expressed in the behavior of the group; and inward, responding to the need and expressed in the behavior of the individual. It is the basis for individual rootedness and coherence and for social choice and association. It is the cement of groups and the prerequisite of common action and effective communication. It relates group cohesiveness *and* psychic coherence on the one side, and private purpose *and* collective choice on the other. It has the functions of satisfying the individual's need for a vision of things and a basis for choice that makes sense, coheres, explains, and invites fidelity; and of satisfying the need of the functional group for a policy blueprint that works. Ideology must, therefore, gear into psychic need and into social circumstance. It follows that an ideological configuration that once commanded commitment and produced psychic equilibrium and functional effectiveness, can break down because there has been a change in psychic need and/or in social circumstance. External circumstances do change; and so do inner needs.

Suppose an ideology that prevails throughout a society is workable and effective as an operating hypothesis and is meaningful in relation to the values and problems of a time. That ideology *must* become cumulatively less workable in relation to action and policy and less meaningful in relation to purpose and problems *because* the universe of action changes, and *because* the individual's values and problems change. The distance between any ideology and existential realities or psychic needs widens simply as an effect of historical time. In consequence functional systems shaped by reference to a blueprint that has become obsolete will cease to achieve the purposes for which they were intended, or to satisfy the expectations of those on whose commitment they depend.

Or time can throw an ideology out of joint with psychic need through its success as a blueprint for policy and action. The very achievement of its purpose forecloses the hope, dedication, sacrifice, aspiration, and adventure that attracted an earlier generation.

Whether one considers the social group or the individual psyche, *an* ideology is but one strand in a fabric where the rupture of a part can lead to the progressive unravelling of the whole. Any change in the psychic structure, or in a component part of the ideological configuration, weakens the under-pinnings of all accepted outlooks and beliefs and creates the base and sets the boundaries for those that will follow.

For these reasons, the prevailing ideology becomes cumulatively less workable, with policy failure and institutional disintegration in its train, and/or less able to satisfy psychic demands and expectations, alienation and ideological disengagement set in. Not all persons or groups will be affected by these forces and events in the same way or to the same degree. And when the effects are the same, the responses will differ. As groups that express a stage or phase of alienation come into being, they produce their opposition. The process divides society; and polarization, confrontation, and conflict will occur.

In the phase of ideological disengagement, the polarization and confrontation will more generally be between categories that are emotionally (psychically) rather than functionally differentiated; i.e., between those who feel the need for change and seek it, and those who are threatened by the prospect of change and recoil from it.

In this sense the generations also will be polarized, with opposition and conflict between youth on the threshold of adulthood (needing a commitment that enlists faith and commands fidelity) and those whose ideological commitment has already been made (being settled in careers and habituated to compromise; being involved in private pursuits and preoccupations; and having status, security, and self-conception vested in existing arrangements).

Even within the oncoming generation there will be polarization and conflict between the "humanists" involved with the world and its values (seeking meaning and purpose and needing to know what it's all about, to know where they're going, and to know what it's worth), and the "technicians," for whom it suffices to acquire skill and to do the job well.

There will be confrontation and conflict also between those whose compulsion to self-destruction and parental defiance produces a repudiation of all that authority represents, whose private malaise merges into the unease and iconoclasm of the age, and whose psychotically-rooted certainty in negation gives them a power of leadership among the wavering; and those who, when threatened with the unknown and unknowable, regress to a total embrace of orthodoxy, and whose fanatic certainties give them a power of leadership among the wavering.

There will be polarization and conflict between those intellectuals who most keenly feel the need for coherence in their vision of things and the need for consistency in what is thought, said, and done against those who are incapable of such abstraction, who are untroubled by ideological incongruities, and who find their security in ritual and convention.

There will be polarization and conflict between those who are victims of the failure of a functional system and feel the cutting edge of its inadequacy, and those who have a vested interest in and are advantaged by an established order.

At this early stage in the process of transformation, the advantages of coercive force and even of reasoned argument are on the side of those who would conserve, resist, or react against change. For at this phase of ideological erosion and institutional breakdown, those most sensitized to the inadequacies and contradictions of things as they are have no coherent ideological alternative. It is for them, rather, to express society's need for one, signalling their readiness to respond and to follow.

If the initial advantage is with those who would conserve, historical time is on the side of those who would destroy. For the distance between the authoritative ideology and the existential reality must continue to grow. As it grows the value of established ideology as an hypothesis for choice and action is continuously degraded. Errors of policy recur, the cost of failure increases, and frustration is magnified. The wavering are alienated; and the chorus of discontent rises in volume and intensity.

Eventually, hopefully, those endowed with creative powers, experiencing the same frustration and driven by the same need, will formulate an alternative way. What new ideologies will be forthcoming? Which of these will come to prevail? In part that will depend on the relevance, the objective truth, the workability, and the implicit potentialities of what is offered. But only in part. Relevance, truth, workability, and potentiality are all conjectures and remain so until the choice has been made and the new vision of things has been incorporated in institutions, formulated as policy, and applied in practice. Then it can turn out that the new truth was a lie and its price was disaster. Which ideologies survive and succeed will depend on the preconditions of acceptance, the processes of collective choice, and the resistance of institutions. It will also depend on the accumulation of memories, the "traditions of the race and the people," and the "primitive categorical conscience"—located by Freud in the superego—as these characterize the psychic structure of the people.

An ideology will invite commitment not only as a basis for coherent choice and effective action, but also for its psychic enticements. These may range from an appeal to the transcendent ethic to the satisfaction of brutal proclivities.

If the resistance of vested powers and the inertia or closure of existing institutions permits no basic change except through force and violence, then only those ideologies that enlist a fanatic allegiance and propose a strategy of violence can survive and succeed; and the social transformation that then occurs will bear the burden of fanaticism and the trauma of violence.

When ideological alternatives stand fully formed on the stage of possibility and choice, then polarization and confrontation are more likely to shift from the cognitive and emotional to the functional, for now presumably it becomes easier to see where individual or group advantage lies.

This chapter has briefly formulated a theory of social change in which ideology plays a central role. In these terms the development of the economic policy of the United States will be examined. The next chapter will glance at the ideologies that prevailed at the onset of the American Republic and will suggest the experience in history that shaped them. The American political system will be conceptualized as a medium for the expression of ideology and of the other determinants of collective choice.

Chapter 2
The Actors
and Their Stage

The chapters that follow will test the value and credibility of this hypothesis: *Political policy is an expression of a prevailing ideology. Hence, policy change reflects ideological change. Therefore, in order to explain and predict change in policy, ideological change must be foreseen and explained.*
This chapter will attempt to:

1. Specify the ideologies that prevailed at the onset of the American Republic. In order to convey the character of these ideologies, their historical source and process of formation will be briefly described. It is with that very limited purpose in mind that these sketches of history should be understood.
2. Analyze the American political system in order to differentiate between ideology and the other determinants of policy in the process of collective choice.

The ideologies with which the American experience begins were produced by Europeans and were the product of European experience. It was, however, in the United States of America that that ideological set, which had been struggling since the Renaissance for expression and domination against a prior Medieval configuration, found its most perfect and complete expression. The Renaissance marked an essential shift from the conception of a God-centered universe where choice derived its legitimacy from authority, to the vision of a universe that is man-centered with legitimacy in human reason — a view of things variously made manifest in the individual's effort to relate directly to his God, to seek his fortune freely in the market, and to participate "democratically" in collective choice. It found expression in home and church, in economy and polity, as Protestantism, as democracy, as nationalism, and as liberalism. Our particular concern here is with the twin ideologies, nationalism and liberalism.

NATIONALISM

Two conceptions are cojoined: that of the *nation* and that of the *state*. The nation is a large "natural" community of individuals who identify with each other. It finds its force, cohesion, and continuity in a sense of sameness and in the shared self-image of those who compose it. Those who feel this sense of self-identification do so perhaps because they have been shaped by a common history and because they perhaps share language, beliefs, traditions, an imagery of heroes and demons, and the other character-forming constituents of a culture. A nation is akin in the biblical meaning of a "people," as the Jews were and are a "people," though dispersed and without a language or a land or even a common belief or any instrument of collective choice and corporate action.

The sense of nationhood need not but can be the basis for a political organization. France was the first European political system based on a sense of nationhood. And in a long-enduring initial phase the role of the national government was simply to secure traditional activities and institutions from alien incursion, and to embody in the monarchy the munificence of a national image.

The French political system, first to express the force of nationhood, dominated Europe. Its invasions and conquests in Italy during the 15th and 16th centuries, and later in Germany during Napoleonic times, stirred the defeated to find a counter-identity. Sensing affinities that differentiated them from the alien, they sought to emulate their conqueror by realizing their nationhood and giving it a political embodiment.

Those most committed to these new nationalist movements were outside the ranks of the feudal aristocracy and the church hierarchs whose status depended on another order of ideological commitment. Nor were they from among the laboring mass who were precluded by ignorance and poverty from indulging in any ideological concerts. The new nationalists came from among the scriveners and scholars, the clerks and clerics, traders, perhaps craftsmen, administrators of estates, and servants of princes. Machiavelli, famous or infamous as an exponent of *realpolitik*, was one of these; and whatever the merits of his work, his views perfectly exemplify the rationale of the new nationalist, who was frustrated before the unachieved potentialities of his nationhood. Called immoral and amoral, Machiavelli was certainly neither. True, he displayed no regard for traditional Christianity; his moral criterion was of another order. For him the highest good was in awakening a sense of nationhood among his (Italian) people and the embodiment of that sense of national identity in an Italian political system. Nor was the criterion of nationhood in his time something apart from a concern for the human condition or for the quality of civilization, for in his time nothing short of a unified nation could secure the Italians from perennial conquest, perennial plunder, perennial humiliation, and cumulative depredation and degradation. Nothing else could give Italy a chance to achieve internal tranquility and prosperity. For these reasons Machiavelli proposed a practical, single-minded strategy for creating an Italian nation.

The strategy he formulated was to be followed by all the new nationalists everywhere who opposed themselves to the existing, entrenched, decentralized power of feudal autonomies. It was simply to render absolute support to the greatest of the feudal lords so that, encouraged to realize upon his ambition and self-interest, that Prince would subjugate and subordinate the others and rule over a whole national domain. As one side of this strategy, those economists of nationhood — now called mercantilists — sought to maximize the flow of treasure into the coffers of the king, so that he could build fleets and hire infantry to crush his enemies.

The nation is not a government. Nor is a national government synonymous with the modern "state." In the "state" the political system acquires an autonomous organizational character, basing itself upon and deriving its energies from the ambitions and dedication of professional technicians, bureaucrats, and administrators. The state was the first professionalized corporate organization, with its origins in Prussia, not then coextensive with the German nation.

The coupling of state and nation produces the modern nation-state. This coalescing of the pride, felt affinities, and cohesiveness of the nation with an autonomous, rational mechanism of control produced political systems of remarkable power and peculiar ferocity.

LIBERALISM

The nation-state, with political authority centralized and rationally organized, destroyed and swept away the autonomous traditional feudal powers and thereby created unprecedented opportunities for private economic gain. Land and labor, once fixed for perpetuity into a pattern of usage, became available for private purchase, for sale, or for hire. In Great Britain the property holder, exercising the new unbounded right of ownership, foreclosed the ancient prerogatives of the village and drove the peasants off the common. A peasantry once bound to the land could now leave and, indeed, were forced to leave by the enclosure of free pasture. They moved to the cities offering their labor for sale.

It was now possible for the self-interested capitalist to mobilize and manipulate all resources and to produce, transport, and offer for sale all goods and services throughout the free trade area of the nation. The tolls and tariffs once imposed by feudal barons at every turn of the river and at every bend of the road were eliminated. The brigandage of bankrupted knights was stopped. National transportation networks were developed. A common currency was created. National lines of credit came into being. Accumulated wealth was available for investment. Uniform weights and standards were established. A national judiciary and a single law for the realm permitted the extension of contract, hence the development of complex industrial and exchange relationships extensive in space and time. National markets invited international trade. The naval power and diplomatic force of national governments provided new security for merchants on the high seas and in foreign lands. Thus, the nation-state produced the framework for a market economy where aggressive individualism could be free of an ancient web of institutional constraints.

Vanished also were the religious constraints on the aggressive use of political power and on the self-interested use of economic power. Luther sanctioned, even sanctified, the secularization (the de-Christianization) of political power. "A prince can be a Christian," he said, "but he is not bound to rule as a Christian. . . . His personality is Christian, but his office or principality has no concern with his being a Christian."[1] Equally, Luther sanctioned and sanctified property as an absolute right beyond and above all human claims, even forbidding Christians enslaved by the Turks from seeking their freedom, "for you are robbing and stealing your body from your master, your body that he has bought or acquired in some other way, so that it be no longer yours but his property like cattle or other goods."[2]

Calvin found God's elect among the thrifty, energetic, capital-accumulating burghers who established their grace by their success. The bourgeoisie, ambitious craftsmen, traders, money lenders, bankers, guildsmen, and shopkeepers — hard-fisted and hard-working; cautious, rational, and self-righteous, with the smell of opportunity in their nostrils — pressed forward in action and found themselves frustrated not only by the traditional institutions and feudal privileges that remained, but also by the policies of those who administered the new nation-state; and who, in the tradition of the initial nation builders, looked upon the economy simply and directly as an instrument of the national (read, the monarch's) power. The king's ships, the king's men, the king's treasure, the king's armies, and the king's supplies: it was all the same. Everything must be kept under close control, subject to quick and easy mobilization, ready for war. The economy, like the soldiery, was to be "run by the book," following established practice and thereby keeping everything in sight, within reach, and subject to the disposition of a centralized administration.

In days of war and crisis, this policy made sense. It still makes sense in times of war and crisis. Indeed, the policies and techniques of mercantilism have been resurrected and reimposed by the modern state in every major war. But given the firm establishment of sovereign national states, and given conditions of peace and security, the mercantilist outlook became less appropriate and, in the longer run, detrimental to the goal of national power.

---

[1]Martin Luther, *Wider die räuberischen und mörderischen Rotten der Bauern*, Vol. 18, 1525 Weimar ed., p. 361.

[2]Martin Luther, *Wochenpredigten uber Matth.*, 5-7, Vol. 32, 1530–1532 Weimar ed., p. 440.

When the state and nation were no longer synonymous with the king's household but encompassed the entire society and were able to mobilize the resources of the entire society, then the source of national power was no longer in the accumulation of gold in the royal treasury, but rather was in the capacity of the economy to produce the sinews of war. Hence, the path to power was not in the accumulation of royal treasure but in the cumulative increase in productive capacity. The real wealth of the nation lay in its power to produce the substance of welfare and, hence (the two were largely interchangeable), the sinews of war. That was the message of Adam Smith. Following the physiocrats in France, he appealed to those who administered the English state. Don't interfere. Let things be. Laissez-faire. Laissez-passer. Rely on us (capitalists, entrepreneurs, bourgeoisie) and on the competition among us. By our energetic self-interest we will introduce rationality into the organization of production. Because we are ambitious and ingenious and ready to invest our wealth and effort we will, if left alone, increase the productive capacity of the economy and, thereby, we will have augmented the power of the nation to raise great armies, to build great navies, and to wage war.

These, he argued, are the true paths to national power.

Let trade be free. The new liberals argued that trade is not, as the mercantilists think, the means whereby one gets the better of another. Trade does not imply that what one gains the other must lose. On the contrary, trade is freely entered into only when both parties to the bargain will gain and know that they will gain thereby. Hence, through the increase in trade, the advantages of all who engage in that trade will be increased. Therefore, promote trade. Make the nation a trading nation. The nation that trades the most gains the most.

Promote free internal and international trade. By maximizing trade and by allowing each firm or region to concentrate on producing what it produces best, the economy will make the most of its resources.

Don't support monopoly. Monopoly restrains trade, reduces output, and therefore reduces the real wealth of the nation.

Don't impose traditional practice on industry and commerce. Let men give full and free rein to their personal ambition and private greed. With each seeking more for himself, all will work harder, avoid waste, and organize the resources they control efficiently. Working thus, they will produce more with the same human and natural resources. Increased production at lower cost, given market competition, will result in greater output at lower prices. More, then, will be available for private consumption or to satisfy public need.

In summary, the new ideology of liberalism pleaded that the public authority give free rein to the natural force of self-interest and private initiative, that it rely on the competitive market to channel private initiative into productive activity, and that it rely on competition to protect the public interest from private greed.

The first thrust of the liberal argument was that to free private initiative in a free market would increase the power of the nation-state. Later some would see it the other way around. The power of the state existed to promote the more perfect happiness of the individual; and the more perfect happiness of the individual required private choice unconstrained by political regulation. The political system was then left with three functions: to protect the security of person, to protect the liberty of individuals, and to protect the rights of property. In the words of the great Blackstone:

> The rights of mankind . . . may be reduced to three principles or primary articles; the right of personal security, the right of personal liberty, and the right of private property; because there is no known method of compulsion or of abridging man's free will but by an infringement or diminution of one or other of these important rights, the preservation of these, inviolate, may justly be said to include the preservation of our civil immunities in their largest and most extensive sense.[3]

Laissez-faire liberalism, like most ideologies, was formed and expressed itself in a particular way by reason of the viewpoint to which it was opposed; it was shaped by what it stood against as well as by what it stood for. Liberalism was formulated as an argument against political intervention in the economy; but intervention of a particular sort. It was the "meddlesome interference" of civil servants who take the market as given and who have no intention of controlling its inner forces

---

[3] J. M. Clark. *Social Control of Business.* (2d ed.; New York: McGraw-Hill Book Company, Inc., 1939), pp. 95–96.

nor of organizing the processes of production and distribution via the instrumentality of political control and central planning.

Given the historical situation, it was the eminently reasonable argument of laissez-faire liberalism that the way to raise the level of production and hence to create an economic surplus (i.e., a national income over and above that required to maintain the essentials of life) which would constitute the tax base and would determine the capacity of the nation to raise armies and to support allies in waging war was: (1) to eliminate the complex of regulations and restraints based on traditional practices and imposed by government and to allow instead the *natural* force of self-interest to motivate hard work, rational adaptation, and technological innovation; (2) to eliminate state-supported monopolies which were created through royal grants of political favor or as a means of collecting taxes, on the grounds that such monopolies restrained the *natural* forces of the market and therefore reduced output, limited the rational management and full utilization of resources, and checked progress; and (3) to eliminate political constraints on international trade since the limitations of imports must correspondingly limit exports and reduce the level of international exchange to the detriment of all. The nation that made the fullest and best use of its peculiar proclivities, skills, and resources through freedom of internal exchange and external trade would, correspondingly, increase its surplus (i.e., the net national output of the requirements of life). The larger the surplus (in the form of private wealth) the larger, presumably, will be the margin of investment. Through investment capital would accumulate and the level of production would be raised.

Liberalism charted a path to higher productivity, to be equated with increased welfare and greater power. This path implied:

1. Increase specialization, both internal and external, achieved through the free movement of resources and the free exchange of outputs.
2. Greater effort and efficiency, motivated by self-interest in the profits to be made through free exchange.
3. A more rational choice of technology and of input combinations under the pressures of competition and the imperatives of survival in a free market economy.

4. More rapid development through the use of wealth gained by business activity and invested under the spur of business ambition.

The increasing national product, supposedly, would be diffused equitably by the *natural* force of market competition, which transmits greater efficiency into lower prices and equates income to the relative value of contribution.

In line with the philosophical style of the age, liberalism was considered by its adherents as an ideology of the *natural* (synonymous with the "good"), juxtaposed against its opposite, the unnatural, the artificial, or the politically contrived. Property, competition, individual self-seeking and initiative were natural. The regulations imposed by the state were artificial. The impositions of the state were considered as barriers, holding back the free flow of effort and ingenuity. The objective of liberal policy was to give free play to individual initiatives and the natural forces of competition. The guardians of liberalism must be forever vigilant against the interventionist proclivities of politicians and officials, and against the importunities of groups demanding the protection of the state. Wisdom and a long-sighted concern for national power and individual welfare demanded that the interferences of the state in the market system and in the economic function be reduced to the absolute minimum. The function of the law was not to check private greed nor to further group interests, but rather to protect private power (property) and prerogative (liberty) and, conversely, to check public intervention in any form.

To the degree that the new class triumphed and capitalism was installed, the liberal ideology was enshrined.

IDEOLOGIES TRANSPLANTED

Nationalism and liberalism, evolved through centuries of European experience, were transplanted to America. There the soil proved uniquely propitious. They took deep root and flourished. In the colonies and then in the new Republic, liberalism found an environment more favorable to its propagation and its successful application than at any other time or in any other place in the world. It was an ideology, after all, that expressed the interests, aspirations, and attitudes of a new class that in Europe had been only a marginal group existing in the fissures of feudalism. But American society belonged to that new class entirely. In Europe the great inert body of the peasantry remained profoundly traditional, and the ideologies and partisans of Catholicism, aristocracy, and monarchy remained entrenched, powerful, and contemptuous of or antagonistic against the upstart bourgeoisie and their greed-glorifying philosophy. In America there were no such enemies. In Europe the feudal and medieval heritage was built inextricably into the social system. In America the field was free of traditional forms, and the vision of liberalism seemed as self-evidently true as that the land itself was broad and filled with opportunities and hardships. In the New World no ancient institutions obstructed the way to the rational organization of social functions with an unchallenged ideology as the blueprint.

The liberal ideology grew strong and persisted in American society for another reason. This was an ideology that evolved out of a universe of experience *preceding* that extraordinary transformation of the economy called the *Industrial Revolution*. It took its form and developed its rationale before the epoch of urban concentration, of a large propertyless proletariat, and of a machine-dominated culture. The heyday of liberalism was not in the epoch of industrialization but in the years that led to it; it proved to be an ideology more appropriate to the achievement of industrialization than for the organization of an industrialized society. But in the United States industrialization was slow in coming so that the new ideology had time to incubate and take deep roots. Industrialization did not come in the United States until the period of the Civil War, and for a time thereafter, some of the problems of an industrialized society were offset by the continued existence of an open frontier where individuals could find an escape from the crunch of economic breakdown and could make their way alone.

The colonies acquired a sense of nationhood. In Europe the ties of nationhood were ethnic and tribal, based on the particularities and attachments of a people in their long, organic development in interaction with the characteristics and continuities of given, circumscribed physical environments. Affinity in the American colonies was of another order. Unlike their European progenitors the Americans were akin not in their common roots, but because they were the unrooted and they shared the trauma and liberation of tearing free of ancient parts, of emigration, and of restless movement over the boundless space of the new continent.

Uniquely in the world, American society was all of a class the Europeans called "bourgeois" or "middle"; the terms are misleading. What distinguished the members of this new class was neither poverty, wealth, manners, nor origin, but rather that none had a place, high or low, in any established, traditional hierarchy. They were mobile in society as they were in space.

If the European was bound to his nation by traditions, habits, and ways of living formed out of the past, the American was bound to his by shared expectations of the future, and by the optimism and confidence with which he faced the future. The past belonged to them; the future was his. The affinities that produced the American nation derived from an extraordinary homogeneity of outlook and culture, astonishing the foreign traveler then as now.

The War of Independence was a nationalist uprising. It asserted a new nationhood, an apartness and distinctiveness from the motherland, and among the rebels it expressed an inner kinship and an American identity. At the same time it was a rebellion of liberalism against state intervention.

The new ideologies of the age were not only in conflict with the old; between and within those new ideologies themselves there was incongruity and conflict. The interests of the individual, the capitalist, and the state need not be in harmony. Liberalism and democracy both emphasized the value of individualized choice and, on that account, both resisted the autonomous power and collectivizing force of the state. But when property was threatened and the institutions of capitalism were shaken by (what the liberal would regard as) the abuse of majorities and the excesses of the rabble, then the liberal needed the organized force of an autonomous state to keep democracy in its place.

In all the societies of that era, ideological elements were differently integrated and ideological conflicts had a different resolution, reflected in a particular structure of power. In Russia on the solid base of an exacerbated, perpetually threatened nationhood, dynasty, religious orthodoxy, and traditional hierarchy came together to support and in the end hopelessly to distort the autonomous power of the state. Poland, bound together by powerful ties of nationhood, could never create a state, and succumbed to the disintegrating force of feudal autonomies. Prussia created a "pure" state, finding its values in order and duty, and in the power and symmetry of a perfectly disciplined collective; a state that eventually imposed itself by conquest upon the German nation, that excluded democracy as irrelevant to its purposes, and that put bourgeois ambition and market incentive to use along with whatever else it considered necessary for economic development. In Italy every ideology was dormant and abortive, and society fell back on the cohesiveness of the clan and the family. In France every ideology was alive and flourishing, and equilibrium of a sort was found in what Stanley Hoffman called a "stalemate society."

An Introduction to the Actors

In our scenario the leading roles will be played not by individuals or classes, but by ideologies — those complex sets of ideas and values through which men see and judge their world, and that provide the cohesive force uniting groups and the guidelines for social choice and policy. Two ideologies destined to be of key importance in the story of American political *cum* economic policy, have now been introduced: *liberalism*, expressing aggressive self interest in pursuit of private gain in a market system, and *nationalism*, coupling the solidarity of the nation with the rationally organized autonomous force of the *state*. Each has been described in its historical context, which may be summarized in the next two paragraphs.

In feudal society the social functions of defense and conquest, of internal security, of adjudication and law, and of production and distribution were performed by fragmented political entities. Under the weight of its own inadequacies, the feudal society was transformed into the nation-state. There the political authority was centralized, professionalized, and rationally organized as the autonomous state that based itself upon and put itself forward as representing the felt affinities of a nation. The successful nation-state created the framework for trade. The disintegration of feudalism released land and manpower for disposition of the market. Unprecedented opportunities for gain-seeking individuals were thereby created. Propelled by bourgeoisie ambition the market developed as the central instrument for the performance of the economic function.

Corresponding to the emergence of the nation-state as the political system and the decentralized market as the economic system, there evolved a twin ideology: (1) nationalism, promulgating a single sovereign power in opposition to the traditional privileges and localized authority of feudalism; and (2) liberalism, promulgating a decentralized price-directed market where individual choice was constrained only by competition and opposing itself to any subordination of enterprise to political control.

THE DETERMINANTS OF POLICY

We have asserted the importance of ideology as a determinant of social policy, but it is no more true for society than for the individual that ideology is the only determinant of policy and choice. Like the individuals and groups that compose it, society also acts in response to emotional forces and nonrational impulses, expediently in ameliorating specific pain and discomfort, intuitively in confronting and in attempting to resolve specific crises, and as a reflex of the ambitions, self-seekings, and conflicts of its constituent parts. To understand and to assess the relative importance of these determinants of social policy requires that we conceive of and comprehend the process of choice, and the particular way that process is organized for the particular political system.

Our concern is with the development of economic policy in the United States. It will be seen in the chapters ahead that, confronted with the same universe of values, problems, and circumstances, the policy enunciated and the choices made by Congress and the President persistently differ from those of the Supreme Court. Indeed, social policy in the United States emerges out of the tension between these branches of American government. We will propose a conceptual basis for explaining this divergence.

Individualized and Organizational Choice

Ordinarily choice is conceived in terms of the individual acting independently in pursuit of his own self-interest. Call this *individualized choice*. Individualized choice has no point of reference beyond the impulse, the values, and the cognitive capacities of the individual who chooses. I do what I want and I take the consequences of what I do. If I fail, I lose. If I succeed, I profit. One way or the other, I have nothing to explain or to justify. Such is the form of choice characteristic of the entrepreneur in the decentralized price-directed market postulated by classical or neo-classical economics.

In contrast to individualized choice there is *organizational choice*, covering what large political or economic entities (the modern corporation or the agencies of government) "choose" to do. Perhaps "choice" is not the right word. It has unwarranted teleological implications — for "choice" suggests that there must be one who chooses. Whereas in large organizations the patterns of action, even policies and laws, need not be an attribute of any distinct and distinguishable choice. (Did anyone choose to engage in a war in Vietnam?) Rather laws, policies, and patterns of organizational action may arise out of the interplay of conflicting interests and intermingled pressures in a stream of disconnected decisions. And even though in such circumstances there is no clear line of relationship between what any individual decides and what eventually emerges as policy and behavior out of the interplay of many decisions, policy and behavior may be predictable nevertheless. When we speak of the "choice" of large organizational entities, what concerns us really is the system that produces policy and behavior.

We discern two forms of organizational choice: Those decisions made by individuals in authority *for* the organization (call this *authoritative decision*) and that policy which emerges not as the consequence of an individual decision but that compounds and reflects the diverse drives, interests, and opinions of the participating group (call this *composite choice*). The mechanism of composite choice may be formally structured, i.e., through voting, or it may be informal and unstructured.

Authoritative Decision and Composite Choice

Authoritative decision is made by an individual but it is not at all the same as individualized choice. Individualized choice, following the instinct, taste, prejudice, "guts" of the choice-maker, is not *answerable*. Whereas those who decide, on the basis of their authority, for a group are "responsible" to those who support their authority. In this sense, to a greater or lesser degree, they are *answerable* to others for their choice and for its consequences. Hence, authoritative decision will be made by reference to that which can be explained, rationalized, or justified. Authoritative decision must be acceptable. Its force depends on organizational response within the boundaries of the acceptable. The boundaries of acceptability are, of course, highly variable but they always set critical limits for the authoritative decision. What then determines these boundaries? What is the point of reference for the explanation, rationalization, or justification of action by authority or, on the other hand, for the evaluation of authoritative decision made by clients and supporters or respondants to authority; and hence, for their acceptance of or resistance to authority? Surely the criteria of evaluation and the boundaries of the acceptable are determined by an ideology shared by those who exercise and those who accept and ultimately support the exercise of authority. Authoritative decision may be made in a government or in an army or in a corporation or in a trade union. In each case the group upon whom the effective exercise of authority depends and to whom those who exercise authority are answerable will be different. Consequently, the ideology in terms of which decisions are made and the values by reference to which the decisions are accepted will differ also.

Individualized choice has its reference point only in the self-interest, the outlook, the tastes, and the values of the decision-maker. Authoritative choice has its reference point in that ideology that links authority to those who follow its imperatives. On the other hand, composite choice, emerging from the diversity of interests and pressures that characterize the group, is without any specific point of reference save in the weight of counterbalanced forces. Composite choice is not tied to any process of rationalization. Its effective expression is not in what the group decides but in what it does and even in what it becomes.

So far as organizational choice is concerned, we have suggested that policy and behavior will reflect both ideology and pragmatic pressures; and that the ideology will have the greatest weight when decision is authoritative, whereas expediency is more likely to prevail when choice is composite. For the American political system then, what are the agencies of authoritative and of composite choice? Where will ideology dominate? Where will expediency prevail?

To answer that question requires that we consider the structure of the American political system.

THE AMERICAN POLITICAL SYSTEM

The political system embodies (1) the organized process of collective choice and policy formulation (and/or choice and policy formulation for and in the name of the whole), and (2) the implementation and administration of choice and policy either through the instrumentality of the law and police controlling activities outside the political system, or through agencies charged with the performance of integral tasks carried on within and as a part of the political system. In the United States both the processes of choice and the means of implementing choice are highly decentralized. Besides the federal government, there are separate state governments. Within the states there are separate governments for the great urban concentrations—the cities, towns, villages, and counties as geographical subdivisions. And at every level decision is further divided among commissions, corporations, boards, agencies, administrations, authorities, departments, bureaus, services, and districts in relation to functional objectives. Aside from the federal judiciary there are state judiciaries with judges and juries participating, and local magistracies and agencies for the prosecution and enforcement of the laws. There are governors, upper and lower houses of legislatures, mayors, councils, boards, trustees, and town meetings. And there are numerous agencies with hosts of administrators, clerks, councilors, and technicians. This massive apparatus serves to preserve order, to express and enforce the collective choice, and to serve various needs of the citizenry. It is, however, the federal government that expresses the force of nationhood, that conceives and speaks for the "national interest," that exercises sovereign power, and that most fully embodies the idea of the state.

The initial position of the American *state* must be understood in terms of rather particular historical circumstances. The War of Independence was an uprising of liberalism and democracy against the British state, and those who had made that war were fearful of another national state that might abridge individual prerogatives. The ex-colonies, moreover, had organized the war and then constituted themselves as independent governments. Each had a long history and often a proud and particular tradition and a claim upon the loyalties and allegiance of its citizenry. The governments of the separate states were destined to play something of the role the feudal powers had played in Europe. They could not embody nationhood nor speak for the nation nor constitute the state, but they were jealous of their established positions and unwilling to subordinate themselves to any other power. At first they tried to make do with a ramshackle confederation that proved unable to deal effectively with foreign nations or (which was the crowning blow) was unable to protect the sanctity of property when farm debtors in the West rose up against the claims of their creditors in the East. Aroused liberals then joined the nationalists to call a constitutional convention. There they laid out the blueprint for a sovereign American state.

It was intended by those who laid out the new governmental design that the powers of the sovereign should be strictly limited. Federal powers and functions were spelled out explicitly in the Constitution. All residual powers and functions (those not explicitly delegated to the federal authority) were to remain with and were to be exercised only by the separate states. The Constitution also spells out the "inalienable rights" of individuals. These were not to be infringed on by any government. The sovereign/state was further constrained by a division of power between branches of the federal government imposed according to a doctrine of checks and balances. A Senate and a House of Representatives were elected by different rules. The President was elected separately, and could exercise a limited veto over Congress. The Supreme Court, in addition to its normal judicial duties, must judge the actions of the several governments and their branches as lawful or unlawful according to the Constitution.

Earlier we differentiated between authoritative decision and composite choice, comparing the relative importance of ideology in each. In these terms then, consider the character of choice by Congress, by the President, and by the Supreme Court in the American political system.

Supreme Court and Congress — The Character of Political Choice

In the American political system the Supreme Court exemplifies authoritative decision. Congress and the President (i.e., the legislative and executive branches of the federal government) exemplify composite choice. Consider the Supreme Court. Its nine members are insulated by life tenure and protected from the pull and tug of politics by an immense prestige. Each Justice decides individually and independently, but each decides not as an individual on his own by reference to his personal tastes and ambitions, but rather *for* American government and *for* American society. Each decides independently and is independently responsible for his decision. Responsible to whom? To his peers, surely — to the thinking men of his time. A Justice gives his opinion in an elaborate effort to justify himself and to rationalize his exercise of authoritative choice. In every opinion he pleads his case before the great bar of his society. And his reference point is an ideology. He brings the implications of an ideology to bear upon the specifics of a concrete case. The willingness of a society to accept the decisions of the Court will depend on its concurrence with the norms of social thought that the Court articulates.

With Congress and the President the process of choice is of another order. The Court is very small but the legislative and executive branches are themselves large, complex organizations that interact and merge with other large organizations (such as political parties; state, regional, and city political machines; clients; partisans; churches and schools; industries and their associations; farm groups; labor groups; ethnic groups; and religious groups endlessly) in the stress and struggle to have their say and to protect their own. In that flux and complexity there are many actors representing many interests. These interests are diverse, equivocal, and often conflicting. The buck is passed and in passing is squeezed, soiled, rubbed, and shaped as it moves from hand to hand. It is never clear where things begin or how they end. There is the ceaseless grouping and regrouping of power relationships. There is the gaming and the counterpoise of strategies. Certainly what emerges is not a consistent expression of a coherent ideology.

Thus, the Supreme Court of the United States exemplifies authoritative decision and articulates an ideology. Congress and the President exemplify composite choice, reflecting a balance of pressures and expressing a universe of mixed and diverse wants and opinions. What then are the strengths and the weaknesses of these two kinds of choice and, therefore, of these two forms of government?

Composite choice *represents*; and in its capacity to represent a real universe of needs and pressure as well as ideas and values, it expresses needs, opinions, aspirations, and discontents as they exist in time and place. It embodies the complexities and contradictions of a real universe and it reacts to these; it balances and juggles; and it responds to private seeking, to group crisis, and to pressure and problem. Flexible, representative, responsive, and pragmatic — such are its virtues — it has also the corresponding vices of expediency. It is meandering and aimless, wasteful, without logical consistency, without vision. It reacts in crisis but not to the anticipation of crisis. It must be kicked into motion. Such are the qualities of composite choice, and such are the characteristics of choice in the congressional and executive branches.

On the other hand, the exercise of authority implies an independent, hence, an *isolated* decision. This must be emphasized. When an authority interacts with and depends upon those upon whom it exercises authority, then authority is diluted. Its powers of decision are diffused. Individual responsibility is lost and the composite tends to emerge. Authoritative choice by the Supreme Court, based upon and justifying itself by reference to an ideology which links governor and governed, is capable of forethought, of rationality, and of consistency. It expresses a system of ideas. It is capable of learning. Such are its virtues. Its vice is in the inescapable inability of the individual to comprehend the social whole and of the ideology to encompass the flux and complexity of a real universe of need and change. The individual masters the philosophy, but a philosophy simplifies and excludes. Urgent needs and critical problems fall outside its purview. And when a dominant ideology is fixed in the face of rapid historical change, then realities will escape its net more and more. Its imperatives will become irrelevant and its concepts will no longer frame the world to which they refer.

These generalizations concerning authoritative decision and composite choice, or concerning the Court and Congress, simplify and exclude. History is full of exceptions. They will be useful, nevertheless, in explaining the decisions of the Supreme Court on the one hand, and the policies and laws emanating from Congress and the President on the other.

Hypothesis Concerning Political Choice

The argument can be put in the form of an hypothesis.

Congress and the President exemplify composite choice in the American political system. Composite choice is a reflex of the balance of interests arising out of group-seeking and social need and reacting to pressures and crises rather than expressing an ideological position. It follows that *when social need and crisis generate pressure for institutional change and those changes conflict with the dominant ideology, the thrust for change and reform will then come first from Congress and the President, while the Supreme Court, exemplifying authoritative decision and, hence, expressing the dominant ideology, will resist change and reform.*

On the other hand, when there is no pressure of crisis but *when there exists a disaccord between ideology and practice, and when the vision is unachieved and the idea unfulfilled, then it will be the Supreme Court, acting by reference to the prevailing ideology, that will take the lead in forcing the pace of social change, and in acting as the spearhead of social reform.*

In following chapters this hypothesis will be tested by reference to the record of events.

LAYING THE SCENE

We have now introduced two of the principal actors of our drama, liberalism and nationalism, and we have laid the scene for the first crisis of policy in American political cum economic history.

To summarize, the American Revolution itself, the great rebellion against the British Crown, was at once an expression of nationalism and of liberalism. It asserted a nationhood. It drew upon the ideology of nationalism in raising its armies and in motivating the colonials in their struggle against British power. But the very conflict against the British was also a struggle against the mercantilist policies of the British Crown; against, that is, the interference of the state in the economy of private choice.

The sense of American nationhood was powerfully felt vis-à-vis the other, the outsider, in the struggle against Britain. But after the rebellion had succeeded, and after the external threat had receded, then the centralizing and unifying power of nationalism diminished and divisive and disintegrative forces built into the political, economic, and cultural circumstances came into play. There were thirteen independent state governments only loosely associated in the war for independence. Each was a well-established political system. Each had strong claims upon the loyalties and allegiances of founding families and resident individuals. And between the inhabitants of the states and regions there were differences in class origin, or in national origin, in religious orientation, and in historical experience. From state to state there were differences in speech and in culture. The states, moreover, were strongly differentiated in their economic structures and economic interests. All this, the underlying differences of culture, the variety of established allegiances, the conflicts in economic interests, and the inertial force of the status quo, constituted a powerful force for political decentralization.

The centralizing counterforce was the ideology of nationalism, based on a larger sense of common identity, on an emotional need for union, and on a rational awareness of the positive advantages of the centralized organization of the political system; i.e., for the establishment of a truly sovereign state in order to protect property, to mobilize power against the alien, to negotiate successfully with other nations, to achieve internal security and stability, and for the development of a more encompassing market system offering greater opportunities for private gain and individual fulfillment.

The federal government was an arrangement made initially by the thirteen states who were reluctant to surrender any of their independent powers. In the first instance so little power had been given to the central government that it broke down under the weight of the problems it confronted. Then, following the Constitutional Convention the federal government was assigned certain definite functional tasks narrowly delineated and carefully spelled out in a written constitution, and was alloted the minimal powers supposedly required to carry out those tasks. All other functions and powers not so delegated were specifically reserved to individuals, or to the states.

Analogous to the struggle between the feudal autonomies and monarchy in Europe, the issue then in the creation of an American political system was whether political authority was to be centralized and truly sovereign for the whole American nation, or whether political power would be dispersed among autonomous states.

Three hypotheses have been postulated:

1. Political policy is an expression of a prevailing ideology. To explain or to predict change in policy, ideological change must be foreseen and explained.
2. When crisis and need press for institutional changes that conflict with the prevailing ideology, the thrust for reform will come from the agencies of composite choice (Congress and the President) against the resistance of the agencies of authoritative choice (the Supreme Court).
3. When in the absence of crisis the imperatives of ideology remain unfulfilled, change and reform will be spearheaded by the agencies of authoritative choice (the Supreme Court) while the agencies of composite choice (Congress and the President) will resist and drag behind.

The rationale of these three hypotheses should be understood and borne in mind. It is an important point of reference for the following discussion.

Chapter 3

The Formation
of the Nation-State:
1800–1860

This chapter will deal with the two major, but related, issues confronting the new American Republic during the first half-century of its existence: (1) what was to be the form of the political system; and (2) where would be the locus of political authority? The court cases to be examined turn on matters of economic policy or control, but the transcendent question to which they relate had not to do with the economy but with the structure and organization of political power. Was the United States to be an integral nation vesting its power in a sovereign state that represented the whole, or was it to be an association of essentially independent and autonomous entities each shaped by a unique history and tradition, and each governed in a manner befitting the peculiarities and special needs of a region and of a stage or direction of economic and social development? For sixty years this question burned, and burned out finally in a terrible war.

Our focus will be on these central issues during the years between 1800 and 1860. The weight of the forces arrayed on either side against each other will be examined and compared, and the roles played in the struggle by Congress and the Court will be summarily described. Since the special concern of this book is to understand the impact of ideology on social choice, and since nowhere is that relationship made so explicit as in the Court's interpretations of the Constitution, the details of judicial interpretation will be emphasized.

AN INTERPRETATION OF INTERPRETATIONS

Most of those who study the judiciary in its interpretation of the fundamental law try to search out the coherence and constancy of the court's decisions. That is not our tack. With the greatest respect for the Court, I nevertheless hold it to be futile to try to deduce pure principles from these decisions abstracted from the circumstances of time and place. Removed from their temporal context, the Court's decisions possess no coherence and consistency. Nor does the law evolve aside from the course of social event. A coherence and consistency will be found in the rulings of the Supreme Court only when they are understood as the expressions of an ideology made manifest in solutions to changing sets of problems. When an issue has been resolved (as that concerning the form of the American political system was resolved between 1800 and 1860) and when fundamental circumstances change and new basic issues arise (as was to occur in the United States after the Civil War and the full onset of industrialization), then the Supreme Court, like the rest of society and like the other constituent parts of the political system, changes its orientation accordingly. Despite the ritual rationale that pretends a continuum of objective reasoning and the precedents by which judges depersonalize their choice, when there comes a time of change in what is sought and what is threatened, the decisions of the Court come to be about something else, to mean something else, to start from a different base, or to express a different rationale than before. Their coherence and consistency must be found not in relation to earlier rulings, but in the logic of problem-solving, in the circumstances of time and place, and on the basis of the ideology which then prevails.

STATE AUTONOMY OR SOVEREIGN NATIONALITY?

On one side were the established governments of the ex-colonies, and on the other the government of an incipient nation. Where would effective power reside?

The states and regions were not alike and their interests were not the same. Slave plantations in the South produced tobacco and cotton for export. There the landed gentry lived a gracious and elegant life, and from among them the greatest men of the revolution had come. Massachusetts and her New England satellites had their population of sturdy yeoman farmers, skilled artisans, and merchant seamen. In villages and towns they arranged their modest dwellings around the white, high-steepled church at the edge of a green common. Seafarers and merchants, they built great sailing ships that criss-crossed the seas and entered every trade. Their town meetings achieved a democracy almost as pure as that of the Athenians. And nowhere in the world was the force of Puritanism so formidable. Among the middle states was New York, with its grand patroons and Dutch patrimony, and Pennsylvania, the extraordinary bastion of religious and political tolerance and of the noble Society of Friends. There were the thriving, westward-reaching cities of New York and Philadelphia, already centers of commerce and financial power.

The states were thus inheritors of great and unique traditions. They each had their own pantheon of heroes and legends of heroisms. They were sharply different in culture, in resources, in economic organization, and in economic potential. Hence, they had different needs and different problems. The state governments were effective agencies of political choice, responsive to the people, whereas the new federal government was yet unorganized and ineffective in responding to the needs and opinions of those who lived in the farms, villages, and cities of the vast land — nor would a federal instrument of responsive administration and effective internal control be forged for a long time to come. The powers of the federal government were only incipient. Its agencies had not yet been created. It was removed from the loci of need and the problems of men in their homes, villages, farms, and regions by geographic space and by a complicated system of representation intended to reduce the force of direct democracy.

The effect of all this was to draw political action and decision, hence power, toward state governments and governments within the states. That, plus the vested power of officialdom, the particularity of regional needs, and the inertia of established institutions tended to perpetuate the decentralization of authority and to augment the power of the individual states.

On the other side, as the counterforce for concentrating authority in a sovereign nation and for diminishing the autonomous power of the states, were the sensed affinities of nationhood. These were intensified by the War of Independence and by the attraction of the idea (an abstraction merely) of an

American nation, with the advantages it promised in confronting the foreigner and in opening opportunities for private gain
and for group power in the New World. On the side of decentralization was pragmatism and the pressure of vested interests;
on the side of centralization was ideology.

The Choice of the Founding Fathers

The Constitutional Convention brought together individuals
of different views, representing the diverse interests of the states
that sent them. After extended negotiation their composite will
produced the famous document. What then was their choice?
Precluding all that happened later, an objective reading of the
Constitution suggests no intention on the part of the states to
surrender their autonomy or independence. Perforce, facing the
impending collapse of the Confederation and responding to the
panicky reaction of the property owners to Shay's Rebellion,
certain narrow, strictly delimited concessions were made to a
central agency which was henceforth to act for the association
as a whole in performing functions that could not be carried
out by the states individually.

The powers granted to Congress are specified in Article I as
follows:

Section 8. (1) The Congress shall have Power To lay and
collect Taxes, Duties, Imposts and Excises, to pay the Debts and
provide for the common Defense and general Welfare of the
United States; but all Duties, Imposts and Excises shall be uniform throughout the United States;

(2) To borrow Money on the credit of the United States;

(3) To regulate Commerce with foreign Nations, and among
the several States, and with the Indian Tribes;

(4) To establish a uniform Rule of Naturalization, and uniform Laws on the subject of Bankruptcies throughout the
United States;

(5) To coin Money, regulate the Value thereof, and of foreign Coin, and fix the Standard of Weights and Measures;

(6) To provide for the Punishment of counterfeiting the
Securities and current Coin of the United States;

(7) To establish Post Offices and post Roads;

(8) To promote the Progress of Science and useful Arts, by
securing for limited Times to Authors and Inventors the exclusive Right to their respective Writings and Discoveries;

(9) To constitute Tribunals inferior to the supreme Court;

(10) To define and punish Piracies and Felonies committed on the high Seas, and Offenses against the Law of Nations;

(11) To declare War, grant Letters of Marque and Reprisal, and make Rules concerning Captures on Land and Water;

(12) To raise and support Armies, but no Appropriation of Money to that Use shall be for a longer Term than two Years;

(13) To provide and maintain a Navy;

(14) To make Rules for the Government and Regulation of the land and naval Forces;

(15) To provide for calling forth the Militia to execute the Laws of the Union, suppress Insurrections and repel Invasions;

(16) To provide for organizing, arming, and disciplining, the Militia, and for governing such Part of them as may be employed in the Service of the United States, reserving to the States respectively, the Appointment of the Officers, and the Authority of training the Militia according to the discipline prescribed by Congress;

(17) To exercise exclusive Legislation in all Cases whatsoever, over such District (not exceeding ten Miles square) as may, by Cession of particular States, and the Acceptance of Congress, become the Seat of the Government of the United States, and to exercise like Authority over all Places purchased by the consent of the Legislature of the State in which the Same shall be, for the Erection of Forts, Magazines, Arsenals, dock-Yards, and other needful Buildings; — And

(18) To make all Laws which shall be necessary and proper for carrying into Execution the foregoing Powers, and all other Powers vested by this Constitution in the Government of the United States, or in any Department or Officer thereof.

The so-called "economic powers," as abstracted from the above, are:

(1) To lay and collect Taxes, Duties, Imposts and Excises, to pay the Debts and provide for the common Defense and general Welfare . . . ;

(2) To borrow Money . . . ;

(3) To regulate Commerce with foreign Nations, and among the several States, and with the Indian tribes;

(4) To establish . . . uniform laws on the subject of Bankruptcies . . . ;

(5) To coin Money, regulate the Value thereof . . . and fix the Standard of Weights and Measures;

(6) To establish Post Offices and post Roads; and

(7) To promote the Progress of Science and useful Arts, by securing for limited Times to Authors and Inventors the exclusive Right to their respective Writings and Discoveries.

Later, Sections 9 and 10 of Article I list a number of constraints upon the activities of the federal and state governments; for example, that "No State shall . . . pass any . . . Law impairing the Obligation of Contract. . . ."

The first nine amendments to the Constitution guarantee "inalienable rights" of individuals vis-à-vis the power of government, and the 10th specifies that, "The powers not delegated to the United States by the Constitution, nor prohibited by it to the States, are reserved to the States respectively, or to the people."

The high degree of specificity, indeed the pettiness of some of the concessions made to the national government, suggests that the founding fathers chose a political system where power was to be decentralized among the autonomous states.

The decisive voices, however, would not be of those who wrote the Constitution but of those who would interpret it.

The Role of the Supreme Court

The founding fathers so arranged the division of responsibilities that each part of the political system was in a position to impose checks and to limit the actions of the other parts. This doctrine of checks and balances reflected the apprehension of the states concerning the possible incursion of the centralized authority upon their domain; and it reflected also the apprehension of liberals concerning the exercise of political power at the expense of private (property) power. Authority was divided between the federal government and the states; and within the federal government authority was divided among Congress, the President, and the Judiciary. The Constitution does not specify how it was to be decided whether any of these three branches of government exceeded its specified powers, or what discipline, if any, should be imposed upon the offending branch.

In *Marbury* v. *Madison*,[1] itself concerned with a matter of small consequence, the Supreme Court asserted itself as guardian

---

[1]*Marbury* v. *Madison*, 5 U.S. 137 (1803).

of the Constitution, able to invalidate the laws of Congress when it found those laws contrary to the provisions of the Constitution. Thus, the high court took on a role of quite unparalleled importance in the political system.

Given the supremacy of a written constitution and the separation of powers among the President, Congress, and the Court, who was to decide by reference to the Constitution whether the laws passed by Congress were "constitutional?" That decision would be made by the Supreme Court.

Who was to decide by reference to the Constitution whether the government infringed on private rights and on the prerogatives of property as these were "guaranteed" by the Constitution? Indeed, who was to determine the concrete meaning of those "guarantees?" The Supreme Court.

Who was to decide by reference to the Constitution whether the Senate was exceeding its powers? Whether Congress was exceeding its powers? Whether the President was exceeding his powers? Whether the Supreme Court was exceeding its powers? The answer again, the Supreme Court. And who was to decide whether or not Congress was meeting or overreaching its responsibilities under the Constitution, or whether or not the executive agencies were carrying out the intent of the law? The Supreme Court.

Who was to decide by reference to the Constitution whether procedural guarantees and organizational requirements, including that of "due process," were duly fulfilled? The Supreme Court.

The Supreme Court had not only the power of censure, but also the power to shape policy. As will be seen, it did shape the development of the American political system and of American society, initially in respect to the overriding issue that faced the new republic — namely, whether the political system was to take the form of decentralized authority exercised by quasi-sovereign states or whether power was to be centralized in the federal government.

Implied Powers

Maryland taxed the notes issued by a national bank established by the federal government. When sued to enjoin the taxation of their banknotes, Maryland demurred, holding that (1) the legitimate powers of the federal government had been carefully specified and strictly limited in the Constitution, with all other powers than those so specified and delegated reserved to the states; and that (2) the power to establish a bank or banks had not been delegated to the federal government by the Constitution and was hence reserved to the states. The case went to the Supreme Court.

Chief Justice John Marshall, who wrote the opinion of the Court in *McCulloch* v. *Maryland*,[2] agreed that there was no constitutional grant of power explicitly permitting the federal government to establish a bank. However, from Article I, Section VIII, which provides that the federal government shall be permitted "to make all laws which shall be necessary and proper for carrying into execution" the specified powers, Marshall deduced the federal right to establish a national bank, arguing that such a bank might be considered as necessary and proper in undertaking, for example, "to declare and wage war." Thus, in addition to those powers specifically delegated, the federal government had by implication the powers to do anything that (in the eye of the Court) could reasonably be related to its delegated powers and functions. "Let the end be legitimate," said Chief Justice Marshall. "Let it be within the scope of the Constitution and all the means which are appropriate, which are not prohibited but consist with the letter and the spirit of the Constitution are constitutional. . . ." This was the doctrine of implied powers.

In *McCulloch* v. *Maryland* Marshall asserted another key principle. The question was not only what the federal government could do above and beyond that which was specifically allowed in the Constitution, but also the converse question as to what powers were denied to the states above and beyond those forbidden or specifically withheld by the Constitution. Here Marshall ruled that since the federal government was sovereign and its power supreme in its proper domain, (1) the states could exercise no power that might constrain, obstruct or conflict with the legitimate functions and the explicit and the implied powers of the federal government, and (2) the states had no parallel right to exercise the explicit or implied powers or to perform the functions that were vested in the federal

---

[2]*McCulloch* v. *Maryland*, 17 U.S. 316 (1819).

government. If these powers implicitly or explicitly vested in the federal government were not being invoked by the federal government, or if those functions that were directly or derivatively the prerogative of the federal government were not being performed by the federal government, could the states then undertake them? In this instance also, Marshall held, the states were excluded from their exercise; for, under those circumstances, it must be inferred that the supreme and ultimate federal authority was not performing these functions because it did not want them performed. If the federal government did not invoke its powers to act, it must be because it wanted no action to be taken.

With this decision the constitutional limits upon the federal authority seem almost to vanish. By this single opinion the constitutional blueprint for an American political system changes from one where the states are powerful and autonomous, with a federal agency designed to play a supplementary role and allowed to do only what the states cannot do independently, to a blueprint for the concentration of virtually all the functions of government into the political center, with federal authority supreme. What powers or functions, after all, could not reasonably be implied from the federal responsibility to develop the military strength of the nation? Wasn't the whole economy and all that relates to its viability and growth, hence all of education and trade, ultimately basic to the capability to "wage war?" Conversely, since all that accrued to the federal government was denied to the states, the states were subordinated, their authority was radically diminished, and the legitimate scope of their powers shrank to the uncertain penumbra beyond the indefinable limits of the implied powers of the national government.

Interstate Commerce

The Constitution had given the federal government the power "to regulate commerce . . . among the several states" and hence the states were implicitly denied that right. But what did "commerce" mean? What did it include? Was the clause intended to prevent the states from imposing tariffs and quotas on each other's goods, allowing only federal regulation of the interstate sale of goods and services? One might have supposed that to be the constitutional intent. Or had the regulation of commerce some other meaning? The question was decided in *Gibbons* v. *Ogden*.[3]

The right of a state to franchise and regulate a ferry crossing a river and carrying passengers between points in New York and New Jersey had been challenged; and the case was brought to the Supreme Court. The Court ruled that transportation must be considered as a part of commerce. Hence, under the commerce clause the regulation of transportation between states belonged to the federal jurisdiction and therefore, that regulatory power was denied to the states. Commerce, said Justice Marshall "is traffic, but it is something more. . . . It describes the commercial intercourse . . . in all its branches." The federal government's power to regulate interstate commerce was thus interpreted very broadly to include trade, transportation, and communication.[4] But at what point do trade, transportation, and communication (commercial intercourse in all its branches) begin or end? Conceivably indeed "commercial intercourse" between the states "in all its branches" would include the sum total of all the interdependent productive-distributive activities of the market (including the hiring and management of labor; the organization of enterprise, the procurement of materials and equipment; and the distribution, sale, and consumption of products) inasmuch as all these were part of an integral system of exchange relationships that extended as a single flow between the states and the nations.[5]

The Open Road to Centralization

In two key cases the Supreme Court swept away the constraints upon centralizing the political authority. It did not create a modern state, but laid the basis for one. The Constitution had allotted a limited number of specific powers to the federal government and had reserved all others to the states. The Supreme Court ruled that all power necessary and proper for the exercise of the specified powers belonged also to the federal government, and asserted, moreover, that whatever specified or

---

[3]*Gibbons* v. *Ogden*, 22 U.S. 1 (1824).
[4]See *Railroad Company* v. *Husen*, 95 U.S. 465 (1877) and *Pensacola Tel. Co.* v. *Western Union Tel. Co.*, 96 U.S. 1 (1877) for later cases.
[5]See *Steamer Daniel Ball* v. *U.S.*, 77 U.S. 557 (1870); *The Shreveport Rate Cases*, 234 U.S. 342 (1914); *Lemke* v. *Farmers Grain Co.*, 258 U.S. 50 (1922); and *Stafford* v. *Wallace*, 258 U.S. 495 (1922) for later developments, generally in a fundamentally alerted context, of the flow of commerce notion.

implied power belonged to the federal government was denied to the states. No other political authority could stand in the way of, nor impinge upon, nor substitute for their exercise.

To understand the implications of the court's rule, consider two of the delegated powers: (1) to wage war and (2) to regulate commerce between the states. Anything relevant to national "strength" (e.g., education, industry, science, and population), unquestionably relates to the power to wage war and hence, by a reasonable interpretation of the doctrine of implied powers, falls within the exclusive domain of the federal government. And everything that has to do with agriculture or industry, with labor or with wages, or with conditions of work, or with prices or profits can be understood as relating to commerce between the states and hence, as falling within the federal domain. Inasmuch as these are subject to the federal authority they are, for that reason, excluded from the powers of the states. The constitutional blueprint for the organization and development of the American political system had been fundamentally changed. The ideology of nationalism, heritage of European experience in its centuries old struggle against tradition-based privileges and the fragmented political powers of feudalism, prevailed.

In its beginning the federal government in the United States was like the European Economic Community is today, or like the United Nations is today—a political agency begrudgingly granted a few limited functions by separate and sovereign political entities. In less than 25 years, under the pressure of the prevailing ideology expressed in the decisions of the Supreme Court, the power structure of the American political system was revolutionized. The federal power became sovereign and that of the states was subordinated. Virtually all political power could now move to the center. And because the Court ruled that what belonged to the sovereign could be exercised only by the sovereign, the federal government was to some degree obliged to act even against the inclinations of its own legislators. The Supreme Court not only permitted but forced power into the hands of the federal government.

So long as the issue was of federal power versus power of the states, the Supreme Court supported a vesting of authority in the nation-state. Not until the *Dred Scott* decision on the verge of the Civil War did the Supreme Court declare a federal law unconstitutional — and then (foreshadowing the issue that would prevail in the epoch that followed), it was not the authority of the states, but the power of property (of slave ownership) that the Court was concerned to protect.

While the way to centralization was opened by the Courts under the sanction of the prevailing ideology, the practices of Congress and the President, and of the states and their legislatures, changed slowly. It was not for another quarter of a century that the issue of union and hence of ultimate federal supremacy was finally settled on the blood-drenched battlefields of the Civil War.

The Interest of Liberalism

Thus, the decisions of the Court concentrated authority in the nation-state. Through the rule of the Court, ideology gained preeminence over the vested interests and the pragmatic pressures to maintain the traditional autonomy of the states. But if the ideology of nationalism gained ascendency over expedience and tradition in this instance, what about liberalism? In our time we have seen the liberal ideologists opposing the power and the intervention of the federal government and, in so doing, taking up the battle cry of "states' rights." Consider, for example, these excerpts from the opinion of Justice Sutherland speaking for the Court more than a century later, in *Carter* v. *Carter Coal Co.*[6] (1935), in a case which dealt a hard blow to the federal power.

> The states were before the Constitution; and consequently their legislative powers antedated the Constitution. Those who framed and those who adopted that instrument meant to carve from the general mass of legislative powers then possessed by the states, only such portions as it was wise to confer upon the Federal government; and in order that there should be no uncertainty in respect of what was taken and what was left, the national powers of legislation were not aggregated but were enumerated — with the result that what was not embraced by enumeration remained vested in the states without change or impairment. . . . And since every addition of the national legislative power to some extent detracts from or invades the power of the states, it is of vital moment that, in order to preserve the fixed balance intended by the Constitution, the powers of the general government be not so extended as to embrace any not

_____
[6]*Carter* v. *Carter Coal Co.*, 298 U.S. 238 (1936).

within the express terms of the several grants or the implications necessarily drawn therefrom. . . . The determination of the Framer's Convention and the ratifying conventions to preserve complete and unimpaired state self-government in all matters not committed to the general government is one of the plainest facts which emerge from the history of their deliberations. And adherence to that determination is incumbent equally upon the Federal government and the states. State powers can neither be appropriated on the one hand nor abdicated on the other. . . . Every journey to a forbidden end begins with a first step; and the danger of such a step by the Federal government in the direction of taking over the power of the states is that the end of the journey may find the states so despoiled of their powers . . . as to reduce them to little more than geographical subdivisions of the national domain . . . if, when the Constitution was under consideration, it had been thought that any such danger lurked behind its plain words, it would never have been ratified.

Yet for the first half century of constitutional development, the whole thrust of the Court was to reduce the power of the states and to invest an increased and seemingly boundless authority in the national government. Was there a contradiction between the nationalism of Marshall and his Court and the interests of liberalism? In fact there was none — at that time. The liberal ideology sought a solid infrastructural base for a viable market system — one that would allow the widest possible sphere for freedom of trade and the unrestricted movement of real and financial resources and goods and commodities, a sound currency, a national system of banking and credit, security for property and the full enforcement of contractual obligation and the claims of creditors throughout the nation. The most likely way to achieve these goals was to shift power from the states to the national government, for if the states had the power to do so, they probably would have restricted trade and finance to protect sectional interests. The states would have strongly expressed in law and institutions the suspicions, the frustrations, and the accumulating resentments against the capitalist middle-man and creditor in the urban centers of the East. Thus, in *McCulloch* v. *Maryland*, whatever the long-run implications of the decision, in respect to the specific, substantive issue the Court was throwing its weight on the side of the party of property and wealth and against the antagonisms of the rural majority that soon would be expressed in the Jacksonian upheaval. To establish a national bank, thereby creating the context and promoting the establishment of a viable and vigorous national market system, was precisely to express the liberal ideology.

Later, resistance to political intervention in economic affairs would become the battle cry of liberalism, but now there was no need for such an outcry. In this first stage of American history, the shift of political authority from the states to the national government had the effect of taking power away from those governments that were more effective interveners and were more subject to democratic pressure for economic intervention to offset specific ills, and giving power to a government that was less effective on that score and was further removed from and, hence, less responsive to the democratic pressure for the amelioration of the difficulties that beset individuals and groups. In the American society of the time, where nearly the whole population was thinly scattered on farms and in rural communities over the vast breadth of the land, the pressure for political action, for political regulation, and for intervention (such as it was) was bound to be scattered and localized. It was only the governments of the states or of governments within the states, long established and responsive to on-the-spot pressures, that could and would intervene in economic affairs. The federal government in the mud flats of Washington was weeks and months away by mule and horseback. It was a new government only slowly taking form; generations would have to pass before it developed agencies capable of complex administrative action. Its capacity to deal with local needs was nil, and virtually all the needs and pressures for intervention in the economy were local. Hence, to deprive state and local governments of power and to vest it instead in the federal government was, at that stage of history, to move away from intervention. Consider, for example, *Gibbons v. Ogden*. At the level of legal abstraction, Marshall's argument was powerful and convincing. Where the federal government was sovereign, it did what it willed to do; and where it did nothing, it must be inferred that it wanted nothing done. But in respect to what was specifically at issue, the argument was ludicrous. Being what and where it was, the federal government could not franchise ferries and regulate their crossing between points in New York and New Jersey, across the Hudson or the Delaware, or elsewhere across the innumerable rivers, bays, lakes, and streams in this vast land. If such control was not to be exercised by governments of or within the states, it would not be exercised at all. Thus, to minimize intervention and the possibility of control was no affront to liberalism.

Nationalism held the stage in the first phase of American political development. But liberalism watched from a box and applauded. Its interests were being served.

The Sovereign National State: A Test of the Hypothesis

In Chapter 2, differentiating between composite choice by Congress and the President and authoritative choice by the Supreme Court, it was hypothesized (in part) that *when there exists a disaccord between ideology and organization or practice, then it will be the Supreme Court, acting by reference to the prevailing ideology, that will take the lead in forcing the pace of social change, acting as the spearhead of social reform.* Consider in these terms the first phase in the development of the American political system that began at the turn of the 19th Century and culminated more than half a century later in the Civil War. During that period the existing organization of the political system, with power vested in the established autonomy of the separate states, was out of kilter with the powerful and prevailing ideology of nationalism. The American Constitution, a product of composite choice, was intended narrowly to limit the federal authority and to protect the substantive power of the states. The Constitution as interpreted by the Supreme Court concentrated political authority in the federal government, thereby redesigning the blueprint for the American political system. If a de facto decentralization of power continued, it was the consequence not of constitutional rule but because the agencies of composite choice remained inert in their established practices and habituated ways.

The drive to centralize political authority and, thereby, to create a coherent, national state was spearheaded by the Supreme Court rather than Congress or the President. In this regard Congress and the President seemed more to follow the paths of expediency and to respond to the resistances and yield to the pressures of sectional particularism.

The Supreme Court led the way in centralizing political authority. In this instance the Supreme Court was the progenitor of radical change and reform. The Court used the cases that came before it to restrict and to limit the powers of the states and to open new horizons for federal responsibility and action. The Court forced the centralization of the political authority because the Court, rather than Congress and the President, articulated and expressed the prevailing ideology; an ideology, nevertheless, that was accepted in principle and "believed in" even by most of those who resisted each particular step along the way toward the centralization of political authority in a sovereign national state. Thinking men could hardly deny the general values of unification in the exercise of the sovereign power. The Supreme Court reshaped the political system because no particular interest or vested power could prevail against the rationale of the nationalist ideology.

Thus, in this first phase of American constitutional development, where the locus of the political power and the form of the political system was at issue, events confirm the hypothesis. Day-to-day pressures, considerations of expediency, vested interests, institutional inertia, and conventional practice all re-enforced the autonomy of the states. Ideology demanded that power be concentrated at the national center. Authoritative choice, expressed through the Supreme Court, made manifest that ideology and forced the transformation of the political system. Congress and the President, instruments of composite choice, followed slowly in the path charted by the Court.

CENTRIPETAL AND CENTRIFUGAL CHANGE IN POLITICAL SYSTEMS: CANADA AND THE UNITED STATES

The concentration of political power at the national center could not have been forced merely by the whim and will of the judges. The judges could require it because they expressed the ideological norms that society accepted. And the national commitment to that ideology was proven in the great testing of the Civil War itself. Why was it that in the United States the mystique of the union was accepted as the ideological norm? What gave force in this country to the ideology of nationalism and the logic of political centralization? The very reverse happened in our northern neighbor, the Dominion of Canada. Beginning with a highly centralized political system, Canada has gradually and persistently fragmented the powers of its government until today it verges on national dissolution. How can this contrast be explained? In attempting to do so, and in explaining the integration and disintegration of social entities generally, one might postulate the following:

1. When the culture (i.e., the prevailing system of values and evaluation) is homogeneous throughout a community, this acts as a centripetal force pulling the parts together; conversely, cultural heterogeneity acts as a centrifugal force. In spite of the diverse origins of its peoples, American culture has been extraordinarily homogeneous. The exception, of course, has been the South; and the South, correspondingly, was generally a divisive force drawing back and pulling away from the centripetal force of union. In Canada, on the other hand, culture is relatively heterogeneous, divided not only between the French Canadian and the English-speaking Canadian, but also among those who retain the cultural cast of the Britisher, of the German, of the Hungarian, of the Pole, and of still others shaped by the cultural mold of the United States.

2. When technology and trade create interdependence between regional groupings and populations, correspondingly those parts are drawn into closer union. Technologies are not always such as to create a web of interdependence corresponding to any given political domain. Trade may pull a system apart rather than together. In the United States trade and technology, on the whole, have been centripetal, drawing the parts together through a condition of interdependence. From the early years of the republic, manufactured goods from the Eastern seaboard moved to supply the western farmer, while the food produced by the latter supported the urban concentrations of the East. Again the South was the exception. The South was not dependent upon western imports of food. Basically agricultural, it could sustain itself. And the southern trade in cotton and tobacco was largely, if not always primarily, with Europe. Hence, at the level of economic interdependence, trade drew the South away from (rather than into) the American orbit. Correspondingly, the South was a divisive counterforce to union.

Later, industrialization spread its iron rings, integrating vast territories and masses of men into integral processes of production. The new industrial technology not only hammered the parts of the American society into a condition of interdependence but also created problems for regulation and control on a national scale that required control powers coextensive with the nation. Again, the South was least encompassed by the integrating and homogenizing force of industrialization.

Canada, on the other hand, was basically agricultural throughout its formative periods. Its scattered farms were not technically interdependent, and its trade flows created ties of exchange not between Canadian and Canadian, but between the Canadian producer or consumer and the United States, or between the Canadian producer or consumer and the economies of Great Britain, Japan, or Western Europe. The new industrialization of Canada is, indeed, de-parochializing and more integrative than the agriculture which it replaces. It draws diverse groups into its vortex and, perhaps, homogenizes their culture. But Canadian industry remains largely an extension — a bulge, so to speak — of American industry, and in some cases, of English and European industry. In that sense the ties of technology draw lines of extra Canadian dependence rather than of Canadian intradependence.

3. A social entity may also be drawn together by the nature and scope of the opportunities or problems it confronts and by the threats to its collective well-being or survival. In Toynbee's terms men may unite in response to a challenge providing that the challenge demands union. The problems and challenges which historically confronted the American — to shake off the British rule; to open, populate, develop, and exploit a vast and rich continent; to defend that whole continent against a threat of European imperialism; to resolve the issue of slavery; to survive the great depression; and to assume leadership in the modern ideological schism — were all vast in scope, requiring the exercise of centralized power. Challenge and the response to challenge was profoundly centripetal. The Canadians, on the other hand, also faced large problems and vast opportunities, so large indeed as to be beyond their national scope and power no matter how power was concentrated. The Canadians have been obliged to depend on the support and power of the United States, Great Britain, or other nations for their defense, for the exploitation of the resources of their enormous territories, and for the opening of those territories for communication and growth. Therefore, such opportunities and problems have not called forth a collective response and brought into play the

exercise of centralized power. Perforce the focus of Canadian effort has been on local issues and sectoral adjustments; and the effect of all this on Canadian society had been centrifugal rather than centripetal.

4. The above suggests some of the underlying forces which provide a sense of nationhood, shape the ideology of nationalism, and produce a strong nation-state. But once the ideology of nationalism, for whatever reason, has been formed and has captured men's imagination, belief, and dedication, the ideology becomes itself a powerful and independent force acting upon social organizations and on the form of political systems. During the years of the founding of the American republic, in Italy a struggle both to propagate the ideology of nationalism and, under its banner, to fight for nationhood was already two centuries old; but that ideology would not sufficiently capture the devotion of the people and congeal their will into a successful fight for independence and national unity for yet another century. In Germany it was to be the confrontation with, and the conquest by, the revolutionary French armies under Napoleon which gave ideological nationalism its force. In India today the ideology of nationalism is the sole centripetal force pitched against the centrifugal powers of cultural diversity and a non-integrative technology. Canadian nationalism in part derives from the real or imagined threat of the American presence. It has acquired new force and centripetal thrust in recent years as a reaction to the brutal mien of cold-war imperialism and to the new ubiquity of the "other" in the guise of the international corporation. This new nationalism may, for awhile at least, turn the tide against the disintegration of an integral Canadian nationhood.

The ideology of nationalism is not always an integrating and centralizing force. Sometimes it is the opposite. For example, in the ancient Austro-Hungarian empire, nationalist ideologies were profoundly centrifugal and after World War I, resulted in the fragmentation of that empire into many small parts. So the nationalist ideology also has been disruptive of the European empires, which contained the different cultures of colonized peoples. And today the ideology of nationalism is a barrier against rational and radical efforts of society to reconstitute itself into more encompassing political systems and to centralize political authority beyond the scope of national governments.

THE OBSOLESCENCE OF THE NATION-STATE:
A POSTSCRIPT

The homogenizing force of industrialization, the shrinking significance of geographical space as a barrier between men and groups, and the force of mass communication have all washed away those particularities which once were the underpinnings of nationhood. Supranational political ideologies, such as Marxism, and felt affinities beyond national groupings, such as "Europeanism," "Arabism," and "Black Africanism," work for an integration at least beyond the nation.

Moreover, the growing importance of supranational phenomena and institutions, such as organized science or even the international corporation, create a web of interdependence in respect to which the traditional organization of power into nation-states, where each is conceived as airtight and self-contained, becomes increasingly inappropriate.

Moreover, in great part political systems have taken their form as a means, through military defense and alliance, of providing security against invasion and conquest. In the past half-century the division of the world into nation-states, each making the mutually incommensurable claim of absolute sovereignty, has generated conflagrations from which none could escape. And as the culmination of this, the development of nuclear weaponry eliminates any possibility that national power could, under any conceivable circumstances, secure its peoples from devastating attack and virtual destruction. If for no other reason than this, the world political system of nation-states has become functionally obsolete.

Chapter 4

The Epoch of Liberalism

Who and what are those persons who have been justices of the Supreme Court? Generally they have been hard-working intellectuals, trained in the law, and believing in the values of its continuity. Believing in continuity, they have given great weight to precedent and to established practices. They have looked upon themselves as those who knew and applied the law—a law which they did not create but which was handed down to them. The Constitution has been for them a supreme law, an objective reality beyond their private discretion. Certainly they have not been philosophers propounding truth and justice from Olympian heights, nor have they considered themselves as such. Yet when the judge interprets the large phrases of the Constitution, he supposes the words to express sound reasoning; that is, reasoning that he considers sound. He understands the words to mean what he thinks they ought to mean if they are to make good sense.

And when the judges have been called upon to make choices which they knew might profoundly affect their society, they have made those choices to the extent that they could and to the extent that they were able to justify and to rationalize their decisions by reference to what they thought was best for society—and by reference to what their peers would accept as being best for society. All this is to say that the judges have made, as judges must always make, their decisions by reference to the ideology prevalent in their time and shared by their peer group.

THE LIBERAL'S UNIVERSE

In the United States during the Nineteenth Century, at least with respect to economic policy, there seems to have been a clear-cut norm—that of ideological liberalism. Of course there were deviations about the norm. Some were more rigid in their adherence, some were "pure" in their orthodoxy, others were more sceptical and ready for exceptions, some were humanistic, and others more mechanistic in response and interpretation. But as a policy guideline, there was no other system of thought, outlook, or coherent set of values to countervail against that of liberalism.[1]

How might one convey the outlook and ideology of liberalism during the latter half of the nineteenth century? Perhaps by reading again the work of a great liberal writer such as John Stuart Mill (1806–1873).[2] Mill was not dogmatic or orthodox. On the contrary, he stood on the left and was considered as a radical reformer, even a "socialist."

Consider, then, Mill's image of the social reality as it appears in his famous *Principles*. He conceived the economy as a universe of small proprietorships, a world of individual sellers and individual buyers all caught in the flux and stress of the market, alike motivated by self-interest in profits or in some other form of private gain, all guided by freely moving flexible price, and all chastised and checked by the salutary force of competition. He saw, or thought he saw, in the real world what the economic theorists today call the "model of pure competition." But this was no theoretical model for him. It was for him, as it was to all liberals of the age, the simple facts, the bald reality, the natural state of affairs, the underlying truth. This is what he saw or thought he saw; and he considered it good.

Liberty and the Market

For Mill the primary social value was "liberty." By liberty he meant individualized choice. The free market was understood to be the central arena for the exercise of individualized choice and, hence, for the significant exercise of "liberty." Not only

---

[1]DeTocqueville's observation, "I know of no country in which there is so little independence of mind and real freedom of discussion as in America," has been explained by Noam Chomsky by reference to what Chomsky calls "a highly restrictive and almost universally shared ideology." *New York Review of Books* (January 2, 1969), p. 29.

[2]John Stuart Mill, *Principles of Political Economy* (London, 1864).

Chapter 4

was individualized choice in the competitive market intrinsically good, but also it was taken as axiomatic that this form of choice was the most efficient way of organizing economic activity. Individualized choice in the competitive market, moreover, was considered as good because it served as a school for self-reliance and initiative, and as a means of initiating the masses into a knowledge of the techniques and the skills of decision-making and choice. It was also taken as axiomatic by Mill that the use of the political system for organizing economic activity was inherently inefficient and uncreative. Moreover, by its natural proclivities the political authority was considered as a threat to liberty. That under democracy government would represent the interests of the majority was not the point. Liberty was what mattered; and under democracy the liberty of the rich would be threatened by the prejudices of poor majorities. Hence, it was inherently desirable to minimize the power of government no matter what its form and no matter to whose interest it was subservient. Under any guise the political authority must be kept from any meddling with the exercise of individualized choice in the market. Only the positive proof of palpable injury to others could justify such meddling; and even when there was proof of such injury, political interference should be undertaken only very reluctantly. "Laissez-faire," said Mill, "should be the general practice; every departure from it, unless required by some greater good, is a certain evil."[3]

Mill did not recognize large voluntary (corporate) organization as significant in the economy. No doubt there were such organizations, but he considered them as marginal, peripheral, and perhaps unnatural. In his *Principles* the only form of monopoly he considered worth writing about was that which had been enfranchised and was protected by the state. Evidently he could not conceive of private monopoly power as existing independently of the state's protection. The only combinations in restraint of trade that he chose to analyze were the trade unions. These he was prepared to tolerate because he supposed that combinations of working men could never be more than transitory and could never exert a significant power against the underlying natural force of competitive price.

The corporation or "joint stock company" he regarded as unnatural; and indeed as a monstrosity that was at least as

_____
[3] *Ibid.*, p. 569.

unprogressive and inefficient as the agencies of government and even less desirable than these as an instrument for the organization of economic activity. He would as soon have seen the activities of private corporations taken over by government agencies.

Yet at the very time that the later editions of Mill's great work were appearing, wherein the market economy is conceived as a universe of small enterprise with the corporation of no significance and private monopoly not worth discussing, there was occurring in the United States the most awesome and rapid movement toward business concentration and monopoly that the world has ever known. Whole industries were amalgamated and brought within the control of massive corporate organizations — the so-called "trusts."

Ideological Lag

Such blindness is amazing and extraordinary only in retrospect. It was a blindness characteristic of the age and a species of blindness that is likely to be characteristic of any age. Finally, every long-established ideology will lag behind change in the social structure, and when such change is spontaneous and rapid, the ideology falls correspondingly out of kilter with the world to which it refers and which it intends to depict.

In his *Principles* Mill took no account of the ugly facts about the competitive market system. He took no account of the dreadful insecurities and wasteful instabilities implicit in this form of economic organization. He hardly saw its raw injustices. The concentration of property and private power and the arbitrary use of that power to constrain the opportunities of others did not detain him. From him one gets no notion of the stunted, degraded lives of the English laboring class during that century. The competitive market was his ideal. He did not judge it but rather judged everything else by reference to its values. Nor could he see that the market system was undergoing revolutionary changes of structure. Mill held the system up as the ideal and argued for it with all his logic and passion as an ideal which provided the general rule for social policy and political conduct. Nevertheless, when he stepped down from the platform of large generalizations and from the role of philosopher and economist to concern himself with concrete problems that happened to arouse his interest (such as the deprivations of small children in factories; the British colonization in Australia, Africa, or Asia; or the question as to whether or not to provide free elementary education), then Mill relaxed his laissez-faire zeal and advocated public intervention, government meddling, and collective controls, rationalizing these as exceptions to the rule.

That is the way it was with Mill and with his milieu. The ideal was universally accepted; but more zealously and absolutely further removed was judgment from concrete problems and from facts in the universe of economic experience.

All this may convey a condemnation of Mill which is not intended. Certainly we have no right to judge his conceptualizations, theories, and judgments by reference to experience and observation in our time—or even by reference to our observation of his time. Conceptualizations of the most perceptive normally lag behind the realities of their own day simply because the notions then present are not based on instant observation but on an accumulation of observations. Hence, the current fund of conception and idea derives preponderantly from experiences and observations of the past, necessarily referring to events and institutions as they were rather than to those that immediately are. Mill's conception of a universe of small enterprise interacting competitively in a price-directed market system was probably an acceptable representation of the world as he had known it over the whole of his long life, and as it had been known and experienced by those "classical" predecessors who shaped his thought. If he took that system of decentralized choice under the direction of competitive price, not only as real but as ideal, it must be said that that system had performed with great success in the historical era within his purview. The possibilities, moreover, of effective control or regulation by a political authority, or of the direct organization of complex activities by government, were quite different in his day than in ours.

Practically all economists *believed*—no matter what they *desired*—that, as J. S. Mill put it, laissez-faire was the general rule for the administration of a nation's economic affairs and that what was significantly called state "interference" was the exception. And though for different reasons in different countries, this was so in actual practice not only as a matter of fact but also as a matter of practical necessity; no responsible administrator could have held then, and no responsible historian should hold now, that, social and economic conditions and the organs of public administration being what they were, any ambitious ventures in regulation and control could have issued in anything but failure.[4]

Mill, moreover, did not experience in his lifetime some of the more striking and painful manifestations of the changing economic structure. The formation of the great trusts in the United States took place during the last quarter of the nineteenth century and the "Great Depression" of that century, with its decades of mass unemployment, did not start until the year of Mill's death in 1873. This depression, according to Maurice Dobb, "has come to be regarded as forming a watershed between the two stages of capitalism: the earlier vigorous, prosperous, and flushed with adventurous optimism; the later more troubled, more hesitant, and, some would say, already bearing the marks of senility and decay."[5]

The purpose here is not to criticize Mill or his theories but through them to suggest that: (1) the nature of the dominant liberal ideology conceived of a universe of small enterprises competitively interacting in a price-directed market system as real, ideal, and natural; (2) consequently, the ideology postulated laissez-faire as the appropriate "rule" for political policy; and (3) there was a widening gap between that ideology and world reality.

Liberalism and Industrialization in the United States

Liberalism was the prevailing ideology in the United States and laissez-faire was accepted as the rule. During the first half-century of the existence of the new American republic, there was no significant controversy concerning the degree and propriety of governmental intervention in economic activity. Presumably, this was because the government was not pressed by need and circumstance to intervene and, thus, did not significantly intervene in the domestic economy. There were tariffs, subsidies of sorts, and taxes but free bargaining, individualized choice, and price movements were the unchallenged regulators of economic activity.

---

[4]Joseph A. Schumpeter, *History of Economic Analysis* (New York: Oxford University Press, 1954), p. 548.

[5]Maurice Dobb, *Studies in the Development of Capitalism* (rev. ed.; New York: International Publishers Co., Inc., 1964), pp. 300–319. For a study of this period, see also Walt W. Rostow, *British Economy of the Nineteenth Century* (New York: Oxford University Press, 1948); and E. H. Phelps-Brown and S. J. Hanfield-Jones, "The Climacteric of the 1890's; A Study in the Expanding Economy," *Oxford Economic Papers* (1952), IV, pp. 266–307.

During that first half century there was no ideological pressure for public intervention in economic affairs nor was significant intervention demanded at the local level by affected parties. There was no need for it. Life was hard enough, but it was simple and full of opportunity. A man could handle things himself; he could do it on his own. Proprietary enterprise served a growing market. Most people lived on farms and produced in good part what they needed for their own living. The level of their lives depended, correspondingly, on their hard work and acquired skill. And always the frontier offered new land, provided an open-ended outlet for individual ambition and hope, and set a minimum condition of life everywhere for the enterprising man.

But the century progressed and America was changing. There was the fundamental economic transformation of *industrialization*. It began before the Civil War but during that war and in its aftermath the economy industrialized with growing momentum. By the third quarter of the nineteenth century America had become an industrialized nation.

What did this mean for markets and men?

It meant the concentration and centralization of economic power, not in governmental agencies but in autonomous corporations. Through the instrumentality of this new business form, human and material resources of unprecedented magnitudes were brought together as integral operating organizations.

With the coming of the great corporation, property lost its former significance. Control was no longer strictly a function of private ownership. That link through property that tied self-interest to the economical use of resources, which for a J. S. Mill was the penultimate virtue of the market, was broken. Business ceased to depend on the life and will of the "natural" man. Rather, temporal power came to reside in a race of "artificial" persons, gigantic, immortal, without souls — the corporations.

Not until after the Civil War and only gradually then did the right of incorporation become a common right and the corporate form become commonplace. In 1886 in the case of Santa Clara County v. Southern Pacific RR,[6] the Supreme Court ruled that the corporation was a person, an artificial person to be sure but nevertheless entitled to all of the rights and prerogatives of the natural man under the Fifth and the Fourteenth Amendments.

---

[6]*Santa Clara County v. Southern Pacific R. R. Co.*, 118 U.S. 394 (1886).

More and more the individual was submerged in organizations, absorbed into a group, planned for, and managed. The managers were managed. Choice was composite or authoritative but in any case was within and through vast organizations. Like it or not, the capacity for problem-solving through individualized choice as it once existed in the market system was gone, or at least was greatly diminished.

Like it or not, men could not make it on their own any more, as once they were able to do. Men were part of organizations. They depended on organizations. What happened to them depended on what happened within the organization and on what happened to the organization, and the fate of the organization itself depended on the shifting winds of world demand and on the onslaught of new technologies — forces outside the control of any private or (then) political agency of choice.

Gone was the hard independence and self-sufficiency of the farm. American society had become urbanized. Its population was crowded into the cities where propertyless masses were tightly packed in slums. Laborers waited outside the factory gate or in the bullpens for the chance to work on the factory benches. And for them there was no escape. The open-ended opportunities of the frontier were no more.

America was a land of immigrants. But the new waves were of a different order than the old. Hundreds of thousands came or were brought in by the corporations from Southern and Eastern Europe to work in the mills and in the mines. Deeply ignorant and habituated to arbitrary rule, they were easy victims and they were ruthlessly victimized.

In an earlier age there had been frequent financial "panics." These were the consequences of changes in the value of money too rapid for the institutional structure to bear. They resulted in the repudiation of debts through bankruptcies, the breakdown of credit, the disruption of contractual arrangements. But now economic crisis was of a different and more terrible order. It had become the phenomenon of depression, with massive and sustained unemployment and a cessation of production threatening social breakdown and driving a part of the population to, or even beyond, the threshold of starvation.[7]

---

[7]Compare the massive unemployment in the great depression referred to in previous footnotes with that described by Douglass C. North, *Economic Growth of the United States, 1790–1860* (New York: W. W. Norton and Co., Inc., 1966), where price fluctuations are described but unemployment is never mentioned.

Outcry of Victims

The rosy ideology of liberalism remained a comfort for those who could afford it, but for a growing number of others it was outside their experience and incongruous in their situation. They were the victims of the system, suffering and desperate with wasted, degraded lives. Not that they had any coherent alternative as a basis for policy. Given the opportunity they would have been glad to bear witness to the splendid vision of uninhibited private liberties and rugged individualism protected by private property and expressed in the free market. They had no countervailing philosophy; only wounds to show for desperate needs and dilemmas that they could not escape through individualized choice and action.

They were not without a voice, however. They could cry out. They could vote, threaten, demand, or ask. And their situation and discontents were, to some degree, reflected in the pressures exerted on the mayors and bosses in the cities; on the legislators and governors of the states; on the congressmen, senators, and executive officials; and on the President himself. In response there emerged some scattered action through the public agencies of composite choice. Laws were passed by the governments of the states and by the federal government that were intended (1) to limit the hours worked by young children and to control the conditions in which children worked in factories and in the mines; (2) to regulate working hours and conditions for women in the factories; (3) to regulate working hours and conditions for men in certain hazardous occupations or in industries where they were easily victimized; (4) to control the fees charged by intermediaries and middlemen who were strategically placed to exploit the ignorance and urgent needs of others; and (5) to control prices and wages or outputs in certain very "sick" industries.

What happened to these laws during this era of liberalism between 1860 and 1935, and to the marginal effort to ameliorate the miseries of an industrialized society that these laws represented? What happened to them when they came before the Supreme Court, that agency of authoritative decision and stronghold of ideology?

Consider some of the cases before the Court. Out of the jigsaw of these decisions a coherent pattern may emerge. Only a few representative cases will be described. Indeed the number of cases dealt with by the Court are relatively few since each case enunciated the supreme law and became the rule that either opened or barred shut the whole range of analogous actions. Thus, a single decision preventing one state from seeking to prevent a particular evil would nip in the bud any effort by any other state to attempt any similar amelioration.

Efforts to Control Child Labor

The most tragic victims of the industrial system were those children of the proletariat who were forced into factories and mines before their bodies and minds had been formed. Their lives were used up as a cheap resource in the production line. Their bodies and minds were stunted and destroyed. Political authorities here and there tried to act to ameliorate extreme conditions; and the Court begrudgingly allowed local governments to act against "excesses" in the same way and on the same grounds that local governments were allowed to prevent barroom fights or prostitution under their "police power," inasmuch as these were to be considered as deviant behavior offensive to the tranquillity and good morals of the citizenry. But local and state governments could not effectively control child labor since employers could always move to another state or to another town or county where "abuses" were allowed; and, of course, the abuses were greatest where people were the poorest and most disorganized and hence least able to resist whatever was demanded of them. Each state or locality, competing to keep business within its borders, was constrained from raising standards very much above the level of the worst and least responsible of its "competitive" neighbor governments.

After generations of suffering and after the proven futility of local efforts, the national government did pass a law forbidding goods to be transported in interstate commerce when such goods were produced in factories that employed children of fourteen years of age or under, or that required fourteen- to sixteen-year-olds to work more than eight hours a day and six days a week. In 1916 in the case of *Hammer* v. *Dagenhart*,[8] this law was challenged before the Supreme Court. And the Supreme Court invalidated the law. In so doing it forbade the federal government to enter into any regulation of manufacturing and its

---

[8]*Hammer* v. *Dagenhart*, 247 U.S. 251 (1918).

practices. The court reasoned that the constitutional power of the federal government to regulate commerce between the states did not cover the *manufacturing* of the commodities which entered into the flow of commerce.

Child labor as an economic condition was inherently beyond control by the decentralized authority of the states and, by the rule of the Supreme Court, control was forbidden to the federal government as well. In effect the use of child labor, no matter that it might be boundlessly evil and socially detrimental, by the ruling of the Supreme Court was permanently immunized from any effective public regulation.

When the issue was not one of meddling with the sacrosanct "economic laws," the Supreme Court was more generous in its interpretation of the powers granted in the Constitution by the commerce clause. It was perfectly willing to allow the federal government's constitutional power over interstate commerce to be used to eliminate all sorts of moral nuisances far less related to interstate commerce than manufacturing is. For example, when the national government forbade cross-state lotteries, the dissemination of obscene literature, or the movement of women for purposes of prostitution, or required standards to preserve purity in foods, the Supreme Court, in each instance, found those things sufficiently related to interstate commerce to bring them within the domain of federal regulation. In each of these instances, the purpose of government was not to regulate commerce as such but was rather to constrain undesirable practices. Nor was there any more (or even as much) of a relationship between such practices and interstate commerce as there was between interstate commerce and the employment of children in manufacturing. It was precisely *commerce* that the Court intended to exclude from regulation, though of course opinion would vary among liberals as to where to draw the line between immoral acts properly controlled by the rule of men and commerce that should be subjected only to natural economic law. That the Court considered the federal government to be empowered under the commerce clause to stop lotteries but not to stop child labor can be explained only in terms of the Court's ideological commitment. The right of government to bar (what it judged to be) immoral acts was ideologically acceptable and would be upheld by the Court by whatever rationale it could find. The right of government to meddle in economic activity and thus to constrain "liberty" and the power of property was not ideologically acceptable, and there could always be found in the wisdom of the Constitution some insurmountable barrier against such meddling. The willingness to allow government to constrain lotteries but not child labor is incomprehensible as a logical deduction from the words of the Constitution; but it is perfectly comprehensible as an expression of the prevailing ideology. The reader will find in this instance and in the others that follow that the Court's decisions cannot be understood as deductions from, nor can they be fitted together as coherent interpretations of, the Constitution; but if one supposes that the Court is interpreting not the Constitution but rather the *Principles* of J. S. Mill (or the similar works of Fawcett or Cairnes, or later, the neoclassical economics of Alfred Marshall, J. B. Clark, Jevons, Walras, Menger, or Wicksell), then its decisions become quite coherent and entirely predictable.

In the prior phase of constitutional development, the Supreme Court had interpreted the commerce clause to vest authority in the national government. From at least 1879[9] onward in industrial America, its interpretations served to deny and to diminish the power of the national government, raising the commerce clause as an iron barrier against effective control over industrial processes. Before, the issue had been whether to vest power in the sovereign national authority or in the state governments, but in the late 19th and 20th century the issue was the power of political authority versus the power vested in property.

The pressure to ameliorate the horrors of child labor continued. Congress tried to find a way around the prohibitions of *Hammer* v. *Dagenhart* through the use of another of the powers specifically delegated by the Constitution, namely to "lay and collect Taxes . . . and provide for the common Defence and general Welfare." A federal excise tax was imposed on goods and commodities produced and sold in interstate commerce under those conditions of child labor that the government wished to outlaw. The new law was challenged. It went to the Supreme Court and in *J. W. Baily* v. *The Drexel Furniture Company*,[10] the Supreme Court struck it down. The Court interpreted the constitutional provision to mean that taxation could not be used by the federal government for purposes of control, but only to collect revenues that would be spent for the general welfare. Since

---

[9] See *Kidd* v. *Pearson*, 128 U.S. 1 (1888).
[10] *J. W. Bailey* v. *Drexel Furniture Company*, 259 U.S. 20 (1922).

the intention of the tax was not to collect revenues, but was rather to control the use of child labor, the law was declared unconstitutional. Yet the Court did not object to the imposition of federal taxes that were intended to check the sale of narcotics,[11] firearms,[12] or oleomargarine.[13] Again, as when under the commerce clause the Court allowed the government to control lotteries and disallowed its power under that clause to control child labor, its decisions in respect to the use of taxation as an instrument of control are only comprehensible ideologically. The Supreme Court would not allow the federal authority under any guise to control the conditions of child labor (such control constituted a substantial and significant "interference" with the free functioning of the market and with property rights). Since the task was beyond the competence of the state governments and was forbidden to the federal government by rule of the Court, child labor as an economic condition was removed from the effective reach of any political agency whatsoever.

In 1924 a constitutional amendment was attempted which would have permitted Congress to regulate child labor, but the pressure for reform was not sufficient to overcome the inertia of composite choice and the countervailing influence of the liberal ideology and of the organized resistance by agricultural and manufacturing interests. The amendment failed. The ills of child labor remained beyond amelioration through the exercise of the political authority during the whole epoch of liberalism.

Power of the States

The constitutional arrangement provides that all the powers of government not delegated to the federal authority, that is, the "residual powers," should remain with the states. This constituted in the eyes of the Court a formidable constraint on federal power. But did it mean that those powers denied to the federal government to impose political authority in the control of economic conditions, i.e., "to meddle with the market," were given to the states? Not at all.

At the turn of the century, New York passed a law which limited the working day of bakers to ten hours and their work week to sixty hours. This law was challenged and came before

---

[11]*U.S. v. Doremus*, 249 U.S. 86 (1919).
[12]*Sonzinsky v. U.S.*, 300 U.S. 506 (1937).
[13]*McCray v. U.S.*, 195 U.S. 27 (1904).

the Supreme Court in the case of *Lochner* v. *New York*.[14] The Court declared the law unconstitutional. Justice Peckham, speaking for the majority, was outraged at New York's "arbitrary interference with freedom to contract." The Court would permit no such "meddlesome interference with the rights of the individual." Rights of the individual? Of course. Peckham reasoned that bakers were not required to work sixty, seventy, or eighty hours a week or ten, fifteen, or twenty hours a day. They weren't slaves, were they? They didn't have to do it if they didn't want to, did they? If they did so, it was because they chose to do so. That was their "freedom," their sacred right of contract. "The question necessarily arises," said Peckham, "is this a fair, reasonable, and appropriate exercise of the police power . . . or . . . unreasonable, unnecessary, and arbitrary interference with the right of the individual to his personal liberty . . . ?" With a touching regard for the bakers' inalienable rights, Justice Peckham declared that they were not "wards of the state" unable "to assert their rights and care for themselves without the protecting arm of the state." The law was called a violation of the Fourteenth Amendment, which forbids the states to deprive any person of life, liberty, or property without *due process of law* (the Fifth Amendment imposes upon the federal government the same constraint of *due process*).[15] And what did the Justices mean by due process of law? They meant, simply, anything that seemed unreasonable to them; and the notion of what was or was not arbitrary and unreasonable was necessarily ideological. In this particular case of *Lochner* v. *New York*, in his dissent Justice Holmes wryly remarked that the "Fourteenth Amendment does not enact Herbert Spencer's social statics." Alas, but it did.

The ideological boundaries were not wholly inflexible in the face of continuing pressure of political demands and felt needs. In 1908 an Oregon law that set maximum hours for working women was allowed by the Supreme Court on the ground that this was a reasonable measure to safeguard the health of mothers and thereby to preserve the health of the community as a whole.[16]

---

[14]*Lochner* v. *New York*, 198 U.S. 45 (1905).

[15]The 5th Amendment requires that "No person shall . . . be deprived of life, liberty, or property, without due process of law; nor shall private property be taken for public use without just compensation." The 14th Amendment, adopted to protect the rights of the black freedmen in the ex-Confederate States, requires that "No State shall make or enforce any law which shall abridge the privileges or . . . deprive any person of life, liberty, or property without due process of law, nor deny to any person within its jurisdiction the equal protection of the laws."

[16]*Muller* v. *Oregon*, 208 U.S. 412 (1908).

In 1917 the Supreme Court allowed Oregon to regulate maximum hours for men and women, holding that this was properly within the police power of the state.[17] But even though in time the Court came reluctantly to accept the regulation of "excess" hours by working men and women, it continued to forbid as contrary to "due process" any effort to fix minimum wages. In 1923 a District of Columbia law to require minimum wages for women was invalidated.[18] Justice Sutherland, speaking for the Court, refused to "accept the doctrine that women of mature age sui juris require or may be subjected to restriction upon their liberty of contract. . . ." And even as late as 1936, a New York law fixing minimum wages for women was overthrown on the same ground.[19]

Not only the "due process" clause but also the commerce clause of the Constitution was used by the Supreme Court to restrict the power of the states to regulate the economy. Midwestern farmers, for example, considered themselves victimized by the owners of grain elevators who were able to exact an undue toll because of a monopolistic position and/or because of ignorance on the part of the farmers of prevailing market conditions. In response to the farmers' demands, governments of grain-producing states passed laws for their protection. North Dakota passed a law to protect its farmers against alleged frauds and unfair practices by the grain elevator operators in that state. That law required the licensing of grain elevators. It required the inspection and grading of grain as a basis for equitable pricing practices, and it required standard markups on grain of specified grades.

The law was called unconstitutional on the ground that the control of granaries was a part of the flow of interstate commerce and that the regulation of interstate commerce was solely the prerogative of the federal government. Whether or not the Supreme Court might have permitted it to do so, the federal government was at that time neither equipped for nor motivated to undertake the tasks of price fixing and policing prices charged by those who bought, warehoused, and resold the farmers' grain. Thus, the Supreme Court used the commerce clause of the Constitution as a doubleheaded hammer, with one head (by what it excluded as commerce)

---

[17]*Bunting v. Oregon,* 243 U.S. 426 (1917).
[18]*Adkins v. Children's Hospital,* 261 U.S. 525 (1923).
[19]*Morehead v. New York ex rel Tipaldo,* 298 U.S. 587 (1936).

to strike down the federal regulation of economic problems of national scope, and with the other head (by what it included as commerce) to strike down attempts by the states to deal with economic problems that were local in nature and with which the federal government was not concerned.[20]

Affected with the Public Interest

The prevailing ideology did not exclude public regulation of price and terms of trade absolutely. Admittedly, there might be anachronism arising in the autonomous functioning of the market. It was understood that in certain peculiar cases the bargaining position of the consumer might be so impaired that competition could not work as the controlling principle or that the technological advantages of concentration might be so great that a condition of monopoly was a practical necessity. Under those special circumstances some public regulation was ideologically acceptable. Such regulation had been a matter of traditional practice under the sanction of the common law for many centuries. Therefore, in its wisdom, the Supreme Court allowed that there were certain industries which it designated as "affected with the public interest" where public regulation was allowable without violating the constitutional guarantee of due process. In spite of heroic efforts to find a rationale for their choice they were never able to discover significant criteria to differentiate these trades and practices from the rest. Nevertheless, they drew their imaginary line and that line became an impassable wall. For example, the state of New Jersey passed a law under which the Commissioner of Labor regulated the fees of employment agencies. Employment agencies were required to submit a schedule of their fees and these could not be changed without the permission of the Commissioner. Many other states also had passed such laws for it had become clear that certain groups of workers, particularly unskilled immigrants who were ignorant of alternative opportunities and who had a desperate need for work during times of mass unemployment and depression, were subject to extreme exploitation by employment agencies. These agencies had become, so to speak, gatekeepers to the workers' survival. In 1928 in the case of *Ribnik v. McBride*,[21]

---

[20]*Lemke v. Farmers' Grain Co.*, 258 U.S. 50 (1922).
[21]*Ribnik v. McBride*, 277 U.S. 350 (1928).

the New Jersey law was challenged before the Supreme Court. The defendent argued for the law on the ground of public necessity, pointing out an "increase in urban population result-ing in great bodies of unemployed in congested areas and the consequent competition for employment, leading to compliance with any fee demanded by employment agencies. . . ."

The Supreme Court invalidated the New Jersey law as violat-ing due process and, thereby, struck down all the similar laws that had been passed throughout the United States. In this case Justice Sutherland, speaking for the majority of the Court, ruled that price fixing was allowed only in businesses "affected by the public interest." According to Sutherland, the fact that a busi-ness lent itself peculiarly to the practice of fraud, extortion, and discrimination did not entitle it to be considered as affected with the public interest. Then what was the criterion? "The phrase," said the judge, "is not capable of exact definition; but, nevertheless, . . . it is the standard by which the validity of price fixing must be tested." If, in the eyes of the Court, the business was not "devoted to a public use," then price fixing was to be considered an arbitrary interference with the right to contract. Holmes and Brandeis dissented but, it should be understood, they did not disagree with the prerogative assumed by the Court of dividing the economy into industries which were and were not affected with the public interest and excluding the exercise of the public authority from all but that small sector thus affected.

The Court and the Depression

By the mid-1930's the epoch of liberalism was drawing to its end. The curtain was being lowered by a terrible breakdown of the industrialized economies of the Western World. The Great Depression was an economic catastrophe of quite unparalleled magnitude. It drove the United States to the edge of mass star-vation while an enormous productive apparatus lay wasting and unused. It made fascism a force throughout the world. In Ger-many it brought the Nazis into power and, thereby, opened the door to World War II.

In the United States the newly-elected administration of Franklin D. Roosevelt attempted to act in the face of an over-whelming crisis. The remedies sought were bold, but hastily contrived and frequently contradictory. Indeed, it was inevitable that radical political action arising out of the intermingled outlooks and conflicting pressures of composite choice must at its incipiency be pragmatic and without a coherent rationale and that it must err in order to learn. The New Deal restricted the "overproduction" of farm products. Through the NRA it introduced a system of "industrial self-government" where trade associations and trade unions collaborated in the fixing of prices and wages and in the control of labor conditions. Codes of "fair competition" variously specifying allowable terms of sale, outputs, distributive systems, production capacities, prices, wages, hours, and work conditions were formulated and were enforced under the law by "code authorities." In the desperately depressed bituminous coal industry the trade association and the trade union formed joint boards to fix wages and prices; and the government supported these by allowing drawbacks on a federal excise tax. Wisely or unwisely, but vigorously, the government was acting to offset the breakdown of the market system and, in so doing, was ignoring the canons of laissez-faire and was violating the ideology of liberalism. And the Supreme Court, in its last total defense of that ideology, invalidated the whole New Deal program kit and caboodle, using all its constitutional weapons in doing so. In a series of cases, it found the government in violation of due process and ruled that the regulation of wages and prices was a violation of states' rights, that the use of taxation as a means of economic control was beyond the allowable limits of the general welfare clause, and that powers had been delegated to agencies of administration that could only be exercised under the Constitution by Congress.[22] Consider two of these cases.

In the Schechter case, which concerned the NRA regulation of a small chicken-slaughtering establishment in New York City, Chief Justice Hughes dismissed the government's contention that its action was warranted by the "grave national crisis," saying that "extraordinary conditions do not create or enlarge constitutional power." He notes first that the NRA process of industrial self-government "is not simply one of voluntary effort. . . . It involves the coercive exercise of the law-making power. The codes of fair competition . . . are codes of law. . . . Violations . . . are punishable as crimes." Congress alone is empowered to make laws, and while some of its laws may require considerable discretion in their administration, the law-making function itself

<hr>

[22]*Schechter Poultry Co.* v. *U.S.*, 295 U.S. 495 (1935); *Carter* v. *Carter Coal Co.*, 298 U.S. 238 (1936); and *U.S.* v. *Butler* (The Hoosac Mills case), 297 U.S. 1 (1936).

cannot be delegated. The Court must determine the point at which an allowable delegation of discretion in the administration of a law becomes an unconstitutional delegation of the law-making function itself, and that determination must depend on the degree to which Congress has made its purpose explicit and its criteria clear. In this instance the Court found that Congress had delegated power without operational criteria or a specificity of purpose sufficient to guide or to serve as a basis for judging the validity of administrative action. In Hughes' words:

> . . . no standards for any trade, industry, or activity. It does not undertake to prescribe rules of conduct to be applied to particular states of fact determined by appropriate administrative procedure. Instead of prescribing rules of conduct it authorizes the making of codes to prescribe them . . . sets up no standards, aside from the general aims of rehabilitation, correction and expansion . . . the discretion of the President . . . is virtually unfettered.

Hence, the Act was unconstitutional.

The Court further ruled that regulation of wages and hours in any form and under any administrative procedure was not within the powers granted by the Constitution to the federal government. The control of wages and hours was central to the NRA. The contention that commerce was a "continuous flow," with working conditions, output, and trade as inextricably interdependent, was rejected.

> The persons employed slaughtering and selling in local trade are not employed in interstate commerce. Their hours and wages have no direct relation to interstate commerce. The question of how many hours these employees should work and what they should be paid differs in no essential respect from similar questions in other local businesses which handle commodities brought into a State and there dealt in as part of its internal commerce. . . .
>
> . . . If the federal government may determine the wages and hours of employees . . . because of their relation to cost and prices and their indirect effect upon interstate commerce . . . a similar control might be exerted over other elements of cost, also affecting prices, such as number of employees, rents, advertising, methods of doing business. . . . All the processes of production and distribution that enter into cost could likewise be controlled.

Aghast at the possible consequences of allowing the government thus to meddle, the Court declared the Act unconstitutional. "There is no penumbra of uncertainty obscuring judgment here. To find immediacy or directness here (in relationship to interstate commerce)," said Justice Cardozo, concurring, "is to find it almost everywhere. If centripetal forces are to be isolated to the exclusion of the forces that oppose and counteract them, there will then be an end to our federal system."

The Carter Coal Company case decided in 1935 related to the New Deal efforts to ameliorate the desperate situation in the bituminous coal industry during the depression. The longstanding conditions of the industry are described by Justice Cardozo in a minority opinion.

Overproduction was at a point where free competition had been degraded into anarchy. Prices had been cut so low that profit had become impossible for all except the lucky handful. Wages came down along with prices and with profits. There were strikes, at times spreading over broad areas, and many mines, with the accompaniment of violence and bloodshed and misery and bitter feeling. The sordid tale is unfolded in many a document and treatise. During the twenty-three years between 1913 and 1935 there were nineteen investigations or hearings by Congress or by specially created commissions with reference to conditions in the coal mines. The hope of betterment was faint unless the industry could be subjected to the compulsion of a code. In the weeks immediately preceding the passage of the Act the country was threatened once more with a strike of ominous proportions. The plight of the industry was not merely a menace to the owners and to the mine workers; it was and had long been a menace to the public deeply concerned in a steady and uniform supply of a fuel so vital to the national economy.

The Bituminous Coal Act of 1935 formed a national commission; designated numerous coal districts; and created district boards to fix all prices for bituminous coal and for wages, hours, and working conditions of the miners throughout the country. Compliance was to be induced through the imposition of an excise tax, with rebates to those sellers who accepted the provisions of the Act. Justice Sutherland, speaking for the Court, first laid it down (1) that the beneficence of the aims of the government and the importance of the problem which confronted it were of no relevance, nor was it relevant (2) that a vital problem required national action and could not be dealt with by the states individually.

> ... for nothing is more certain than that beneficent aims, however great or well directed, can never serve in lieu of constitutional power.

> ... to a constitutional end many ways are open; but to an end not within the terms of the Constitution, all ways are closed.

> The proposition, often advanced and as often discredited, that the power of the federal government inherently extends to purposes affecting the nation as a whole with which the states severally cannot deal, and the related notion that Congress, entirely apart from those powers delegated by the Constitution, may enact laws to promote the general welfare, have never been accepted but always definitely rejected by this Court.

The issue then was whether the federal government had the constitutional power to do what the Act intended doing. Since the Act contemplated regulating the wages, hours, and working conditions of the miners, and since the wages, hours, and working conditions of the miners were in the opinion of the Court only "indirectly" related to interstate commerce, the intervention of the federal government could not be justified by reference to the commerce clause in the Constitution. Hence, the Act was unconstitutional.

Yet, the justices were not entirely unaffected by the catastrophic proportions of the economic disaster, by the evidence of a society in turmoil, or by the political clamoring at their gates. There is evidence of psychic uncertainty and of fissures in the ideological allegiance. Even Justice Sutherland, a hard-nosed adherent of old style liberalism, wrestled with his soul for sixteen pages in trying to justify and to find some solidity in his distinction between direct and indirect effects upon interstate commerce. And Justice Cardozo's opinion (concurred in by Brandeis and Stone), which would not have nullified the Act entirely, gives witness of an inner struggle to find ideological moorings.

> Sometimes it is said that the relation [to interstate commerce] must be "direct" to bring that [commerce] power into play. In many circumstances such a description will be sufficiently precise to meet the needs of the occasion. But a great principle of constitutional law is not susceptible of comprehensive

statement in an adjective. The underlying thought is merely this, that "the law is not indifferent to consideration of degree".... It cannot be indifferent to them without an expansion of the commerce clause that would absorb or imperil the reserved power of the states. At times ... the waves of causation will have radiated so far that their undulatory motion, if not discernible at all, will be too faint or obscure, too broken by cross-currents to be heeded by the law. In such circumstances the holding is not directed at prices or wages considered in the abstract, but at prices or wages in particular conditions. The relation may be tenuous or the opposite according to the facts. Always the setting of the facts is to be viewed if one would know the closeness of the tie. Perhaps, if one group of adjectives is to be chosen in preference to another "intimate" and "remote" will be found to be as good as any. In all events "direct" and "indirect," even if accepted as sufficient, must not be read too narrowly.

Whether the New Deal efforts to deal with economic breakdown were well-chosen or not is beside the point. The action of the Supreme Court lay bare a situation which could not continue for much longer. Ideology was incommensurate with reality. The whole effort of the Court as upholder of the liberal ideology was to keep the powers of the political authority at bay and to protect the "freedom" and "liberties" of the market system. But now the industrialized economy and its market system was collapsing and, with the liberal ideology imposed by the Court as an iron law of the Constitution, the political authority was unable to act. Action was absolutely necessary and yet, under the constitutional rule, effective action was made impossible. The political authority was rendered impotent.

THE CONSTITUTION AS A BARRIER TO ECONOMIC "MEDDLING"

During this period between the Civil War and the Great Depression of the 1930's, the Supreme Court acted as the guardian of ideological liberalism and the defender of the prerogatives of property against all political interference. In so doing it converted the Constitution into a series of interlocked barriers that precluded effective action by any political authority, state or federal. These barriers, diagrammed in Figure 4-1, are enumerated and described as follows:

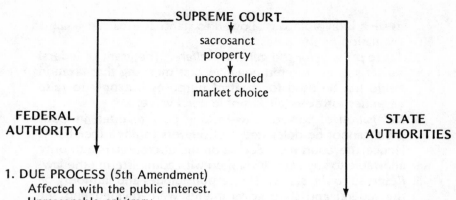

FEDERAL
AUTHORITY

STATE
AUTHORITIES

1. DUE PROCESS (5th Amendment)
   Affected with the public interest.
   Unreasonable, arbitrary.
2. COMMERCE CLAUSE
   Manufacturing excluded.
3. TAXATION . . . TO PROVIDE
   FOR THE GENERAL WELFARE
   Taxation not to be used
   for purpose of control.
4. DELEGATION OF POWER
   Congress cannot vest its power
   in agencies of administration.
5. RESERVED TO THE STATES
   All powers not specifically
   delegated to the federal authority
   are reserved to the states.

1. DUE PROCESS (14th Amendment)
   Affected with the public interest.
   Unreasonable, arbitrary.
2. COMMERCE CLAUSE
   Commercial intercourse between
   the states, in all its branches
   excluded from state control.

Figure 4-1

The Liberal Ideology

1. *Due process.* The federal government by reference to the
   5th Amendment, and the state governments by reference to
   the 14th Amendment, were barred from any regulation of
   enterprise that the Court considered not to be "affected
   with the public interest," and from any form of economic
   action which the Court considered "unreasonable," "arbitrary," or substantively unwarranted and unnecessary.
2. *The commerce clause.* The constitutional grant of power to
   the federal government to regulate interstate commerce,
   following the logic of early rulings, would have given the
   federal government power over virtually all economic activity. It was now narrowly confined to that which affected interstate commerce "directly." Manufacturing and all that
   related to the processes of production were specifically
   excluded. At the same time the earlier rulings that commerce was commercial intercourse in all its branches, and

as such indivisible, was allowed to stand as a barrier against regulation by the states.

3. *Tax to provide for the general welfare.* The grant of federal power was interpreted negatively, as meaning that taxation could not be used for control purposes but only to raise revenues for expenditures of general value.

4. *Delegation of power.* Law-making power vested in Congress cannot be delegated by Congress to any other body. Hence, the Court must decide on the discretionary authority allowable to any agency charged with administering the law.

5. *Reserved to the states.* The responsibilities and authority of the federal and state governments were divided and set apart in airtight boxes and, regardless of functional necessity or the nature of the problems and phenomena to be dealt with, neither government was permitted to extend its powers beyond its constitutional confines.

THE COURT IN THE EPOCH OF LAISSEZ-FAIRE LIBERALISM

It is not possible to find any logical reconciliation between the decision of the Supreme Court in 1819 that the power to establish a national bank belonged to the federal government because it was deducible from, and hence implied in, the delegated power "to wage war" and the decision of the Supreme Court in 1935 not to allow the federal government to try to salvage the bituminous coal industry as a political right and responsibility to be deduced from the same delegated power "to wage war."

To understand the rationale of the decisions of the Supreme Court during the period between the end of the Civil War and the onset of the Great Depression, one needs to look not at the words of the Constitution or at the precedents of the law, but rather at the substantive stakes and the prevading and dominant ideology of laissez-faire liberalism. The judges were generally hard-working, dedicated, and able professionals. Nor were they unsympathetic to moral right and human need. They were willing to permit "police action" to outlaw an immoral practice or a particular abuse of private rights. But what they could not accept—or even comprehend—was the substitution of political authority for the market system or any generalized political control of economic activities. Such a substitution of the political authority for the market system seemed to them a breach of faith or a kind of blasphemy. And they were the keepers of the faith. Those cases which came before them in which the public authority attempted the control of economic activity were proposed as exception to the rule. The Supreme Court blocked the exceptions and asserted the rule. It was the Court's function to assert and to maintain the integrity of the rule, to keep it from being evaded, broken, or eroded.

And if the Court frustrated Congress, the President, and the electorate, why did an aroused Congress and electorate not change the Constitution and deprive the Court of its powers? Because, basically, nearly everyone accepted the rightness of the rule. They believed what the Court asserted. The social philosophy expressed by the Court was accepted by the public and there was no other coherent body of values and concepts that could be set against it. That was the Court's strength; that it expressed an ideology and society accepted that ideology even if, here and there, many would have liked to have found a way of getting around it.

Thus, during this period the Supreme Court was the defender of laissez-faire. It shackled the political authority. It destroyed at its incipiency every effort at political control or reform of the economy. It foreclosed the experimental search for the means to ameliorate the miseries, to salvage the human debris, or to offset crisis and imminent economic disaster which were the consequences and dangers of an industrialized market economy.

The Court interpreted the Constitution in terms of the prevailing ideology and in so doing shaped the law and the Constitution in the image of that ideology. During the first phase of constitutional development, from the birth of the republic through the Civil War, it was the Supreme Court that spearheaded the trend of change and reform in centralizing and rationalizing political authority. In this first phase the Court expressed the ideology of nationalism and Congress and the President reflected the resistances of the vested powers, established governments, and traditional loyalties.

During the second phase of constitutional development, from 1860 to about 1935, it was Congress and the President who pressed for reform and change while the Supreme Court was the bastion of status. This also confirms the hypothesis as to the character of composite choice and of authoritative decision. During this period the composite choice of Congress and the President reflected the immediate and specific pressures growing out of crisis and deprivation, and sought for some amelioration of these. The authoritative decisions of the Court, on the other hand, asserted the dominant ideology of laissez-faire liberalism, and by reference to that ideology constrained the political authority from "meddling" in the market system.

In retrospect the Court was wrong. Eventually, given the growing distance between ideology and existential reality, it would have to yield and if it had yielded sooner, generations might have been spared some of the waste and deprivation that they were, in fact, obliged to suffer. But this is not to say that the justices were less wise or less compassionate than the congressmen and presidents. Rather, by the nature of its position and by the nature of its office, the decisions of the Court necessarily reflected the dominant social philosophy, which had become obsolete. There was the crux and the tragedy. The prevailing idea of what the world was like, the shadows in the cave through which intellectuals conceived and "saw" the economy, no longer approximated what the economy had become. Inevitably, the crisis of minunderstanding became greater and the burden of dogma more unbearable until the ideology itself burst asunder.

A Test of the Hypothesis

In Chapter 2 it was hypothesized that "Congress and the President exemplify composite choice in the American political system. Composite choice is a reflex of the balance of interests arising out of group-seeking and social need and reacting not to belief but to the balance of pressures and to the force of crisis. It follows that when social need and crisis generate pressures for institutional change and for forms of action in conflict with the imperatives of the dominant ideology, the thrust for change and reform will then come first from Congress and the President while the Supreme Court, exemplifying authoritative decision and, hence, expressing the dominant ideology, will resist such change and reform."

This period between the Civil War and the Great Depression of the 1930's surely substantiates the hypothesis. All the pressures for change and reform, reflecting need, crisis, and breakdown, came from the agencies of composite choice. The authoritative choice of the Supreme Court, expressing the prevailing ideology, resisted change and reform from first to last.

Chapter 5

Control of Monopoly
and Restraint of Trade:
1890–1935

During the period between the end of the Civil War and the onset of the Great Depression in the United States, the ideology of liberalism was dominant and unchallenged; it was expressed as the credo of the Court. It stood foursquare against government meddling with the market on the grounds that such meddling would interfere with the salutary force of competition. Yet there was another danger to the force of competition, arising not from the interferences of the political authority but from the exercise of private power within the market economy itself.

THE LIBERALS' DILEMMA

Given that price competition was the great and beneficent regulator of economic activity, what then was to be done when such competition was hampered or even destroyed by the exercise of private power within the market system itself? What political action was allowable and appropriate when the force of competition was subverted not by government but by private, self-seeking interests in the market? Should government intervene not to displace, replace, or regulate the force of market competition, but rather to maintain and preserve that competition? British liberals, like J. S. Mill, or later Alfred Marshall, would have answered, "It can't happen here." They supposed that the efforts of an individual or even of any group of individuals could not for long withstand the natural force of competition. Left alone, the market system would make things right in due course. Such was the response of the British and, indeed of liberalism throughout Western Europe. No vigorous effort was ever made there to eliminate or prevent private monopoly or business combinations in restraint of trade. Parenthetically, it should be said that the absolute reliance of European liberalism on "natural" forces of the market coincided with the material self-interest of those who exercised, or who thought they stood to gain from the exercise of, monopoly power; and these constituted a powerful group in all societies. In the United States there was perhaps a greater countervailing political force exercised by consumers and small enterprises. The rigors of competition were more admired, and the ethic of competition was more fully sanctioned here. In Europe the feudal ideology remained in a transmuted form as a powerful force among political elites, coexisting with that of liberalism. It found competition repugnant and welcomed concentration, conceiving proper society as a pyramid-like hierarchy of stabilized social classes wherein the rich man ruled his factory as the aristocrat ruled his estate.

In any case, in the United States at the turn of the century it would have been hard to say of the subversion of the competitive economy by private monopoly, "It can't happen here," because it was happening here. This was the period of the trusts, with the concentration of industrial power proceeding at a rate quite unparalleled in history. Aggressive and ruthless, the financial and industrial powers of the economy were herding independent businesses into gigantic amalgamations like cattle being driven into pens. And indeed the cattle often flocked happily into the pens, for these were decades of falling prices and depression, and the trusts seemed to offer a comfortable and safe sanctuary from "destructive competition." Vital industrial sectors were monopolized, and the powers of monopoly were used to force prices up and thereby to squeeze enormous profits at the expense of consumers and workers. These profits were in large part siphoned off through stock manipulation and the sale of securities, as great fortunes grew in the possession of financiers and promoters.[1]

---

[1]See Elliot Jones, *The Trust Problem in the United States* (New York: The Macmillan Company, 1921); Myron W. Watkins, *Industrial Combinations and Public Policy: A Study of Combination, Competition, and the Common Welfare* (New York: Burt Franklin, reprint of 1927 ed.); and Henry Rogers Seager and C. A. Gulick, *Trust and Corporation Problems* (New York: Harper and Brothers, 1929).

Chapter 5

THE STEEL TRUST

The term "trust" describes a now obsolete technique of business combination. In it the owners of the controlling interests in the common stock of competing corporations transferred legal titles to their shares to "trustees" and received trust certificates in return. The trustees elected a set of directors to control the trust and to run it as an integral enterprise. The holders of the trust certificates participated in the profits of the combined corporation. This form was devised by the promoters of the Standard Oil combination in 1879 and subsequently adopted in a number of other industries. Shortly thereafter the term was generalized to cover all monopolistic combinations, howsoever the combination was achieved. The word "trust," striking a popular chord, was subsequently immortalized as the generic term for monopoly in a series of antimonopoly laws.

The steel combinations which took place at the turn of the century illustrate the general nature of this trust movement. The United States Steel Corporation, created in 1901, was a combination of 12 large concerns, many of them monopolizing a branch of industry, following upon earlier combinations of 180 separate companies. The most important of these merging corporations was the Carnegie Company of New Jersey, then the biggest steel producer in the United States. The second largest of the combining companies, which was also the nation's second largest steel producer, was the Federal Steel Company. Federal had been formed through the combination of the Illinois Steel Company and several steel companies in the vicinity of Chicago, one in Milwaukee, one in Ohio, one in Pennsylvania, and the Minnesota Iron Company, which possessed very large iron ore deposits, an iron ore railroad, and a fleet of lake vessels. The third largest company in the combination was the National Steel Company, itself the result of a series of consolidations of a number of Ohio companies. The American Tinplate Company was another of the merging corporations. This was a trust proper, which brought together 39 firms controlling 279 mills, including virtually every plant in the country that made tinplate in 1898. Another member of the combination was the American Steel and Wire Company with a virtual monopoly of barbed and woven wire, producing about four fifths of the national output of nails and wire fencing. The National Tube Company also joined; this was the "tube trust" which controlled about 90 percent of the nation's capacity to produce steel tubing and about 75 percent of the capacity to produce wrought tubing. Also included was the American Steel Hoop Company, which was formed through the consolidation of nine companies producing iron and steel bars, hoops, bands, cotton ties, and iron skelp.

Other members were the American Sheet Steel Company, a trust proper that controlled about 70 percent of the country's capacity for producing sheet steel; the American Bridge Company, a combination of firms engaged in erecting steel bridges and steel construction for building; the Shelby Steel Tube Company, which controlled 90 percent of the country's output of seamless steel tubing; and the Lake Superior Consolidated Iron Mines, with enormous reserves of iron ore and an important iron ore railroad. Affiliated with the latter was the Bessemer Steamship Company, the largest owner of ore vessels on the Great Lakes.

The formation of these combinations, which at a later stage were amalgamated into the United States Steel Corporation, had themselves been the source of enormous profits for their promoters. For example, in the formation of the National Tube Company trust, one quarter of the $80 million stock issue was turned over to the promoters. Out of the $33 million in stock issued at the formation of the American Sheet Steel Company, $5 million accrued to the promoters.

The advent of these earlier combinations had signalled a very sharp rise in the price of steel products. Bessemer pig iron, averaging $10.32 per gross ton in 1898, went up to $18.88 per ton in 1899 and to $24.72 in 1900. Steel billets went from $15.18 per gross ton in 1898 to $20.81 per ton in 1899, and to $33 in 1900. Steel rails went from $17.63 per gross ton in 1898 to $28.13 in 1899, and to $35 in 1900. Tinplate averaged $64.08 per gross ton in 1898; the next year it rose to $95.48. Prior to the formation of the tube trust, the price of tubes had been $30 per ton. During 1899, the very year of the formation of the trust, the price went up to $67 per ton, and in early 1900 to $89 per ton. High prices and enormous profits were an invitation to vertical integration as a means of cutting costs, and also the cross-invasion and capture of lush markets. The industry was not in equilibrium. Between March and October of 1900, competition forced prices down to a level of about that of 1899. Pressure arose to create a super trust that would keep monopoly in the saddle and competition at bay. The United States Steel Corporation was formed, offering to exchange its securities for those of the companies to be brought into the combination. After the trusts had thus been merged into a super trust, prices were raised again. In this process of reorganization, the underwriting syndicate made a profit of nearly $63 million. The new company controlled three fifths of the steel business of the country, producing about 60 percent of the pig iron, about 66 percent of the crude steel, and about 50 percent of the finished steel products. It owned over 1,000 miles of railroad, more than 50,000 acres of the best coking coal lands, and reserves of hundreds of millions of tons of iron ore.

The Bureau of Corporations, studying the financing of the combination, concluded that out of the total capitalization of the United States Steel Company of $1.4 billion, only about $676 million represented actual investment in concrete assets of any sort. The rest was pure water. Subsequently the steel corporation continued to grow through internal investment and through external purchases. Nevertheless, there was to be a gradual decline in United States Steel's proportion of the total national output of steel products.

THE ANTITRUST LAWS

The trust movement must have been a terrifying phenomena. It hurt powerful sections of the electorate, small businessmen, producers of raw materials, workers, and consumers. Popular apprehension and accumulating injuries crystallized into a political protest that already had roots in the farmers' organizations in the West and the South. During the 1880's the antimonopoly movement came to control the legislatures of several states, elected a number of members to Congress, and even ran a candidate for the presidency. As is to be expected when an issue has so proven its popularity at the polls, it was taken up by the major parties. By 1889 eighteen states had enacted antitrust laws. And in 1890 the Sherman Antitrust Act was passed by Congress and signed by the President. The major provisions of the Sherman Act are as follows:

Section 1—Every contract, combination in the form of a trust or otherwise, or conspiracy, in restraint of trade or commerce among several states, or with foreign nations, is hereby declared to be illegal. Every person who shall make any such contract or engage in any such combination or conspiracy shall be deemed guilty of a misdemeanor. . . .

Section 2—Every person who shall monopolize or attempt to monopolize or combine or conspire with any other person or persons, to monopolize any part of the trade or commerce among the several states or with foreign nations shall be deemed guilty of a misdemeanor. . . .

Was the Law Constitutional? The E. C. Knight Case

The American Sugar Refining Company, which controlled 65 percent of the sugar refined in the United States, purchased the stock of the E. C. Knight Company and three other independent refiners in Philadelphia, thus increasing its control of sugar refining to 98 percent of the national output. The government attacked the American Sugar Refining Company under the Sherman Act, seeking to compel it to dispose of its newly-acquired stock in the four competing concerns. The case was taken to the Supreme Court.[2] The Court recognized that the sugar trust was a monopoly but decided that it was a monopoly in manufacturing and manufacturing was not commerce; hence, the activity was outside the scope of federal jurisdiction. This decision, which was entirely consistent with the rule of the Court from *Kidd* v. *Pearson*[3] to *Carter* v. *Carter Coal Company*,[4] virtually declared the Sherman Act to be unconstitutional. But after a brief pause the Supreme Court looked around, took a deep breath, and reversed its interpretation of the commerce clause—but only in respect to the antitrust law. To disallow the federal regulation of child labor on the grounds that manufacturing was not commerce, and to allow the application of the antitrust laws to manufacturing on the grounds that the federal government had the power to regulate commerce between the states, was certainly an inconsistent interpretation of the words of the Constitution. But inconsistent interpretation of the Constitution or not, the decision of the Court to allow government action in the latter instance and not in the former was entirely consistent with ideological liberalism. Regardless of the words of the Constitution, *ideologically* it was right that the public authority should be constrained from controlling the

---

[2]*U.S.* v. *E. C. Knight Company*, 156 U.S. 1 (1895).
[3]*Kidd* v. *Pearson*, 128 U.S. 1 (1888).
[4]*Carter* v. *Carter Coal Company*, 298 U.S. 238 (1936).

conditions of employment in manufacturing but should be permitted to impose its controls in the interest of promoting competition in manufacturing. Believing in the beneficent force of competition and being aware of the trend towards combination and monopoly, the judges deemed it reasonable and appropriate that government act to safeguard competition.

In sum, antitrust legislation was consistent with the liberal ideology but was entirely inconsistent with coexisting judicial interpretations of the constitutional powers of government. The Court accepted constitutional inconsistency in order to permit ideological consistency. After the *E. C. Knight* case the Supreme Court allowed no challenge of the power of the federal government to attack monopolistic arrangements by manufacturing enterprise. It was accepted that the political authority could regulate the practices of manufacturing companies in order to preserve competition, but not for other purposes.

Common Law Precedents

The Sherman Act introduced no new notions of injury and wrong. From ancient times the common law, i.e., the de facto law made through the accumulating precedents of judicial decisions, had held conspiracy in restraint of trade and monopoly or monopolization to be a wrong; and individuals who considered themselves victimized by such monopolization or conspiracy could sue under the common law (and sometimes did sue) to recover damages for their injury. Such private suits in fact were (and are) rare and of themselves could hardly be more than peripheral in their effect on the structure of industry.

In the Sherman Act restraint of trade and monopoly were made statutory crimes and it became a task of the government, specifically of the Department of Justice, to require and enforce competition as the general condition of the market economy. The Sherman Act also reinforced private antimonopoly suits. It provided that "any person . . . injured . . . by reason of anything forbidden in the antitrust laws may sue . . . and shall recover threefold the damages by him sustained."

This triple damage provision, designed to encourage private prosecutions, also lends force to public prosecution since a convictions under government attack is prima facie evidence of guilt in future suits by those seeking to recover damages on private account. For example, if a group of companies are convicted of a price conspiracy under the Sherman Act, the customers of those companies can then sue (under the presumption that the general guilt of those whom they sue had already been established) to recover triple the damages of the higher costs they have been obliged to incur on account of the conspiracy. For this reason companies attacked by government as antitrust violators are often anxious to settle out of court, pleading nolo contendere and accepting "consent decrees," and hence avoiding the presumption of guilt in private suits. The threat of triple damage suits may coerce firms to accept what they consider to be unjust decrees.

The Sherman Act can be enforced through criminal or civil prosecution. Where the prosecution is criminal, an indictment must first be sought before a grand jury. This indictment gives the Department of Justice the power to seek and obtain from the defendant data which may be necessary for its case. The trial is then brought before a jury in a district court. Before trial the defendant can plead nolo contendere and accept a consent decree through agreement with the Department of Justice, or the Department of Justice can plead nolle prosequi and drop the case. If the case is tried and the defendant is judged not guilty by the jury, the Department of Justice cannot appeal; but if the defendant is found to be guilty, he can appeal and the case is then heard by a higher court. If the higher court acquits the defendant, the Department of Justice cannot appeal; but if the defendant is found guilty again, he can ask that his case be heard by the Supreme Court. The Supreme Court can, at its discretion, hear the case. A civil suit, on the other hand, is heard before a judge and both sides have the right of appeal. Where the prosecution is successful, the enforcement of the court's decree in restructuring the industry or in requiring a change in the practices of the firm must be through processes of civil law, and is handled by the judges of the lower courts.

The Clayton and Federal Trade Commission Acts

Subsequent to the Sherman Act, two other antimonopoly laws were passed in 1914. The Clayton Act outlawed certain specified business practices as "unfair competition." These included exclusive and tying contracts, interlocking directorates, discrimination in pricing, selective price cutting, and intercorporate stockholdings when the effect of any of these "may be

substantially to lessen competition or tend to create a monopoly."
In the Federal Trade Commission Act an independent commission
was established to enforce the provisions of the Clayton Act.[5]
In 1936 the provisions of the Clayton Act were revised with the
passage of the Robinson-Patman Act.[6] And in 1938 the Wheeler-
Lea Act was passed, increasing the powers of the Federal Trade

---

[5]Among the important provisions of the Clayton Act are the following. Section Two forbids sellers "to discriminate in price between different purchasers of commodities" except where there are "differences in the grade, quality or quantity of the commodity sold" or where price concessions were made giving "due allowance for differences in the cost of selling or transportation" or where they were offered "in good faith to meet competition."

Section Three forbids sellers "to lease or make a sale or contract for sale . . . on the condition that the lessee or purchaser thereof shall not use or deal in the . . . commodity . . . of a competitor."

Section Seven forbids any corporation engaged in commerce from acquiring the shares of a competing corporation or from purchasing the stocks of two or more corporations that are competitors.

The aforementioned practices are not forbidden absolutely, but only where their effect "may be substantially to lessen competition or tend to create a monopoly. . . ." Unlike the Sherman Act, what must be established here is only a tendency, probability, or significant possibility, rather than the actual restraint of competition and the existence of monopoly.

Section Eight prohibits interlocking directorates between corporations engaged in commerce, if one of them has a capital and surplus with a value of $1 million or more, and where "the elimination of competition . . . between them would constitute a violation of any of the provisions of the antitrust laws."

The Federal Trade Commission Act, in Section Five, simply provides "that unfair methods of competition in commerce are hereby declared unlawful." The presumption is that unfair methods of competition are already defined in the common law, or can be decided upon by the courts in the process of litigation. What the act does then is to place the onus of enforcement on a public agency rather than relying solely on private suits. It also gives to private suits the greater force of triple damages, by bringing unfair methods of competition within the scope of the antitrust laws.

[6]Robinson-Patman revises Section Two of the Clayton Act, the purpose of which was to prevent large manufacturers from eliminating or disciplining their smaller rivals through selective price cutting. The purpose of the new act is to prevent big buyers, particularly chain stores, from securing an unwarranted cost advantage through their greater (monopsonistic) bargaining power with suppliers. Such concessions can take many forms, e.g., in broker's commissions when no broker was employed, in special services obtained from suppliers, and in allowances in lieu of advertising. The objective of Robinson-Patman is to prevent such discriminations when they are not justified by seller-cost differentials or, even where they can be so justified, where they may create a monopoly.

Section Two of Robinson-Patman forbids any payments of broker's commissions when no independent brokers are employed, and forbids supplementary services or allowances in lieu of such services unless these are available to all buyers on "proportionately equal terms." Quantity discounts and other forms of discrimination are forbidden where the effect "may be substantially to lessen competition or tend to create a monopoly." Those accused of such discrimination are allowed to offer in defense proof that they acted "in good faith to meet an equally low price of a competitor." It is made unlawful for any person "knowingly to induce or to receive" a prohibited discrimination in price. The Federal Trade Commission is also authorized to establish quantity limits beyond which discounts cannot be given.

(Continued on next page)

Commission.[7] The effects of the later legislation will be treated in Chapter 10.

The establishment of the Federal Trade Commission reflected a political theory that was then very popular. According to this theory politicians and public officials were to be distrusted as creatures of "pressure groups" and "the interests." Judges were to be distrusted as technically uninformed; therefore it was supposed that the complex problems of social policy and control must be entrusted to objective and independent "experts." The Federal Trade Commission was to be such a body of experts. The commissioners were given a relatively long tenure. They were not subordinated in their operations either to Congress or the President. They would, it was supposed, make the studies and produce the information that Congress needed to enact better laws and to develop wiser policies. They were to confer with the representatives of industry, and in tandem with the representatives of industry were to formulate codes (guidelines) of fair competition. When they disapproved the practice of firms, they might issue "cease and desist" orders, but they could not enforce those orders. For that they must go to the courts.

Reasonable Restraints

The Sherman Act is very broadly worded. The Court had to give substantive meaning to its terms and define the boundaries of its application. Whatever its wording, no one could suppose

---

Section Three specifies substantial penalties for violations. It forbids the giving or receiving of a larger discount than that received by a competing buyer for a sale of the same magnitude. It forbids selling the same good at a different price in one locality than the price established in another; and forbids the sale of goods at "unreasonably low prices" where these practices are "for the purpose of destroying competition or eliminating a competitor."

Robinson-Patman must be understood as a political reaction of independent retailers against the incursion of the chain store. It expresses and capitalizes upon an ideology that is against bigness and would preserve a universe of choice decentralized among small enterprises, rather than an ideology that is against monopoly and would preserve the cutting edge of efficiency-producing competition.

[7]In the common law the only injury that is taken into account in cases of "unfair methods of competition" are injuries to a competitor or to competitors. Given this well-established precedent, the Federal Trade Commission found that it could not prosecute where the welfare of the consumer rather than of business competitors was at issue. Thus when the Commission ordered the Raladam Company to cease and desist from representing their product Marmola falsely as a remedy for obesity, the Supreme Court in FTC v. Raladam Co., 283 U.S. 643, (1931), vacated the order on the grounds that while the Raladam advertising was indeed deceptive, such misrepresentation was commonplace and hence that no injury had been done to Raladam's competitors. The Wheeler-Lea Act of 1938 closed this loophole so that Section Five as amended outlaws not only "unfair methods of competition" but "unfair or deceptive acts or practices" as well.

that *every* contract and combination in restraint of trade could be made illegal, since virtually any contract can be interpreted as a constraint of trade. If you should make a contract with a builder to work on your house for the next six weeks, you would remove that contractor and his crew from the market and ipso facto restrain trade.

Consider an actual case which came before the Court. A photographer in a certain southern town sold his business including his trade name and goodwill to an outsider. As part of the terms of sale the photographer agreed and signed a contract to the effect that he would not open a competing business in that town for seven years. But after he had taken his money, the photographer opened a competing business, in violation of his contract. The purchaser sued. The photographer defended himself on the ground that their contract was illegal since it was in restraint of trade and hence could not be enforced. The Court held to the contrary.

In this instance the Court applied the "rule of reason," interpreting the agreement in terms of prevailing notions as to the operational requirements of a legitimate contract. Certainly the contract between the seller and the buyer of the photography shop did restrain trade, but not "unreasonably," not "unduly." Restraint was not the purpose of the contract. On the contrary, the purpose of the contract was the legitimate sale and meaningful transference of a going business which, under the circumstances, would not have been possible without some such contractual provision safeguarding the investment of the new buyer. The restraints implicit in the contract were not regarded as direct but were considered to be *ancillary*, that is, incidental to a legitimate purpose. Nevertheless, the terms of sale might have been such that the Court would have considered them, according to its rule of reason as "unduly restrictive," and hence illegal.

THE ANTITRUST LOGIC OF THE COURT

The courts did undertake to define and to enforce the antitrust laws. Before analyzing the historical development of judicial interpretation, it might be well to reconstruct what came to be the antitrust logic of the Court; a logic that would guide specific and concrete applications of the law during the period from 1890 to 1935.

Take the following as significant components of judicial judgments: (1) a more or less complete ignorance of technology on the part of the judges; (2) their more or less complete trust in the technological knowledge and organizational acumen of the businessman; (3) a deep faith in the ultimate rightness of unconstrained private choice competitively exercised in the free market; (4) an underlying distrust of the competence and judgment of political authority; and (5) antagonism toward monopoly.

A wide range of practices and arrangements can be construed as monopoly restraints. But the removal of those restraints can interfere with legitimate business arrangements and, therefore, hurt efficiency, lower productivity, or check progress. The Court knew that it was unable to judge the probable damage to technology implicit in a particular application of the antitrust law, nor did it trust the opinions of public officials on this matter. Hence, the Court was reluctant to disturb business arrangements, though these could be construed as monopoly restraints, whenever it had reason to fear that to do so might reduce efficiency or impede technological progress. When it was convinced that those restraints could be eliminated without ill effects on efficiency or technological progress, the Court was vigorous and positive in its antitrust actions. Conversely, to the degree that the judges had reason to suppose that there might be substantial costs and significant risks of disrupting rational organization and hampering technological progress, they were reluctant to impose the antitrust law. The statutes took no account of the requisites of organizational efficiency and technological progress, but the judges tried to do so.

The opinions of the courts, always balancing the benefits from competition against the risks and costs of antitrust enforcement, depend not only on the facts of the case but also on the very limited and peculiar judicial competence to evaluate those facts. Since judges are trained in law and not in technology, they are reluctant to enforce action and require change which might have any significant effect on an integral operation simply because they do not understand and are unprepared to assess the possibility of an unfavorable effect of such action upon technology.

The control of prices maintained through agreements between independent firms evidently can be forbidden without any significant effect on operating organization or technology. Thus, the Court was willing to enjoin price-fixing agreements wherever they existed without equivocation or hesitation. In the same spirit and with the same freedom, the Court was willing to invalidate agreements between otherwise independent firms to exclude competitors, divide markets, restrict outputs or purchases, or eliminate opportunities or incentives to compete, for example, through agreements to pool profits.

But control over price and output can be achieved not only through agreement between independent competitors but also, and much more effectively, through the concentration of power over price and production into the hands of a single enterprise or even of a very few enterprises where a tacit accommodation in respect to price and output is inevitable or at least is very easy to arrive at without overt agreements. The courts, no doubt, would concede that control of price and output achieved through concentration is of itself undesirable. They would surely agree that other things being equal, it is always better to have more rather than fewer competitors. But to break up a great company into many smaller ones runs the risk of destroying technical advantages and operating efficiencies in ways that the judges are unable to foresee or assess. For that reason the Court was extremely reluctant to sanction the dissolution of an integral business operation. If all the pluses were on the side of more competition, then the Court did not hesitate. But if there were possible minuses on the side of operating efficiency, the Court treaded with care. And during these years under review, when technological fragmentation and restructuring of a complex business operation were at issue, the Court was reluctant to move against monopoly power at all.

Such would appear to be the logic of the judicial approach to antitrust enforcement. Consider the specifics.[8]

The Per Se Illegality of Restrictive Agreements Between Independents

The first cases dealing with agreements among competitors to restrain trade were those of the Trans-Missouri

---

[8]For the reader who is not really interested in the specifics, it would be as well to simply take note of the fact that during the period under review, the Supreme Court (1) rigorously suppressed anticompetitive agreements, such as price fixing, between independent firms, and (2) under the "rule of reason" acted equivocally in respect to a range of business practices and interfirm relationships, such as patent pooling and exclusive dealerships; and then turn to the section on *Combinations and Monopoly Power* on page 118.

Freight Association (1897),[9] the Joint Traffic Association (1898),[10] and the Addyston Pipe and Steel Company (1899).[11] In every case the defendants pleaded that their action was only taken to prevent ruinous competition, and that the prices agreed upon were reasonable. The Court refused to consider the reasonableness of the prices, holding that it was only necessary to establish that the power and the intent to fix prices for a significant sector of the market existed in order for an agreement between competitors to be declared illegal. It was thus established as a principle that the onerous effects of constraints on competition need not be proven or even considered in order to quell price-restrictive agreements under the antitrust acts. It is also notable, and certainly an ill omen for much that was to follow, that in the landmark *Addyston Pipe* case the six defendants immediately merged to become the United States Cast Iron Pipe and Foundry Company. In the *Trenton Potteries* case in 1927, the Court specifically ruled that with respect to a price agreement, the level of prices was not at issue and the reasonableness of price was not a defense.[12] Price-fixing agreements, regardless of their effects, were an unreasonable restraint and hence were illegal per se. In this regard the position of the Court has not changed over the years. Thus, in 1940 in the *Socony-Vacuum Oil* case the Court dealt with a complex arrangement where major oil companies agreed to purchase "distress" supplies of gasoline from smaller independents in order to stabilize spot prices.[13] These spot prices, in turn, determined the price at which the large integrated oil companies contracted to sell gasoline to jobbers for retail redistribution. While not an agreement to fix prices, this was certainly a system intended to influence prices. The Court invalidated the arrangement ruling that a "combination formed for the purpose and with the effect of raising, depressing, fixing, pegging, or stabilizing the price of a commodity in interstate commerce is illegal per se." It was not necessary to establish

---

[9]*U.S. v. Trans-Missouri Freight Assn.*, 166 U.S. 290 (1897).

[10]*U.S. v. Joint Traffic Assn.*, 171 U.S. 505 (1898).

[11]*Addyston Pipe and Steel Co. v. U.S.*, 175 U.S. 211 (1899). Other cases developing this precedent are *Swift and Co. v. U.S.*, 196 U.S. 375 (1905), against collusive bidding in the purchase of livestock; *U.S. v. Terminal R. R. Assn.*, 224 U.S. 383 (1912), preventing the exclusion of competing railways from a terminal; *Standard Sanitary Mfg. Co. v. U.S.*, 226 U.S. 20 (1912), using patent licenses to fix the price of bathtubs; and *Eastern States Retail Lumber Assn. v. U.S.*, 234 U.S. 600 (1914), a boycott by retail lumber dealers.

[12]*U.S. v. Trenton Potteries Co.*, 273 U.S. 392 (1927).

[13]*U.S. v. Socony-Vacuum Oil Co.*, 310 U.S. 150 (1940).

Chapter 5

monopoly or even the power to fix and control prices effectively. That the combination existed for the purpose of influencing price sufficed for it to be stricken down. As *Socony-Vacuum* suggests, the principle of per se illegality respecting competition-constraining agreements between independent firms was re-asserted, and even more strongly than before, in the period after 1935.

The per se illegality of price fixing and related agreements has been the general rule. Nevertheless, there have been occasional exceptions. The Court validated an agreement between the National Association of Window Glass Manufacturers and the National Window Glass Workers, a trade union, to limit the operations of the plants in the industry to four and a half months of the year, with half of the firms being closed at any one time and workers moving from one set of plants to the other.[14] The industry, producing hand-blown glass windows, was a technological anachronism. The agreement, in effect, arranged for the more orderly demise of a dying industry, reducing costs by concentrating operations and stabilizing the employment of the remaining craftsmen.

Again in 1933 in the midst of the Great Depression, the Court validated an agreement of a group of bituminous coal producers.[15] This included 137 producers whose output constituted 74 percent of the coal produced in the Appalachian regions and 12 percent of the national tonnage of bituminous coal. The agreement organized an exclusive selling agency which would market the coal of those who participated, selling it at the "best price obtainable." If all the coal available could not be sold, the obtainable business would be allocated among parties to the agreement. At the time of the agreement, economic conditions in the bituminous coal industry were quite desperate. The Court recognized as possibly valid the claims made by the defendants that their arrangement could produce greater operating and marketing efficiency. Taking the stated "intention" of the agreement into account and recognizing the "unfortunate state of the industry," the Court permitted the agreement with the proviso that "if actual operation should prove undue restraint," the government was not precluded from seeking an appropriate remedy.

---

[14]*National Association of Window Glass Manufacturers* v. *U.S.*, 263 U.S. 403 (1923).
[15]*Appalachian Coals, Inc.* v. *U.S.*, 344 (1933).

Thus, the Court has on at least two occasions been willing to modify the per se rule when there were clear doubts that intensive competition was socially justifiable. In both instances consideration of equity suggested that it was the producer's rather than the consumer's share that needed protection. There is another *possible* exception to the per se rule that is consistent with the prevailing conceptions of workable competition. Consider J. K. Galbraith's notion of "countervailing power" which holds that when there is a seller or buyer that, through its size in respect to its market, controls price and output, then effective competition would require that that seller or buyer be countervailed against by a seller or buyer with an equivalent, offsetting bargaining power. This is the rationale, after all, for supporting the development of trade unions as agencies able to bargain effectively against corporate employers. It would not be difficult to imagine a powerfully concentrated industry supplying a basic material to numerous small competitive fabricators. Suppose that the latter, through an association, established a common purchasing agency to bargain against the large firms who are their suppliers. Or suppose that a group of small sellers combined to bargain more effectively against a large buyer. Would the Court invalidate such agreements? It might not, given the criterion of achieving more effective competition.

Trade Associations

The Court has held agreements between individual competitors to be generally suspect. Nevertheless, there are numerous trade associations where arrangements between competitors exist and are allowed. Firms can associate for purposes which do not reduce the effectiveness of competition but which raise the general level of decision-making and improve technical organization. A trade association, for example, may conduct joint research into problems of mutual concern. It might deal with legislation that affects the industry or undertake advertising that is intended to shape the public image of the industry or to promote consumer acceptance of the industry product. The association may serve as the agency which standardizes parts and products. It might gather and disseminate information useful to the individual firms for the rational planning of production, distribution, and investment. On the other hand, it might act through the promulgation of standards, information gathering, and dissemination to restrain competition and to fight price cutting.

During the early 1920's a series of cases concerning the so-called "open competition plan" carried on under trade association auspices was brought before the Court. *The American Column and Lumber Company* case dealt with a trade association of hardwood producers.[16] In this industry there were a large number of small firms. The members of the trade association accounted for about one third of the hardwood production and included about 5 percent of the number of firms producing hardwood. The "plan" required that each member firm provide full information about its output, sales, shipments, stocks on hand, and prices. Each firm received this information about competing firms who were participating in the plan. Firms also were continually bombarded with advice from the trade association secretary, generally urging restraint in production and resistance to price cutting.

The Court enjoined the association's open pricing plan, holding that the effect of the plan was to reduce price competition. Since the elimination of the plan did not threaten the existing technological and managerial organization, the decision was quite consistent with the "antitrust logic" of the Court. There were strong dissents by Holmes and Brandeis, and in two later cases the Court allowed modified variants of the open competition plan.[17]

Thus, while the Supreme Court has forbidden agreements between competitors when such agreements directly and specifically regulate price, control output, or otherwise restrict competition (at least 500 of such agreements have been enjoined

---

[16]*American Column and Lumber Co. v. U.S.,* 257 U.S. 377 (1921). *U.S. v. American Linseed Oil Company,* 262 U.S. 371 (1923) was decided in the same way.

[17]*Maple Flooring Manufacturers Assn. v. U.S.,* 268 U.S. 563 (1925), and *Cement Manufacturers Protective Association v. U.S.,* 268 U.S. 588 (1925). Another important trade association case to reach the Supreme Court was the *U.S. v. Sugar Institute,* 15 F. Supp. 817 (1934), and *Sugar Institute v. U.S.,* 297 U.S. 553 (1936). In that case the Court enjoined a number of the institute's practices. Since this decision, the Justice Department has normally settled its cases involving trade associations through consent decrees; this is true also of the cease and desist orders of the Federal Trade Commission. On a number of occasions, however, these cease and desist orders have been challenged and have normally been upheld by the courts except in one case, *In re Tag Manufacturers Institute,* 43 FTC 499 (1947), *Tag Manufacturers Institute v. FTC,* 174 F. 2d 452 (1949), where the court of appeals held for the trade association.

under the Sherman Act[18]), it has not forbidden all agreements between competitors even though these may have a restraining influence on competition when they are conceded to have some inherent value independent of their effect upon competition.

Workable Competition

The trade association cases raise some interesting questions as to the viability of "perfect competition" as a criterion in anti-trust enforcement.

In the classical conception the ideal condition of the market is one of *perfect* competition, where choice is fully rational, waste is minimal, and the allocation of resources is allegedly optimal. A precondition of perfect competition is that decision-makers have full and immediate knowledge of all variables relevant to their producing and selling plans. According to this venerable conception, it would follow that the active dissemination of information by the trade association should have perfected competition rather than stifling it. The point is made by Justice Holmes in his dissent in the *American Column and Lumber Company* case.

> But I should have supposed the Sherman Act did not set itself against knowledge — did not aim at a transitory cheapness unprofitable to the community as a whole because not corresponding to the actual conditions of the country. I should have thought that the ideal of commerce was intelligent interchange made with full knowledge of the facts as the basis for a forecast of the future on both sides. A combination to get and distribute such knowledge, notwithstanding its tendency to equalize, not necessarily to raise prices, is very far from a combination in unreasonable restraint of trade. It is true that it is a combination of sellers only, but the knowledge acquired is not secret; it is public, and the buyers, I think I may assume, are not less active in their efforts to know the facts. A combination in unreasonable restraint of trade imports an attempt

---

[18]Arthur T. Dietz, in "An Analysis of Decrees under the Sherman Act" (Doctoral dissertation, Princeton University, 1953), found that by 1951, 437 restrictive agreements — price fixing, market sharing, control of output, collusive bidding, and the use of a common buying or selling agent — had been enjoined, 69 through litigation and 368 by consent decrees.

to override normal market conditions. An attempt to conform to them seems to me the most reasonable thing in the world.

Similarly, in the dissent of Justice Brandeis:

> The Plan is a voluntary system for collecting from those independent concerns detailed information concerning the business operations of each, and its opinions as to trade conditions, prospects, and policy, and of collating, interpreting, and distributing the data so received among the members of the Association and others. No information gathered under the Plan was kept secret from any producer, any buyer, or the public. . . . The Sherman law does not prohibit every lessening of competition; and it certainly does not command that competition shall be pursued blindly, that business rivals shall remain ignorant of trade facts, or be denied aid in weighing their significance . . . but it was neither the aim of the Plan nor the practice under it to regulate competition in any way. Its purpose was to make rational competition possible, by supplying data not otherwise available, and without which most of those engaged in the trade would be unable to trade intelligently. . . . No official or other public means have been established for collecting from these mills and from dealers data as to current production, stocks on hand, and market prices. Concerning grain, cotton, coal, and oil, the government collects and publishes regularly, at frequent intervals, current information on production, consumption, and stocks on hand; and Boards of Trade furnish freely to the public details of current market prices of those commodities, the volume of sales, and even individual sales as recorded in daily transactions. Persons interested in such commodities are enabled through this information to deal with one another on an equal footing.

How indeed could more and better information reduce competition rather than perfecting it? Economics, during those decades, was also troubled by this dilemma, and as a response produced the theories of "imperfect competition" and "monopolistic competition" and the criteria of "workable competition."

Monopolistic competition contrasts with the condition of *pure competition*. In pure competition sellers are so numerous, and output so homogeneous, that no one seller considers it possible that his production policies and his output can have any effect whatsoever on price. Autonomous, free-moving price is taken by all individual sellers and buyers as a parameter of their output choice. Under conditions of pure competition, more complete and more rapidly disseminated knowledge of all information relevant to choice would make competition more *perfect* as well as pure. But according to the rationale of monopolistic competition, sellers in the modern industrial and mercantile economy can influence price without conspiracy and without anything like the power of the classical monopolist. Price is not autonomous but is controlled to some degree. When such is the case, a more complete knowledge by one seller of the effects of his output on price or of his price on sales will lead not toward more perfect competition but toward more effective control by the individual seller of output and price; i.e., toward a more perfect monopoly. And the seller's awareness that others will learn easily and quickly of price concessions that he makes will deter him from making such concessions. After all, what incentive would a seller have to cut his prices in order to gain more business if his competitors were to know (and he knew they were to know) immediately of his actions or even of his intentions, and were to cut their prices correspondingly to keep him from increasing his business at their expense? That which is more likely to break a common price line is the expectation of a seller that by concessions to buyers he can gain a larger share of the market for himself at the expense of his competitors, coupled with his uncertainty as to whether competitors are making concessions to buyers so as to increase their share of the market at his expense. If every seller knows that none of his competitors can make price concessions without his being aware of it and that no price concession that he can make will escape the attention of his competitors, his strongest motivation to cut his prices will be removed; and the members of the industry, united now by common rather than rival objectives, will presumably push prices up toward the monopoly level.

The new theorists supposed that competition in industrial markets was not pure and could never be made pure in the classical sense. Rather, accepting a degree of price control as intrinsic, social policy must try to make competition "workable." Workable competition is competition where prices are significantly responsive to changing conditions of supply and demand; e.g., to slackened purchasing and excess capacity. Such responsiveness requires, as an offset to the power to control prices implicit in a market structure, a substantial degree of seller ignorance and uncertainty. Hence, it becomes an objective of workable competition to preserve a necessary margin of ignorance and uncertainty. Yet, aside from their effects on pricing policy, uncertainty and ignorance can exact a heavy cost in irrational organization and in the misallocation of resources. From a company's viewpoint the same information that is relevant to the choice of a more rational monopoly policy is also relevant to the efficient, progressive, and foresightful organization of resources. This is one of the dilemmas of workable competition.

The Curse of Bigness

We have supposed hitherto that the ideology of liberalism favored a price-guided market because of its alleged progressiveness and efficiency. The ideology implied something more. Private ownership, the self-sufficiency and independence of men who run their own businesses and make their own choices, was considered by many liberals to be good in itself. Conversely, "bigness," the swallowing up of individualism into organization, was considered inherently evil.

When Justice Brandeis wrote his most famous book, he did not call it *The Curse of Monopoly*. He called it *The Curse of Bigness*. The undercurrents of antibigness and antimonopoly both run through the history of American liberalism, sometimes coalescing, sometimes drawing apart — for antibigness can sometimes be anticompetitive. Antibigness, as it has been expressed in the law and in the decisions of the Court, sometimes deliberately dampens competition and pays the price of comparative inefficiency in order to preserve the social environment of small enterprise as an intrinsic good.

The *American Column and Lumber Company* case illustrates this issue. The hardwood industry was highly decentralized, containing numerous small independent concerns. To Justice Brandeis the danger was that unless this industry was enabled to create institutions that eliminate "destructive" price wars and the like, the number of independents would be progressively reduced. Through consolidation a few gigantic corporations would replace the thousands of independent producers.

Price control would then not be problematic but automatic — a function of market shares. In that way price stability finally would be achieved, and the cherished environment of small independent enterprise would have vanished. According to Brandeis' dissent in the *American Column and Lumber* case:

> The absence of such information in the hardwood lumber trade enables dealers in the large centers more readily to secure advantage over the isolated producer. And the large concerns, which are able to establish their own bureaus of statistics, secure an advantage over small concerns. . . . In making such information available to the smallest concern, it creates among producers equality of opportunity. In making it available, also, to purchasers and the general public, it does all that can actually be done to protect the community from extortion. If, as alleged, the Plan tends to substitute stability in prices for violent fluctuations, its influence, in this respect, is not against the public interest. The evidence in this case far from establishing an illegal restraint of trade, presents in my opinion, an instance of commendable effort by concerns engaged in a chaotic industry to make possible its intelligent conduct under competitive conditions.

> The refusal to permit a multitude of small rivals to cooperate, as they have done here, in order to protect themselves and the public from the chaos and havoc wrought in their trade by ignorance, may result in suppressing competition in the hardwood industry. These keen business rivals, who sought through cooperative exchange of trade information to create conditions under which alone rational competition is possible, produce in the aggregate about one third of the hardwood lumber of the country. . . . May not these hardwood lumber concerns, frustrated in their efforts to rationalize competition, be led to enter the inviting field of consolidation? And if they do, may not another huge trust, with highly centralized control over vast resources, natural, manufacturing, and financial, become so powerful as to dominate competitors, wholesalers, retailers, consumers, employees, and, in large measure, the community?

That ideology, which would preserve small enterprise and decentralized choice as intrinsic goods to be preserved, if necessary, at the expense of competition and efficiency, is expressed in the Robinson-Patman Act of 1936. It attempts to neutralize the bargaining power of large buyers that might enable them to secure an advantage over their smaller competitors.[19]   The ideology of smallness at the expense of aggressive competition also had a day of triumph in court in the *A & P* case.[20]

Cross-Product and Cross-Market Leverage

There is a body of business activities and arrangements usually designated as *unfair trade practices* that have been attacked and held to be illegal under the Sherman Act, Clayton Act, Federal Trade Commission Act, and in a subsequent period to be described in Chapter 10, the Robinson-Patman Act. These activities and arrangements constitute quite a mixed bag, reflecting not only the interest of economic liberalism in the preservation of market competition, but also the sentiment of antibigness and the self-concern of consumers and competitors for adherence to the acknowledged rules of the game and of consumers for fair-dealing and honesty on the part of sellers. Many of these specific unfair trade practices and particularly the unelaborated prohibition of "unfair methods of competition," incorporate into statutes the precedents of the common law.

Inasmuch as they relate to the preservation of market competition, unfair trade laws can, in large part, be understood as an attempt to constrain the use of a quite general business strategy, namely the use of an entrenched position in one market or industry as leverage to gain a competitive advantage elsewhere. This strategy can appear in such guises as exclusion, discrimination, tying contracts, restrictive licenses, and vertical integration. The use of cross-market or cross-product leverage will always constrain competition, but such strategies are often interwoven with the legitimate objectives and practices of the firm. Thus, when patents are used as a means of cross-market or cross-product leverage, the detriments to competition must be weighed against considerations of equity in exploiting a legal grant of monopoly (which a patent is), and in a larger sense weighed against the prerequisites and viability of the patent system as a means of promoting invention and innovation.

The Court had rigorously suppressed cross-market and cross-product leverage proportionately as this could be done without

---

[19]See footnote 6, pp. 99–100, for a discussion of the Robinson-Patman Act.
[20]*U.S. v. New York Great A & P Tea Company,* 67 F. Supp. 626 (1946).

imperiling the organizational and technological viability of enterprise or overriding consideration of equity. Consider some specifics.

The possibilities (from the viewpoint of business strategy) and the problems (from the viewpoint of the antitrust law) implicit in cross-market and cross-product leverage are most clearly demonstrated in relation to the possession of a patent monopoly. The patent grant conveys exclusive rights in the use, sale, or licensing of a specified invention. When a patentee licenses an invention, what controls can be imposed on the licensee? The Court has held that the patent owner can impose virtually any conditions in the use of the licensed invention. The patentee can control the licensee's level of output, sales territory, and the prices charged for the products produced with the licensed invention. The licensees are considered to be agents in the exercise of a legitimate monopoly right.[21] The powers of control, however, cannot be extended by attaching any conditions to the sale of the patented device or product.[22] Once the item is sold, the fact that it is patented or was produced through a patented process can have no effect upon what the new owner can do with it.

But what if a patented good is offered for sale only in combination with some unpatented item, in whose output and sales the patent owner presumably has an interest? Has the patent owner the right to use his legitimate monopoly in item A as leverage to secure a competitive advantage in unpatented item B by tying the sale of B to that of A? Or, suppose that the owner licenses patented process A; can he require that his licensees use unpatented, or separately patented, material C or component D in process A as a condition for the licensed right to use A? In the Clayton Act Congress specifically outlawed tying clauses whether the leased tying items were patented or unpatented.[23] Thereafter, the Court acted rigorously in preventing the extension of patent monopolies through tying contracts.

---

[21]U.S. v. General Electric Co., 272 U.S. 476 (1926); Rubber Tire Wheel Company v. Milwaukee Rubber Works Co., 154 F. 358 (1907) and 210 U.S. 439 (1908); General Talking Picture Corporation v. Western Electric Corportion, 304 U.S. 175 (1938); Providence Rubber Company v. Goodyear, 76 U.S. 788 (1869).

[22]Bauer & Cie v. O'Donnell, 229 U. S. 1 (1913).

[23]Section 3 of the Clayton Act of 1914: ". . . to lease or make a sale or contract for sale of goods, wares, merchandise, machinery supplies, or other commodities, whether patented or unpatented. . . ."

Thus, in 1928 contracts requiring that only RCA radio tubes should be used by those manufacturing radios under RCA licenses were invalidated.[24] In 1936 contracts requiring those who leased IBM tabulating machines to use IBM tabulating cards were invalidated.[25]

A producer who dominates the market or who possesses some other bargaining advantage is in a position to fortify and extend his advantages by arrangements with dealers that exclude his competitors from distributional outlets. Any arrangements with dealers excluding competitors will, for that reason, constrain competition. At the same time, exclusive arrangements between a producer and dealers or sales agents might be advantageous or necessary from the point of view of technological organization and managerial efficiency. To disturb or prevent such arrangements, whatever their constraints on competition, might do more harm than good. Hence, in its approach to exclusive dealerships, the Court has been cautious, balancing technical and organizational values against competitive constraints.[26] In the period before World War II, a seller had to be "dominant" in his market before any exclusive dealer arrangements he might make could be considered illicit. In 1923 the Court refused to enjoin the Curtis Publishing Company from forbidding its delivery boys to deliver other than Curtis publications.[27] It refused to enjoin big oil refiners from forbidding the filling stations to which they leased tanks and pumps from using those tanks and pumps for other than the leasing company's gasoline.[28] On the other hand, the Court did outlaw exclusive dealer arrangements in the *Standard Fashion* and *Butterick* cases in 1923 for firms dominating the dress pattern industry[29] and in the *Q.R.S. Music* case in 1926 for a firm dominating the production of player piano rolls.[30] In the *Eastman Kodak* case in 1927, a firm dominant in producing motion picture film was forbidden from making arrangements with

---

[24]*Lord* v. *Radio Corporation of America*, 24 F. 2d 565 (1928).
[25]*International Business Machines Corp.* v. *U.S.*, 298 U.S. 131 (1936).
[26]*B. S. Pearsall Butter Company* v. *FTC*, 292 F. 720 (1923).
[27]*FTC* v. *Curtis Publishing Company*, 260 U.S. 568 (1923).
[28]*FTC* v. *Sinclair Refining Company*, 261 U.S. 463 (1923).
[29]*Standard Fashion Company* v. *Magrane-Houston Company*, 258 U.S. 346 (1922); *Butterick Company* v. *FTC*, 4 F. 2d 910 (1925), certiorari denied, 267 U.S. 602 (1925).
[30]*Q.R.S. Music Company* v. *FTC*, 12 F. 2d 730 (1926).
[31]*FTC* v. *Eastman Kodak*, 269 U.S. 546 (1927).

its processors which had the effect of excluding the processing of foreign film.[31] But in 1936, taking technological and organizational considerations into account, the Court refused to enjoin General Motors from forbidding its dealers to sell or use other than GM parts in making repairs. The Court held that "while it may be that competition would have increased more rapidly in the absence of such provisions," they were nevertheless justified in maintaining quality control in repairs, protecting the reputation of the company, and maintaining the goodwill of its car buyers.[32]

Similarly, it was held that patent pooling might serve either beneficient or pernicious purposes. In effect, such pools might be conspiracies to bar new entry into an industry and exploit an industry-wide monopoly. On the other hand (indeed, at the same time), such patent pooling might advance technology and increase productivity by facilitating the dissemination of information and more widespread use of inventions and by eliminating duplicative research or the need for firms to work around patent blockages. As in the instance of exclusive dealerships or trade association information-dissemination schemes, the Court considered each case pragmatically under the rule of reason, weighing and balancing the values and dangers that might inhere in a particular arrangement. In 1912 when firms producing some 85 percent of enameled iron bathtubs and related sanitary wares pooled their patents through a trade association which issued licenses fixing output, prices, discounts, and channels of distribution, the arrangement was declared illegal.[33] In 1931, on the other hand, following disputes between petroleum companies an arrangement for the interchange of their process patents for the catalytic cracking of oil was approved by the Court as having "resulted in no monopoly or restriction of competition in . . . licensing . . . or in production."[34]

> The need for patent interchanges and conversely the antitrust risks which may accompany their use, has been judicially recognized . . . may help . . . make assembled patents available to others . . . thus promote rather than restrain competition. On the other hand the interchange . . . created with illicit purpose,

---

[32]*Pick Mfg. Company v. General Motors Corporation*, 299 U.S. 3 (1936).
[33]*Standard Sanitary Manufacturing Co. v. U.S.*, 266 U.S. 20 (1912).
[34]*Standard Oil Company (Indiana) v. U.S.*, 283 U.S. 163 (1931).

or misused . . . may lead to unreasonable restraints of trade. . . . Separating a licit from an illicit purpose in inception, the courts emphasize an interchange's activities as evidence of intent underlying its formation. An absence of restrictive practices evidences lack of improper intent. Contrariwise, an interchange is unlawful if formed with the purpose of regimenting an industry, fixing prices and eliminating competition, or threatening litigation with accompanying undue restraint of trade.[35]

It is also possible for cross-market or cross-product leverage to be exercised through vertical integration. In 1920 two railroad lines owned mines that produced nearly half of the country's anthracite coal supply; hence, they were in a position to use their monopoly of important transport routes to favor their own mining operations over those of independents. The railroads were found to be in violation of the Sherman Act and were required to divest themselves of their mine ownership.[36] It was quite evident in this instance that there was no relationship of technological necessity and no advantage of coherent organization in the binding together of anthracite coal mines and railroads. Therefore, the Court forced dissolution and divestiture without concern for possible ill consequences on operations. Normally, corporate organizations attacked as monopolies under the Sherman Act could not be fragmented without such apprehension.

Price Discrimination under the Clayton Act

Price discrimination, a common phenomenon, exists when there are differences in the seller's net realization upon the sale of the same product or service to different buyers, or when price variations of products are not in proportion to the variations in their costs. Section Two of the Clayton Act forbids discrimination in price "between different purchasers of commodities of like grade and quality . . . where the effect of such discrimination may be substantially to lessen competition or tend to create a monopoly in any line of commerce."

---

[35]Report of the Attorney General's National Committee to Study the Antitrust Laws (Washington: U.S. Government Printing Office, 1955), pp. 242–247.

[36]U.S. v. Reading Company, 253 U.S. 26 (1920); U.S. v. Lehigh Valley Railroad Co., 254 U.S. 255 (1920).

It specifically allows "differentials which make only due allowance for differences in the cost of manufacture, sale, or delivery resulting from the differing methods or quantities in which such commodities are . . . sold or delivered." The prohibition does not apply when discrimination "was made in good faith to meet the equally low price of a competitor."

What the authors of the Clayton Act no doubt intended by all this was to proscribe the use of selective price cutting by a powerful seller to discipline or to eliminate his weaker rivals. Under this section of the Clayton Act the Court has also allowed buyers to demand equal discounts with rivals who are "in the same line of commerce" and who buy in equivalent quantities.[37] The Court, however, invalidated Federal Trade Commission efforts to require equal discounts for purchasers of the same commodity in equivalent quantities when the Court did not consider purchasers to be "in the same line of commerce;" i.e., where one was a cooperative and the other a commercial wholesaler[38] or where one was a chain store and the other an association of retailers.[39] Nor would it allow the Federal Trade Commission to require discounts proportionate to cost variations when the product of a single seller was sold to different categories of buyers or when the quality of the product differed.[40]

The prohibition of price discrimination was to become much more important later, after passage of the Robinson-Patman Act in 1936.

Combinations and Monopoly Power

Monopoly is conceived in economic theory as a species of market power — namely, the ability of a particular seller to control or substantially to influence the aggregate output and hence the price of a product in a given market, a power which in turn depends on the comparative size or output share of that seller in respect to that market. Monopoly power depends also on the relative costs and difficulties that others have in entering the market. In other words, it is a function of the

---

[37]*Van Camp* v. *American Can Company*, 278 U.S. 245 (1929).
[38]*Mennen Company* v. *FTC*, 288 F. 774, certiorari denied (1923).
[39]*National Biscuit Company* v. *FTC*, 299 F. 733, certiorari denied (1924).
[40]*Goodyear Tire and Rubber Company* v. *FTC*, 101 F. 2d 620 (1939), certiorari denied, 308 U.S. 557 (1939).

absence of both actual and potential competition as a constraint on the exercise of market power.

Monopoly implies a significant control by a given seller over price and output and hence, of production, the employment of labor, and the use of other resources in the industry. On the assumption that pricing policy follows entrepreneurial self-interest in maximizing profits, the economist has deduced a priori that monopoly power will result in "monopoly prices" and that monopoly pricing distorts the allocation of resources and, through the exploitation of consumers, maldistributes wealth. Therefore, in the eyes of the antitrust economist, the evil that must be attacked is the monopoly power itself, and consequently, the fewness of sellers from which monopoly power derives. But economics has not attempted to evaluate and has certainly never succeeded in measuring the social costs of such an attack in respect to its effect upon organizational and technological efficiency and on the capacity for progressive innovation. Nor has economics ever clearly established or meaningfully measured the benefits that have been or could be derived from the fragmentation of enterprise and the segmentation of economic choice. Nor has economics established any appropriate or approximate limits for a policy of fragmentation; i.e., for a policy of breaking up monopolies.

The judges, less bound to academic doctrine and carrying the burden of responsibility for the concrete effects of their decisions, have looked at monopoly somewhat differently. In implementing the Sherman Act they started with a highly conservative assumption designed to minimize the changes they would be required to enforce in the structure of organizations, and hence to minimize the risks to technology of antitrust enforcement. Their assumption was this: it is not possible to achieve and maintain an economic power beyond that which is required for efficient organization and for optimal technological progress except by concerted (i.e., "conspiratorial") efforts backed up with coercive pressure and strategies that are outside the pale of normal business practice. According to this assumption there are underlying forces that, in the absence of such untoward conspiracy and coercion, would surely shape the economy into its optimal structure and organization. Justice Day, in the *Standard Oil of New Jersey* case,[41] put it this way:

---

[41]*Standard Oil Company of New Jersey v. U.S.*, 221 U.S. 1 (1911).

[The Sherman Act by its] comprehensiveness . . . makes it certain that its purpose was to prevent undue restraint of every kind and nature, nevertheless by the omission of any direct prohibition against the monopoly in the concrete it indicates a consciousness that the freedom of the individual right to contract, when not unduly or improperly exercised, was the most efficient means for the prevention of monopoly, since the operation of the centrifugal and centripetal forces resulting from the right to freely contract was the means by which monopoly would be inevitably prevented if no extraneous or sovereign power imposed it and no right to make unlawful contracts having a monopolistic tendency were permitted.

If, as the judges thought, "monopoly is inevitably prevented" by those "forces resulting from the right to freely contract," it follows that an undue, socially harmful business concentration can only be created or maintained by the exertion of "extraneous . . . power" made manifest in coercion, pressure, and conspiracy. Hence, the test of monopoly was not to be the market power of the business entity itself in its ability to influence or to control prices, but was rather whether or not there existed visible props to such power in the form of conspiracy and coercion to constrain free contract. Since, supposedly, these were inevitably required to maintain an undue and socially harmful concentration of power, their existence could be taken as a test of whether any given concentration was a socially harmful monopoly. If the Court was convinced that a combination rested upon and required those props, it was willing to order dissolution, divestiture, and segmentation; otherwise, not.

Very simply, the judges chose to stand on what seemed safe ground to them. They were willing to suppose that a given concentration of power was not an organizational and technological requisite of high productivity only when it was evident that such a concentration had been "artificially" contrived and maintained through force and coercion extraneous to legitimate market relationships. The concentration of power was permissible when it had evolved out of free and voluntary contract in the normal course of business and/or had withstood the buffeting and test of market competition. In 1911 the Supreme Court ruled on the legality of two of the great trusts of the period, the Standard Oil Trust and the Tobacco Trust.[42] Both had been recently formed

---

[42]*U.S. v. American Tobacco Company,* 221 U.S. 106 (1911).

through the ruthless coercion of independents. Standard Oil of New Jersey, for example, had made extensive use of railroad rebates, industrial spying and sabotage, and selective price cutting. The Supreme Court declared the two trusts illegal and required that each be broken into several parts. In both cases the test of monopoly was not the existence, degree, or exercise of monopoly power, but rather the visible and unmistakably coercive *props* to power. The existence of these props as evidence of coercion and monopolistic conspiracy established to the satisfaction of the Court that the Standard Oil Company of New Jersey and the American Tobacco Company were artificial contrivances *not* based on superior technology and organizational efficiency, but rather that they had been imposed through extraneous means and devices.

Good Trusts

As time passed there was a competitive shakedown of the great trustified industries. Because of internal resistance within industry, the revulsion of society against overt coercion, and the limits laid down by the courts in the *Standard Oil* and *Tobacco* cases, the business behavior of the great trusts mellowed. Their aggressiveness was replaced by an attitude of live and let live; they became "dominant firms," centers of an industrial "establishment," representing the group interest in "orderly" production, the maintenance of high stable prices, and industrial peace. They grew but they chose to grow at a slower rate than the industry as a whole, yielding a larger proportion of the production increment to aggressive newcomers. Hence, their share of the market declined. Such were the characteristics of these companies when the second wave of antitrust prosecution against them reached the courts in the 1920's.

The trusts brought before the Court in the second wave of prosecutions no longer had the aspect of devouring monsters. Now they were conservative pater familias, responsible for vast and complex commercial and technical operations, having survived and surviving in the stream of normal commercial intercourse and imposing no visible extraneous constraints or illicit pressures on voluntary contract and competitive practice. To bust these trusts was to risk the loss to society of industrial productivity and a capacity for technical progress. Under these circumstances the Court would not countenance their dissolution.

In two leading cases of the second generation of anti-monopoly suits, efforts were made to break up the United States Steel Corporation and the American Can Company, which controlled nine tenths of the output of tin cans.[43] Deciding the case in 1916, a lower court refused to take action against the American Can Company because it had "done nothing of which any competitor or consumer of cans complains or anything which strikes a disinterested outsider as unfair or unethical."

In its 1920 decision the Supreme Court reviewed the history of the United States Steel Corporation and recognized an initial intent on its part to monopolize.[44] It recognized also that a substantial part of the industry had remained independent of U.S. Steel and that during the intervening years the corporation had lost something of its market share. At the time of the second antitrust suit it controlled about half of the industry's output of steel and steel products. The Court also recognized that U.S. Steel had once engaged in conspiratorial efforts to control the price of steel but that these overt arrangements had since been abandoned. Nor was there evidence of coercive pressure or ruthless tactics beyond the conventional bounds of business practice, no "brutalities or tyranny." "It did not secure freight rebates; it did not increase its profits by reducing the wages of its employees, . . . by lowering the quality of its products nor by creating an artificial scarcity of them; . . . it did not undersell its competitors in some localities by reducing its prices there below those maintained elsewhere; . . . there was no evidence that it attempted to crush its competitors or drive them from the market." But the steel company was not being accused of any such wickednesses. The issue before the Court was simply and specifically that of monopoly; whether the size and share of the market of the United States Steel Corporation, which certainly permitted that company significantly to influence output and price in the industry, was to be considered an offense under the Sherman Act.

Justice McKenna, speaking for the majority of the Court, refused to accept market power as a criterion of monopoly

---

[43]U.S. v. American Can Company, 230 F. 859 (1916).
[44]U.S. v. United States Steel Corporation, 251 U.S. 417 (1920).

under the antitrust law. The criterion of market power was not subject to measurement. It afforded no clear boundaries for the application of the law nor guidelines for legitimate corporation policy and business planning. "The law does not make mere size an offense . . . (but) requires overt acts and trusts to its prohibition of them and the power to repress or punish them."

Justice Day, who wrote the dissent, agreed "that the act offers no objection to the mere size of a corporation nor to the continued exertion of . . . power, when that size and power have been obtained by lawful means and developed by natural growth." For Day, however, the U. S. Steel trust had been established "for illegal purposes" through practices "made upon a scale that was huge and a manner that was wild." In his view the United States Steel Corporation had through its past "overt acts" been placed in a relatively invulnerable position, and it remained a product of coercion and conspiracy.

Neither the majority of the Court nor Justice Day were concerned with monopoly power as conceived by the economist, but rather with whether overt acts committed in the past should or should not be punished, and whether conditions as they existed prior to the commitment of those acts should be restored. McKenna and the majority agreed that overt acts and illegal purposes had led to the formation of the company, but they gave credence to the contention of the lower court that "the concentration of powers . . . was . . . necessary, and immediately manifested . . . in improved methods and products and in an increase of domestic and foreign trade." The trust had been formed a decade before, and account must be taken "of the many millions of dollars spent, the developments made, and the enterprises undertaken" as well as the changes in equity holdings and the increments of new public investment which had occurred since that time. Those who had perpetuated the overt acts a decade ago had in great part taken their loot and left. To punish those overt acts of the past would penalize a new generation of "shareholders as well as thousands of workers and consumers." The Court would not undertake to "enforce abstractions and do injury thereby." To yield to the "prayer of the government" would mean "not only a disruption of present conditions, but the restoration of the conditions of 20 years ago" which, in the view of the Court, would not serve the public interest but rather would "risk injury to the public interest."

In the steel case the Supreme Court enunciated the doctrine of the "good trusts." Market power was legitimate so long as it was not manifestly employed in overt acts of conspiracy and coercion. Following that decision, the government withdrew its pending and ongoing prosecutions against other alleged monopolies. Not until 1927 was the issue of monopoly power raised again. And again the Supreme Court, in the *International Harvester* case, held that "the law does not make the mere size of a corporation, however impressive, or the existence of unexerted power on its part, an offense when unaccompanied by unlawful conduct in the exercise of power. . . ."[45] Nor would the Court accept price leadership as evidence of monopoly power. "The fact that competitors may see proper, in the exercise of their own judgment, to follow the prices of another manufacturer, does not establish any suppression of competition or show any sinister domination."[46]

Academic economists, in doctrinaire righteousness, have ridiculed the notion of "good trusts." How can monopoly be good when a priori the action of any rational monopolist must contravene against the public interest? Yet not even among academic economists was there consensus as to what ought to be done in respect to the market power of the great industrial corporation, or even as to how to measure that alleged power. The economists, indifferent to and ignorant of technological considerations, neither reckoned the social risks and costs of industrial disruption nor determined the feasibility of alternatives. Everything else being the same, it would have been preferable (following the precepts of liberalism) that the United States Steel Corporation be divided into ten companies, or better still that it be divided into a hundred companies, or even better that it be divided into a thousand companies. The more the competitors, the more intense and pure would competition become. All this would be preferable if pure competition was taken as the norm and if everything else remained the same. But nothing else would remain the same, particularly the

---

[45]*U.S.* v. *International Harvester*, 274 U.S. 693 (1927).

[46]This does not settle the question as to whether price leadership is evidence of a conspiracy to restrain competition rather than evidence of the "sinister domination" of monopoly.

technological and organizational capacities. Nor is it clear what increase in the number of competitors is required before the plateau of satisfactory, sufficient, or optimal competition is reached.

It is again to be emphasized that underlying the rule of the "good trust" was a more fundamental rationale. The Court had weighed the detriments of monopoly power (detriments they accepted as real and significant) against the unknowable but formidable dangers implicit in the enforced fragmentation of a massive corporate enterprise, and by their scale of measurement the potential dangers normally outweighed the possible benefits. When the dangers implicit in a policy of fragmentation were appreciably less than in those heavy industries where most of the tests of monopoly power came, then the Court correspondingly was more receptive to the alternative of dissolution and divestiture. Thus, in a series of cases the Court was confronted with railroad combinations attacked by the Justice Department as monopolies under the Sherman Act. These combinations were in an industry of regulated monopoly and hence were not obliged to withstand the "survival" test of market competition that the Court had posited in other cases; moreover, the combined entities were technically and organizationally distinct and spatially separated, and their ownership had in fact been popping in and out of investment house portfolios in a gigantic financial game for half a century, so that no intelligent observer could be apprehensive of the effects on operating organization or on viable technological relationships of dissolving the combinations. Hence, in these railroad cases settled in 1904,[47] 1912,[48] 1920,[49] and 1922,[50] the

---

[47]*Northern Securities Company* v. *U.S.*, 193 U.S. 197 (1904). The Court ordered the dissolution of a holding company controlling through the ownership of their shares the Great Northern and Northern Pacific Railroads, running parallel routes in competition with other transcontinental lines.

[48]*U.S.* v. *Terminal Railroad Association*, 224 U.S. 383 (1912), relating to a combination to exclude other roads from terminal facilities; also, *U.S.* v. *Union Pacific Railroad Company*, 226 U.S. 61 (1912), relating to the acquisition of a noncompeting line, which might provide the basis for future competition.

[49]*U.S.* v. *Reading Company*, 253 U.S. 26 (1920); *U.S.* v. *Lehigh Valley Railroad Co.*, 254 U.S. 255 (1920), concerning railroad-anthracite coal combinations. These were devices intended presumably to evade the provisions of the Hepburn Act of 1906 which forbade railways to haul goods produced by themselves (except when those goods were used by themselves) and aimed specifically at the advantages of anthracite coal mines owned by railroads over their competitors.

[50]*U.S.* v. *Southern Pacific Co.*, 259 U.S. 214 (1922).

Court resorted to dissolution and divestiture without hesitancy and without requiring proof of coercive or exploitative behavior.

Stock Acquisitions and Mergers

Competition can be restrained through means other than formal agreement; for example, through interlocking directorates (the same individuals on the boards of directors of competing companies) or through the acquisition by one company of the common stock of another, and hence the power to influence or eventually to control the policy of its competitor. Competition might be restricted not only by acquiring the stock of a competitor but also by acquiring shares of other corporations that sell to or buy from the stock-acquiring company since such cross-corporate influence or control could close off a part of the sales outlets or the sources of procurement of competitors. If, for example, a company producing steel pipe should secure stock control or otherwise be in a position to influence the policies of natural gas companies who were about to build large pipelines, then conceivably, through such influence the company producing steel pipes could restrain competition by preempting for itself the sale of pipe to the natural gas companies. The logical extension of control through stock acquisition is merger. And merger is the highroad to concentration and monopoly. If, as we have seen, the Court was unwilling to allow the Sherman Act to be used as an instrument for shattering those concentrations of economic power deemed "monopolistic," would it allow preventive measures to be taken that would check the emergence through mergers of new loci of monopolistic power?

The Clayton Act specifically forbids "any corporation engaged in commerce to acquire the shares of a competing corporation or to purchase the stocks of two or more corporations that were competitors . . . where effect may be substantially to lessen competition." Here the government is not required to establish monopoly or monopolization but the far less stringent condition that the "effect may be to substantially lessen competition." The effect of this more permissive provision for antitrust enforcement in the prevention of monopoly was nullified when companies, acquiring control over their competitors by acquiring the voting stock of the competing company, stumbled onto a gimmick which permitted them to evade the intent of the Clayton Act. In the *Thatcher Manufacturing* case a company "unlawfully acquired" the common stock of a competitor and used this control to transfer to itself ownership of the assets of the controlled competitor.[51] Thus, the real properties of the two corporations were merged. The eggs, so far as the Court was concerned, were scrambled and the Court refused to unscramble them. The Court ruled that the section of the Clayton Act forbidding the acquisition of the stock of a competitor had "no application to ownership of a competitor's property and business . . . even though this was brought about through stock improperly held." The Court said, in effect, that it was quite willing to force a company to divest itself of the stock that it had acquired in a competitor's business if there was the suspicion that through the ownership of those shares the policies of the competitor could be so influenced as to lessen competition. To force the divestiture of mere stock is no threat to operating organizations and technology, but when the stocks are used to merge real assets, the companies have crossed the Rubicon of paper relationships and have become an integral technological and organizational entity. Then, in the eyes of the Court, divestiture involves significant risks and possible costs.

The Court, not itself competent to evaluate the costs and risks of technological dismemberment, was not prepared to undertake those risks merely on evidence that the "effect may be to substantially lessen competition." The Court decided that after an actual merger of assets, the company could no longer be attacked under the Clayton Act. If it was to be attacked at all, it must be as a monopoly under the Sherman Act. Thus, the preventive measures written into the Clayton Act were of no avail as a check on merger.

THE ENFORCEMENT OF ANTITRUST, 1890–1935

For the period between the Civil War and the Great Depression, the rulings of the Supreme Court were (1) ideologically negative, aborting all efforts of government to ameliorate the miseries or to deal with breakdowns produced in an

---

[51]*Thatcher Manufacturing Company v. FTC*, 272 U.S. 554 (1926).

industrialized economy, and (2) operational and pragmatic with respect to the effort to preserve market competition under the antitrust laws. In the first instance the Court interpreted the Constitution as an absolute defense of ideological liberalism. In the second it accepted the antitrust laws as supporting the precepts of liberalism and, within the framework of the ideology, tried to develop workable rules that would permit the achievement of antitrust objectives without unduly detrimental effects on business organization and technology.

The Court's antitrust rationale during this period (1890–1935) is illustrated in Figure 5-1, which suggests a spectrum of enforcement. The implementation of the law ranges from absolute enforcement to nonenforcement, depending on the Court's evaluation of the implicit dangers of disrupting viable technological and organizational relationships. The scale

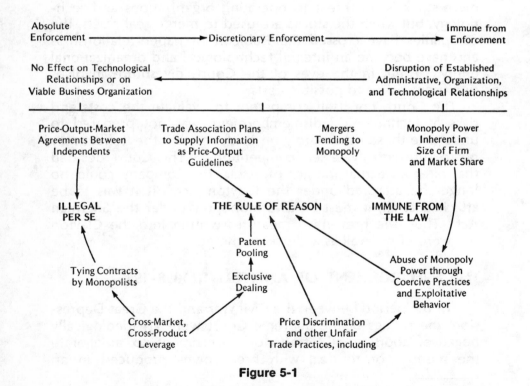

Figure 5-1

Scale of Antitrust Enforcement: 1890–1935

of enforcement shown includes those categories of practices and arrangements which are:

1. *Illegal Per Se*—In this category of per se constraints, antitrust enforcement is without evident effect on technology or business organization agreements between independent firms to fix prices, to share markets, or to control production, and tying contracts where the tying product or process is monopolized.
2. *Subject to the Rule of Reason*—The rule of reason means in effect "subject to the discretionary choice of the court." A zone of enforcement subject to discretionary judgments is always less satisfactory, ipso facto, than one where the rules are clear-cut, both from the point of view of those who enforce the law and those who are subject to it. Nevertheless, where pernicious effect and significant values intermingle, some judgment and discretion in the administration of the law is probably inescapable. In any case, precedents provide cumulating evidence of what business intent the court considers permissible, what business activities it looks upon with suspicion, and what sorts of arrangements it regards as pernicious. This rule of reason applies to trade association activities that provide information, costing techniques, and guide-lines influencing price and production policies of business enterprise, exclusive dealer arrangements, price discrimination, patent pooling, and a variety of possible coercive and "unfair" trade practices.
3. *Immune from Enforcement*—Enterprise that possesses the "monopoly" power to control output and price, or mergers leading to the acquisition of such power, so long as there is no evidence that this power has been sustained through coercive or illicit practices. Clearly the remedies that might be applied, namely dissolution and divestiture, must necessarily threaten the viability of technology and the effectiveness of organization.

ANTITRUST POLICY, 1890–1935: A SUMMARY

This chapter has examined the antitrust laws and their enforcement from 1890 when the Sherman Act was passed by

Congress to 1935-36 when the United States was in the throes of the Great Depression and on the threshold of war. In summary the following can be said:

1. The Supreme Court sanctioned a positive role for the federal government in eliminating constraints upon market competition. The Court, however, exercised a decisive authority in fixing the boundaries and in determining the nature of such antitrust enforcement.
2. Its interpretation of the law reflects the Court's intention of weighing the substantive effects on the economy of any effort to enforce competition.
3. The Court only permitted a per se or absolute enforcement of the words of the law when it was satisfied that the prohibition was such as not adversely to affect technology and operating organization.
4. Because the dissolution of agreements between independent companies seemed to pose no threat to technological or operating organization, the Court absolutely prohibited such agreements between independent companies for the purpose of fixing prices or production, sharing markets, excluding new competitors, or sharing profits as a means of dampening the incentive to compete.
5. The Court would not forbid all institutionalized arrangements between independent companies, such as trade associations, for the Court recognized that such arrangements might have legitimate and socially useful purposes. But the Court did examine such arrangements and, under the rule of reason, sometimes judged them to be illegal, trying to balance their possible values for efficient operation and technical progress against the possible detriments to competition.
6. As a precautionary measure, the court was willing to enjoin intercorporate stockholding, but once control had been acquired through such intercorporate stockholding and that control had been used to merge the assets of competing companies, the Court was faced with the possibility that divestiture would require physical dismemberment and a technological or organizational disruption. In view of the possible social costs thereof, the Court refused to act whenever control acquired through intercorporate stockholding had been used to merge the ownership of assets. Hence, the antitrust laws could not be used to prevent the trend toward combination.

7. Nor would the Court permit the dismemberment of large, going concerns on account of their alleged monopoly power. The benefits of such dismemberment were considered too hypothetical to offset the risk of a positive loss of technological and organizational advantages. Rather, the Court took as a test of monopoly the exercise of overt acts presumably required to create and to maintain concentrations of monopoly power in opposition to the normal force of free and voluntary contract. While academic economists frequently condemned the reluctance of the Court to dismember the trusts, economics in fact evolved no criterion of competition, workable as law, by reference to which the judges could have differentiated between unlawful monopoly and lawful competition; nor did economics succeed in any specific instance in assessing the social gains through increased competition as a consequence of dismemberment compared to the loss of productivity and organizational efficiency that might also be a consequence of dismemberment.

8. The outstanding achievement of the antitrust laws during this period was the prevention of any general and systematic sets of agreements between independent companies to fix prices, control output, or otherwise limit competition. At least partly on account of these laws, there never occurred in the United States the cartelization of enterprise characteristic of Western Europe and Great Britain in the years before World War II.

9. As an expression of social ethos, the antitrust laws had an effect on corporate policy and business behavior. The Courts, moreover, put the great corporations on notice that the legitimacy of their power depended on the propriety with which it was exercised. Monopoly power was allowable so long as it was not joined with overt coercion. And while this did not attack the monopoly power itself, it did tend to set boundaries on the exercise of that power. Economists frowned on the idea of allowing good trusts. But a good trust, after all, is to be preferred to a bad one.

10. Probably, during the period under study, the antitrust laws accelerated the process of merger and combination, since merger and combination which the law did not inhibit was the alternative to cartelization which it forbade. The question as to whether the emergence of markets

dominated by massive corporate organizations is to be preferred to the cartelization of small enterprise is a relevant question, but one that has hardly been asked — at least not in the American context.

11. The Populist subcurrent of ideological liberalism was anti-bigness as well as procompetition. The two were not necessarily commensurable, for the big organization could represent the force of vigorous competition. In some instances where the large threatened the small, competition was squelched by censure or the fear of censure.[52]

---

[52]See Simon N. Whitney, *Antitrust Policies* (New York: Twentieth Century Fund, 1958), p. 84. "This suggests that the big packers may have some justification for their suspicion that their competitors occasionally use complaints to the government as competitive weapons, for instance to 'scare off' the big one from encroaching on their market."

Chapter 6

Affected with the Public Interest: 1860–1935

It was earlier shown how the Supreme Court raised the constitutional requirement of "due process" as a barrier against political meddling in the market economy. There was an exception. For many centuries it had been established in British (then American) practice and sanctioned in the common law that the prices charged in certain industries and trades were properly subject to public regulation. In 1877 in the case of *Munn* v. *Illinois*, this common law tradition was incorporated into constitutional interpretation.[1] For certain industries and trades, demarcated as "affected with the public interest," the constitutional barrier of due process was lifted, and the political authority was allowed by the Court to regulate prices. The others, not so affected with the public interest, remained outside the scope of permissible public regulation. Industries considered as affected with the public interest and hence subject to regulation, were of two sorts. There were first the "natural monopolies," where the economies of large-scale operations were such that, in respect to the relevant market, operations must be concentrated in a single integral business entity if production was to be carried on at lowest average cost; e.g., urban transit lines, metropolitan light and power companies, and telephone companies. And there were those industries where an individual buyer or seller was liable to be caught in a "distress position," and subjected to extreme exploitation, with charges widely deviating

---

[1] *Munn v. Illinois*, 94 U.S. 113 (1877).

from an equilibrium market price. Granaries, stockyards, docks, hotels, and inns are examples.

Thus, the court allowed the public authority to regulate prices within a narrowly (and arbitrarily) bounded sector of the economy. But that was not the end of the matter. As guardian of due process and defender of property, the Court undertook to protect the regulated company from undue deprivation at the hands of the public authority, thus regulating the regulators.[2]

THE AGENCIES OF REGULATION

Under the common law industries traditionally recognized as "common callings" have been liable for failing to provide all comers with adequate service at reasonable rates. Sometimes these industries have been regulated by statutory enactment; for example, state laws fixing rates and service requirements for in-state railways or urban transit lines. Industries have also been regulated by contractual arrangement incorporated into franchises. But ordinarily in the United States, regulation has been through administrative agencies operating under a broad statutory grant of powers. For the public utilities, to be considered here, regulation characteristically has been through public utility or public service commissions, usually bipartisan and quasi-autonomous. A commission to regulate granaries was formed in Illinois in 1871; commissions to regulate railroad rates were established in Illinois, Wisconsin, and Minnesota in 1874. By 1913 twenty-eight states had public utility or public service commissions, and by 1927 all the states except Delaware had them. The federal government created the Interstate Commerce Commission (ICC) in 1887 to regulate interstate railways, and the Federal Power Commission (FPC) in 1920, although not until 1936 was an autonomous FPC first given the right to regulate the transmission of electric power, and in 1938, the right to regulate the interstate movement of natural gas. The Federal Radio Commission was established in 1927, and in 1933 its functions and those of the ICC pertaining to the regulation of interstate telephone communications were taken over by the Federal Communications Commission (FCC).

---

[2]*Stone v. Farmers Loan and Trust Co.*, 116 U.S. 307 (1886); *Reagan v. Farmers Loan and Trust Co.*, 154 U.S. 362 (1894).

PROTECTION FOR MONOPOLY

It was supposed that a public utility must be regulated because it is a monopoly, and hence, immunized from the market competition that otherwise would protect the consumer. It is allowed a position of monopoly so that the public might realize the advantages of large-scale output and low production costs. It becomes then the task of regulation to insure that low average costs will be reflected in correspondingly low prices. The monopoly is regulated, but it is also protected. In return for surrendering the possibility of above-normal profits, the regulated monopoly is assured of market security; i.e., that competitors will not be allowed to invade its market.

Such competition normally is excluded through the public utility commission's issuance or nonissuance of certificates "of convenience or necessity," which permit a company to operate in the regulated market. The courts have, of course, been concerned with the basis for and propriety of issuing such certificates[3] and with the transfer of rights once given.[4] The point to be emphasized is this: the public utility commission preserves and protects the monopolist's position. That, indeed, may be all that it does. As a regulator of monopoly it may be impotent; as a barrier against competition, it can be insurmountable. Hence, it has been in the interest of the private utility companies to capture, control, or influence the public utility commission in order to (1) minimize or eliminate the constraints that the commission might impose on its own profit seeking; and (2) minimize, prevent, or eliminate competitive threats from outside.

THE REGULATION OF FAIR RETURN

It has been the objective of regulation to fix rates so that the regulated companies will receive no more or no less than a "fair return" on their investment. When profits are greater than "fair return," rates are to be reduced. When profits are less than "fair return," the public service commission is obliged to raise rates so that investors get their due.

---

[3]*Slaughter House Cases*, 83 U.S. 36 (1873); *New State Ice Co. v. Liebmann*, 285 U.S. 262 (1932); *Frost v. Corporation Commission of Oklahoma*, 278 U.S. 515 (1929).
[4]*In Re Powell Crosley, Jr.*, 11 F.C.C. 3.

Efficient low-cost operations are assumed. No effort is made to determine whether technology is progressive. The regulatory agency is simply concerned that rates to consumers and profits to ownerships are "fair." What return is "fair"? One percent? Five percent? Ten percent? There is no clear criterion, nor has this been an important issue. Both regulators and regulated have been inclined to accept some conventional percentage associated with the return on "gilt-edge" securities.

Even if there is no problem as to what percentage should be allowed, what is the value to which that percentage return should be applied? There's the rub. The difficult question and the crux of a long-lasting controversy had to do with the valuation of shareholders' ownership. The determination not of the rate of return but of the *rate base* has been at issue. The Supreme Court laid down criteria for determining the rate base in *Smyth v. Ames* in 1898.[5] Justice Harlan, speaking for the majority, postulated that the following must be taken into account in fixing the value of the equity holders' investment:

1. The original costs of construction and the funds expended in permanent improvements.
2. The amount and market value of the company's stocks and bonds.
3. The costs of reproducing the actual construction and permanent equipment and improvements.
4. The company's probable earning capacity.
5. The sums required to meet operating expenses.

All these were "matters for consideration . . . to be given such weight as may be just and right in each case." Consider these five criteria. The fifth, the sums required to meet operating expenses, is obviously irrelevant to the determination of the value of the rate base since the rate base and the "fair return" to investors is something allowed *after* all operating costs have been covered. Criteria 2 and 4 are also irrelevant. The amount and market value of stocks and bonds and probable earning capacity will depend on the "fair return" that the company is allowed to earn. This leaves two criteria: 1, the original cost of the investment; and 3, the current costs of reproducing that investment. For many years the emphasis of the court wavered between these

---

[5]*Smyth v. Ames*, 169 U.S. 466 (1898).

two. How much weight has to be given to reproduction costs as against original costs was never specified. The Court preserved the mystery, saying that, "Each must be given such weight as may be right and just in each case." But how is that determined? Public utility commissions, it is said, were obliged to use a "trance" method for property valuation. From the turn of the century, with prices rising rapidly private companies emphasized the criterion of reproduction costs as the standard for determining the value of the rate base, and the courts were generally sympathetic to their pleas.[6]

Justice Brandeis described the process of determining fair returns, hence, fair rates, as follows:

> To decide whether a proposed rate is confiscatory the tribunal must determine both what sum would be earned under it and whether that sum would be a fair return. The decision involves ordinarily the making of four subsidiary ones:
>
> 1. What gross earnings from operating the utility under the rate in controversy would be (a prediction).
> 2. What the operating expenses and charges, while so operating, would be (a prediction).
> 3. The rate base; that is, what the amount is on which a return should be earned (under *Smyth* v. *Ames*, an opinion, largely).
> 4. What rate of return should be deemed fair (an opinion, largely).[7]

The Prudent Investment Criterion

In a series of brilliant dissents, Justice Brandeis developed a prudent investment criterion for evaluating the rate base as an alternative to the rule of *Smyth* v. *Ames*. He argued that the value of the rate base should exactly equal actual cumulative dollars of investment made by shareholders, where the invested funds had been used with common prudence by management. The value of the rate base would then equal the money received through the sale of common stock and no separate evaluation of tangible property would be required.

---

[6]*McCardle* v. *Indianapolis Water Company*, 272 U.S. 400 (1926); *St. Louis and O'Fallon Railway Co.* v. *U.S.*, 279 U.S. 461 (1929).
[7]The dissenting opinion of Justice Brandeis, *Southwestern Bell Telephone Co.* v. *Public Service Commission of Missouri*, 262 U.S. 289 (1923).

The so-called rule of *Smyth* v. *Ames*, is, in my opinion, legally and economically unsound. The thing devoted by the investor to the public use is not specific property, tangible or intangible, but capital embarked upon by an enterprise. . . . The investor agrees, by embarking capital in a utility, that its charges to the public shall be reasonable. His company is the substitute for the state in the performance of a public service; . . . the Constitution guarantees an opportunity to earn . . . the reasonable cost of conducting business. Cost includes, not only operating expenses, but also capital charges. . . . The experience of the 25 years since [*Smyth* v. *Ames*] has demonstrated that the rule there enunciated is delusive. In the attempt to apply it insuperable obstacles have been encountered. . . . It is essential that the rate base be definite, stable, and readily ascertainable, and that the percentage to be earned on the rate base be measured by the cost, or charge, of the capital employed in the enterprise.

. . . Under the rule of *Smyth* v. *Ames* it is usually sought to prove the present value of a utility by ascertaining what it actually cost to construct and install it, or by estimating what it should have cost to reproduce or replace it. To this end an enumeration is made of the component elements of the utility tangible and intangible; then the actual, or the proper cost of producing or of reproducing each part is sought; and finally it is estimated how much less than the new each part, or the whole, is worth. That is, depreciation is estimated. Obviously each step in the process of estimating the cost of reproduction, or replacement, involves forming an opinion, or exercising judgment, as distinguished from merely ascertaining the facts.

. . . A sound conclusion as to the actual value of a utility is not to be reached by a meticulous study of conflicting estimates of the cost of reproducing new the congeries of old machinery and equipment, called the plant, and the still more fanciful estimates concerning the value of the intangible assets of an established business.

. . . Capital honestly and prudently invested must . . . be taken as the controlling factor in fixing the basis for computing fair and reasonable rates. . . . In essence there is no difference between the capital charge and operating expense . . . for interest on the floating debt; . . . this is readily seen. But it is no less true . . . of the economic obligation to pay dividends on stock, preferred or common. . . . Where the financing has been proper, the cost to the utility of the capital required to construct, equip and operate its plant should measure the rate of return which the Constitution guarantees opportunity to earn. The adoption of the amount prudently invested as the rate base and the amount of capital charge as the measure of the rate of return would give definiteness to these two factors . . . which are now shifting and treacherous . . . and offer a basis for decision which is certain and stable. The rate base would be ascertained as a fact, not determined as a matter of opinion; it would not fluctuate with the market price of labor, or materials, or money. It would not change with hard times or shifting populations. It would not be distorted by the fickle and varying judgments of appraisers, commissions or courts. The wild uncertainties of the present method . . . would be avoided.[8]

John Bauer further developed the Brandeis criterion.[9] Investment in a public utility is substantially guaranteed by the government's protection of the enfranchised monopoly from competitive incursions, and by the legal obligation of the public utility commission to permit such rates as will allow a fair return. In a situation where the return on an investment is *fixed* (at the "fair return" level, whatever that may be) and is protected (by the rate enforcement and market security provided by the public authority), then that investment necessarily takes on the actual character of a debt, a debenture, a fixed obligation. So why not strip the matter of its pretension of being a species of equity ownership in a competitive market where profit and loss is part of the game and treat investment in regulated public utilities for what in fact it is; namely, a publicly-supported obligation to pay an objectively determinable sum annually — hence, a form of debt. True, no promise to pay made by a private company is ever wholly secure. There is always some risk that a company will not be able to earn enough to pay the interest on its debt or the dividends on its preferred shares. Nor would the guaranteed return on public utility investment be wholly secure. Regardless of how accommodating the public utility commission may be, a public utility may not be able to earn a "fair return" on its investment, no matter what the level of rates, when the demand for its output shrinks enough. In other words, there is always some risk; and the degree of the risk, as investors appraise it, will be reflected in the price that the security (guaranteeing the payment of any sum annually) will bring.

---

[8]Brandeis, *op. cit.*
[9]John Bauer, *Transforming Public Utility Regulation* (New York: Harper and Row, 1950).

In the Bauer plan public utilities would raise all their funds by offering shares that would be like preferred stock in that they carried a fixed return, and like common stock in that they conveyed the normal control or voting rights of ownership. The market value of the shares would reflect in each specific instance the current rate of interest and the investor's appraisal of the company's capacity to meet its pledge, given a protected market and the regulation of "fair return" by the public utility commission. Thus, if the company needed capital and offered debentures paying $5 per share per annum, it would then be the market that determined whether that guaranteed annual payment would bring $50 or $80 or $100 as the purchase price of the shares, depending upon the current costs of capital, the preferences of investors for this type of security, and the investor's assessment of risk. Supposing only that shares are sold in good faith and that the money (secured from the sale of shares) is used to finance legitimate expansion, the public utility commission would allow rates at a level sufficient to cover all obligations thus incurred, no more and no less. Fair return would be precisely and continuously determined as a basis for rate regulation. No separate evaluation of the rate base or determination of a percentage return would be needed. A financial commitment would have been incurred in the raising of funds; and "fair return" would be specifically the amount required annually to meet that commitment. Under these circumstances there is no problem at all in determining precisely the fair return on investment; and hence, none in knowing precisely when to allow the company to raise or require it to lower rates.

An Inflation Hedge

Advocates of reproduction costs as the criterion for determining the value of the rate base have argued that during prosperity both profits and prices normally rise. Hence, they say that (1) if investors in public utility companies are to be treated fairly in comparison to equity holders in nonregulated companies, and (2) if the credit of the utility companies is to be maintained, then the income on their shares must be allowed to go up correspondingly as profits rise in unregulated industry. They contend that by using the reproduction cost criterion this would be done automatically, for presumably the value of the rate base would rise as construction costs moved upward. Construction costs reflected in a rate base valued under the reproduction cost criterion would serve as an approximate index of consumer pricing and business profits.

This argument is fallacious. Inasmuch as the utility is offering a type of debenture with a fixed return, its "credit" depends solely on its ability to fulfill the commitment. Nor is there any issue of fairness. A public utility debenture, like a government bond or a corporation preferred stock, is simply one type of security that investors are free to buy or to sell according to their own assessment of its comparative advantages. If they prefer an inflation hedge to a fixed money return, they are free to buy shares in industrial companies. The price they pay for any given type of security will reflect their preferences and their evaluation of the balance of advantages between this type and another. Their preferences will be reflected in the relative prices of shares. Fairness requires only that the terms and conditions of sale are made clear and that obligations incurred in good faith are met. Unfairness is only in falsehood and deceit.

Should it be considered as a more efficient way of raising money, it is entirely within the scope of the prudent investment approach that a company, with the sanction of the public utility commission, build some inflation hedge into the securities it offers, perhaps relating the guaranteed return to a cost of living index. The price of the security thus offered then would find its price level on the market in accord with investor preferences for a debenture of that sort. In this instance also, fair return would be a market-determined contractual obligation as easily and precisely determinable as when securities have no inflation hedge.

Requisites of Effective Regulation

But these considerations of equity are, in fact, peripheral. The real reason that the prudent investment criterion made sense while the criterion of reproduction costs made no sense is of another order. Effective regulation was possible using the prudent investment criterion. Using a reproduction cost criterion, effective regulation was not possible. Effective regulation means simply that the public utility commission does what it was meant to do; namely, to fix rates at such levels that ownership continuously receives a fair and no more than a fair return.

Consider the regulators, usually obscure governmental agencies outside the public eye dealing with questions too technical for the laymen or legislator to comprehend and too dull for the newspapers to bother with. The state commission consists, perhaps, of three or four commissioners and a staff of a few lawyers and accountants, and an engineer or two up from the municipal waterworks. Their work is unnoticed. Their roles are unglamorous and their pay is low. The commissioners are themselves, perhaps, faithful hacks, worn-out politicians, or city employees ready for retirement. The most to be hoped for (and this is to hope for a lot) is the careful work and disinterested service of honest bureaucrats.[10]

Now consider the *task* of continuously evaluating the property of a large utility company on the basis of "reproduction costs." There are dams and turbines, generators and transmission lines, bridges, roads and ditches, cleared land and buildings, and a great range of equipment and tools — manufactured, fabricated, or constructed some five, ten, twenty, fifty, sixty, or more years ago. How much would it cost to reproduce an obsolete and worn-down turbine, out of production for half a century? How much would it cost to reproduce an underground transmission line laid decades earlier through the open country on land that has long since been urbanized? And the task of evaluation would be not one of determining the cost of reproducing a single turbine or a single transmission line, but one of evaluating the whole vast complex of properties, mechanisms, and improvements; and not for one company but for every utility in the state. An unequivocal valuation would be impossible. Because it was impossible for commissions to determine reproduction costs in any clear and unequivocal way, it was impossible for them to

---

[10]"In size the commissions range from one member in Oregon and Rhode Island to seven in Massachusetts, New York and South Carolina; the usual number is three to five. Their members are chosen by the governor in 33 states . . . by the legislature in 2, . . . elected . . . in 15, . . . usually bipartisan . . . without financial interests in the regulated industries. . . . Few commissioners, in fact, have had technical competence. Elections are won through other qualities, and appointments are often made as a reward for political services. The salaries paid commissioners are low. In 1964 . . . the median salary was $12,500. . . . The tenure of commissioners, finally is short, . . . the term in three quarters of the states is 6 years; . . . most . . . serve a single term or even less . . . Appropriations are inadequate; in 1961 the total appropriated to all state commissions was $45 million, but of this, half went to six (New York, Pennsylvania, Virginia, Minnesota, Texas, and California) leaving an average of less than $500,000 for each of the others. A utility corporation may spend far more than this to fight a single case." Clair Wilcox, *Public Policies Toward Business* (3d. ed.; Homewood, Ill.: Richard D. Irwin, Inc., 1966). See also Charles F. Phillips, *Economics of Regulation* (rev. ed.; Homewood, Ill.: Richard D. Irwin, Inc., 1969).

make clear unequivocal determination of the value of the rate base, and therefore impossible for them to determine fair return. Effective regulation, as the law intended it and as the judges envisaged it, was inconceivable so long as the rate base criterion was that of "reproduction costs."

To be sure, if the public utility commission could not meaningfully evaluate properties on the basis of reproduction costs, neither were companies able to make that evaluation, and between estimates of the company and estimates of the commission the judges were utterly unequipped to render a competent decision. There were endless and costly struggles in court, and in these court fights it was the companies rather than the commissions that had the upper hand for they possessed the technical facts about their properties and they had greater technical expertise at their command.[11] The best the commissions could hope to do was to fight a blind delaying action resisting the upward pressure on rates and holding fast to conventional norms.

Under the prudent investment criterion public utility commissions might have regulated effectively. The rate base might indeed have been "definite, stable, and readily ascertainable" with the "percentage to be earned measured by the cost . . . of the capital employed." Hence, there might have been a precise and continuous determination of fair return with rates automatically adjusted upward or downward accordingly as net income was greater or less than the called-for return. Under the prudent investment criterion the precise and continuous determination of fair return becomes a manageable task for a competent accountant. To determine the rate base nothing more is required than to add up the actual receipt of funds from the sale of securities, disallowing subsequent investments by the company only on grounds of gross incompetence and fraud.

Through the 1930's, however, under the rule laid down by the courts, reproduction costs remained a prime criterion and regulation was universally ineffective. It is not possible to say that regulation, such as it was, had any positive value.

The context of regulation has changed since the period surveyed here. The constraints that then paralyzed rate-making no longer do so. It was, nevertheless, those formative generations when virtual impotence and ritualized performance were the

---

[11]*Lindheimer v. Illinois Bell Telephone Co.*, 292 U.S. 151, for example, was begun in 1921 and was decided in 1934.

rule that shaped the character of the public utility commissions—
their self-image, their accepted role, and respect for and expectations of them by governors, legislators, business, and the public.

CORRUPTION OF THE REGULATORS

It was not only the imposition of the reproduction costs criterion that posed a problem for the regulation of public utilities. There was an even more fundamental difficulty. Public utility commissions were small and obscure, ignored by legislators, humbled in the courts, and forgotten by the public. Politically impotent and technically incompetent, they were charged with protecting the public against the greed of powerful, technically-sophisticated, and aggressive private agencies who had huge profits at stake. The commissions had a negative power. They could resist and delay change but they could not impose it. As a barrier to private objectives they had to be reckoned with, pressured, pushed aside, perhaps bought, and controlled. And if they could be bought or controlled, they could be used to sanctify and cover up covert manipulation and to keep the field clear of competition. Nearly all the great public scandals of the period derived from this situation.

In the days of the muckrakers during the early years of the 20th century, when there still were franchises (local monopolies) to be captured, the temptation to control the public utility commissions in order to secure the franchises and then to exploit them was a primary force leading to the corruption of the city and state political machines.

THE TEST OF PERFORMANCE

The direct expense of the utility in maintaining an army of experts and counsel is appalling. The indirect costs are far greater. The attention of officials high and low is, necessarily, diverted from the constructive task of efficient operation and development.[12]

---

[12]Brandeis, *op. cit.* "The fact that the conception of fair value is purely arbitrary appears from the records in numerous rate cases. A conspicuous case . . . was that of the New York Telephone Co. The litigation lasted for nine years, accumulated 62,864 pages of testimony and 4,323 exhibits and cost the company alone about $6,000,000. There existed as of the same date six different valuations all purporting to be based on the principles laid down by the United States Supreme Court." *Report of Joint Committee Investigation of the Tennessee Valley Authority*, S. Doc. No. 56, 76th Cong., 1st Session (1930).

A priori it would seem reasonable to hypothesize that the system of regulation (1) insulated industries from the pressure of competition without providing consumers with sufficient protection to offset the exploitative power of enfranchised monopoly; (2) drew the skills, interests, and energies of management away from the tasks of market entrepreneurship, organization, and technological innovation, and diverted their skills, interests, and energies instead to perpetual legal dueling and political manipulation; and (3) introduced no motivation or pressure in lieu of competition to reduce costs and promote service. Whatever the a priori reasonableness of this hypothesis, it also ought to be related to and tested against experience with regulated companies. Consider then, with reference to observation and experience, the aforementioned propositions, taking into account not only the period 1860–1935 surveyed in this chapter, but recent experience as well.

(1) *Monopoly power, inadequately controlled, has produced exploitative prices and exorbitant profits.*

The proposition might be supported in the instance of the railroads or urban transit lines for the period before World War I. It would not apply to the experience of recent years. Since the mid-twenties at least, with markets shrunken through the competitive incursion of the truck and the automobile, railroads, and urban transit have been on the industry sick list.

The telephone company has, through research, so diversified itself that many of its activities are outside the scope of regulation. Under the jurisdiction both of the FCC and state commissions, regulation of the telephone company according to John Bauer, has been "far less effective than that of the other local utilities."[13] Nevertheless, the company's record does not support the proposition that admittedly ineffective regulation has resulted in exploitative prices or exorbitant profits. Its earnings have been moderately high and very secure. The quality of service has been high and price performance, measured by secular price trends, compares favorably with unregulated industries.

Price performance in electric utilities where demand has been expanding and where firms have a real monopolistic advantage vis-à-vis local and regional markets, is more difficult to interpret.[14] There are very large price variations between different

---

[13]Bauer, *op. cit.*

[14]Twentieth Century Fund, Inc., Power Committee, *Electric Power and Government Policy* (New York: Twentieth Century Fund, 1948).

companies and regions not explicable by differences in fuel, transportation, or technological advantage, which suggests that price may be more a function of demand elasticity than of cost. It also seems generally true that public power is cheaper than private power, despite the anachronistic character of government-owned utilities in the American economy.

In electrical utilities it remained for the Tennessee Valley Authority to force through a major reduction in the prevailing rate structure that proved advantageous not only for consumers, but also (such was the elasticity of demand) highly profitable for the private companies.[15] It took the Rural Electrification Administration, financing rural cooperatives, to establish the fact that massive farm electrification was feasible and was not only advantageous for the farmer and the consumer, but also could be profitable for private operations as well.[16]

During periods of generally declining cost, as between 1920 and 1930, electric utility earnings seemed excessively high.[17] On the other hand, during periods of cost inflation, price rise in electrical utilities has been relatively laggard. Nevertheless, profits have been high. For example, in the period of rapidly rising price between 1940 and 1967, the composite retail price index for electricity rose only slightly, from 98.5 to 102.9. The wholesale price index for electric power declined from 101.9 in 1960 (1958 = 100) to 100.7 in 1967. On the other hand, the retail price index for petroleum and solid fuels rose from 42.6 in 1940 to 111.6 in 1967. There was also a very substantial increase in the regulated price of "gas fuels" during the period.[18]

In sum, we cannot on the whole account for price performance by public utilities either by the rationale of effective regulation nor by that of rapacious monopoly. It would seem that price performance was in large part shaped by the same determinants as characterized "big business" generally. If anything, regulation has added an element of (downward and upward) price inflexibility to the price structure. Perhaps it is fairer to say that regulation has checked the upward movement of price,

---

[15]The TVA was established by Congress in 1933 to develop the Tennessee River system and to aid in the development of other resources of the Tennessee Valley region.

[16]The Rural Electrification Administration was instituted by the federal government in 1935.

[17]Clair Wilcox, *Competition and Monopoly in American Industry*, T.N.E.C. Monograph No. 21 (Washington: U.S. Government Printing Office, 1940).

[18]U.S. Bureau of the Census, *Statistical Abstract of the United States*, 1968 (Washington: U.S. Government Printing Office, 1968).

forcing such price increases to pass, so to speak, a test of public convenience and necessity.

(2) *Managerial energies have been diverted from their proper tasks of entrepreneurial control and technological innovation to buck, beat down, or buy off the agencies of regulation and to manipulate the political authority for their private advantage.*

This proposition can be supported with the evident use of talent and energy in the endless controversies before the courts during the period surveyed here, and in the well-recorded relationships between franchise seekers and the corruption of state and city officials, political bosses, and political machines. It is evidenced by the very extensive lobbying activities of the "power trust."[19] And also presumably as a consequence of the ineffective regulation plus protected monopoly, the distortion of managerial energies is evidenced by the fantastic railroad and electric power holding company empires that came into being during the 1920's — for example, the Associated Gas and Electric Company, where operating companies and holding companies were piled twelve layers deep. In the case of the Insull group, one operating company was controlled by holding one two-hundredth of one percent of the value of its equity. These enormous and complex organizational structures had not a vestigial relationship to the requisites of organizational efficiency and technological progress. Indeed, given such a system of control, efficient management and effective technological organization is not conceivable. These holding-company empires occurred in railroads and in electric light and power companies; that is, only in the protected monopolies under public regulation. The shock of the Great Depression brought them down like castles of cards, and exposed them as vast systems for stock watering and profit siphoning.

The experience led to the Public Utility Holding Company Act of 1935. In this act a Security and Exchange Commission (SEC) was given very extensive power to restructure the holding-company systems of ownership and control. The greatly simplified corporate structures that the SEC produced were designed to control contiguous and technologically related activities and to facilitate the task of regulation. The effect was not to weaken but greatly to strengthen the industry's financial base, as well as

---

[19]See Jack Levin, *Power Ethics* (New York: Alfred A. Knopf, Inc., 1931), and Carl D. Thompson, *Confessions of the Power Trust* (New York: E. P. Dutton and Co., Inc., 1932).

its technical and operating viability. This lesson, showing how management can be distorted through the imposition of a superstructure of control unrelated to functional need and showing how that distorted structure can finally collapse and require a radical and painful industrial reconstruction, has evidently been lost upon policy makers so far as conglomerate mergers today are concerned.

(3) *Competition has been excluded, and even (or particularly) with effective regulation, no pressure or motivation is substituted for competition to force the pace of technological advance and to eliminate inefficient operations.*

In examining utility performance economists have been mostly concerned with the relationship between costs and rates. This has to do only with the sharing of benefits between the consumer on the one side and the producer (including manager, shareholder, and worker) on the other. Far more important as a measure of the industrial contribution to welfare is the secular trend in productivity which measures the benefits for producers, consumers, and the whole society.

By the available measures of secular change in productivity, the performance of the regulated sector has been rather good, and better over the long haul than the performance of the nonregulated sector. For example, between 1899 and 1953, measuring productivity as "average annual rates of change of output per unit of labor input," electric utilities scored the highest with an average annual increase of 4.7 percent. Natural gas companies followed with a 3.0 percent increase; railroads, 2.8 percent; local transit, 2.4 percent; and telephone companies, 2.0 percent. This was compared to a 1.7 percent increase for farming, 2.2 percent for manufacturing, and 2.5 percent for mining.[20]

In so-called "total productivity" measures where secular changes in capital labor ratios are discounted, the results are substantially the same, with electric utilities increasing at 5.5 percent; manufactured gas, 2.0 percent; railroads, 2.6 percent; and local transit, 2.5 percent. This was compared to 1.1 percent for farming, 2.0 percent for manufacturing, and 2.2 percent for mining.[21]

These statistics, however, are highly suspect, particularly when used in interindustry comparisons and even more so when

---

[20]John Kendrick, *Productivity Trends in the United States* (Princeton: Princeton University Press, 1961).
[21]*Ibid.*

what is sought is a measure that will serve to compare the relative contributions of industries to technological advance.

In these measures, for example, a new dynamo produced by the electrical machinery industry that greatly increases the output of electrical power per unit of resource input will be shown as an increase in the productivity *not* of the electrical machinery industry which is responsible for the innovation, but of the electrical power industry. It must be admitted, however, that even in this instance the electrical power industry must also be credited with having contributed to technological advance by accepting the new technology (even though it had not produced it) and transforming its operations accordingly.

Moreover, the standardized outputs that are characteristic of utilities, e.g., ton miles of goods transported or kilowatt hours of power transmitted, totally embody and fully reflect in productivity measures the extent of technological advance in a way that is not even approximately possible in those industries where technological advance results in totally new outputs or in a basic change in the quality of products. Hence, available measures will relatively overstate productivity increases in public utilities or wherever outputs are standardized.

While electric utilities seem not to have generated significant technological advances themselves, nor do they support any significant research and development, they have been receptive to technological opportunities. The telephone industry, through Bell Laboratories, has created perhaps the most successful single research organization in the world, whose contribution to technological advance (for example, in creating the transistor technology) far transcends its measurable impact on the company's own productivity.

The railroads and urban transit have clearly lagged in the progress of technology. In their case the statistics are clearly false and misleading, so much so as to cast fundamental doubt on the analytic procedure that produced them. The productivity measure of the railroads is distorted by an evident deterioration in the quality of outputs, including the diminution and often total elimination of passenger services as an output. The railroads that once spearheaded the industrial revolution became incapable of generating any significant technological innovation within themselves and resisted the infiltration of innovation from the outside. By the 1920's the railroads had become a backward industry.

REGULATION IN RETROSPECT

This chapter has focussed on the problems and policies of public utility regulation, as these developed in the period before the Great Depression of the 1930's. Now, in taking a bird's eye view of that period, the time horizon will occasionally shift to the present.

(1) Regulation, understood as the systematic control of rates to hold revenues at a predetermined level of "fair return," was not effective. It was ineffective because the Court, oversolicitous for the rights of property, meddled grossly in matters beyond its technical competence and laid down rules that were beyond the scope of any rational administration.

(2) Given a reasonable relaxation of the constraints imposed by the Court, regulation could have been effective, with fair return determined precisely and continuously through automatic rate raises when income was below the norm and automatic rate decreases when income was above the norm.

(3) What if effective regulation had been achieved? Then (given a well-situated monopoly) there would have been absolutely no profit incentive to efficient operations or technological advances. This would be true no matter how generous or over-generous the allowance to ownership was, since the very objective of regulation was to keep fair return constant, whether technology advanced or was static and whether costs were high or low. If regulation was effective in controlling rates so as to provide ownership with no more or no less than a fair return, then another dimension of control would be required to impose incentives and penalties in lieu of profit and loss.

(4) But could such a system (not only controlling rates effectively, but also imposing the penalties and incentives needed to spur progress and produce efficiency) have been created, given a weak political bureaucracy and the bad standing of political intervention in the era of liberalism? It is extremely doubtful that it could have been. Yet, unless it embodied effective penalties and incentives for performance as well as the effective control of fair return, it was better that regulation failed completely than that it succeeded fully. For in failing, the pressure and promise of profit and loss as a motivating, driving force was not lost entirely.

(5) The system of regulation not only failed in what was intended; it also at certain times and in certain areas baited the

corruption of the political authority and provided a shelter and cover-up for the manipulations of speculators and for financial finagling on a gigantic scale.

(6) The record of regulated industry, taking secular price or productivity trends as the measure, shows great variations in performance with the regulated sector being sometimes much better, and sometimes far worse, than the nonregulated norm. The presumption is inescapable that regulation itself is only one variable and probably has been of minor importance in determining the level of industrial performance. Corporate behavior and performance in both the regulated and the nonregulated sectors has been determined by more fundamental forces common to both. Thus, the period of time in which a particular industry came into being, and whether or not its initial technology is "science based" (hence, the nature of its managerial competence, the fund of experience on which management draws, and the ties of technology to academic science) are far more significant for an understanding of the response of an industry to emerging technological potentials than whether or not it is regulated.

(7) During the postwar years of inflationary pressure and rising demand, the system of regulation has acted as a brake on the upward movement of price in electrical utilities. Electrical utilities have been required to justify price increases by a public exposition of their profit and cost situation. This has been useful all around. But the value of this exercise has nothing to do with the alleged monopoly position of electric utilities as compared, for example, to steel, cement, or automobiles. That the electric utilities have been required to justify themselves and the others have not is a matter of pure happenstance. Nevertheless, that this control has worked to the public advantage in electric utilities gives us an a priori reason to suppose that it might work to the public advantage in other oligopolistic industries as well. Indeed, the system of price control installed in the United States in 1972 operated for awhile in this fashion.

(8) No doubt each of the great regulated (as well as the unregulated) industries present problems or potentialities for betterment that are of public concern. During the years of bankruptcy and receivership, a commission like the ICC might have installed a technologically competent, progressive management in the railroads, and might have insisted on high quality performance and a steady rise in productivity as precondition to

any rate-making appeal, and might have rationalized organization of railroad transport. A commission like the FPC might
have created national and regional electric grids, and might
have rationalized the interstate flow of natural gas. But to have
done these things would have required a competence, a purpose,
public expectations, and a context of authority very different
from that which characterized the regulatory commissions
during the era of liberalism.

Chapter 7

Interregnum

For time changes the nature of the whole world, and all things must pass on from one condition to another, and nothing like unto itself.

Lucretius

LIBERALISM IN RETROSPECT

The period 1860–1936, roughly between the end of the Civil War and the Great Depression, was a time when a massive new industrialization was producing problems and needs that could not be encompassed by the prevailing ideology of laissez-faire liberalism. Congress and the President responded with piecemeal efforts to extend the scope of public responsibility. The Supreme Court, whose decisions reflected the dominant ideology of laissez-faire liberalism, broke every political effort to ameliorate economic conditions. Thus, as hypothesized, it was the composite choice of Congress and the President that was sensitive to crisis and need while the authoritative decisions of the Supreme Court were firm in expressing the prevailing ideology. When mass needs and discontents pressed for change and the dominant ideology stood for the status quo, the authoritative decision of the Court resisted, and the composite choice of the President and Congress took the lead in structural change and reform.

By its interpretation of the due process clause and of the rights reserved to the states, the Supreme Court aborted the

153

federal effort to control wages, hours, production, price, and employment practices in manufacturing. By reference to federal sovereignty and due process, the Supreme Court aborted the efforts of the states to regulate economic activity. In the mid-1930's the political authority in the United States was virtually without power to control the strategic functions of the market economy, nor was it itself able to undertake those functions.

The antitrust laws were consistent with the liberal ideology though inconsistent with the prevailing interpretations of the Constitution. The Supreme Court allowed their implementation and, through its decisions, gave the antitrust laws their substantive meaning and determined the range of their application. Those laws prevented the cartelization of small-scale industry. They limited the "anti-competitive" activities of trade associations. They enjoined certain "unfair" business practices. The Court nullified all efforts to check merger; neither did it permit the law to strike down the power that inheres in the size of an enterprise and its share of a market.

The Supreme Court allowed price regulation in industries traditionally considered as "affected by the public interest." In its solicitude for private property and its distrust of the political authority, the Court imposed standards which made effective regulation, i.e., regulation that did what it set out to do, impossible.

Throughout the period surveyed, ideology exercised a powerfull and autonomous force aside from and even in opposition to rational pragmatism and the pressures of interested groups. How much did ideology change during these years? Compare J. S. Mill's *Principles of Political Economy*,[1] written within the last half of the 19th century, with John Maurice Clark's *Social Control of Business*,[2] appearing earlier but much read in the late 1930's. Clark was among the most "advanced" liberals of his time. He raised new questions with respect to the nature and limits of competition. He considered "grades of competition," "unfair competition," "potential competition," and "competition between different systems of economic organization" — meaning competition between such entities as independent stores, chain stores, and cooperatives. Such distinctions were foreign to the thought of J. S. Mill. In his chapter "Economic Constitution for

---

[1] John Stewart Mill. *Principles of Political Economy* (London, 1864).
[2] John Maurice Clark. *Social Control of Business* (2d ed.; New York: McGraw-Hill Book Co., 1939).

Chapter 7

the State," Clark postulates grounds for permissible economic control or action by the political authority. He includes national defense, the protection of person and property, the regulation and appropriation of goods which remain in the public domain, the control of inheritance, and the raising of revenues. All of these presumably would have been acceptable to J. S. Mill. But Clark then goes on with "further grounds for public action transcending the traditional criteria." Among these are the need to maintain competition and to act against monopoly. He concedes that public action may be needed to protect those who are not competent to undertake the responsibilities that a system of "individualism" lays upon them; because they are persons of low mentality or lacking the "economic virtues" or because the character of the problem and the nature of the decision are such that they lie beyond individual capabilities, or because the information required for rational choice cannot be made available to each individual. He holds that there may be a need for public intervention to regulate the internal affairs of autonomous organizations, e.g., the trade union or corporation whose members may have to be protected against each other. He justifies public intervention to save the victims of social and physical catastrophe. In this category he includes not only the victims of economic upheaval and technological obsolescence. He would have the public authority protect "human wreckage" and uphold a "social minimum," thus justifying minimum wage laws within the penumbra of supply and demand. He maintains the need for some economic guidance, e.g., in supplying information to consumers so as to promote more rational choice or in providing technological information to small enterprises and farms who are not in a position to support research in order to produce the information for themselves. He suggests a continual effort by the public authority to maintain "equality of opportunity." He holds that the public authority should offset distortions of choice arising from discrepancies between private and social accounting. He recognizes competitive wastes, e.g., advertising which serves simply to cancel out the effect of other advertising. He suggests also the need to remedy the failure to use industrial capacity and human resources during depression.

But with all the range of new tasks and responsibilities for government, and all the weaknesses and failures he recognizes in the uncontrolled market system, Clark shares with Mill a deep and general antagonism against political intervention, a distrust of the political authority, and an emphasis on the unimpeded choice of the individual property holder in market exchange.

> No large state yet seen on earth has given evidence of sufficient collective wisdom to devise a system which would work anything like as effectively as the competitive struggle does. . . . In spite of its limitations the state may command enough wisdom . . . to see where [the competitive system's] worst wastes and perversions lie and to modify it here and there.
>
> . . . The most fundamental limitation on control arises out of the fact that the paramount human value is liberty. Hence liberty should be limited only to increase liberty, that is, the true and effective sum of liberty for the people as a whole.
>
> . . . The presumption should always be against allowing the state to substitute its judgment for that of any individual in matters which primarily concern him. . . . No power of control should ever be presumed to exist unless there is a specific need for the exercise of that power.[3]

Thus, on the threshold of the 1930's the ideology of liberalism remains preeminent, but purity and simplicity of conception are gone; and there is no longer the certainty of the beneficence of market forces that once prevailed. Cracks and fissures cover the walls; imperfections and malfunctions have been observed in the machinery. It is conceded that government, inherently inferior, corruptible, and limited though it admittedly was, might "command enough wisdom," nevertheless, to tidy up the dirty corners, fix the leaks, remove the garbage, and salvage some debris of the market system.

THE WALLS OF JERICHO

> *And it shall come to pass, that when they make a*
> *long blast with the ram's horn and when you hear*
> *the sound of the trumpet, all the people shall*
> *shout with a great shout; and the wall of the*
> *city shall fall flat, and the people shall ascend*
> *up every man straight before him.*
>
> Joshua 6:5

---

[3]Clark, *op. cit.*

Joshua had sounded his trumpet and to the sound of the ram's horn and shouting of the people, the great walls that for so long had stood invulnerable to every assault, came tumbling.

The Reinterpretation of Due Process

Beginning with *Munn* v. *Illinois* in 1877 the Supreme Court, following traditional criteria, set apart a small sector of industry as "affected with the public interest," where public regulation of private activities was permissible.[4] Political interference in, meddling with, or regulation of private activity in the rest of the economy was forbidden by Constitutional fiat. The judges drew their authority to proscribe political meddling in the market system from the 5th and 14th amendments to the Constitution, which provide that no person (taken by the Court to include the corporation) shall be deprived of life, liberty, or property without due process of law.

Thus, in 1923 it invalidated a Kansas law requiring compulsory arbitration of labor disputes in basic industries as a violation of due process.[5] In 1927 it invalidated, on the same grounds, a New York law intended to eliminate ticket scalping by fixing the markup on theater tickets.[6] In *Ribnick* v. *McBride*, as was earlier seen, the Court declared a New Jersey law regulating the fees of employment agencies to be unconstitutional.[7] Thereby it quashed laws that had been enacted throughout the United States to protect groups of laborers who were particularly vulnerable to exploitation by employment agencies in times of rampant unemployment. In 1928 it also threw out a Tennessee act controlling the price of gasoline.[8] In 1932 it invalidated an Oklahoma law having to do with the entry of newcomers into the ice business.[9] All these invalidations were based on the grounds that such public intervention violated due process.

Then, in 1934 in *Nebbia* v. *New York*, the Supreme Court reversed its position entirely.[10] A New York law fixed the price of milk. The milk industry was in a highly chaotic condition. Milk prices had fallen very low, and "destructive competition"

---

[4]*Munn v. Illinois*, 94 U.S. 113 (1877).
[5]*Wolff Packing Company v. Court of Industrial Relations*, 262 U.S. 522 (1923).
[6]*Tyson v. Banton*, 273 U.S. 418 (1927).
[7]*Ribnick v. McBride*, 277 U.S. 350 (1928).
[8]*Williams v. Standard Oil Company*, 278 U.S. 235 (1928).
[9]*New State Ice Company v. Liebman*, 282 U.S. 262 (1932).
[10]*Nebbia v. New York*, 291 U.S. 502 (1934).

was said to threaten long-run supply. The law was challenged by Nebbia, a grocer in Rochester, who had sold milk below the price set by a control board. Nebbia argued, and quite rightly, that the milk industry was not "affected with the public interest" in the sense that the Court had used the term hitherto; i.e., it was neither a "natural monopoly" nor one of those industries where consumers were subject to a peculiar bargaining disadvantage, traditionally subject to price regulation under the common law. The Court, nevertheless, upheld the New York law. The Court ruled, in effect, that there was no trade or industry peculiarly "affected with the public interest," but rather that so long as there was "reasonable relationship to a proper legislative purpose" and so long as the law was "neither arbitrary nor discriminatory," the requirement of due process was satisfied.

Justice Roberts, speaking for a majority of five, said, "It is clear that there is no closed class or category of business affected with a public interest. . . . The phrase, 'affected with the public interest' can, in the nature of things, mean no more than that an industry, for adequate reasons, is subject to control for the public good. . . . So far as the requirement of due process is concerned . . . a state is free to adopt whatever economic policy may reasonably be deemed to promote public welfare."

Subsequently, the Court upheld a state law fixing warehouse charges for tobacco.[11] It upheld federal laws requiring the inspection of tobacco[12] and restricting the quantities of tobacco that could be sold.[13] It allowed the federal government to establish minimum prices for milk[14] and bituminous coal,[15] and allowed states to require the curtailment of the output of petroleum.[16] Thus vanished the wall of "due process" that had barred from public regulation all but a small number of trades and industries traditionally "affected with the public interest."

INTERSTATE COMMERCE

In *Gibbons* v. *Ogden* in 1824,[17] and in subsequent decisions, the Supreme Court ruled that the federal government had

[11]*Townsend* v. *Yeomans*, 301 U.S. 441 (1937).
[12]*Currin* v. *Wallace*, 306 U.S. 1 (1939).
[13]*Mulford* v. *Smith*, 307 U.S. 38 (1939).
[14]*U.S.* v. *Rock Royal Cooperative*, 307 U.S. 533 (1939).
[15]*Sunshine Anthracite Coal Company* v. *Adkins*, 310 U.S. 318 (1940).
[16]*R.R. Commission* v. *Rowan and Nichols Oil Company*, 310 U.S. 573 (1940).
[17]*Gibbons* v. *Ogden*, 9 Wheaton 1 (1824).

exclusive jurisdiction over commerce between states.[18] This interpretation was used to chop down efforts by the states to regulate economic activity, as in *Lemke* v. *Farmers Grain Co.*, where state regulation of grain elevators and stockyards was forbidden.[19] At the same time the commerce clause was so interpreted as to nullify federal control of industry. In 1887 the Court ruled that manufacturing was not directly related to commerce and, hence, was beyond the scope of federal regulation.[20] In 1918 the Court invalidated a federal law prohibiting the interstate shipment of goods produced with child labor on the grounds that such regulation was not sufficiently related to the flow of interstate commerce to fall within the scope of federal power.[21] In 1935, in the Schechter Case, the Court's interpretation of the limitations implicit in the interstate commerce clause was one of its reasons for invalidating the National Recovery Act.[22] And again in 1936 a federal law fixing wages in the coal industry was called unconstitutional on the same grounds.[23]

In 1937 the Supreme Court reversed itself. The National Labor Relations Act required collective bargaining and delegated to a federal agency the power to regulate certain employer-employee relationships. The act was challenged on the grounds that such regulation was, as it had previously been held to be, not directly related to interstate commerce; hence, it was outside the scope of federal regulation. But now, in a series of cases[24] the court ruled that labor strife affects the flow of commerce; hence, whatever might be required to avoid or minimize such strife was sufficiently related to the flow of commerce to bring it under the jurisdiction of the interstate commerce clause, making it subject to federal regulation. The federal authority's power must, the Court insisted, be equal to the problems with which it was confronted; a whole functional relationship must be taken into account. Given a legitimate objective for public action, the appropriate agency of regulation, federal or state, was that one

[18]*Railway* v. *Van Husen*, 95 U.S. 465 (1872); *Pensacola Tel. Co.* v. *Western Union*, 96 U.S. 1 (1877); *Steamer Daniel Bell* v. *U.S.*, 10 Wallace 557 (1871); *The Shreveport Rate Cases*, 234 U.S. 342 (1914).

[19]*Lemke* v. *Farmers Grain Co.*, 258 U.S. 50 (1922).

[20]*Kidd* v. *Pearson*, 128 U.S. 1 (1889).

[21]*Hammer* v. *Dagenhart*, 247 U.S. 251 (1918).

[22]*Schechter Poultry Co.* v. *U.S.*, 295 U.S. 495 (1935).

[23]*Carter* v. *Carter Coal Company*, 298 U.S. 238 (1936).

[24]*NLRB* v. *Jones & Laughlin Steel Corp.*, 301 U.S. 1 (1937); *NLRB* v. *Freuhauf Trailer Company*, 301 U.S. 49 (1937); *NLRB* v. *Friedman-Harry Marx Clothing Company*, 301 U.S. 58 (1937).

best able to achieve the objective. "When industries organize themselves on a national scale, making their relation to interstate commerce the dominant factor in their activities," then a national power commensurate with the phenomenon to be controlled must be accepted as the appropriate agency of control.

The interstate commerce clause was subsequently held to bring within the scope of federal jurisdiction a cannery that shipped only a third of its output to other states[25] and a power company that sold only a fraction of its output across state lines.[26] In the case of *U.S. v. Darby Lumber Company*[27] in 1941, the Supreme Court approved the Fair Labor Standards Act which forbids interstate shipment of goods made by persons paid less than legally determined wages or required to work more than the legally determined number of hours, reversing its position from that in *Hammer v. Dagenhart* in 1918. In 1942 the Supreme Court upheld the use of penalties by the federal government to control the output on a farm, even where that output was for use by the farmer himself. In this instance it was considered that on-farm consumption of farm produce significantly affected the national market for the output in question, and hence was properly subject to federal control.[28] Thus, by the mid-1940's the interstate commerce clause of the Constitution had ceased to impose any significant limitation on the exercise of the public authority. Under this clause every economic activity of national significance fell within the scope of federal regulation.

THE GENERAL WELFARE

The Court had interpreted the general welfare clause to mean that taxation could not be used as an instrument of political control. Taxation must be only a means of raising the revenues required in order to spend for appropriate national objectives. Thus, in 1922 the Supreme Court struck down the effort of the federal government to control the use of child labor through its tax powers.[29] And in 1933 the Supreme Court outlawed the use of taxation to control the level of agricultural output.[30]

---

[25]*Santa Cruz Packing Company v. NLRB*, 303 U.S. 453 (1938).
[26]*Consolidated Edison Company v. NLRB*, 305 U.S. 197 (1938).
[27]*U.S. v. Darby Lumber Company*, 312 U.S. 100 (1941).
[28]Related to the Agricultural Adjustment Act of 1938, upheld in *Wickard v. Filburn*, 317 U.S. 111 (1942).
[29]*Bailey v. Drexel Furniture Company*, 259 U.S. 20 (1922).
[30]*U.S. v. Butler*, U.S. 1 (1932).

In 1937 the Court reversed itself. In that year the Court ruled on two social insurance programs. To provide for a national system of unemployment compensation, the federal government taxed the states but returned the revenues collected to the state governments, provided that the unemployment compensation laws of the state met the requirements laid down by the federal authority. The Court held that this was not an "unconstitutional attempt to coerce the states." The objective sought was considered to be legitimate and the method used was deemed not coercion but "temptation." In respect to Article I Section 8 of the Constitution — which holds that "If the tax is a direct one it shall be apportioned according to the census or enumeration. If it is a duty, import or excise, it should be uniform throughout the United States." — the Court ruled that an "excise" need not be on a product. It could also be on an activity or on a set of relationships. Nor need it be the same for all such sets of relationships. It was required simply that it be uniform in classification or in conditions of imposition throughout the country; i.e., that the "rule of liability shall be the same."[31] The government had also levied taxes on wages and payrolls in order to provide a post-retirement income to wage earners. The Court held that special provision for the aged was not a violation of the constitutional injunction that spending should be for the "general welfare." The general welfare need not signify that which is universally beneficial, but simply that which is collectively valued. Thus, the federal government could tax though it was unequivocally recognized that the purpose of such taxation was *not* to collect revenue but to control economic activity. And the government could collect revenues where it was unequivocally intended that those revenues be used to support a particular group in the population. It sufficed that the tax power was rationally exercised in dealing with problems of national concern. No bar remained on the use of taxation as an instrument of deliberate control.

RESERVED TO THE STATES

The Court had held that the Constitution had either delegated power to the federal government or else reserved it for the states; neither government dared act in the domain reserved to the other. But now the Court had taken a different view. The

---

[31]*Steward Machine Company v. Davis*, 301 U.S. 548 (1937).

exercise of power was justified by the legitimacy of the objective. The appropriateness of the agency of control, federal or state, was to be judged in relationship to the nature of the phenomenon to be controlled and the functional requisites of control. The Court rejected the concept of two closed boxes between which the power of government had been once and forever divided. Rather the distribution of power must be judged by its functional appropriateness. In the National Labor Relations Board cases the Court recognized that labor strife had national implications and that the protection of the worker's right to bargain was a problem that was national in scope and therefore must, appropriately, be dealt with by the federal authority. In the case of *Helvering* v. *Davis*, which upheld the Social Security Act, Justice Cardozo based his decision on the significance and scope of the problem and on the functional need for a national authority to deal with it.[32] To control unemployment required the "resources of the nation," and the resources of the nation were needed to "save men and women from the rigors of the poorhouse as well as from the haunting fears that such a lot awaits them when the journey's end is near." Piecemeal, local arrangements could always be disrupted by the migration of the needy and the movement of employers. "The purge of nationwide calamity," reflected Cardozo, "that began in 1929 has taught us many lessons. Not the least is the solidarity of interests that once may have seemed divided."

Thus, the old notion of an inviolable division between state and federal power disappeared. In dealing with unemployment insurance,[33] through "temptation" or "coercion," the federal and the state power in fact merged, and it was not possible to say where one began and the other ended. Nor did this concern the Court. It sufficed that the problem was real and significant and that the arrangements for dealing with it were functionally appropriate. The hard and fast line between federal and state responsibility had vanished; and constitutional interpretation on this score had ceased to be a significant impediment to the exercise of political authority, nationally or locally, in the control of economic activity.

The whole turning is exemplified in *Wickard* v. *Filburn* in 1942,[34] where the federal right to regulate a farmer in the use of

---

[32]*Helvering* v. *Davis*, 301 U.S. 619 (1937).
[33]*Steward Machine Company v. Davis*, 301 U.S. 548 (1937).
[34]*Wickard* v. *Filburn*, 317 U.S. 111 (1942).

his own land to raise crops for his own consumption was allowed by the Court on the ground that such action by the individual farmer would affect the national market and the national level of prices which the government was seeking legitimately to control.

Before and After

The decade of 1935–1945 constitutes a great divide in the constitutional interpretations by the Supreme Court. Before, a wall had been raised between the political authority and the economic function, with the political authority allowed only rare and exceptional incursions into market-directed territory. After, there was no longer any significant constitutional restraint on the substantive exercise of economic control by the political authority.

Before, government was on the periphery of the economy. After, government was deeply involved in and committed to the achievement of a range of complex economic objectives. Its authority was pervasive. Its potentials were unbounded. Its competencies were formidable.

Before, the property power was sacrosanct, a natural right not to be abridged except in extraordinary circumstances. After, the rights of property had become equivocal both in concept and in fact.

Before, the political authority was constrained by an almost universally accepted economic ideology that was expressed in and enforced through constitutional interpretation. The Supreme Court, articulating that ideology, forbade every tentative political effort to respond to economic need, forbade every experimental move to find the political means of ameliorating economic crisis and misery. All that had changed. The changes were not merely in form, but in underlying conceptions. This radical reinterpretation of the Constitution reflected a new set of values and a different way of conceiving reality. A new ideology was emerging.

JOSHUA'S TRUMPET

The administration of Franklin D. Roosevelt marks the time when ideological liberalism was subverted by events and driven from its throne. During those years the barriers to political intervention were breached and broken. The walls of Jericho came down. What caused the ancient walls to crumble?

Depression

There was the experience of the Great Depression. It was like a dreadful disease on the body of capitalist societies. For more than a decade it lay like a slow devourer on the British economy, the sad England of the dole and the hunger marchers. Then it erupted in a more virulent form, as though it had reached the vital organs and must bring capitalist societies to a quick and agonizing death. This second terrible stage began in the United States, precipitated by the application of traditional restrictive monetary policies as a "cure" to "overheating." It spread in a catastrophic increase of unemployment and a breakdown of production throughout the whole Western world. It was Marx's dread prophecy near fulfillment. Germany, at the hub of Europe, turned fascist, imposed centralized controls upon its economy, and boasted of its prosperity. Everywhere were undercurrents of revolution, communist or fascist. In Spain the struggle between the two seemed to presage Armageddon.

The Great Depression taught the lesson that given an economy based on the complex interdependencies of modern technology, the market system, left alone, is vulnerable to complete collapse. It has not the regenerative capacities, working through the self-interested choices of a universe of property owners, to prevent or to overcome such a breakdown. The traditional values of liberalism, postulating the sanctity of property rights and liberty of contract, pale in significance beside the political dangers, the human miseries, and the economic costs of a major depression. Capitalist societies, with individualized choice working through the market system, must find the means to overcome and to prevent major depressions or they must die.

Our world learned another lesson. The market system is only one of the ways to organize complex economic activities. Experience has shown that a productive, technically-progressive economy could also be organized under centralized political direction. Socialist or fascist planning was not the fantastic dream of crackpots, but a practical alternative. This was proven not only by the achievements of the Communists and the Fascists, but also by the war-time experience of Western democracies. It was also quite clear that unless the private enterprise economy could avoid the depredations of major depressions, many Americans would prefer an economic system of centralized political direction. If the values of individualism were to be preserved and the virtues of the market to be salvaged, it must and could only be through the deliberate effort of government.

Maintain the functional integrity and the operational effectiveness of the market-based economy, ameliorate the miseries of those cast into the pit of unemployment, prevent depression — this the government must do and must be allowed to do.

What had to be done to maintain full employment without inflation in the market system was not clear then and is not clear now. But few could doubt that the problem had to be dealt with, and could only be dealt with by the political authority. Nor was this a problem for local governments. The phenomenon of depression was a national, even a world, phenomenon. A power of control commensurate with the phenomenon to be controlled was required. Local autonomy and state sovereignty must be subordinated, and the national government must be permitted to act with force and responsibility and with wide discretion in its choice of means and measures.

The old ideology of liberalism was shattered by the experience of the Great Depression. To accept it meant to remain impotent in the face of catastrophe — impotent not only to save the values of the traditional system, but also to satisfy men's basic material needs.

War

Ideology was reshaped not only by the terrible experience of depression, but also by the impact of a global war. War taught the lesson that military power now depends upon the command of an advanced technology specific to the military function, and generally unrelated to and not created through a consumer-oriented market system. This military technology must be produced through scientific research, which in turn requires an enormous R&D establishment under the aegis of the political authority.

The Imperative of Economic Growth

To avoid depression was the first command. But in the postwar decades, pressed by rising expectations for material betterment and by the rivalry of an upsurgent socialist Russia, there emerged a new political imperative: to guarantee a sufficient rate of economic growth. It became the task of the political authority to underwrite and enforce the pace of technological advance and the continual rise of productivity in the private sector.

The Organizational Revolution

Postwar America is, and increasingly conceives itself as being, a society dominated by the large organization. In place of a universe of free-acting, self-seeking individuals, each on his own and out for himself, has come a mass amalgamation of energies and ambitions within the operation of the great corporation and political agency. This is the age of the organizational revolution and the organizational man.

A first response of professional economists, for so long apologists of liberalism and philosophers of laissez-faire, was to look on bigness as synonymous with monopoly; or at least to suppose that bigness is worth worrying about only if and when it signifies monopoly. In fact, the great modern corporation is not synonymous with monopoly; its share of the vast markets in which it competes may be smaller than the share of man-sized enterprises of the smaller, segmented markets of another age. The prime importance of bigness is the size itself where man-to-man relationships are of another order; where the old virtues and vices of rugged individualism become irrelevant; where the nature and the structure of power changes; where property loses its former significance; where the process of choice must be differently understood; where confrontation is between corporation and corporation, corporation and trade union, and private and public organizations; and where the individual needs to be protected against them all, both as outsider and as participant in the great organizations that constitute the matrix of modern life.

Chapter 8
At the Turning

The ideology of laissez-faire liberalism has not vanished from our intellectual scene. Social philosophies, alas, never entirely disappear but this one has ceased to be central to the American outlook. It no longer has the status of a body of self-evident truths, common coin in the world of thought. Rather, it has become what Marxist Communism was in the 1920's and 1930's in the United States—namely, the battle whoop of a tribe of Neanderthals and, at once, the utopianism of an esoteric cult. But if the old philosophy has moved from center stage, it is not clear what has come to take its place or, rather, it is not yet clear what will come to take its place. For this is a time of experimental searching, groping, and uncertainty.

The old ideology is shattered and the new ideology, which must shape tomorrow's law and mode of political action, is still unformed. In this light, as a taking-off point for our own thought, it is of interest to consider the attempt of Joseph Schumpeter to foresee the future configuration of society.

SCHUMPETER'S LIBERALISM

Joseph Schumpeter was perhaps the greatest economist and social philosopher of his time. His fame is chiefly based on a work, *The Theory of Capitalist Development*, published in English in the 1930's and written earlier in Austria.[1] In this work

---

[1]Joseph Schumpeter, *The Theory of Capitalist Development* (Cambridge, Mass.: Harvard University Press, 1934).

Schumpeter looks at the market system in a way and from an angle that departs radically from neoclassical economics. Neoclassical economists considered the economic system as the means of allocating resources in relationship to consumer wants. Schumpeter saw the matter differently. His measure of its worth was not how well the competitive market brought consumer demand and resource utilization into an appropriate balance. Rather, he believed that the primary function of the economic system was continuously to upgrade technology. The criterion of classical and neoclassical economics was efficiency—to make the most of the available resources with the given technology. For Schumpeter the appropriate measure of welfare was productivity, or rather the capacity continuously to raise the level of productivity through technological advance. Indeed, the capacity to change technology was the key to his system.

As he saw things, the process of technological change required not only the inauguration of the new but also the elimination of the old. The waves of change that created also annihilated; hence, that which advanced the economy inevitably disturbed and disrupted it. Expectations, habits, and established relationships worked into the fabric of living must be crudely torn apart. Before the "gales of creative destruction," acquired skills lost their value, prosperous enterprises were gutted, and capital structures were rendered obsolete. But on the other hand, new opportunities were born and the greater technological potential made possible higher standards of life for society as a whole.

Though he asked a different question and saw the economic function from a different angle than did the classical and neoclassical economist, in his ideological commitment Schumpeter was a laissez-faire liberal. He was not examining the process of economic development with the notion of changing it, controlling it, or finding some exogenous means for accelerating it. What he saw seemed to him good. He counted our blessings. For him the overriding reason why capitalism should be left alone, why meddling by the political authority should be avoided, was to allow this process of creative destruction and destructive creation to continue unhampered within the free market system. As a social scientist, Schumpeter analyzed this process of economic development in order to explain (and to rationalize) business fluctuations in the long and short cycles of prosperity and depression.

Schumpeter liked capitalism and he wanted to preserve it. But what did he mean by capitalism? He meant a system where economic power was based on the ownership of property; and where property was held as private privilege and a personal prerogative and was exercised through the market mechanism. In his conception of capitalism, power was privately exercised, personally possessed, and rooted in ownership. It was neither a function of political authority nor of organizational status. That, for Schumpeter, was the essence and the value of capitalism —the unimpeded economic power of the capitalist (of the many capitalists) derived from accumulated property and the prerogative of ownership. The firm, the entity of business choice and action, was the property of the individual in possession — of the proprietor. It was the instrument of the proprietor's ambition and his will. What the firm did or could do depended entirely on what the proprietor wanted and on the resources he could mobilize in support of his objectives. How then, with this vision of things, did Schumpeter explain the process of economic development?

As Schumpeter saw it, the vast bulk of economic activity was organized by individual proprietors, investors, coupon clippers, buyers and sellers, speculators, and entrepreneurs manipulating input and output combinations and trying to run their affairs efficiently. Schumpeter had little regard for this mass of capitalists and participants in the market system, busy in their optimizing preoccupations in the manner described by classical and neo-classical economics. All their busy activities changed nothing in the technological understructure. They did not contribute to the process of economic development.

Aside from the mass of ordinary optimizing activities in the market system, Schumpeter also assumed, as given, a world of intellectual ferment and invention. He does not explain the source of invention; he does not speculate on the preconditions of invention, nor does he describe the process of inventing. Just as he assumes a flux of economic activity, he also assumes a stream of inventions. Both are parameters. Inventions are made because some men happen to be inventive. Inventions, new ideas, odd notions — mostly useless, mostly facetious, mostly untimely — are always available as possibilities to be explored, as notions that might be made concrete, as potentialities that might be realized.

The Innovator

There then steps out from the mass of manipulating, money-grubbing capitalists, the rare man — the innovator. The innovator is the giant on whose shoulders justification for the whole system rests: the Schumpeterian hero. He has the unique capacities to see the practical potentialities of inventions generated through the obsessional curiosity and fevered imaginations of dreamers and tinkerers. It is the innovator who has the guts to move into the unknown and the inherently unpredictable, risking his possessions on an intuitive belief in an idea and its potentials. He has the strength to ram through a radical change in technological organization in the face of resistance from workers, trade unions, competitors, business associates, investors, bankers, and consumers. He has the organizational and creative capacity to adapt and to put complex new processes into motion.

What is the bait that induces the innovator to swim against the tide, and what induces investors to back the risky venture? According to Schumpeter, the bait that induces this extraordinary effort and the undertaking of the risks inherent in innovation is the possibility of great gains that might accrue if the innovation is successful. And such gains from innovation can only exist if first-comers can maintain, for a significantly long period of time, a substantial monopoly power; i.e., if they possess the power to maintain prices substantially above costs in the innovative venture. Eventually, competitors will enter the field, output will be expanded, and price will be forced down to the level of normal costs. Then the yield to the innovators and the profits that provide the incentive to innovate will have vanished.

It is Schumpeter's view that without some degree of monopoly or some power to resist the incursion of imitators, there can be no gain from innovation and hence no innovators, innovation, or economic progress. For that reason Schumpeter opposed the price theorists with their ideology of pure competition in which there was no room for profit through innovation. For that reason also he was suspicious of an antitrust policy that took pure competition as its norm, though he was very much aware that monopoly can also serve to resist innovation and suffocate progressive change. Naturally, Schumpeter would have a different norm or ideal for the organization of industry than that of the neoclassical economists and antitrusters who thought in terms of efficiency and low current prices for consumers. Above all, Schumpeter was concerned with the capacity to generate technological advance.

Again, it should be emphasized that the Schumpeterian innovator was a man of property. He exercised independent power through the prerogatives of ownership, and not because he belonged to an organization or because he possessed political authority. Capitalism, and economic progress under capitalism, in Schumpeter's way of seeing things, required the unimpeded personalized exercise of the property power. It required a form of power that could be exercised by a maverick expressing a unique, personal vision. If in many instances the property power was misused and abused, that was the price that had to be paid to allow this rare man, the innovator, to exercise his vision in providing the forward thrust of technological change in the dynamism of economic development.

The justification of capitalism in Schumpeter's eyes was its capacity to generate technological innovation and hence economic progress. The Roman Catholic church is said to exist for the sake of its saints. Just so, in Schumpeter's view, capitalism existed for the sake of its innovators. For progress there must be innovation. Capitalism was the means for generating innovation. The innovators, a few among the mass of drones, busy beavers, speculators, and manipulators, made the system worthwhile.

Such was Schumpeter's view of the capitalist system as he formulated it in Austria during the first quarter of the 20th century.

SCHUMPETER'S PROPHECY

And then in *Capitalism, Socialism and Democracy*, written in the midst of the Great Depression and published in 1942 in the midst of World War II, Schumpeter looked again at the system and sadly prophesized the end of capitalism.[2]
Why?

---

[2]Joseph Schumpeter, *Capitalism, Socialism and Democracy* (New York: Harper and Row, Publishers, Inc., 1942).

Not at all for the usual reasons. Schumpeter did not see any proletarian mass rising out of their miseries. On the contrary he considered that the system had greatly improved the lot of the common man and would continue to do so. And he shrugged off the then popular "stagnation thesis" that the drying up of investment opportunity had brought capitalism to the end of its rope. Schumpeter saw no end of investment opportunity. Rather, he reasoned that in the process of its evolution, capitalism — particularly American capitalism — had produced very large and successful corporate organizations. These corporate entities dominated the industrial economy. In consequence the fundamental nature of property had changed. Ownership was no longer the basis of control. Real power no longer resided in property. The functional significance of property had changed. In consequence, the emotional attachment and personal meaning of property as the embodiment of achievement and as the projection of human will and aspiration had vanished. Property claims remained but much of their meaning had slipped away. An individual would have fought and died to hold control of his own bit of land or his own shop, but what does it mean to the shareholder to control his own corporation? Masses or classes would no longer struggle, or be willing to sacrifice their lives as once they did, for the principle of property.

The great corporations which had come into being through an unprecedented accumulation of property claims were indeed doing very well — even though power was no longer vested in property, even though power was exercised instead by corporate officials and bureaucrats, and even though property could no longer have the old functional justification of dispersing and personalizing power and using the self-interest in aggrandizement as a motivation to innovate. The great corporation was not the vehicle of a property owner; i.e., of a proprietor, proprietors, or a capitalistic entrepreneur. It was not the reflex of the will and ambition of an individual, nor of an integral group so bound by a common point of view and a unifying objective that it might be counted as an individual. Rather, the great corporation was an autonomous, self-perpetuating organization embodying a diversity of interests, and controlled by a species of bureaucrats and officials whose power was based on status and was exercised as authority.

The key, for Schumpeter, was not that these corporations succeeded in running things efficiently but rather that they had been able to generate technological advance from within themselves and to organize and to regularize innovation.

Demise of the Hero

Through research and development, through competition in the quality and novelty of products, and through the use of advertising to overcome consumer resistance, the great corporations had bureaucratically organized technological advance. They had "routinized" innovation and economic progress. They had learned to generate technological advance without the capitalist innovator. The Schumpeterian hero had become superfluous, or at least no longer necessary in the new scheme of things.

The capitalist has not and never has had an esthetically appealing or glorious image. In the eye of the populace he was no knight in shining armor, no dashing aristocrat, no soldier on horseback; rather, he was the fat man with the black vest sitting on the bag of gold. Capitalism, that is to say a system based on the unimpeded exercise of the property power, had survived not because of traditional loyalties or sentimental attachments but because of its incomparable, unapproachable superiority of performance; and that performance had depended on the free-wheeling innovator. But now entities spawned of capitalism proved that the capitalist innovator was no longer necessary. Invention and innovation were organized as a process wherein property rights had lost their relationship to decision-making. The individual capitalist was supernumerary. Power based on property had become obsolete.

This did not mean that energetic and creative individuals (innovators, in that sense) were no longer needed. Of course they were and always would be. Robert McNamara is an energetic and creative man — an innovator — whether as president of the Ford Motor Company or as Secretary of Defense in the United States government. In both cases he was an official and his power was based on status; he was not a capitalist whose power was based on ownership.

And if capitalism is no longer necessary? If the economy can perform (can generate technological advance and the rise in productivity) just as well or even better without the property-based dispersion of personal power, then what? Then there would be no emotional attachment, lingering romanticism, or coherent force that could for long preserve the capitalist system as once feudalism had been preserved, long after its functional justification was gone. In fact, and almost unnoticed, individualized choice based on unimpeded property power had in large part already vanished in the world of massive autonomous organization. In awhile the old universe of competitive striving by property owners in a market system would be gone forever.

What did Schumpeter imagine would happen to the autonomous corporation that replaced the mass of individually owned proprietorships? Certainly he did not suppose its takeover through a proletarian uprising. He postulated simply that corporate and trade union officialdom would inevitably be made more responsible to society at large for their decisions and policies, and would become *answerable* to those who were affected by their choice and action — to a public authority that spoke for the general interest. Both the trade union that accepts the wage directive and the corporation that accepts the price directive of a national wage-price board signal the evolutionary transformation of the economy towards socialism, as prophesized by Schumpeter.

AN IDEOLOGICAL FORETASTE

What is the role of the Supreme Court in the process of ideological transformation? It may be clear enough that they express an established ideology, but what part have they to play in creating a new one?

Given the form of their choice and the nature of their task, the judges of the Supreme Court have a particular and continuing need for an integrated and coherent set of values and concepts. They require a clear idea of what is and what ought to be; that is, an "ideology" on which to base judgment and to justify judgments before their peers. Yet in the postwar era there was no coherent, articulated, and accepted ideology, not for them or for anyone else. This is at the heart of the modern malaise.

Most of us manage without any clear idea of how things are or of how they should be. From day to day we do our work and make our way. We act pragmatically. We accept the current state of confusion; we pass over the contradiction; we follow orders, act on directive, do what we're told, do what we've been doing, hope to please, try to score, and get what we're after. Not so with the justices. They are at the very summit of authoritative choice. They are confronted with critical questions that they must answer without external directive. They cannot dodge the questions, they must answer them clearly. And what they answer today, they will be answerable for tomorrow. To render judgment, the judge needs an ideology; if none prevails, he must try to find or produce one.

The Court, by reason of its own needs and its function, is pushed to the fore in formulating a new ideology that is acceptable and appropriate for our time. This is a task in which many participate and which concerns us all. On the other hand, Congress, the administrative departments, and the public commissions operate pragmatically in response to counterbalancing pressures of their supporters and critics, of the ins and the outs, and to sporadic voter demands that reflect the equivocation, confusions, and contradictory expectations of the electorate. These agencies of composite choice are not similarly driven to construct an ideological framework as a basis for decision, nor does the acceptance of a set of ideas and values constitute a policy imperative for them as it does for the Court.

In this time of ideological transition, it is the Court that must grope for and express the incipient ideology. What ideological elements explain the postwar decisions of the Supreme Court?

Under ideological liberalism the political authority was considered inherently incompetent, virtually unnecessary, and generally dangerous in its proclivity for meddling in the self-balancing, autonomous universe of individualized choice. But under the new dispensation, with the belief in a self-balancing and ultimately beneficent universe of individualized choice gone, correspondingly, that which is expected of the political authority has changed. The political authority is seen as indispensible; it is the agency responsible for the general condition of society. It alone has the potential capability for dealing with problems that are national or supranational in scope.

Not all the judges of the Supreme Court give the same weight or accept in the same degree those elements of ideology that are to be specified here. But none would now deny the need for strong, creative, experimental government and all look with respect upon its sovereign powers. These new attitudes toward, and expectations concerning, the political authority have produced fundamental changes in the rule of the Supreme Court. Whereas before the Court interpreted the Constitution as an absolute barrier against political meddling with individu   d choice and the prerogatives of property, now the Court conceives its task as eliminating constitutional barriers to any rational effort by the political authority to achieve an acknowledged public purpose. Whereas before the Court had imposed its own standards, "down to the dotting of the *i* and the crossing of the *t*" upon the administrative agencies of government, now it treats those agencies as masters in their own houses, refusing to substitute its judgment on substantive issues for theirs. It has transferred to them that discretionary authority that for over a century was the prerogative of the Court. This is fundamental. Such administrative agencies of government as the Department of Justice, the Federal Trade Commission, or the regulatory commissions become answerable not to the Court, but to Congress and the electorate for guidelines of action.

It was, of course, one thing for the Court to *allow* an administrative agency or executive department to become the master of its own house, responsible for its own choice and answerable for results to the President and to Congress. It is quite another for a commission or department, after serving so long as an advocate or prosecutor before the almighty Court, to become the master of its own house and to assume the responsibilities, autonomies, and independence of choice that the Court at long last permits.

In any case the Court has cleared the decks for political action. It has thrust independence and autonomy upon the agencies of economic regulation and control. If the Court now imposes itself, it is likely to do so not as a constraining force but as an intercedent for political initiative beyond the intent of regulatory agencies and executive departments.

The judges of the Supreme Court have no full-fledged ideology. They cannot answer, any more than can the rest of us, such essential questions as: What are the conditions for personal fulfillment and collective or group achievement? How does and how should organization interact with the individual? Inasmuch as organization does or can shape a person, and inasmuch as it is the task of the political authority to control these character-shaping force, by what model should the individual be shaped? How should the individual participate in shaping the organization? And how in this process of organizational restructuring should the interest of one be reconciled with or balanced against that of another? And how should the rationale proper to the ulterior achievements of organization be reconciled with and balanced against the values inherent in the nature of its internal relationships?

But even if the justices are without any full-fledged ideology, we may deduce from their decisions over the past quarter century the incipient conceptions in terms of which they interpret the Constitution and read the law. Before, the individual was understood as the self-contained, irreducible, atomic particle of a social universe, the best (if not the only possible) judge of his own well-being. In the new dispensation the individual is seen as embedded within an immense complexity of social organizations that shape his values and his tastes, determine his capabilities and proclivities, and define the range of his opportunities and the scope of his meaningful choice. In a word, it is the social complex into which he is born or otherwise placed that makes him or breaks him. It becomes then the responsibility of the sovereign power to use the instruments of government to protect the individual from whatever is arbitrary and oppressive in social organization, and to reshape the organizational complex to produce the conditions most conducive to personal fulfillment and individual or group achievement. Government too is joined into that organizational complex wherein the individual is embedded and upon which he depends. Government must, therefore, regulate and impose constraints that will protect the individual from that which is arbitrary and oppressive, and governments qua organizations must themselves be shaped or controlled to protect those who participate within, as well as those who are affected without.

Implicit in the opinions of the Court is a manner of seeing man and society, with the individual as both creature and creation of organization, needing organization and yet needing to be protected from organization. Thus, the Court decided that segregation of white and black in the organization of education ipso facto shapes the attitudes of segregators and segregated, perpetuates the psychology of black inferiority, and fails to offer the black child the equality (and the fullness) of opportunity that the Constitution demands. This decision, so evident and sensible (and indeed, inevitable given their, and our, new and still incipient conception of man and society), produced a rule of law that leaped far ahead of anything that Congress, the President, or any of the other agencies of composite choice had yet ventured.

The new rule of the Supreme Court has been accepted because the experience of the age has produced the same psychic ferment and the same elements of ideology in the thinking community at large as among the justices of the Supreme Court. So, in the civil rights cases the Court repeatedly intercedes to protect the individual against the organization, even when that protection interferes with or limits the effectiveness of the organization (the State Department, the FBI, the army, the police) in the pursuit of acknowledged public goals.

To protect the individual within and in relation to the organization is an objective of a different order than that of protecting individualized choice and the property power from meddling by political authority, which once was the obsessive purpose of the Supreme Court.

That which differentiates the conservatives and the radicals of the Court today is primarily the question of how much to constrain the legitimate objectives of public and private organization in order to protect the individual. The conservatives are on the side of organizational effectiveness and of strength for political authority. The radicals, or "liberals," give greater weight to the claims of the individual within and outside the organization.

Chapter 9

Antitrust
Across the Divide

> ... the Sherman Act is a humbug based on economic
> ignorance and incompetence.
>
> Justice Oliver Wendell Holmes

This chapter will deal with the current status and significance of the antitrust laws and the appropriate means of their enforcement. Subsequent chapters will be concerned with the historical particulars.

THE DISCRETIONARY AUTHORITY

During the half century before the Depression and World War II, the Supreme Court of the United States accepted the necessity of antitrust legislation. The Court, however, gave its support to the enforcement of the antitrust laws only insofar as those laws posed no present danger to viable business organizations. When there seemed to be no threat to a business organization, the antitrust agencies were permitted to prosecute freely on the assumption that, from society's viewpoint, nothing could be lost and something might be gained. But when a viable organization was endangered, the Court reserved the right to decide for itself how far enforcement could go and whether it was to be allowed at all.

Now there has been a fundamental change in the attitude of society generally, and of the Supreme Court particularly, concerning the responsibilities of the political authority and the powers required for the exercise of those responsibilities. Correspondingly, the Court has been prepared to give more credence to the choice of the agencies of administration. It has been willing to allow those agencies far more latitude than before in subordinating the prerogatives of property to social policy and in interposing demands upon the market system. There is on the part of the Court a new presumption that the political authority will act reasonably and in the public interest, and a willingness to allow the agencies of the political authority an exercise of discretion that the Court once held as its own prerogative.

The Department of Justice and the Federal Trade Commission, no longer tightly bound by judicial constraints, have acted in striking down what before was invulnerable — mergers, monopoly power, behavior presumed to be conspiratorial without hard evidence of agreement or monopolistic intent, vertical integration, and nonconspiratorial pricing institutions.

The Court shows good sense in thus yielding its discretionary authority. The new dispensation recognizes the need for political responsibility and public intervention in the intricate and delicate task of restructuring or controlling the behavior of modern industry with all its vast dynamic complexities, at a level that the judiciary is neither trained to achieve nor can be organized to undertake. It is, however, perilous to free the hands of the agencies of antitrust enforcement unless these agencies are themselves prepared to do without a judicial master and to assume independent responsibility for the consequences of their actions. In fact the agencies of antitrust enforcement have been shaped for quite another role.

Land of the Wicked Giants

The Antitrust Division of the Department of Justice and the Federal Trade Commission (along with the Sherman and the Clayton Acts) were born of the conception of an economy where the symmetries of price-directed competition could only be disturbed by the wicked plots of conspirators and by the brutal power of the monopolist, despoiling and devouring his prey. Given this conception, the political authority was to be policeman and prosecutor, punishing conspirators and destroying monopoly so that all others would take warning. The giant would be chopped into little bits; and if the pieces came to life and existed independently, so much the better. If not, others would come to fill the vacancy, and the harmonies of the competitive universe would be restored.

The agencies of enforcement were the giant killers. Their duty was to catch and punish sinners and to destroy monstrosities. The courts were there simply to see to it that the guilty and not the innocent were punished. But the Court did not wholly accept the tale of Jack the giant killer. When brought before the bar, the giants did not look like monsters but seemed quite useful fellows doing important work. To chop them into little pieces might have dangerous and unpleasant consequences. And so the Court constrained the agencies of antitrust enforcement. This was sensible, but negative. If it prevented anything very dangerous from happening, it also prevented anything very constructive from happening. The Court could not itself initiate change nor evaluate proposals to raise the level of industrial performance. Rather, specialized agencies were required with that, specifically, as their task and responsibility. To do the job, such agencies had to exercise discretion. Given the new dispensation, the Court was willing to allow them discretion rather than itself attempting to balance the detriments and dangers of antitrust enforcement against possible benefits to performance. But would the agencies accept such responsibility?

Giant Killer or Social Engineer?

What is the political authority to be: Jack the giant killer or Jack the social engineer?

If the task is to unmask and chase away conspirators and to hunt down and chop up wicked giants who terrorize innocents and devour busy little businesses, so that all will work perfectly of its own accord, then Jack the giant killer is our man. I will argue that the Land of the Giants belongs in fairy tales, and so does Jack; that the American reality, hence, the task of the public authority, is of an entirely different order. Nevertheless, it must be recognized (regretfully) that the Department of Justice and the Federal Trade Commission are still made up to play the role, not of the social engineer, but of the giant killer.

Certainly the great corporation has had its defenders[1] but the role of the giant killer has long been the academic norm, and no doubt men of great sincerity and social concern have been attracted to this crusade against the wicked giants. In recent years that crusade has lost some of its old fervor, and the newest recruits have taken a fundamentally different tack. Leaving behind the effort to re-create the land of the little people, they accept and seek entrée into the interior decision processes of the large corporate and government organizations. From there, using what pressures or persuasions are open to them, they attempt to influence organizational policies on matters of social concern. That, at least to me, seems to be the essence and viable element of Naderism.

Characteristically, today the economist remains nominally a giant killer. He still approaches the issue through the neoclassical mental apparatus in which a price-directed universe of decentralized, individual choice is conceived as the norm, with the antitrust imperatives as its logical consequence. And yet, now he is profoundly uncertain as to the relevance of the first and the applicability of the second. This temper can be illustrated with two examples. After making the most exhaustive study extant on the application of the antitrust laws and their effects, Simon Whitney states:

> One influential viewpoint among economists [holds] that dissolution has been far too seldom applied — that is "in less than a hundred cases" (mostly covering trade associations or common selling agencies) in the first sixty years of the Sherman Act. According to the viewpoint "we should make dissolution the normal method of eliminating restrictive practices in oligopolistic industries." How men of this opinion analyze Sherman Act history is well expressed in the title of an article by Walter Adams, "Dissolution, Divorcement, Divestiture: The Pyrrhic Victories of Antitrust." After deploring the failure to break up the oil and tobacco trusts more effectively, and the steel and harvester trusts at all, Adams cites the *Alcoa, National Lead, Timken,* and *Pullman* cases as examples of regrettable postwar failures to require dissolution (in the last named case in the failure to prevent railroad ownership of the new sleeping-car company). In this

---

[1]See John Kenneth Galbraith, *The New Industrial State* (Boston: Houghton Mifflin Company, 1967); David Lilienthal, *Big Business: A New Era* (New York: Harper and Brothers, 1953).

view only an economy of many small companies in each industry can ensure "workable competition."

The viewpoint of the present study is different primarily because no evidence was found that the industries in which these "Pyrrhic victories" occurred, or others containing big corporations that might seem ripe for dissolution under these principles, operate less efficiently for the public welfare than industries composed of many small firms. Nor does the authoritative book edited by Adams himself, *The Structure of American Industry*, show that the performance of cotton textiles, bituminous coal, residential construction, or agriculture industries with many small firms, has been superior, from the consumers standpoint, to that of the seven oligopoly-type industries it treats.[2]

A new uncertainty and "loss of faith" is suggested also in comparing the first and third editions of Clair Wilcox's *Public Policies Toward Business*.[3] Wilcox was one of the most trustworthy of antitrusters and perhaps the most knowledgeable. In his third edition a new chapter appears, "Antitrust Appraised," where he introduces the following:

Perfect Competition

It is the responsibility of antitrust to restore competition where it does not exist and to maintain it where it does. Is such an undertaking really feasible? The answer will depend upon the way in which competition is defined. If the economist's ideal of perfect competition is accepted as the goal, five conditions must be satisfied:

1. The commodity dealt in must consist of innumerable units, each identical with the others, so that buyers can shift quickly from one seller to another in order to obtain a lower price; the advantages offered by different buyers must also be uniform, so that sellers can shift quickly from one buyer to another in order to obtain a higher price.
2. The market in which the commodity is bought and sold must be well organized, trading must be continuous, and traders must be so well informed that every unit sold at the same time will sell at the same price.

---

[2]Simon N. Whitney, *Antitrust Policies* (New York: Twentieth Century Fund, 1958), II, 391–392.
[3]Clair Wilcox, *Public Policies Toward Business* (Homewood, Ill.: Richard D. Irwin, Inc., 1955); *ibid.* (3d ed., 1966).

3. Sellers and buyers must be numerous, each of them must be small, and the quantity supplied or demanded by any one of them must be so insignificant a part of the total supply or demand that no increase or decrease in his sales or purchases can appreciably affect the price.

4. There must be no restraint upon the independence of any seller or buyer, whether by custom, contract, collusion, the fear of reprisals by competitors, or otherwise; each one must be free to act in his own interest without regard for the interests of any of the others.

5. There must be no friction to impede the movement of resources from industry to industry, from product to product, or from firm to firm; investment must be speedily withdrawn from unsuccessful undertakings and transferred to those that promise a profit. There must be no barrier to entrance into the market; access must be granted to all sellers and all buyers at home and abroad.

Perfect competition, thus defined, never has existed and never can exist. An attempt to realize it in practice would require an atomization of industry that is not within the bounds of possibility. The concept is useful merely as a standard by which to measure the varying degrees of imperfection that must always characterize the actual markets in which goods are bought and sold. It cannot be taken as a practical objective of public policy.

Effective Competition

Another concept, developed more recently by economists, defines competition in terms, not of perfection, but of workability, thus establishing a standard that is more nearly attainable. A market may be regarded as effectively competitive when it is characterized by conditions that afford to buyers and sellers real opportunities to protect themselves, each against the other. Effective competition may be produced by conditions that are less exacting than those demanded for perfection:

1. It need not involve the standardization of commodities; it does require the availability of products so closely related that they may be readily substituted, one for another. It does not require that the advantages offered by all buyers be identical; it does require that they differ so little that sellers will not hesitate to shift from one to another.

2. It does not require that markets be formally organized, that trading be continuous, or that all buyers and sellers be intelligent, educated, and equally well informed; it does require

that information be available and that no action be taken to grant it to some traders and withhold it from others.

3. It does not require that traders be present in such numbers and limited to such a size that none of them has an appreciable influence on supply, demand, or price; it does require that traders be sufficiently numerous to offer to buyers and to sellers, respectively, a considerable number of genuine alternatives in sources of supply and demand, so that, by shifting their purchases or sales, they can substantially influence quality, service, and price.

4. It does not require emancipation from custom or isolation from contacts with competitors; it does require substantial independence of action; each trader must be free to adopt his own policy governing output, purchases, and price; traders must not take part in formal agreements or tacit understandings; power must not be so distributed that lack of resources or fear of retaliation prevent one trader from encroaching on the sales or the purchases of another.

5. It does not require that transference of resources be frictionless or instantaneous or that entry to the market be unimpeded by such natural obstacles as the cost of facilities and sales promotion or the experience and contacts of existing firms; it does require that transference and entry be unobstructed by artificial barriers and that no preferences be accorded or handicaps imposed.

Effective competition cannot be expected to insure complete flexibility or optimum economy in the use of resources. In a rough way, however, it can contribute toward these ends. By subjecting traders to its discipline, it can prevent deliberate curtailment of output and the survival of extremes of inefficiency. By affording access to genuine alternatives, it can protect the weaker trader against the worst of the bargains that might otherwise be imposed upon him by the stronger one. By holding open the door to opportunity, it can encourage experimentation in products, processes, and prices, and forestall the suppression of innovation by established firms. This concept, admittedly, is less precise than that of perfect competition. It is more useful, however, as a goal for public policy.[4]

While "workable competition" in Wilcox's meaning is more descriptive of what one observes in business performance,

---

[4]Wilcox, *op. cit.* 3d ed., pp. 251–253.

correspondingly, it is less viable as a basis for antitrust enforcement. Indeed, I know of no market structure in American industry today that, as a matter of judgment, could or could not be justified within its strictures. So equivocal are the preceding criteria that competition in any industrial market could be considered workable or unworkable as a matter of judgment.

Thus, big business or the organizational sector has its attackers, its defenders, and those who are uncertain. But more important than that which exists is that which lacks. There is a lack of any systematic effort to explore the operation of industries and firms in order to measure and evaluate performance, or to discern what causes failure or determines achievement or promotes technological advance in order to devise techniques and standards that will permit the public authority to raise the performance level and to harness the beneficent potentialities or to curb inherent dangers in resolving what Galbraith refers to as "the problem of how we are to survive, and in a civilized fashion, in a world of great organizations, which, not surprisingly, impose both their values and their needs on the society they are assumed to serve."[5]

THE ORGANIZATIONAL SECTOR

We are confronted in the American economy with a number of coexisting and interacting systems of production, distribution, and consumption. Not all of these are part of the market system. Households, universities, and governments are all engaged in organizing production and consumption outside the process of market exchange. And within the market system there are diverse forms ranging from that of the agricultural sector, where choice is highly decentralized and price-directed in the classical mode, to the very different organization of large-scale manufacturing where the primary producing-distributing agencies are very large corporations, each employing many thousands of persons. That part of its labor which is not highly specialized and is without managerial or supervisory responsibility is separately organized

---

[5]John Kenneth Galbraith, from a paper presented in 1967 before a subcommittee of the Senate Committee on Small Business to discuss some of the ideas in Galbraith's *The New Industrial State*, reproduced in Edwin Mansfield (ed.), *Monopoly Power and Economic Performance* (Rev. ed.; New York: W. W. Norton and Co., Inc., 1968), p. 127.

through trade unions. Wages and working conditions are negotiated by trade union and management representatives. It is with respect to this "organizational sector" that the antitrust controversy rages.

Organizational Choice

Through its sheer size and complexity the great corporation outstrips the control powers of any individual or collegium. Choice is organizational rather than individual. The great corporation constitutes a community of sorts, a society in microcosm. Its decision-making and control processes are analogous to those of government. Indeed its activities and responsibilities overlap and, in important areas, merge with those of the political authority. Unlike the political system, however, individuals interacting and participating in the organizational sector do not relate as subjects of the same sovereign power; nor do they, as in the decentralized, price-directed economy, interact as self-interested bargainers out to buy for as little as possible and to sell for as much as possible. Rather, they relate as colleagues, associates, and partisans, sharing an "identification with" the idea of the company; as superior and subordinate in a provisional chain of authority; or as bargaining agents representing interests that are not, in an individualized sense, their own. Power resides in status within, and as a part of, the organization rather than in the possession of property or the claims of ownership.

Optimal Scale and Mix

The great corporation is normally engaged in many different markets; i.e., it participates simultaneously in numerous, integral producing-distributing-procuring systems. In participating in such systems, the corporation performs not a single task but a wide diversity of tasks. It may be, for example, an R&D agent, generating innovation or operationally relevant information. It may be an advertising agent or a distribution and sales agent organized to reach a mass of consumers. It may be a procurement agent, concentrating its buying or integrating backward in order to secure a steady low-cost input of resources. It may be a financial agent, floating securities, arranging for loans, managing an investment portfolio, and extending mass credit. Under contract it may be, in effect, an agency of the government; a transportation agent; a merchandising agent; a personnel relations agent; and, of course, an agent of planning and management for any number of different operations. Each of these functional activities has its own organizational requisites, including perhaps a more or less appropriate system of decision-making and control and scale of operations. Under these circumstances there can be no uniquely optimal organizational scheme or scale of operations for all the firms in an industry. Optimal organization and optimal size are conceivable only in relation to the embodied combination of functions. And each firm will be composed of a different combination. It is to be expected, therefore, that in any market there will be a variety of quite different but competitively equivalent organizations, each of a form and size appropriate to its peculiar functional combination. Some will be able to work more quickly and easily in the nooks and crannies where the waters of opportunity are shallow. Some will plow through heavy storms, while others follow safely in their wake. Some will operate successfully as satellites, supporters, and indeed as parasites. It is futile to look for an optimal scale of operations or a single organizational format as the industry norm. What might be sought is an optimal mix of sizes and structures for the performance of the diverse functions that together constitute any specified procuring-producing-distributing (industrial) system.

In the organizational sector the market (i.e., the body of exchange relationships and the institutional arrangements for purchase and sale) is not the master of choice. The market is rather a negotiating arena, a showcase for the display of capabilities and outputs, a place for maneuver and the exercise of strategy by entities that interrelate in a manner analogous to that of rival or allied states. There is presumably a drive to survive, to hold position, to grow, to win. Their competition, which is of many dimensions and not necessarily in accord with the public interest, very rarely erupts in the mutual catastrophe of a "price war."

Prices and wages are set as a function of corporation and trade union policy. They may not reflect resource availability and end-product demand, but rather a negotiated balance of autonomous powers. Hence, price need no longer be an index of real scarcities as once it might have been; nevertheless, it does continue to guide resource utilization and to shape the patterns of consumption.

Organizational Performance

By the test of performance the organizational sector has shown itself to have unique advantages relative to such alternatives as "pure competition" in the agricultural sector or to centralized planning and operation under the political authority. Given the cultural correlates of American society, the great corporation has established its capacity to motivate efficiency and progress, to self-recruit, and to self-perpetuate. It is flexible and adaptable, able to change shape and form rapidly in response to opportunity and pressure. It can mobilize vast resources in complex operations, planning for the achievement of fairly long-range objectives. It combines these technical advantages of large-scale operations and of rational time-projected planning with a considerable freedom for the individual in his choice of work and association.

Arbitrary Power and the Dangers of Drift

The organizational sector has also its peculiar problems and comparative disadvantages. There is here neither the mechanism of responsibility and answerability that holds the political agency in line, nor the forces of price competition that keep the small enterprise of the decentralized market to the straight and narrow. For the great corporation and the trade union there is a wide range of options and no built-in force to assure that choice will be brought into accord with the public interest. Among the variables that determine corporate decision the interests of financial manipulators may overbalance the interest of managers in efficient operations. Internecine struggles for advantage and power can distort the structure of operations and control. The prejudices and the corruptibility of management and of trade unionists can distort organization, tyrannize individuals, and foreclose opportunity. A corporate organization, indeed the whole procuring-producing-distributing complex of an industry, can exhaust itself in sterile pursuits; it can stagnate, regress, and fail in its performance potential. In a word, there is in the organizational sector a dangerous arbitrariness of power and a capacity to drift into swamp waters and quicksands, greatly to the detriment of society at large.

ACTING UPON THE MARKET ECONOMY

Suppose it is the intention of the political authority to act upon the organizational sector in order to promote technological advance and otherwise to raise the level of performance. How should the political authority organize itself for that purpose? Whatever the administrative guise, this task, which is the task of social engineering, would require that: (1) each industry and each firm if size and power warrants, be monitored and its performance evaluated by measures of creativity, efficiency, technological progress, equity in income distribution, and price formation; (2) the preconditions or determinants of performance be hypothesized; (3) on the basis of that hypothesis, the political authority take action in order to raise or to maintain the level of performance; and (4) that such action by the political authority, in turn, be evaluated by its effects, thus testing the underlying hypotheses. At the level of what is now called "technological assessment," this sort of social engineering would also require that real costs and benefits external to private (and corporate) accounting be brought to bear in evaluating performance and in influencing corporate choice and action. What is indeed at issue is the superimposition of a process of social planning upon a universe of autonomous, corporate decision-making and operation. As part of that it is necessary to develop criteria by reference to which performance, resource allocation, and the environmental effects of operations can be judged and a strategy of offsets and control designed. This includes the imposition of structural change in particular markets where circumstances warrant in order to raise the level of performance and in order to bring activities and outputs into closer accord with social values. All this differs fundamentally from the traditional system of political intervention in the market, which has as its purpose the imposition of a predetermined pattern of behavior and the punishment of crimes, and not (as here) of finding the means to solve a continuum of problems with the continuing objective of evaluating and progressively raising the level of industrial performance. The development and design of an instrument of choice and control should depend on the nature of the choice and the objective control. Thus, what is critically at issue is the purpose of political action and the nature of political responsibility with respect to the market system.

There is no intrinsic worth or moral value in actions taken to forbid delivered pricing, to require f.o.b. mill pricing, to forbid vertical integration, to limit leasing, to force the disposition of patents, or to transform a single-firm industry into a multi-firm industry (and these are the sum and substance of postwar antitrust enforcement) unless these serve to raise the level of industrial performance. The actions taken by the Department of Justice and the Federal Trade Commission are justified *if* they raise the level of performance. Did they do so? Alas, the agencies of government have never asked the question. They have never attempted to monitor or evaluate performance, or to base antitrust intervention on an analysis of performance. Nor have they ever looked back to ponder the results of intervention, not even with respect to the competition they were trying to create, let alone the performance of goals of productivity and equity to which competition allegedly relates.

> During the nearly seventy years that the antitrust laws have been on the statute books many cases have been brought and much money, time and effort have been expended in determining whether violations have occurred. An investment of large magnitude in the enforcement of a body of legislation so central to the functioning of our economy is inevitable, but it has seemed to the author of this research study, and the Committee, that a serious lack of balance is evident between the attention given to the question whether violation has occurred and to the questions whether, and in what way, legal procedures could be expected noticeably to improve, or have improved, the situation. By this time several hundred cases have ended in decrees of various sorts designed to bring about changes in market structures and business practices.

> Yet very little time and effort have been spent, either inside the government or out, in assessing the effects of these decrees on the behavior of firms or the status of competition in the affected industries. How differently do the firms encompassed act from the way they would if a case had never been brought? Is competition, in some meaningful sense of the word, noticeably improved? Almost no one has bothered to inquire.[6]

The antitrust agencies have remained policemen and giant killers. They still ride into battle with their tattered dogma as a

---

[6]Whitney, *op. cit.*, p. 442.

banner, attacking the giants and breaking their lances against windmills, ending in a swamp of futility only to rally their forces again and attack the enemy who are now just over another hill.

In the following chapters let us consider the particulars of antitrust enforcement during the decades after World War II before returning to a consideration of the reformulation of policy and the transformation of the system of control.

Chapter 10
Continuities

Chapters that follow this one will describe the novelties introduced into the substance of antitrust enforcement during the period of ideological transformation after World War II. There have been radical changes, as will be seen, but not in every aspect of the law. In some respects antitrust enforcement and interpretation has been continuous with that of prewar decades. This chapter will examine only those developments continuous with the past (continuities) where recent interpretations remain consistent with the earlier "antitrust logic" of the Court. This includes (1) conspiracies between independents, (2) price discrimination, and (3) the use of cross-product and cross-market leverage to gain a competitive advantage. While for these categories the interpretation of the law remained in line with what it had been before, the greater permissiveness of the Court led the antitrust agencies to more far reaching enforcement and also to the exercise of great deliberation in the exercise of their authority. This augmentation of power and evolution of responsibility of the agencies of antitrust for enforcement signals an important change in the structure and character of the political authority.

AGREEMENTS IN RESTRAINT OF TRADE

After World War II the per se prohibition against price-fixing, market-sharing, and profit-sharing agreements was reasserted strongly to include complex interfirm arrangements indirectly stabilizing prices, as in the *Socony-Vacuum Oil Company* case.[1]

The largest crude oil discovery ever made in the United States was in east Texas in the 1930's. In "skimming the crude" a number of independent producers and refiners came into being. Lacking other sales outlets, they dumped their output in the midcontinental market with consequences on prices and on marketing arrangements that can only be described as "chaotic." The National Recovery Administration (NRA) authority representing the industry tried to cope by setting up a system where each large refiner bought the surplus or "distress" fuel of a particular small producer, known as his "dancing partner." When the NRA was declared unconstitutional, the Refiners Committee set up under the NRA code authority continued the program on its own. On this account, in 1936, 18 large petroleum companies were indicted under the Sherman Act. The Supreme Court upheld the convictions of 12 oil companies and 5 individuals. Fines of more than half a million dollars were levied. The arrangement was dissolved. Justice Douglas, speaking for the Court, said:

> Any combination which tampers with price structures is engaged in an unlawful activity. Even though the members of the price-fixing group were in no position to control the market, to the extent that they raised, lowered, or stabilized prices they would be directly interfering with the free play of market forces. The Act places all such schemes beyond the pale. . . . They are banned because of their actual or potential threat to the central nervous system of the economy.[2]

Justice Douglas' notion that a "free play of market forces" (manifested presumably in the up and down movement of price) is the "central nervous system" of the organizational sector is surely a naive one, and brings into question the ideological understructure of the antitrust laws. In any case the dance was over, and the partners left the floor. One result was the bankruptcy and shutdown of scores of small refineries that had once provided outlets for independent producers of crude oil. The total number in operation declined from 76 in 1936 to 14 in 1940.

---

[1]*U.S.* v. *Socony-Vacuum Oil Co.*, 310 U.S. 150 (1940).
[2]*Ibid.*

The most spectacular case of price agreement during the postwar decades did not turn on legal principle and, hence, never found its way to the Supreme Court. In 1961, 29 manufacturers of heavy electrical equipment (turbines, generators, etc.), including the General Electric Company and Westinghouse, were convicted of price fixing. Their conspiracy seemed to have been in effect for a decade or more. District Court Judge J. Cullen Ganey imposed fines of $1,787,000, sentenced 7 executives to prison, and imposed suspended sentences on 23 others. About this case there are some provocative questions concerning:

1. The tremors of horror and indignation which the discovery of this particular conspiracy aroused. Were they at the shock of seeing the establishment with its pants down? Were they caused by the discomfort that comes with the realization that things are not as they are popularly imagined? Said Judge Ganey in imposing sentence ". . . what is really at stake here is the survival of the kind of economy under which America has grown to greatness, the free enterprise system. The conduct of the corporate and individual defendants . . . has flagrantly mocked the image of that economic system of free enterprise which we profess to the country and destroyed the model which we offer today as a free world alternative to state control and eventual dictatorship." I am afraid, Judge Ganey, that what was at stake was not the survival of the kind of economy under which America has grown to greatness, but was rather the survival of an illusion.

2. The stubbornly asserted claim by high officials of big companies, whose testimony was unshaken by the evidence submitted, that the long-existing conspiracy had been hidden from them, that it was carried out in defiance of official policy, and that they had known nothing of it. Antitrusters greeted this claim with considerable jocularity. I would argue that it is entirely credible and important, because it gives evidence of the nature of decision making and of the source of initiative in large organizations. That matter will be developed further in Chapter 14.

3. The fact that no effort was made by economists, politicians or lawyers to determine, and no question was asked concerning, the *performance* in this industry, measured by its productivity and its price trends or by those technological advances that show up in the industries that procured

electrical equipment during the period of the conspiracy and during the period that followed its elimination.

The state of the present law against collusion (paraphrasing Corwin Edwards) can be summarized as follows.[3] It is presumed illegal to exclude competition, to restrict output or procurement, to divide markets, to fix prices, or to dampen the opportunity or incentive to compete through *agreements* between independent firms. Illicit agreements may take the form of boycotts, selective price cutting and other forms of coercion, control of access to an industry or a market, preferential dealing, pooling and profit sharing, or reciprocal purchasing.

PER SE VIOLATIONS UNDER THE ROBINSON-PATMAN ACT

The provisions of the Robinson-Patman Act, passed in 1936, were described earlier in Chapter 5. Its primary objective was to protect small retailers from the competition of the chain stores. It was prosmall and antibig rather than procompetitive and antimonopoly in its purpose, and could serve to reduce rather than to increase the intensity of competition. The act imposes certain absolute prohibitions. The seller is forbidden to pay a brokerage commission or its equivalent to anyone but a bona fide broker, hopefully cancelling the advantage to the buyer who is large enough to do without the intermediary of a broker. In addition, the seller cannot make price allowances in lieu of services rendered to other buyers (e.g., allowances in lieu of brand name advertising for those who do their own advertising or for services rendered by the buyer — for example, those who undertake brand name promotion on their own account), unless these concessions are made to competitors on "proportionately equal terms." (The Federal Trade Commission calculates proportionality as a ratio to dollar volume.) In respect to allowances the Federal Trade Commission operates under its own rule of reason, in principle requiring that such allowances be bona fide cost trade-offs and not concessions to strong bargainers. For that reason such allowances must be published, made available to all, and must be congruent with services rendered.

---

[3]Corwin Edwards, *Maintaining Competition* (New York: McGraw-Hill Book Co., 1949).

In spite of the problems of interpretation, when the Federal Trade Commission's regulations pertaining to brokerage fees and allowances have been appealed, they have almost invariably been upheld by the courts. The social value of these rules on allowances and brokerage fees is open to question. A priori they protect and perpetuate certain established systems of distribution though these may have become obsolete.[4] All this does not necessarily accrue to the advantage of the small buyer. There have been instances when purchasing agencies designed to serve small clients (such as the Biddle Purchasing Company, which served 2,400 clients and passed on its purchasing commission as lower prices[5]) and purchasing cooperatives set up to reduce the costs of small independent enterprises (such as a cooperative arrangement of bakers, Quality Bakers of America, that was intended to economize in the purchasing of flour, equipment, and supplies[6]) have been penalized under the Robinson-Patman Act. However, in another case the court chose to blink at the letter of the law in observing its spirit. A cooperative organization of independent retail grocers was allowed "price concessions, discounts, and allowances" even though these could be "correlated mathematically with the normal rates of brokerage which suppliers pay their brokers on regular sales," said the court. "Reason does not permit our ignoring these facts in order to declare illegal a worthy effort by a number of wholesale grocers, owned by retailers, to reduce the ultimate sales prices to consumers by entering into an arrangement with Central, which made them stronger in their competition with the large chain stores."[7] This interpretation implies, of course, that what is forbidden to one form of organization (chain stores) is open to another form of organization (cooperative associations of retailers). The beneficiaries, presumably, are the entrenched and perhaps parasitical middlemen.

The most "successful" prosecution under the Robinson-Patman Act, especially in disallowing any economies implicit in absorbing the brokerage function into the regular operations

---

[4]*FTC v. Henry Broch & Co.*, 363 U.S. 166 (1960), wherein brokers themselves are forbidden to make concessions on their fees.

[5]*Biddle Purchasing Company v. FTC*, 96 F. 2d 687 (1938), certiorari denied, 305 U.S. 634 (1938).

[6]*Quality Bakers of America v. FTC*, 114 F. 2d 393 (1940).

[7]*Central Retailer-Owned Grocers, Inc. v. FTC*, United States Court of Appeals for the Seventh Circuit, 319 F. 2d 410 (1963).

of the chain store, was the indictment and conviction of A&P.[8] The attack on A&P appeared to destroy the elan of an aggressive competitor, which subsequently regressed into routinized practice and financial distress, greatly to the detriment of consumers. It is not evident that the cutting down of A&P benefited the small independent retailer.

Injury to a Competitor

The Robinson-Patman Act, unlike the Clayton Act, makes discrimination illegal not only when its effect "may be substantially to lessen competition or tend to create a monopoly," but also where it may tend "to injure, destroy, or prevent competition with any person who either grants or knowingly receives the benefit of such discrimination, or with the customers of either of them." Illegal discrimination has then a new test — did it injure a competitor? Injury to a competitor is much easier to prove than is injury to competition; it is also less likely to be relevant to the public weal. The accused discriminator is permitted to justify his price concessions on the grounds that (1) the price concession was "made in good faith to meet an equally low price of a competitor," or (2) "the price differential makes only due allowance for differences in the cost of manufacture, sale, or delivery resulting from different methods or quantities in which such commodities are to such purchasers sold or delivered."

The rule of the Commission and the response of the Court can be illustrated by two cases. Morton Salt Company priced its product, after discounts, as follows:

	per case
Less-than-carload purchases	$1.60
Carload purchases	1.50
5,000 case purchases in any consecutive 12 months	1.40
50,000 case purchases in any consecutive 12 months	1.35

Justice Black, speaking for the Court, put aside the "Respondent's basic contention" that it was offering "standard quantity discounts available to all on equal terms. . . . Theoretically these discounts are equally available to all, but functionally they are not . . . no single independent retail grocery

---

[8] *A&P* v. *FTC*, 106 F. 2d 667 (1939); certiorari denied, 308 U.S. 625 (1940).

store, and probably no single wholesaler, bought as many as 50,000 cases or as much as $50,000 worth of salt in a given year."[9] Hence, there was a discrimination in price which was injurious to certain competitors and, inferentially, to competition. Such discrimination might be justified if it could be equated to the cost savings made by the seller as a consequence of the sale of larger quantities of salt; but, if this was to be the justification, the respondent would have to prove to the Commission that there were such savings. The burden of proof was on those who wished to be exempted from a forbidden act, not on the enforcement agency.

It turns out to be a very hard thing to prove such savings, especially when quantity discounts are not related to differential shipping costs. (A discount on carload as compared to less-than-carload-lots can be related to shipping cost differentials, but not the requirement that X number of units be purchased over the course of a year.) Hitherto, the Federal Trade Commission has permitted discounts that can be justified by ascertainable differences in selling or shipping costs, but it has refused to impute per-unit differences in manufacturing costs to differences in the scale of purchasing.[10]

In his opinion Justice Black asked the lower courts to accept the authority of the Federal Trade Commission in respect to questions of fact and, indeed, in the inferences to be made from the facts concerning circumstance and intent.

> One of the reasons for entrusting enforcement of this Act primarily to the Commission, a body of experts, was to authorize it to hear evidence as to given differential practices and to make findings concerning possible injury to competition. Such findings are to form the basis for cease and desist orders. . . . The effective administration of the Act . . . would be greatly impaired if . . . the Commission's cease and desist orders did no more than shift to the courts in subsequent contempt proceedings for their volition the very fact questions of injury to competition, etc., which the Act requires the Commission to determine as the basis for its order. The enforcement responsibility of the courts . . . is to adjudicate questions concerning the order's violation, not questions of fact which support that valid order.[11]

[9]*FTC v. Morton Salt Co.*, 334 U.S. 37 (1948).
[10]See *United States v. Borden Co.*, 350 U.S. 460 (1962), and *In re Sylvania Products, Inc.*, 51 FTC 282 (1954).
[11]*Op. cit., FTC v. Morton Salt Co.*

The Federal Trade Commission is authorized under the Robinson-Patman Act to fix absolute limits on quantity discounts "where purchasers in greater quantities are so few as to render differentials . . . promotive of monopoly." For 15 years this authority was not exercised by the Commission. Finally, under the pressure of 48,000 independent tire dealers and Congressmen who were responsive to the demands of those dealers, the Commission forbade that category of quantity discounts then being obtained by 62 of the largest distributors. The Commission's order was reversed by the courts.[12]

The Commission allows "functional" discounts; i.e., it permits a seller to set different prices for functionally differentiated groups of buyers, e.g., manufacturers, jobbers, wholesalers, and retailers. But functionally differentiated groups may compete together, just as alternative systems for the organization of the same basic functions may compete together. Then complications arise as exemplified in the *Standard Oil of Indiana* cases.[13] Standard Oil operated no service stations in the Detroit area but sold at both retail and wholesale prices: wagonload lots to jobbers at one price and tank wagon lots to retailers at another price. One of the jobbers who purchased in wagonload lots operated his own cut-rate chain of retail stations, selling gasoline under the brand name "Neds." The Federal Trade Commission ruled that although this jobber bought in wagonload lots, the discount he received was illegal inasmuch as he operated retail outlets. Standard was ordered to cease and desist from selling to Neds at the jobber rate. Standard resisted the order, offering the cost difference as a defense. The Commission rejected the argument. Standard then defended its price to Neds on the ground that it was made in good faith to meet the equally low price of a competitor. The Commission accepted the fact but adjudged the argument insufficient and held that the discrimination was illegal on the grounds that competition had been injured. The decision was appealed. In this rare instance, too, the Court reversed the Commission's decision holding that a seller could not be penalized for lowering a price in good faith to meet the equally low price of a competitor; hence, if the "good faith" argument is accepted as a fact, it must be considered as a sufficient defense.

---

[12]*FTC v. B. F. Goodrich & Co.*, 242 F. 2d 31 (1957).

[13]*Standard Oil Co. (Indiana) v. FTC*, 173 F. 2d 210 (1949); *Standard Oil Co. (Indiana) v. FTC*, 340 U.S. 231 (1951); *FTC v. Standard Oil Co. (Indiana)*, 355 U.S. 396 (1958).

Can the "good faith" defense be used to justify aggressive (getting new customer) price cutting as well as defensive (keeping old customers) price cutting? In the *Sunshine Biscuit* case the Commission ruled that only defensive price cutting was allowable, with one commissioner strongly dissenting. In 1962 a circuit court pondered the question of how in a competitive struggle a distinction could be made between new customers and old ones, with price concessions made to the latter and withheld from the former. It considered the differentiation unworkable and reversed the Commission's decision.[14] The "good faith" defense remains equivocal. Presumably, it cannot be used to justify a price below that of a competitor in the strategy of price cutting. It cannot be used to justify a lower price to a customer when it is the customer and not the discriminating seller who is obliged to meet the lower price of the customer's competitor.[15]

Discrimination through local price cutting has come before the courts in private suits. Where local price cutting was required to stay in a regional market, the Court allowed it.[16] Where the Court saw such price cutting used by a chain baker to drive a local competitor out of business, it disallowed it.[17] In 1960 the Court found injury when Anheuser-Busch, a national brewer of premium beer, lowered its margin in one region so that its premium beer was sold at a price equal to the normally lower prices of certain regional competitors, in what was evidently an effort to coerce these competitors to follow its price leadership upward.[18]

THE LAW AS A FOOTBALL IN THE COMPETITIVE GAME

Given the complexity of the laws controlling business behavior and selling arrangements, the triple damage provisions of the Sherman and Clayton Acts, and the broad and imprecise grounds for claiming injury under the Robinson-Patman Act, there arises a continual danger that the law will become a football in the business game. Lawsuits can be instruments of interfirm coercion and competition of a peculiarly debilitating and

[14]*Sunshine Biscuits Inc.* v. *FTC*, 306 F. 2d 48 (7th Cir. 1962).
[15]*FTC* v. *Sun Oil Co.*, 371 U.S. 505 (1963).
[16]*Balian Ice Cream* v. *Arden Farms Co.*, 104 F. Supp. 796 (1952); certiorari denied, 231 F. 2d 356 (1955).
[17]*L. L. More* v. *Mead's Fine Breads Co.*, 347 U.S. 1012 (1954).
[18]*FTC* v. *Anheuser-Busch, Inc.*, 363 U.S. 536 (1960).

unhealthy sort that serves no useful purpose but is wasteful and costly. Such lawsuits may substitute shyster skill for managerial competence in the struggle for business survival and success. One example of this is the *Paramount Pictures* case, to be described later in this chapter, in which motion picture exhibitors were solicited by law firms to undertake triple damage suits against filmmakers to take advantage of the presumption of guilt established by the government's successful prosecution of an antitrust case against them. In 1953 total claims under such suits amounted to $600 million — an amount sufficient to wipe out the industry several times — for practices which the exhibitors were themselves then trying desperately to resuscitate.

The Court has somewhat narrowed the range of litigation under the Robinson-Patman Act. It has ruled that Section 3 of that act, which forbids as a criminal offense different prices for the sale of otherwise identical items, and local price cutting or "unreasonably low prices . . . for the purpose of destroying competition or eliminating a competitor," does not admit triple damage suits since, unlike Section 2, it is not worded as an amendment to the Clayton Act.[19] The Court has also ruled that only purchasers directly discriminated against (not purchasers who have purchased from discriminated-against purchasers) can collect damages under this act.[20]

THE VALUE OF A BRAND NAME

A case that might have far-reaching implications is the Federal Trade Commission's order against the Borden Company charging discrimination because evaporated milk was sold under the Borden label at a higher price than the same milk in the same can under the private brand labels of several retailers. The Supreme Court upheld the Commission's order, holding that ". . . labels do not differentiate products for the purpose of determining grade or quality, even though one label may have more customer appeal and command a higher price in the market place. . . ."[21] The case was remanded to the lower court to consider Borden's cost justification defense. There the court ruled that "a manufacturer may sell a privately labeled

---

[19]*Nashville Milk Co. v. Carnation Co.*, 355 U.S. 373 (1958).
[20]*Klein v. Lionel Corp.*, 237 F. 2d 13 (3d Cir. 1956).
[21]*FTC v. The Borden Co.*, 382 U.S. 807 (1965).

product for less than he sells a chemically identical premium brand, so long as the difference doesn't exceed the benefit by way of the seller's national advertising and promotion which the purchaser of the . . . brand product enjoys."[22] The intriguing question is whether a brand per se, which may have acquired its market impact as the result of years of prior promotion, has any intrinsic value under the law, or whether all that is allowable is an offset equivalent to current costs of advertising. If the latter is to be the rule, what will be the implications, say, for the sale of branded and unbranded gasoline, "physically and chemically the same" but sold at different prices?

THE USE OF MARKET LEVERAGE

It was earlier established that the use of a favored position in one market as leverage to gain advantage in other markets can be, and has been, constrained by the antitrust laws. Tying contracts, forbidden under Section 3 of the Clayton Act when their effect may be "substantially to lessen competition," are favorite leverage devices, particularly for tie-ins to the use of a patented product. The Court has been vigorous in constraining such tying contracts, even more so in the postwar decades than earlier. Thus, in 1942 the Court took the drastic step of refusing to allow a patentee to defend his patent against infringement, because control of the patented product (a dispensing machine that deposited salt tablets in cans during the canning process) had been used to gain an advantage in the sale of an unpatented product (the dispenser was leased only on the condition that the lessee would use unpatented salt tablets produced by the lessor).[23] In 1947 the Court declared a contract illegal that tied the use of a patented salt dispenser to the use of salt sold by the company owning the patent to that dispenser. In this case the Court held that such tying arrangements were illegal per se; i.e., illegality did not require that harm to competition be established.[24] In 1954 Eastman Kodak agreed under a consent decree to split off its sale of color film from its charge for developing this film, and to instruct competitors on the technique of color film finishing.[25] In 1957 District Court Judge Leahy ruled that

---

[22]"Price Differentials on Brands Upheld," *Business Week* (July 29, 1967).
[23]*Morton Salt Co.* v. *G. S. Suppiger Co.,* 314 U.S. 488 (1942).
[24]*International Salt Co.* v. *U.S.,* 332 U.S. 392 (1947).
[25]*1954 Trade Cases,* Par. 67, 920.

the refusal to license patents individually rather than in a block constituted an "unlawful coercion contrary to public policy as announced by the courts."[26] In the *Mercoid* case, going beyond its previous position forbidding unpatented items to be drawn into the orbit of a patented one through a tying contract, the Court held that the possession of a patent on a "system" or "combination" could not be used to control the unpatented items that made up the combination.[27]   Hence, the Court may have eliminated the practical viability of a "system" patent in the sense of being able to secure a commercial payoff from the possession of that patent.

These instances refer to the use of the patent as a legal grant of monopoly to gain advantages in other markets or in the sale of other products through some tying arrangement.   Tying arrangements are not the only means through which the patent monopoly may serve as the fulcrum for leverage to gain advantages beyond those that fall within the always tenuous boundaries of the patent grant.   The Court has opened the door to the prosecution of patent licensing used for the purpose of controlling or influencing the price structure of an entire industry or product line where patents are strategically related to, but do not wholly comprehend, that which is offered for sale.[28] In the *Besser* and *Singer* cases the Court ruled against patent-based agreements between independent firms for purposes of market strategy and control.[29] In 1945 the Court upheld in part the prosecution of Hartford-Empire, which had dominated the glass container industry through a patent-pooling arrangement, and required that company to license its patents at reasonable royalties.   This was the first imposition of compulsory licensing by the courts.   Here, the Supreme Court implicity recognized a threshold beyond which the industrial power consequent upon the sheer agglomeration of patents becomes intolerable.[30]   Through their agglomeration the legal control over patented items is levered into the control of the output of an entire industry or technology — and that leverage

---

[26] *American Security Co.* v. *Shatterproof Glass Corp.*, 154 F. Supp. 890 (1957); aff'd. 268 F. 2d 769 (3d Cir. 1959).

[27] *Mercoid Corp.* v. *Minneapolis-Honeywell Regulator Co.*, 320 U.S. 680 (1944).

[28] *U.S.* v. *Line Material Co.*, 333 U.S. 287 (1948); *U.S.* v. *United States Gypsum Co.*, 333 U.S. 364 (1948).

[29] *Besser Mfg. Co.* v. *U.S.*, 343 U.S. 444 (1952); *U.S.* v. *Singer Mfg. Co.*, 374 U.S. 174 (1963).

[30] *Hartford-Empire Co.* v. *U.S.*, 323 U.S. 386 (1945).

is ruled illicit. The National Lead Company was the American leg of an international cartel producing titanium compounds. The cartel used its cross-licensing of patents to control prices and to allocate markets. It was convicted under the antitrust laws and eventually agreed under a consent decree to offer its patents, royalty-free, and to supply supplementary technical "know how" to competitors as well.[31] In the General Electric case concerning the production of incandescent light bulbs the courts refused to allow the company to perpetuate its monopoly of incandescent bulbs, after the expiration of its basic patents, through its accumulation of supplementary and improvement patents which it alone was in a position to generate or accumulate because of its monopoly position. The control of an integral technology carries with it the power to control the market for supplementary inventions and to control and take possession of patented advances in that technology since such advances, to be commercially viable, must in part incorporate and proceed from the base of the existing technology. In 1958 the courts required that General Electric license all its existing patents royalty free (surrendering its monopoly claims entirely), and make its future patents universally available at a reasonable royalty.[32] In this instance the control over a technology during one time period can be, and presumably was, used as leverage to acquire control over the evolving technology during future time periods — and that leverage was ruled illicit. Consent decrees requiring royalty-free licensing, and often requiring also the provisions of supplementary "know how," have been entered into by Standard Oil of New Jersey, Aluminum Company of America, Merck and Co., A. B. Dick, Libby-Owens-Ford, Owens-Corning Fiberglas, Eastman Kodak, American Can Co., Western Electric, IBM, and RCA.

The illicit leverage need not have a patent monopoly as its fulcrum. The base for the exercise of leverage may simply be dominance in one market which can be extended to advantages in another whether or not the holding of patents is involved. Thus, in the *Times-Picayune* case the Court ruled that tying contracts are illegal per se whenever sellers have a monopoly in the tying product and when the tied product affects a substantial volume of trade.[33] The case itself showed

[31]*U.S.* v. *National Lead Co.*, 332 U.S. 319 (1947).
[32]*U.S.* v. *General Electric Co.*, 115 F. Supp. 835 (1953).
[33]*Times-Picayune Publishing Co.* v. *U.S.*, 345 U.S. 594 (1953).

that the rule could be a paper tiger. There were two afternoon papers and one morning paper in New Orleans. The morning newspaper, the *Times-Picayune*, was dominant, with about half the city's total circulation and 40 percent of the total advertising. The publisher of the *Times-Picayune* also owned *The States*, an afternoon newspaper which competed with the other afternoon paper, *The Item*. The publisher of the two newspapers instituted a "unit plan" under which no advertiser could buy space in one (e.g., the highly valued morning paper, the *Times-Picayune*) without also buying space and inserting the same copy in the less valued paper, *The States*. Thus, the power of the morning newspaper was used as a lever to shift advertisers to *The States* and away from its competitor *The Item*. The practice was condemned by the Federal Trade Commission but was upheld by the Supreme Court. Shortly thereafter, blaming the unit rule *The Item* went out of business and New Orleans, like so many other cities in the United States, became the domain of a single publisher.

In the sale and lease of 40 million acres of land along a right of way initially donated to it by the federal government, the Northern Pacific Railway had followed the practice of requiring purchasers or lessees to agree that they would use its lines for their shipping needs unless competing carriers offered better rates or services.[34] The Court held such "preferential routing agreements" to be illegal. To establish illegality it was now only necessary to show that there was "sufficient economic power to impose an appreciable restraint on free competition in a tied product." The Court restated its classic rationale succinctly. Certain practices "because of their pernicious effects on competition and lack of any redeeming virtues are conclusively presumed to be unreasonable." It is when there are pernicious effects on competition but, at the same time, when there are also "redeeming virtues" that the law becomes equivocal.

Closely related as a technique of market leverage to the tying contract is the use of exclusive dealing arrangements. The essence of a tying contract is that if the buyer wants *A* produced by Firm *Y*, he must also take *B* from Firm *Y*, which is competitive with *C* produced by Firm *Z* and with *D* produced by Firm *F*. With an exclusive dealing arrangement, if a dealer wants to sell *A* produced by Firm *Y*, that dealer may be obliged to offer for

---

[34]*Northern Pacific Railway Co. v. U.S.*, 356 U.S. 1 (1958).

sale *B* produced by Firm *Y*, and may not be allowed to sell any competitive products *C, D, E, F, . . . N.* Hence, exclusive dealerships constrain competition and, depending upon the breadth of such arrangements, the constraint can be substantial. On the other hand, along with the pernicious effect on competition, there may be "redeeming virtues." The exclusive dealer arrangements may be intended and necessary for the organization of a rational, reliable system of marketing and sales promotion. Inasmuch as this is so, to eliminate such arrangements would regress organization and reduce productivity and/or the seller would be pressed into alternative arrangements, such as the outright ownership of his retail outlets. This would bring about an even greater constraint on competition than that of exclusive dealerships.

In the years before the turning the Court permitted a limited attack on exclusive dealing arrangements. In the *Standard Fashions, Butterick, Q.R.S. Music,* and *Eastman Kodak* cases described earlier in Chapter 5, arrangements were forbidden where the seller was clearly dominant in his market and where his exclusive demands on dealers were not part of an integrated marketing organization. In the postwar period, in the spirit of its pronouncement in the *International Salt* case that ". . . it is unreasonable per se to foreclose competitors from any substantial market," the Court opened wide the doors for a massive attack on exclusive dealing by the agencies of antitrust enforcement.[35]

In 1940 the Carter Carburetor Company was enjoined from giving discounts to those dealers who dealt exclusively in its products.[36] In 1941 an association of 176 dress manufacturers, considered as "design originators," were enjoined from a contract with 12,000 retailers that would have forbidden the latter from buying design imitators; i.e., from the "style pirates" who copy designs without paying the costs or running the risks involved in originating them.[37]

In the 1947 *Standard Oil of California* case a major west coast refiner producing some 23 percent of the gasoline sold in seven western states had exclusive contracts with 6,000 dealers covering petroleum products and, in some cases, tires, tubes, batteries, and other auto accessories.[38] The Federal Trade Commission

[35]*International Salt Co.* v. *U.S.,* 332 U.S. 392, 396 (1947).
[36]*Carter Carburetor* v. *FTC,* 112 F. 2d 722 (1940).
[37]*Fashion Originator's Guild of America, Inc.* v. *FTC,* 312 U.S. 457 (1941).
[38]*Standard Oil of California* v. *U.S.,* 337 U.S. 293 (1949).

enjoined the arrangements between the oil company and its dealers, and the Supreme Court upheld the decision. Justice Frankfurter's reasoning was straightforward. Competitors were excluded from a substantial number of outlets. That sufficed. Justices Jackson, Warren, Burton, and Douglas thought otherwise. In his dissent Justice Jackson argued:

> I cannot agree that the requirements contract is per se an illegal one under the antitrust law, and that is the substance of what the Court seems to hold. I am not convinced that the requirements contract as here used is a device for suppressing competition instead of a device for waging competition. . . . Many contracts have the effect of taking a purchaser out of the market for goods he has bought or contracted to take. But the retailer in this industry is only a conduit from the oil fields to the driver's tank, a means by which the oil companies compete to get the business of the ultimate consumer — the man in whose automobile the gas is used. It means to me, if I must decide without evidence, that these contracts are an almost necessary means to maintain this all-important competition for consumer business, in which it is admitted competition is keen.
>
> It does not seem to me inherently to lessen this real competition when an oil company tries to establish superior service by providing the consumer with a responsible dealer from which the public can purchase adequate and timely supplies of oil, gasoline, and car accessories of some known and reliable standard of quality. . . . The Government can hardly force someone to contract to stand by, ever ready to fill fluctuating demands of dealers who will not in turn undertake to buy from that supplier all their requirements. And it is important to the driving public to be able to rely on retailers to have gas to sell. It is equally important that the wholesaler have some incentive to carry stocks and have the transport facilities to make the irregular deliveries caused by varied consumer demands.
>
> It may be that the Government . . . could prove that this is a bad system. . . . But on the present record the Government has not made a case.

Said Justice Douglas in his dissent:

> The elimination of these requirements contracts sets the stage . . . to build service-station empires. . . . The opinion of the

Court . . . is an advisory opinion as well, stating to the oil companies how they can with impunity build their empires. The formula suggested by the Court is either the use of the "agency" device, which in practical effect means control of filling stations by the oil companies . . . or the outright acquisition of them. . . .

When the choice is thus given, I dissent from the outlawry of the requirements contract on the present facts. The effect which it has on competition . . . is minor compared to the damage which will flow. . . . The small independent business man will be supplanted by clerks. Competition between suppliers of accessories . . . will diminish or cease altogether.

In fact, disaster did not follow the Commission's attack; neither did any change in the nature of competition. The company retained control of its pumps and tanks; the dealers needed and valued their affiliation with the company. The judicial thunder, ominous as it seemed, rolled over the landscape of organization and operation and left it as before.[39]

Again, in the *Richfield Oil Corporation* case exclusive dealerships were declared unlawful on a showing of "substantiality."[40] In this instance Richfield did only 3 percent of the gasoline business in the area.

Evidently the Court in its permissiveness had given the agencies of antitrust enforcement full discretion to attack exclusive dealing as they chose to. With power comes responsibility — and blame. The Commission was raked over by its peers.[41] Under this pressure the Commission undertook a study of the economic effects of exclusive requirements contracts, and in due course evolved its own rules of reason, upholding exclusive dealing requirements or condemning them by reference to their economic effects.[42] When faced with private suits rather

---

[39]Simon N. Whitney, *Antitrust Policies, Vol. II* (New York: The Twentieth Century Fund, 1958), pp. 126–128.

[40]*U.S. v. Richfield Oil Corp.*, 99 F. Supp. 280 (1951); sustained per curiam, 343 U.S. 922 (1952).

[41]For example, *Report of the Attorney General's National Committee to Study the Antitrust Laws* (Washington: Government Printing Office, 1950), pp. 242–47; Kintner, "The Revitalized Federal Trade Commission," 30 *N.Y.U. Law Review*, 1143 (1955); Lockhart and Sachs, "The Relevance of Economic Factors in Determining Whether Exclusive Arrangements Violate Section 3 of the Clayton Act." 65 *Harvard Law Review*, 913 (1952); Schwartz, "Potential Impairment of Competition — the Impact of *Standard Oil Company v. United States* on the Standard of Legality under the Clayton Act," 98 *U. Penna. Law Review*, 10 (1949).

[42]See *Carvel Corp.*, FTC Docket 8574, July 19, 1965.

than with the exercise of public authority, the Court would not allow any per se rule against exclusive dealing.[43]

In 1965 the Supreme Court upheld the Federal Trade Commission in the case of *Atlantic Refining Company* v. *Federal Trade Commission,* where a combination of dealer control and a tying relationship was at issue.[44] In this instance the Federal Trade Commission had examined an arrangement between the Atlantic Refining Company and the Goodyear Rubber Company, both giants in their industries wherein Atlantic sponsored the sale of Goodyear products through its independent wholesale and retail dealers. For this Atlantic received a commission on the sale of all Goodyear products through Atlantic's distributors. Taking into account the overt and covert pressure exerted on Atlantic's dealers and wholesalers, and considering the considerable elinimation of sales outlets for competitors as a consequence thereof, the Commission enjoined the arrangement. Goodyear was forbidden from entering into any like sales-commission plan with other companies having the capacity to control or influence their independent distributors.

The case is of peculiar interest because, in speaking for the Court, Justice Clark spells out two points of general importance that have been emphasized throughout this chapter. First, that underlying the complexities of the law in relation to a wide variety of business practices and arrangements is the effort to forestall the use of leverage from strength in one market to gain advantage in another. Thus

> . . . the Commission considered the coercive practices to be symptomatic of a more fundamental restraint of trade and found the sales-commission plan illegal in itself as "a classic example of the use of economic power in one market . . . to destroy competition in another market. . . ."
>
> . . . notwithstanding Atlantic's contention that it and its dealers are mutually dependent upon each other, they simply do not bargain as equals. Among the sources of leverage in Atlantic's hands are its lease and equipment loan contracts with their cancellation and short-term provisions . . . Atlantic controlled the supply of gasoline and oil to its wholesalers and dealers. This was an additional source of economic leverage . . . as was its extensive control of all advertising in

---

[43]*Tampa Electric Co.* v. *Nashville Coal Co.,* 365 U.S. 320 (1961).
[44]*Atlantic Refining Co.* v. *FTC,* 381 U.S. 357 (1965).

the premises of its dealers. . . . Furthermore, there was abundant evidence that Atlantic not only exerted the persuasion that is a natural incident of its economic power, but coupled it with direct and overt threats of reprisal. . . . Indeed the Commission could properly have concluded that it was for this bundle of persuasion that Goodyear paid Atlantic its commission. . . .

We recognize that the Goodyear-Atlantic contract is not a tying arrangement . . . nor does [Atlantic] expressly require such purchases of its dealers. But neither do we understand that either the Commission or the Court of Appeals held that the sales-commission arrangement was a tying scheme. What they did find was that the central competitive characteristic was the same in both cases — the utilization of economic power in one market to curtail competition in another.

Secondly, Justice Clark spells out the Court's conception of the role of agencies of antitrust enforcement. Under the new dispensation these agencies were to exercise the discretionary authority, basing their judgment on an independent study and evaluation of the impact of the behavior and arrangements at issue, on equity, and on economic performance. Respecting these judgments, the Court was to satisfy itself only that the agency's decision "has warrant in the record and a reasonable basis in the law."

The Congress intentionally left the development of the term "unfair" to the Commission rather than attempting to define the "many and variable practices which prevail in commerce." . . . As the House Report stated, "Unfair competition could best be prevented through the action of an administrative body of practical men. . . who will be able to apply the rule enacted by Congress to particular business situations, so as to eradicate evil with the least risk of interfering with legitimate business operations." . . . In thus divining that there is no limit to business ingenuity and legal gymnastics the Congress displayed much foresight. . . . Where the Congress has provided that an administrative agency initially apply a broad statutory term to a particular situation, our function is limited to determining whether the Commission's decision has warrant in the record and a reasonable basis in law.

. . . the Commission . . . expressly rejected a mechanical application of the law. . . . Rather it looked to the entire record as a basis for its conclusion that the activity . . . impaired competition. . . .

Vertical Integration as Market Leverage

The most savage and telling attack by the agencies of antitrust enforcement, on what was considered to be a prejudicial use of market leverage, was against the vertical integration of film-makers and exhibitors in the booking and showing of motion pictures. The fulcrum of power was conceived to be the production and ownership of motion picture films. The victimized competitors were conceived to be the independent exhibitors; i.e., the private movie house owners. Complaints were made that exhibitors were obliged to book films in blocks, taking the good with the bad, and hence, being denied freedom of choice. It was thought that if block booking was eliminated, the consequent freedom of choice would open new outlets to independent film producers. There were also complaints as to the time interval between first-, second-, and third-run showings and other conditions imposed on exhibitors by the movie makers. It was supposed that these worked to the particular disadvantage of independents as compared to the first-run houses that were largely owned by companies that also produced films.

In a series of cases the Department of Justice attacked the industry and forced it to accept the complete divorcement of theatre ownership from the production and distribution of films, shattering vertical integration in the industry and forbidding the institutionalized procedures for block booking or for control by film producers of the practices of movie exhibitors.[45]

> The principal prohibitions were the following: (1) tying the sale of one picture with that of another; (2) stipulating admission prices; (3) establishing any fixed system of clearances, and unreasonably long clearances, or any clearances at all between theatres not in substantial competition; and (4) granting to circuits any franchise agreements, formula deals, master agreements or other privileges — in short any contract at all except theatre by theatre and picture by picture.[46]

It was a great victory. Alas, there remains some question as to whether the government's action had not incidently

---

[45]*U.S.* v. *Paramount Pictures Inc.*, 334 U.S. 131 (1948); *Schine Theatres Chain* v. *U.S.*, 334 U.S. 110 (1948); *U.S.* v. *Griffith Amusement Co.*, 68 F. Supp. 180 (D. Okla. 1946), 334 U.S. 100 (1948); *Loew's Inc.* v. *U.S.*, 339 U.S. 974 (1950); *Interstate Circuit Co.* v. *U.S..*, 306 U.S. 208 (1939).
[46]Whitney, *op. cit.*, p. 160.

destroyed a quite efficient, even irreplaceable, system for planning and organizing the distribution of film outputs, to the detriment of consumers, producers, and ultimately the exhibitors on whose behalf the battle had been fought.

Simon Whitney, surveying the aftermath of the decrees, found that most of the independent exhibitors wanted a return to block booking.[47] Among independents with an opinion on the matter, most regretted the decision in the key Paramount Pictures case. Suffering from a film shortage and higher film rentals, from 1953 onward the exhibitors worked through their two principle trade associations in an effort to recreate something like the old system. They sought to reverse the principal of separating production and exhibition that the government's antitrust prosecutor had established, supposedly in their interest. They sought to integrate backwards, returning to the "blind buying" of the block-booking days so that they might secure an assured supply of pictures geared to their needs. Evidently the film producers, no longer responsible for, interested in, or concerned about the booking and billing requirements of movie houses, and no longer able legally to contract with exhibitors for a continuous output of films, chose to cut down on the number of films they produced and to concentrate on sure-fire "spectaculars" that they released at high rentals. This for a while at least proved to be good business for them, and was perhaps a rational response to the competition of television. But for the exhibitors the solution was not a happy one. Film rentals increased sharply, from 27.7 percent of total receipts in 1948 to 33.6 percent in 1955. The number of feature films released dropped sharply, from 406 in 1948 to 283 in 1955. The proportion of pictures produced by smaller companies declined from more than 40 percent of the total in 1948 to less than 13 percent in 1955. Theatre attendance dropped from 59 percent of the population in 1946 to 27 percent in 1955. Exhibitor profits fell from an estimated $325 million in 1946 to a deficit estimated at $12 million in 1955. Increased costs of distribution, higher film rental costs, and pressure by exhibitors to get into earlier-run, higher-price categories caused a sharp increase in admission prices; from 1947–49 to 1956 the BLS indices show a 23.6 point rise in the movie admission prices as compared to a 14.7 point rise in consumer prices generally. To

---

[47]Quotations and data which follow are from Whitney, *ibid.*, pp. 163–195.

judge by trends in those regions where television was slow in coming, television might have accounted for 50 percent of the actual decline in attendance. Subsequently, film producers were more inclined to sell their film libraries to television, to the detriment of exhibitors, than they would have been if they had continued to have a stake in the exhibitor function.

Given the impact of television, it is, of course, difficult to isolate the effects of the antitrust decrees on the decline of the industry. But this much seems clear. The antitrust attack was a random blow that found its justification in ideology and was delivered in complete disregard of technology and organization. Looking at the record of subsequent economic performance, a prayer might be offered that we be spared the fruits of such "great victories."

CONTINUITIES AND CONSEQUENCES

In those areas where the Court permitted rigorous antitrust enforcement during the epoch of liberalism, the range of antitrust enforcement has been steadily, even radically, extended during subsequent postwar decades. Policy has evolved at the discretion of the agencies of enforcement, with the Court shaping the law in accomodation to those policies. Unfortunately, the analytic and conceptual base that underlies the policies of the antitrust agencies has not developed as the scope of their power has increased and the range of their enforcement has been extended. Too often simplistic notions of pure competition, incongruous in the economy of large organizations, have been applied blindly, with no ex post or ex ante attempt to take account of effects on economic performance. The problem of differentiating between those practices and arrangements that can or cannot be forbidden without detrimental effect upon performance has been shifted from the Court to the agencies of enforcement—but a problem it remains. Its solution is particularly difficult and critical in respect to the injunction against the application of cross-market leverage where position and strength in one market is used to exercise control or to gain advantage in another, inasmuch as cross-market relationships also have a functional rationale and to destroy them may imperil performance.

Chapter 11

The Persisting Spectre
of Monopoly

Under the ideology of laissez-faire liberalism the Supreme Court was not unsympathetic to the attack on private monopoly. But in its concern for the integrity of business operations and its fear that to disrupt them might have a pernicious effect upon the economy, the monopoly power itself as a function of size and the magnitude of market control was excluded from prosecution under the antitrust laws. Only the coercive use of the monopoly power was open to antitrust action. But now, after the turning of the 1940's, the Court took a different position, reflecting a basic change in what it accepted as the role of the political authority vis-à-vis the market system.

THE ALCOA CASE

In 1937 the Aluminum Company of America was indicted as a monopoly and hence was illegal under the Sherman Act. When the case finally reached the Supreme Court, after years in the lower courts, so many of the justices disqualified themselves on grounds of prior involvement that there was not the required quorum of six to consider the case.[1] Under Congressional order the case was remanded to the Second United States Circuit Court where Justice Learned Hand's 1945 decision had the effect of a Supreme Court ruling.[2] This case represented

---

[1]*U.S. v. Aluminum Company of America*, 44 F. Supp. 97 (1941).
[2]*U.S. v. Aluminum Company of America*, 148 F. 2d 416 (1945).

the first high court ruling on the issue of monopoly after the decisive turning of the 1940's.

Justice Hand had considerable difficulties with the definition and measurement of monopoly. But after having defined and measured it to his satisfaction, he accepted the Justice Department's allegation that the Aluminum Company of America did indeed have monopoly power and that it did not matter how that power had been used; the monopoly power was forbidden per se. The monopoly power itself, rather than its use or abuse, was thereby opened to antitrust attack. Justice Hand held also that it was not only market power, but also the form of social relationships that was at issue. The Sherman Act had come down in favor of "a system of small producers, each dependent for his success upon his own skill and character." Thus, Hand echoed Brandeis' "curse of bigness." Yet, surely this argument was strangely archaic in the circumstances of the Alcoa case. Bigness indeed is not the same as monopoly. A relatively small company could possess monopoly power, depending upon the scope of the effective market for its product, while enormous corporations are not necessarily monopolies as Hand understood the term. But who could imagine that Alcoa would ever be so fragmented as to create a "system of small producers" — proprietorships where each man owned and ran his little business and where each firm was the reflex of the skill and character of a single entrepreneur? Certainly not Justice Hand.

There was another preplexing question in this case. If Alcoa was indeed a monopoly, had it sought to "monopolize" or had monopoly been "thrust upon it"? It seemed evident to Justice Hand that a monopoly is permissible, that it must be regarded if not as good then at least as necessary and inescapable when the monopolist achieves his position "without having intended either to put an end to existing competition or to prevent competition from arising when none had existed; they may become monopolists by force of accident . . . (or) merely by virtue of . . . superior skill, foresight, and industry. . . . The successful competitor, having been urged to compete, must not be turned upon when he wins. . . ."

Taking this as the criterion, did Alcoa attempt to monopolize? Of course it did, answered Learned Hand. How so? Simply by being so efficient and selling at so low a price and by anticipating demand so that it was always ready to supply what was wanted at prices that tempted no newcomers to enter the industry. In other words, Alcoa monopolized by acting exactly like the ideal competitor. "We can think of no more effective exclusion," said Hand, "than progressively to embrace each new opportunity as it opened and to face each newcomer with new capacity already geared into a great organization having the advantages of experience, trade connections, and the elite of personnel."

It was thus decided that monopoly is a form of power; and that Alcoa, having maintained possession of that power by its own deliberate design, was an illegal monopoly. What then was to be done to destroy this illegal power, called monopoly, possessed by the Aluminum Company of America?

The action against Alcoa had been started in 1937. Since then new aluminum capacity had been built by the government in response to wartime needs. That capacity had been operated under contract with independent companies. Now, presumably, the Surplus Property Administration would sell that capacity to those independents. This it did. Kaiser and Reynolds Aluminum companies came into being in competition with Alcoa. In addition, the Court forced the separation of the American and Canadian branches of the Aluminum Company of America. Both the Court and the Department of Justice were satisfied, though economic theorists would hardly consider that the transition from one producer of primary aluminum to three (or four, taking Aluminum, Ltd. in Canada into account) created a competitive market. Alcoa was warned by the Court not to compete so hard as to threaten its two new competitors. The Department of Justice was given the right to petition for further relief if the new competition proved to be "feeble and ineffective."

Under government sponsorship and subsidy Alcoa's competitors expanded rapidly in size; and subsequently, three other companies, Anaconda, Harvey, and Ormet, entered the market so that from 1949 to 1958 Alcoa's share of primary aluminum capacity was further reduced from 51% to 38% of the total. This transformation of the industrial structure from a monopoly to an oligopoly was achieved at very substantial real costs to the American public in the form of a massive and otherwise unnecessary subsidy. Thus, Reynolds built its initial reduction plants under a politically sponsored RFC "loan" of $52,000,000. Reynolds then purchased an aluminum plant built by the government during the war at a cost of $174,000,000, with current reproduction costs higher still, for a cash payment of $3,000,000 plus a long-term "note" to the government of $55,000,000. Kaiser purchased a government plant built at a cost of $127,000,000, with higher current reproduction costs, for $3,500,000 in cash plus a long-term "note" to the government for $43,500,000. During the postwar period of severe aluminum shortage, the government aluminum stockpile was released through Kaiser and Reynolds, to be sold by them at a profit. After 1948 only Alcoa undertook an independent expansion of capacity with the Korean War mobilization. From 1950 to 1955 an 84.2% increase in Reynolds' capacity and a 140.1% increase in Kaiser's constituted sheer "giveaway," with accelerated depreciation allowing the cost of the new plants to be written off in the prices charged for an assured government procurement. It was indeed the "businessman's version of a welfare state."[3]

Not only were there heavy social costs related to the transformation of the industrial structure, but all these vast expenditures were to benefit two families, Kaiser and Reynolds, who acquired incredible wealth and industrial empires over which they presided with their relatives installed in positions of power, able to skim the cream for their private advantage. And this happened at the very time when Alcoa, qua autonomous organization, was passing from the monarchical stage of corporate government to one of self-perpetuating technocracy that selected its leadership through promotions up from the ranks. These costs and social distortions might be justified if they resulted in better performance. But did they?

The New View

In respect to antitrust action the Court was more *permissive* than before. It opened the door to extensive prosecution and stern enforcement by the agency of the political authority. The gates were down. But Joshua had seemed fiercer when blowing his trumpet from the outside than he did now that the walls had tumbled.

In the Aluminum Company case the Justice Department had won its victory and established the principle that the possession

---

[3]Merton J. Peck, *Competition in the Aluminum Industry 1945–1958* (Cambridge: Harvard University Press, 1961), p. 219.

of monopoly power was illegal per se. It pressed for no radical reconstruction of industry because, inadvertently, basic changes in the structure of industry had already occurred of precisely the sort the Justice Department was seeking. Instead of one there were now three, and later six, substantial producers of aluminum ingot serving the American market. Here, then, the value of antitrust prosecution could be tested, although the cards were stacked in favor of the antitrusters in this instance because monopoly was transcended without the necessity of disrupting the technology and organization of the monopolist. One would have hoped that the Department of Justice would have taken the occasion to analyze the effects of thus restructuring an industry. Alas, there is no evidence that such a test was ever undertaken or contemplated, or that the Department of Justice ever considered itself as operating under theories that are properly subject to examination. It behooves us then to consider, if only superficially, the effect of the transition from monopoly to oligopoly on the economic performance in the industry.

1. The movements of aluminum ingot prices and the wholesale price index from 1895 to 1968 are shown in Figure 11-1. Until World War I aluminum prices declined very sharply while wholesale prices generally rose. After World War I the price of aluminum continued its sharp and steady decline until the outbreak of World War II in 1941. Only after the "end of monopoly" in 1948 did aluminum prices rise, continuing upward until 1958 when they stabilized and declined slightly.

   The price trends are shown in Figure 11-1 as M-M' during the period of monopoly, and as 0L-0L' during the period of oligopoly. Once oligopoly was installed the sharp reversal from the downward price trend of the monopoly period is unmistakable. It is also significant that the price rise for aluminum since the "end of monopoly" has been much more rapid than that of the index of wholesale prices. During the period when the wholesale price index went from 100 to a high of 124, a price index constructed for aluminum on the same basis would have gone up from 100 to a high of 173.

2. The changes in the production of primary aluminum and in the domestic consumption of aluminum from 1895 to 1968 are shown in Figure 11-2, along with an index of industrial production. The production and consumption of aluminum

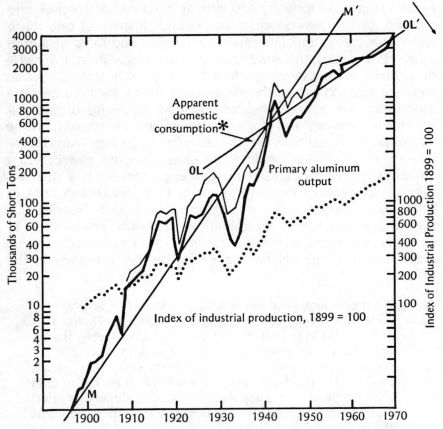

*Apparent domestic consumption is output plus scrap recovery plus imports minus exports. 1959 production and consumption estimates.

Figure 11-1

Aluminum Price Trends and Wholesale Price Index, 1895–1968

follows the general contours of the index of industrial production, except that during the period of monopoly the rate of increase was much more rapid than during the period of oligopoly. In the latter phase the rate of increase tends to approximate the rate of increase of industrial production. This decline in the rate at which output increases took place in spite of a massive government subsidization of plant expansion between 1950–55. The output-consumption trend during the period of monopoly is shown as M-M', and during the period of oligopoly as 0L-0L'.

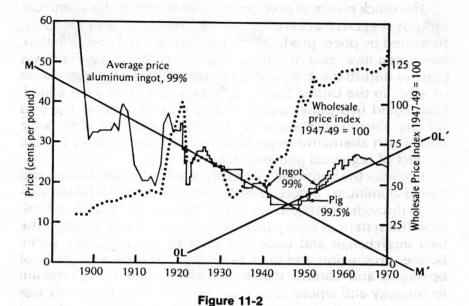

Figure 11-2

Aluminum Production and Consumption, 1895–1968

3. The major advances in technology were made during the period of monopoly. The phase that followed was characterized by product adaptations. What of productivity? Data on mill costs suggest a sharp regression in the rate of productivity increase after the transition from monopoly to oligopoly. Sample data from Alcoa show that mill costs were reduced by a third between 1926–37, and increased by half between 1947–56.[4]

---

[4]Justice Department Exhibit 718 in *U.S.* v. *Alcoa,* quoted in Leonard Weiss, *Economics and American Industry* (New York: John Wiley & Sons, 1961), p. 220; and N. H. Engle, E. E. Gregory, and R. Mosse, *Aluminum and Industrial Marketing Appraisal* (Chicago: Richard D. Irwin, Inc., 1944).

According to Peck, *op. cit.,* there were "more major inventions to enliven the record" during the monopoly period than during the oligopolistic phase that followed. However, he found that "A historical comparison between the prewar and postwar period indicates that inventions have occurred at a higher rate [presumably rate per annum] in the postwar oligopolistic era." (p. 210) This would hardly be surprising since the size of the industry has increased eightfold. Was there then an eightfold increase in the annual number of inventions? In fact, we aren't given a clue as to the absolute or relative change in the numbers of inventions except that at "the reduction stage [the primary stage in the production of aluminum] the changes in the market structure made no observable difference in the rate and nature of invention," (p. 201) which suggests a sharp reduction in the inventions made as a ratio of industrial activity. Moreover, Peck's invention count is (*sic*) based on the numbers of publicity releases to the two trade journals and, hence, tells us nothing at all about the contribution to technological advance. No effort is made to measure productivity as an index of technological advance.

This quick glance at economic performance in the aluminum industry suggests that the effects of the breakup of the monopoly, measured by price, productivity, production, and consumption, have been invariably negative. This is surprising. Nothing was done to disturb the organization or technology of the operation of Alcoa in the United States. And two new firms were added. How could two pluses and no minuses, and another big plus for the alleged increase in competition, produce a negative result? An alternative hypothesis is possible that does explain the fact of regressed performance.

Consider the body of activities involved in the production and sale of aluminum. Before, production and sales had been organized through an integral agency of policy making and control. Now the system of policy making and control was through the tacit interchange and uncertain rules of the oligopoly game. Before, production and sales were organized by an agency of operation and control that had itself created the aluminum technology and whose total focus of interest and concern was on aluminum making, and whose path to power, industrial affluence, and corporate prestige had been solely through lowering the costs and increasing the consumption of aluminum. Now, participating in the process of composite choice and control were the two new junior partners, both large conglomerates with only a marginal interest in aluminum. Neither had taken any part in the creation of the aluminum technology; neither was research-based or science-oriented. Management in both was highly skilled in wheeling-dealing and in political in-fighting and, moreover, each had an established "in" with government. They were the protégés of the various agencies of government who had dealt them into the game. And the Court had invited them to invoke the punitive powers of the Department of Justice in case Alcoa should compete too hard. Before, Alcoa had been an unbounded aggressor fighting to establish its place and to expand its power in the universe of industrial metals. It became the dominant firm expected to play the role of mother hen or face the wrath of the law.[5] Subsequently, it was just another of the oligarchs concerned with the preservation of status, order,

---

[5]Peck, *op. cit.*, Chapter 11 supports this hypothesis in observing that Alcoa was the "low-price preference firm," and that Reynolds and Kaiser agitated for a high-price, high-profit margin and a low volume policy even before they were brought into the industry, and that they continued to press for continually higher prices during the years that followed.

and balance, so that none would be pressed, all would be content, and each would get his share. Is it surprising that under these circumstances the industry lost its élan and performance regressed?

It would seem appropriate at this point to mention another fallacy—or naiveté at least—that underlies the antitrust outlook. It is expressed in Simon Whitney's precept that "it is simple logic that progress should be faster when there is competition"[6] or Carl Kaysen's principal that "several independent centers of effort produce a greater variety of ideas."[7]

The fallacy dervies from equating the firm to a thinking, inventing, experiencing individual; hence, the supposition that more firms, meaning more individuals, do more independent thinking and therefore must produce more inventions and innovations. But the firm, in the sense of the modern corporation, is not synonomous with an individual; and fragmentation of a firm does not increase the number of thinking, experiencing, inventing individuals, or even the number of integral operations that constitute the industry. It is simply that after fragmentation the activities of the same number of individuals are organized differently. Adding Reynolds and Kaiser to the aluminum industry did not mean ipso facto that more individuals would be engaged in the production and sale of aluminum or that more scientists and engineers would be engaged in aluminum-focused research. On the contrary, inferring from the rate at which production and consumption increased during the monopoly as compared to the oligopoly phase, there might well have been more individuals engaged in the production and sale of aluminum and aluminum-related research and development if Reynolds and Kaiser had not been brought into the industry. The certain difference was that before, workers, managers, salesmen, engineers, and researchers were all engaged in an integral system of policy making and control; whereas, later, they were split among three such systems. Given such a change, we might ask these questions: (1) Would the competition and interaction of a given number of individual scientists and research engineers be more fruitful if they worked under a single roof or if they were set apart from each other, separated by geographical space and isolated within walls of proprietary

---

[6]Whitney, op. cit., p. 142.
[7]Carl Kaysen, United States v. United Shoe Machinery Corporation: An Economic Analysis of an Antitrust Case (Cambridge: Harvard University Press, 1956), p. 196.

secrecy so that each group was denied access to the information produced by the others? (2) Would the scientists and scholars at, say, Harvard be more productive if Harvard were divested and divorced, fragmented into a few or a few hundred separate colleges and junior colleges scattered over the land with no communication allowed among them? (3) Would the aggregate investment in R&D be greater when the investment maker was able to realize on the benefits to a whole industry of an innovation, or when investment in the R&D function was divided among several agencies none of which was able to realize upon all the potential benefits to the industry of any invention and innovation forthcoming? To answer these questions is to say why no simple inference can be made that "several independent centers of effort produce a greater variety of ideas."

In the following paragraphs some representative cases will be examined in an effort to understand and evaluate the nature of an emerging antimonopoly policy.

THE SHOE MACHINERY CASE

In 1947 the Department of Justice launched a full-scale antitrust attack against the United Shoe Machinery Company for "monopoly" and "monopolizing." The case was decided in the district court in 1953 and sustained by the Supreme Court in 1954.[8] The company was the lineal descendent of the old Shoe Machinery Trust. Between the time of its incipiency in 1915 and 1953 the company's share of the shoe machinery market had "somewhat declined" but in 1953 it was still "supplying over 75% and probably 85% of the current demand in the American shoe machinery market." It had only one important competitor.

Initially the power of the trust had been based on an unassailable patent position. "At the turn of the century United's patents covered the fundamentals of shoe machinery manufacture. Those fundamental patents have expired." It was possible now to "invent around" United's aggregation of patent holdings which included for the most part "only minor developments." United remained the only company in the industry with a broad R&D organization whose efforts covered all

---

[8]U.S. v. United Shoe Machinery Company, 110 F. Supp. 295 (1953); and United Shoe Machinery Company v. U.S., 347 U.S. 521 (1954).

aspects of shoe machinery manufacture. United did not sell but leased its machinery. Service and repairs were covered by the lease. Allegedly, lease prices were low on those items of machinery where competition threatened and were higher where competition was not a consideration. All this was in the tradition of the trade. No coercion of competitors was claimed, nor was any "immoral intent" adduced. The Court accepted the Justice Department's allegation that the company possessed monopoly power, and that it had monopolized. "United is denied the right to exercise effective control of the market (when such control is) . . . not the inevitable consequences of its capacities or natural advantages." What was to be done?

The Department of Justice asked that the company be broken up into "three separate manufacturing companies." This demand was denied by the court as "unrealistic." United was an integral technical operation. "It takes," said Justice Wyzanski, "no wisdom of Solomon to see that this organism cannot be cut into three equal and viable parts." The judge noted particularly that the attorney general had not committed himself to any consistent plan for the proposed means of dissolution other than those made by his assistants in "divergent proposals . . . in briefs and oral arguments." By way of relief the court required that United sell as well as lease its machinery under the supposition that a market in secondhand machinery would develop and this would "gradually weaken the prohibited market power." It required that the terms of leases be shortened and that repair and servicing be divorced from the leasing contract. It required that United grant licenses on its patents at "reasonable" royalties. The Court also required that United dispose of its facilities for making tacks, nails, and eyelets, which accounted for 80 to 90 percent of the national production of these items and for 11 percent of United's gross revenue.

Another "victory!" This time it had been established that even a monopoly "thrust upon" a company was illegal. For in this instance no wrongdoing, abuse, deliberated exclusion, or design to forestall competition and seize and hold the monopoly power was found. This was the new neo-Calvinist doctrine. Cleared of evil intent and abuse, except for the original sin of possessing the power itself, the company was found to be without the grace of competition; hence, it was doomed. Innocent of wrongdoing or not, its defenses had been torn down and its competitors and customers moved in with triple damage suits to rend its financial flesh.

"United's power does not rest on predatory practices. Probably few monopolies could produce a record so free from any taint of that kind of wrongdoing. The violations depend not on moral . . . but on solely economic considerations," said Judge Wyzanski. "The three principal sources of United's power have been the original constitution of the company, the superiority of United's products and services, and the leasing system. The first two of these are plainly above reproach." As for the leasing system "under the system, entry into shoe manufacture has been easy. The rates charged to all customers have been uniform. The machines supplied have performed excellently. United has, without charge, promptly and efficiently supplied repair service and many kinds of other service." Another reason for its dominance was allegedly its high annual investment in research and its "research organization of efficiency, intelligence, and vision." The antitrust conclusion was obvious. With its irreproachable record of technological progress, high efficiency, and fair dealing, the company must be destroyed as an integral organization and dismembered.

In 1965 the Department of Justice reopened the case and demanded further divorcement and divestiture, claiming that the diminution of the company's share of the market from 85 percent to 65 percent was not sufficient. The district court rejected the Department's demand but the Supreme Court overruled the district court and remanded the case to be reconsidered on the facts. In 1969, under the pressure of the Department of Justice and under the threat of a new barrage of triple damage suits (only in that very year had the last of the original triple damage claims been settled for another $6 million), the company agreed to divest itself of nearly half of its remaining shoemaking equipment business. But in the meantime what had happened to the company and to the industry and to the consumers of its products under the antitrust decree?

By 1968 the United Shoe Machinery Corporation had become the USM Corp., a giant conglomerate with annual sales totaling $350 million of which only $23 million came from the sale of shoe machinery. Divestiture of half of its remaining shoe machinery business would represent less than 3% of its current sales.[9] Thus, there was another "victory" in chopping up the once great producer of shoemaking machines. But no one asks the hard questions, the questions that are significant for the real well-being of the people. What effect has the old decree had, and what effect is the new one likely to have on industrial *performance*? Is our society better served by USM Corporation, the giant conglomerate shifting shareholdings and manipulating equities, with fingers in ten dozen pies, or was it better served by the United Shoe Machinery Corporation that had created a key technology and whose whole focus was on the advance and promotion of that technology? What has happened to USM's research and to research in the industry? What has happened to productivity? Here the important effect is not so much what has happened to the shoemaking machine industry itself, but what has happened to productivity and costs of footwear since these are the machines that make the shoes.

All the gross statistical indicators suggest a steady decline in the relative level of industrial performance of the footwear and the shoe machinery industry. Hence, it can be inferred that the heavy blow against the dominant firm, which eventually changed its structure and focal interest, has been detrimental to performance and that antitrust victory has damaged the economy. Consider the fact that the shoe machinery industry itself has declined from annual gross sales well in excess of $100 million before the attack to less than $50 million in 1968–69.[10] The trend of imports of the category, textile and leather machinery, has increased with extraordinary rapidity, rising from $103 million in 1960 to $572 million in 1967, as compared to an increase in general imports from $15 billion to $26.8 billion during the same period. Industrial production of leather products has lagged far behind the general increase in industrial production. Leather products production rose from an index of 91.0 in 1950 to 107.0 in 1968, whereas nondurable manufacturers rose from 76 to 157 and durable manufacturers from 76 to 163 during the same period. While production lagged, prices soared. As compared to the wholesale price index, which rose from 86.8 in 1950 to 106.1 in 1967, the price of footwear rose from 85.7 in 1950 to 122.1 in 1967 (the deviation from the general price trend shows itself after 1955). All this happened in spite of the fact that the price of leather

---

[9]*Business Week* (January 25, 1969), p. 37.
[10]*Ibid.*

remained virtually unchanged. All consumers know about the price inflation and quality depreciation in shoe repair. Output per man hour as a measure of productivity in the private economy as a whole rose from 78.5 in 1950 to 94.7 in 1965 and to 131.5 in 1967. For footwear the increase was only from 84.5 in 1950 to 92.7 in 1955 and to 107.5 in 1965. Of all the 26 industrial categories reported by the Bureau of Labor Statistics, the record of productivity (output per man hour) between 1950 and 1965 for footwear is the worst on the list, equalled only in poor performance by glass containers; from 1955 to 1967 the footwear industry is unmatched in the poverty of performance.[11]

In noting that the production of domestic shoes dropped to a 20-year low in 1971, *Business Week* reported that:

> No American industry more desperately needs to increase its productivity than the labor-intensive shoe industry, which is being engulfed by a flood of low-cost imports. Imports of nonrubber footwear climbed dramatically from just 27-million pairs in 1960 to 260-million last year and now account for one third of total U.S. sales
>
> . . . A recent government survey that compared productivity gains in 27 industries between 1957 and 1970 found footwear dead last, barely gaining at all.

The hope was offered that with the use of injection-molding equipment, footwear might succeed in its "desperate drive for productivity."

> In the 1960's, Compo introduced injection-molding equipment to the U.S. shoe industry. Henry Hardy, a German-born, French-raised entrepreneur who took over as president in 1963, says that Compo still is the leading supplier of this equipment, with 400 machines at work. He estimates that 150-million to 200-million pairs, or as much as 37% of last year's domestic shoe production, were made on injection-molding equipment.
>
> . . . Compo gets its injection-molding equipment from Germany.[12]

---

[11]Data on productivity, price, production, and imports are from the U.S. Bureau of the Census, *Statistical Abstract of the United States, 1968* (Washington: U.S. Government Printing Office, 1968).

[12]"Footwear's Desperate Drive for Productivity," *Business Week* (June 10, 1972), p. 68.

These are the gains from the competition produced by the antitrust victories! May we be spared their beneficence.

THE TOBACCO CASES

The *American Tobacco Company* v. *U.S.* was the culmination of an attack by the Department of Justice on the three largest cigarette manufacturers in the United States; it was begun in 1940 and was finally decided in 1946.[13] The "Big Three" were accused of monopoly and monopolization. The accusation of monopoly was not based on the magnitude of a single seller's share of the market, but rather on the "dominance" of the three companies considered together. It was not claimed that new competition had been excluded. It was not even claimed that there existed an illegal agreement among the three accused companies. Rather the existence of monopoly and monopolization were deduced from patterns of behavior that were not in accord with classical notions of competition, but which reflected the sort of action that might be expected of oligopolists who are conscious of a certain mutuality of interest and who are sensitive to the effects of their own actions on the competitive counteractions of their rivals. What was at issue, in other words, was the commonplace behavior of firms in the big business sector of American industry.

Price movements, for example, did not follow the contours of classical theory. In the face of the disastrous depression of the 30's, with demand for cigarettes rapidly shrinking, the prices of the regular brand-name cigarettes remained fixed and inflexible. Then in 1932, following the price leader, the three largest cigarette companies raised the prices of their brand-name cigarettes. As a result the three companies made large profits, but as a consequence of their actions they opened the way for the entry of a host of cheap brands (10¢ a pack), whose share of the market shot up from two percent to 22 percent. The large companies responded not only by cutting the prices of their own established brands below cost, but also by buying up stocks of low-grade tobacco supposedly in order to force up the costs of the producers of the ten-cent brands. In buying tobacco for their own use it was customary for each of the "Big Three" to

---

[13]*The American Tobacco Company* v. *U.S.*, 328 U.S. 781 (1946).

send its buyers to the tobacco auctions to be sure that the price paid by its competitors for tobacco was no lower than the price it had itself been obliged to pay. The objective evidently was not to depress prices by oligopsonistic conspiracy but rather to maintain a uniform floor on prices, and hence, a uniform floor on costs.

On this basis a lower court agreed to the charge of monopoly. The case was appealed and the Supreme Court upheld the lower court's decision. Some inferred from this that parallelism of price behavior established oligopoly and oligopoly equalled monopoly; hence, oligopoly was illegal and must be destroyed.[14] In fact the reasoning of the Court and the prosecution was rather that parallelism established conspiracy and a conspiracy with the power and intent of excluding competitors was equivalent to monopolization. So far as the alleged conspiracy is concerned Simon Whitney holds that of the four buying practices on which Judge Burton based his charge of conspiracy, "Only one . . . was unambiguously proved to exist, and this— location of leaf markets by agreement—was a natural consequence of both the size of the defendants and the desires of the growers."[15]

Another victory. Fines were imposed and the alleged conspiracy was forbidden. The Court had again shown itself pliable, ready to yield to the pressure of the Department of Justice. But now the Justice Department, with prerogatives that had once been exercised alone by the Court, found itself in the dilemma of the Court and it responded as the old Court had done. Behavior was censored, but power remained intact. The structure of the industry did not change as a consequence of the antitrust attack. During 1931 and 1939, cited by the Supreme Court as the period of monopoly and monopolization, the share in cigarette production of the three largest firms declined from 90.5 percent to 68.0 percent. Between 1939 and 1955 their share increased from 68 percent to 74 percent. Nor has price parallelism changed. Demands of the law have no doubt introduced new ritualisms into business behavior. "All agreements

---

[14]Edward H. Levi, "The Antitrust Laws and Monopoly," *University of Chicago Law Review* (February, 1947), pp. 153–183; Eugene V. Rostow, "The New Sherman Act: A Positive Instrument for Progress," *University of Chicago Law Review* (June, 1947), pp. 567–600; William H. Nicholls, *Price Policies in the Cigarette Industry* (Vanderbilt University Press, 1951), pp. 398–399.

[15]Simon Whitney, *op. cit.*, p. 35.

as to the establishment of market towns were abandoned, so that many more auction markets were soon in operation — and consequently warehouse facilities and expert buyers were inefficiently scattered. One company is said to have given its buyers no price instructions one season, with the result that growers complained of erratic price movements until buyers learned from market news services what their associates were paying elsewhere and adjusted their own bids. Another company began to notify the Department of Agriculture of the amount of tobacco it planned to purchase during the year. All defendants ceased attending meetings sponsored by the Department of Agriculture if their competitors were to be present. Salesmen began to avoid each other; joint meetings ceased. Resale prices were never mentioned in conversations of salesmen with dealers and various producers reduced or nearly eliminated direct shipments to retailers. . . ."[16] Aside from such trivia the pattern of behavior remained as before.

THE NEW DISPENSATION

Before the turning of the 1940's the Court had protected the monopoly power of large enterprises from antitrust attack and dissolution unless such power was used to coerce competitiors or to exclude competition. So long as the trusts were well-behaved they were safe. But now the Court accepted monopoly power as illegal per se without regard to its abusive exercise. Moreover, the Court became very flexible and permissive in allowing the Department of Justice to define and to identify the monopoly power. In the *Alcoa* case it chose to identify the market in a manner most favorable to the Department of Justice's case, considering the relevant market for virgin ingots alone and excluding the competition of scrap aluminum. In the *United Shoe Machinery* case the Court ruled the existence of monopoly without establishing the exclusion of competitors. In the *American Tobacco* case monopoly power was considered not to be a function of market share or of established agreement but rather of alleged deviations by the three large companies from the classical pattern of competitive behavior. In these cases it would seem that the Court was not defining and imposing a

[16]*Ibid.*, pp. 39–40.

criterion of monopoly power but rather, in each instance, accommodating its rule to the regulatory objectives and criteria put forward by the Department of Justice. As once the Court had displayed its ingenuity in interpreting the words of the law so as to protect the property power from political authority, now it interpreted the law, case by case, to justify the thrust of public intervention and to open the gates to the political authority.

The Exercise of Authority

Thus, control of the monopoly power was brought within the scope of the political authority. What then was to be done by that authority? Was monopoly to be tamed or destroyed? The rationale of antitrust economics held that monopoly could not be tamed; it had to be destroyed. Monopoly power was not a question of the stratagems of the firm but rather of the capacity to effectuate these stratagems and, hence, the only meaningful attack on monopoly meant a restructuring of industry so that the power to control and influence price itself was eliminated. But although the Department of Justice carried this antitrust ideology as its banner, when it had at last attained the commanding heights, it did not so fragment industry that none could control or influence price; so that competition in the context of autonomous price change guided the movement of all resources. Fortunately so.

Certainly the Department of Justice has demonstrated a power, backed up by the ravages of triple damage suits, to strike heavy blows that could destroy a firm or an industry. Certainly it has introduced new and costly risks and uncertainties into the universe of business choice and calculation. Conceivably, its great authority could have been used to restructure industry and control behavior so as to raise the level of economic performance. Unfortunately, it acted in blind obedience to an obsolete ideology and a false conception of the world. The Department of Justice has *never* attempted to measure the actual and comparative contributions of the firm or industry. It has *never* tried to understand or evaluate the character of economic performance. It has *never* looked back to assess the effects of its actions on performance, thereby to test the worth of its policy and the truth of its theory. On the face of it, it would appear that its "successes" and "victories" in the pursuit of monopoly have invariably damaged the economy.

THE CELLOPHANE CASE

The cellophane case decided by the Supreme Court in 1956 deserves special attention.[17]   Of all the antitrust attacks on monopoly, it is the most interesting. So far as the response of the Court is concerned it represents an exception to, a deviation from, or perhaps a reversal of the rule of permissiveness in respect to action by political authority.

DuPont was prosecuted for its control over the production of cellophane. It controlled 80 percent of the output of this product and Sylvania (later acquired by the American Viscose Corporation) controlled the other 20 percent.   Control was based on the patent holdings by the two companies and cross-licensing agreements between them. The Department of Justice brought action against duPont charging "monopolizing . . . in violation of Section II of the Sherman Act." Relief was sought by injunction "forbidding monopolizing, (and) action to dissipate the effect of monopolization by divestiture and other steps." The question before the Court was whether or not "duPont had monopolized trade in cellophane." The Court ruled that duPont indeed had a monopoly over cellophane but that cellophane was competitive with a variety of other wrapping materials that constitute more or less close substitutes. In terms of the "relevant market" it held that this control over the output of cellophane could not be considered as a monopoly within the meaning of the Sherman Act.

Four justices ruled against the government. Two justices took no part in the consideration of the case. The three dissenting judges followed the prior line of permissiveness in upholding the government's attack. The dissenters argued that cellophane was a distinctive product embodying a unique combination of qualities, and that duPont had a significant degree of latitude in fixing the price of cellophane. Therefore, the substitutes for cellophane were not sufficiently close to preclude considering the cellophane market as an integral

---

[17]*U.S.* v. *E. I. duPont de Nemours and Co.*, 351 U.S. 377 (1956), affirming the judgment of Justice Leahy; *U.S.* v. *E. I. duPont de Nemours and Co.*, 118 F. Supp. 41, 123 (D. Del 1953).

one subject to monopolization. Hence, the three dissenting judges held that the monopoly of cellophane was properly subject to antitrust action under the Sherman Act.

The Emptiness of a Criterion

The cellophane case suggests the bankruptcy of the concept of monopoly power used as a criterion for public control. The attack against duPont carried with it the notion of monopoly as an aberration from a competitive norm, something unnatural, extraordinary, an exception to the rule, or an artificial contrivance set up as a barrier against the progressive force of development and change. But in fact a monopoly such as cellophane is not the aberration but the norm in the organizational sector. It is the usual thing. The world of modern industrial enterprise is a world of monopolies — of outputs that have distinctive qualities, of firms possessing independent power and a significant latitude in their pricing policies — yet undoubtedly interacting competitively together. In the sense that cellophane is a monopoly, Saran Wrap is a monopoly, Scotch Tape is a monopoly, Coca-Cola is a monopoly, Bayer aspirin is a monopoly, and Volkswagen is a monopoly. And far from constituting an artificial contrivance set against the normal forces of change and development, the cellophane monopoly exemplifies the mechanism of change and development in modern capitalism.

If the attack was ideological, premised on the idea that all monopoly power is evil and that wherever it is found it must be rooted out and destroyed, then the antitrust task is impossible short of a full-scale destruction and an entire reconstruction of the American industrial and mercantile economy. The use of brand names or the strategy of product differentiation is not compatible with that ideology.

If the attack was not merely ideological, expressing the conviction that the power to control and influence price is inherently and intrinsically evil, but based on operational considerations — with its objective not to root out the corruption of "monopoly" but rather to improve the level of economic performance — then, surely, in a universe with so many sluggard firms and static industries, duPont made a strange target for attack. By a measure of comparative performance duPont, particularly in the instance of cellophane, has done remarkably well. The original invention of cellophane was not a product of duPont laboratories but through the duPont laboratories and the R&D competence embodied therein, duPont found and evaluated the original invention and gave it its most distinctive feature of being at once moisture-proof and transparent. Through its R&D it developed a series of defensive patents that secured a "monopoly" position for itself. Then, from the security of that position, it launched a major product innovation that set in motion chains of effects and responses throughout the whole economy. This was innovation in the Schumpeterian sense, the dynamism of a capitalist economy. It brought into being what had not been there before. It offered new options and a wider range of choice to industry and the consumer. In so doing it raised the real value of the national product with gains accruing both as consumer values and producer opportunities. It organized what must have been a massive program of promotion and producer and consumer education, and involved itself in the development of a range of new end uses for its product. In consequence the output of cellophane enormously increased and, as a matter of company policy, the price of cellophane was continuously and drastically reduced. Nevertheless, the sale of the new product redounded greatly to the company's benefit resulting, presumably, in higher wages, higher salaries, and most certainly in higher taxes and profits. Consequently, dividends were higher and there was more corporate investment. But is that bad?

DuPont's performance was remarkable, but that is not to say that it could not have been better. Nor is it to say that duPont's experience does not suggest the need for institutional reforms. Perhaps, for example, the patent system gives too much protection and for too long a period of time. That question, which is legitimate and rational, is on a different plane than the attack on monopoly carried on in pursuit of an 18th-century ideal.

THE PERSISTING SPECTRE OF MONOPOLY

The antitrust attacks on monopoly have something of the aspect of a symbolic sacrifice to idols in whom no one really believes any more. Still, though the rationale of belief has faded the symbolism has acquired a value of its own and the ritual has its own inertial force. So the priests proceed as before; the sacrifices are made, the worship continues, and the populace accepts as they accept so much else of the unbelievable. The images of demons remain long after the theology is forgotten and the faith is lost. Many are still haunted by the fearsome spectre of monopoly. The witch hunt is not over. The knives are being sharpened and the stake prepared for the International Business Machines Corporation, which might conceivably be described as the most effective, creative, and progressive business organization in the world. That attack is not being made in the name of or for the benefit of consumers, suppliers, or small independent enterprise. It is being egged on by other large, powerful corporations who have been less successful than IBM, and to whom the antitrust laws offer a means of weakening, muzzling, or striking down their great competitor. There has been no attempt by the Department of Justice to analyze or evaluate IBM's level of economic performance or its economic contribution. In a suit filed by the Justice Department in 1969 against IBM, complaints were made about four practices: (1) a single price policy for equipment, programming, and "related support" (subsequently discontinued by the company); (2) the competitive advantages of IBM's accumulated "softwear and related support;" (3) a claim that the company has introduced low-profit lines and new models when it "knew" that it was not likely that these could be delivered on time; and (4) that IBM has charged low prices (sic) to colleges and universities.[18] On that account the Department of Justice demands "divorcement and divestiture."

Only a society as rich as ours could affort such fantasy and waste.

At this writing the case against IBM is not yet resolved, and whatever is written concerning it will be incomplete by the time this book appears. Nevertheless, it is worth a backward glance from this point in midstream to understand better the character of the attack on monopoly in the modern economy.

Certainly IBM dominates the market for computers, or at least those of average size. Nevertheless, it competes with technically advanced and financially powerful rivals including General Electric, RCA, Honeywell, Sperry Rand Corp., National

---

[18]"IBM Girds for Battle," *Business Week* (January 25, 1969), pp. 36–38.

Cash Register, Burroughs, and Control Data Corporation. It is different from these others in that its total commitment and the whole thrust of its technology has been in the field of data processing and in the development of computers, a field in which IBM was the industrial pioneer.

And unlike the others, IBM has not grown by merger and conglomeration in the wheeling-dealing of stock deals and financial manipulation. Rather, it has grown through internal expansion achieved through technological superiority and competitive force in its chosen market. Competitors felt the bite. Control Data, a conglomerate dominating the production of super-sized computers that had in a single decade from 1958 increased its value of assets 25 fold, blamed IBM's competition for a $1.9 million loss in 1966. "IBM has been out to get us, and you can print that," said William Norris, the president of Control Data.[19]

In 1967, evidently under Control Data pressure, the Department of Jutice undertook another investigation of IBM. (As a result of a prior investigation, IBM had accepted the consent decree of 1956.) In December, 1968, Control Data brought its own antitrust suit against IBM charging "monopoly power" and "price leadership," and demanding dissolution and divestiture. It also asked triple damages from the losses it allegedly suffered through IBM competition, holding that "there had been excess competition which was contrary to the public interest and unfair to Control Data."[20]

Among the IBM practices that Control Data complained of were "prematurely introducing new models," discounts and free technical services offered to customers, the buying back of unused data processing time, "making lease prices more attractive than sales prices, trading on a user's fear of technological obsolescence, discriminating against the competitor that buys replacement parts, and attempting to switch customers to another model after committing itself to a particular model."[21]

A month after Control Data filed suit, another enormous conglomerate, Data Processing Financial and General Corporation,

---

[19]"Control Data Sues IBM for Damages in Antitrust Suit," *Wall Street Journal* (December 12, 1968), p. 2.

[20]"IBM Claims 'Inconsistent, Baseless' Accusations," *Wall Street Journal* (January 13, 1968), p. 2.

[21]*Wall Street Journal, op. cit.* (December 12, 1968).

joined in the attack. It accused IBM of possessing the forbidden monopoly power, and demanded that IBM be excluded from the manufacture of peripheral computer equipment; i.e., that it be eliminated as Data Processing's competitor. It also demanded that IBM be forbidden from offering free services and free information, i.e., "software programs" to IBM clients.[22] And Data Processing asked the courts to award it a billion dollars in damages allegedly suffered as a consequence of IBM's aggressive competition. Not that the survival of Data Processing was at stake or even that its operations had been unprofitable. On the contrary this huge and fast-growing conglomerate had increased its profits in the very year it filed suit from $641,700 to $1.9 million. It simply contended that its profits, large as they were, were not large enough. According to its president it had not been permitted to realize its "full profit potential." Data Processing bought IBM equipment and leased it to others; at the time it filed its suit it was $175 million in debt to IBM.[23]

It was that same month of January, 1969, that the Department of Justice charged IBM with monopoly and monopolizing and asked the courts for "dissolution and divestiture." The specific complaints of the Justice Department were in every instance against the aggressive competition of the company and a pricing policy that "failed to reflect a reasonable profit."[24] In the words of the editorial writer, IBM was "too good for its own good."[25]

In the wake of the Justice Department's suit, Applied Research Data, Inc., also joined in the hunt[26] and in the month

---

[22]The giving away of software programs, i.e., computer programs worked out by IBM at considerable expense and having some general value in business practice, presents an interesting problem. One might wonder why any company would give away something free when that something was costly to produce, unless there was some illicit intent. It should be remembered, however, that no matter how costly it might be to produce information, e.g., a computer program, the marginal costs of distribution and use are zero and hence it is in the social interest that such information be treated as a public good and made freely available. From the point of view of a company such as IBM, in serving a great number of customers no other way could be devised that would at once increase the value-in-use and the desirability and salability of computers in general, and of IBM's computers in particular, than the free and universal dissemination of such computer software. Alas, as will be seen, IBM has been forced under the antitrust bludgeon to stop the free distribution of such information.

[23]"Data Processing Financial Sues IBM: Asks $1 Billion Damages. Demands Split," Wall Street Journal (January 6, 1969), p. 34.

[24]"Justice Department Charges IBM with Monopolizing Computer Field," Wall Street Journal (January 20, 1969), p. 3.

[25]"The Assault on IBM," Wall Street Journal (January 27, 1969), p. 14.

[26]"IBM Hit with 4th Civil Antitrust Suit As Software Firm Alleges Monopoly," Wall Street Journal (April 23, 1969), p. 5.

that followed Programmatics, Inc., a subsidiary of Applied Data, sued IBM on the same grounds.[27]

The five-pronged antitrust attack by the Department of Justice, Control Data, Data Processing, Applied Data and Programmatics, brought the giant to bay. In August, 1970, IBM "settled" out of court with Applied Data and its subsidiary, Programmatics. The settlement was in fact a payoff to its attackers. IBM paid out $1.4 million cash to Applied Data, plus a $600,000 contract for developing an "autoflow" program for IBM.[28] That same month IBM settled with Data Processing Financial out of court, again with a fat payoff to its pursuer. This time IBM refinanced the rich conglomerate's $42 million debt at "highly favorable" interest rates. The settlement, according to the president of Data Processing, would improve their "cash flow over the coming 24 months by $30 million."[29] What better way of doing business than entering into an antitrust suit against IBM, charging monopoly and monopolizing, asking dissolution and divestiture, and being bought off.

No doubt inspired by Data Processing's manner of escaping the pressure of its debts, VIP Systems, which had failed to pay $300,000 in rental fees for IBM equipment, filed an antitrust suit against its creditor, asking $15 million in damages on grounds that IBM had sold a competing "text-editing service" at artificially low prices.[30] The VIP suit is still outstanding.

In 1971 IBM filed an antitrust countersuit against Control Data, charging anticompetitive practices and the monopolization of the market for very large computers, and asking for the divestiture of its subsidiary, Commercial Credit. IBM's concern was to find some counterthreat as an instrument of defense and for that reason, perhaps, here antitrust charges were different from Control Data's in that while the sum and substance of Control Data's complaint was the over-aggressive competitiveness of its rival, IBM put its finger on strategies and practices that were truly anticompetitive and without the saving grace of a technological value or an organizational rationale. Among these

---

[27]"IBM Sued by Programmatics, Inc. Action Seeks To End Free Computer Sort Program," *Wall Street Journal* (May 22, 1969), p. 5.

[28]"Applied Data Unit and IBM Settle Antitrust Suit," *Wall Street Journal* (August 21, 1970), p. 2.

[29]"Data Processing, IBM End Antitrust Suit. Settle Out of Court," *Wall Street Journal* (September 1, 1970), p. 4.

[30]"VIP Systems Files an Antitrust Suit Action Against IBM," *Wall Street Journal* (October 30, 1970), p. 14.

were Control Data's reciprocal buying; its acquisition of and combination with more than fifty competitors, customers, and suppliers; and its leadership in the formation of an international cartel known as "the club."[31]

With the new year Telex Corporation, a manufacturer of "peripheral equipment" designed to be plugged into and used as part of IBM computers, filed suit, charging IBM with monopolizing and accusing IBM of "sharply cutting prices to knock Telex out of business." Telex asked $877 million in damages.[32]

Between 1969 and 1972 five other antitrust suits were filed against IBM besides those covered in this survey.[33]

During the month of October, 1972, a series of meetings were held between IBM and the Justice Department in which IBM sought for a clarification of the charges and a definition of the monopoly and monopolizing of which it stood accused. Though it was six years since the investigation of IBM had begun, and four years since the case against IBM had been filed, during which time 27 million documents had been obtained from IBM and processed by the Department, nevertheless, the Department of Justice still was unable to state the crimes at issue, to define the market monopolized, or to state the objectives of the suit or the relief it would ask for. It refused to bring the case to trial, contending that it "still had a lot to learn about computers."[34]

In spite of its incapacity to explain the why or wherefore of its charges, the Department of Justice did reiterate its ultimate intention of breaking IBM into an unspecified number and variety of independent parts.[35]

---

[31]"IBM Gets Clearance to File Counter Suit Against Control Data," *Wall Street Journal* (April 22, 1971), p. 3 and "IBM Has Again Filed Antitrust Counterclaim Against Control Data," *Wall Street Journal* (August 9, 1971), p. 12.

[32]"Telex Asks $877 Million in Damages from IBM for Alleged Monopoly," *Wall Street Journal* (January 25, 1972), p. 25.

[33]Advanced Memory Systems sued for antitrust violation in 1971, demanding that IBM withdraw an alleged threat not to provide maintenance services for computers to which the peripheral equipment of other manufacturers had been added. IBM almost immediately complied and the case was settled out of court in a month. Additionally, according to "The Giant Takes a Big Loss," *Business Week* (September, 1973), p. 19, antitrust suits were filed against IBM by Levine Townsend Computer Corporation in 1969, by the Greyhound Computer Corporation in 1969, by Memorex Corporation in 1971, and by Itel Corporation in 1971. Because the antitrust character of these suits is not clear from the available reports, they have not been included in this survey.

[34]"Justice Agency Lawyers Meet Today to Define Aims of 1969 Antitrust Case," *Wall Street Journal* (October 6, 1972), p. 4.

[35]"Breakup of IBM Is Tentative Goal of Pending Suit," *Wall Street Journal* (October 17, 1972), p. 3.

In January, 1973, it was announced that IBM had settled out of court with Control Data. The settlement was entirely unrelated to the correction of the alleged monopoly, to monopolization, or to the objectionable practices nominally at issue. It was pay-off, pure and simple. A threat to destroy the great company, perpetually so vulnerable under the law, was put aside "in exchange for a variety of benefits" — $100 million on the barrel head to leave IBM in peace. Control Data received "some $96 million in reimbursements and contracts from IBM over ten years" including four R&D contracts "to run five years each at $6 million a year" with the technology produced belonging to Control Data as much as to IBM. Control Data took over IBM's Service Bureau for a payment of $16 million, with IBM agreeing to drop out of computer servicing for at least six years. William Norris, president of Control Data, was gleeful over the results as well he should have been, knocking a competitor out of an important market and receiving a huge payoff besides, all in the name of the Sherman Act. He said the case "has proved to be one of the best management decisions in our history. We are extremely pleased with the settlement . . . our company will receive substantial long-term benefits from the business transaction."[36]

In late September, 1973, IBM took a hard blow. In deciding the Telex case, Judge A. Sherman Christensen held that IBM had engaged in predatory pricing (though the prices charged were high enough to earn a comfortable profit for the seller) and that its price reductions and marketing practices were directed "not at competition in an appropriate competitive sense, but at competitors and their viability as such." Telex was awarded $352.5 million in damages and more than $20 million for costs and attorney's fees. Further, IBM was ordered to price separately and with "substantially uniform" markups, all the fuctionally different devices that make up the computer, including central processors and memories. IBM was ordered to reveal all technical specifications for the interconnections of all computer devices immediately upon time of product announcement or of internal release to manufacture, whichever comes first. This was done evidently to facilitate imitation and copying of all IBM innovations and developments in the design

---

[36]"Control Data Settles Its Antitrust Suit Against IBM Buying Subsidiary and Relying on U.S. Case for Relief," *Wall Street Journal* (January 16, 1973), p. 3.

of peripheral equipment. IBM was required to eliminate all penalties for premature termination of long-term leases, provided only that lessees give a 90-day notice of termination. This was intended to facilitate "competitive substitutions," presumably by copiers and imitators of the peripheral equipment developed and designed by IBM. It incidently destroys the rationale of long-term leasing. These injunctions cannot but have a negative effect on the company's incentive to develop and to innovate as well as to reduce prices below the conventional norm. Finally, IBM was enjoined from antitrust sinning in general, and particularly from the sin of aggressive competition. It must henceforth "refrain from predatory pricing, leasing, or other practices and strategies intended to obtain or to maintain a monopoly for equipment compatible with computers, or any relevant submarket."

At the same time Judge Christensen found Telex guilty of illegal copying of IBM products, obtaining proprietary information by hiring IBM employees, and otherwise appropriating trade secrets and confidential proprietary information and violating IBM copyrights. On this account Telex was ordered to pay IBM $21.9 million in damages plus attorney's fees.[37]

If one supposes that Judge Christensen's findings in both cases to be factually correct, then an impression of the two firms emerges. Telex is seen (so far as this aspect of its business is concerned) as a parasite that lives upon IBM's R&D and product innovation, obtaining information by forms of spying and bribery that skirt the edges of legality, or by outright theft and illegal practice. Because it copies product designs and feeds upon another's R&D, Telex presumably has a cost advantage in the sale of some peripheral equipment. IBM has fought back with long-term leasing and low prices on vulnerable items to ward off the incursions of the other.

The orders of the court would certainly serve to raise prices and reduce concessions to customers and to reduce the incentive to invest in R&D and product innovation. And the decision itself would have an even greater and more dangerous effect in opening the way for a free-for-all rending of IBM's financial flesh, with claims for triple damages on all the profits that might have been if IBM had so priced and so marketed its products as to surrender the market to its rivals.

---

[37]"The Giant Takes a Big Loss," *Business Week* (September 22, 1973), pp. 18–20.

More likely, the Telex decision will spawn a host of similiar actions against IBM. Chief executives of Itel, California Computer Products, and Potter Instruments Co. are all pushing their lawyers to investigate possible suits. Says Lester L. Kirkpatrick, chairman of California Computer Products: "I think almost any company in the computer industry has got to be thinking about bringing suit against IBM, even the big mainframe companies."

A. G. W. "Jack" Biddle, executive director of the Computer Industry Assn., primarily made up of peripheral products manufacturers, says: "As many as 40 companies are in a position to bring suit. All you'd need if the decision stands is a Xerox machine and a month of discovery to bring the record up to date."[38]

IBM appealed and Judge Christensen recalled and revised his reckoning of the damages against them.[39] In the meantime California Products launched its antitrust suit against IBM, claiming $300 million in damages; and by threatening suit Potter Instruments collected a quick $3.5 million payoff in the form of a development contract. Said John C. Potter, chief executive, "We're canceling our previous suit in return for our contract."[40]

That is the tale of IBM so far. What inferences can be drawn? What lessons are to be learned?

1. The Department of Justice has accused IBM of the crime of monopoly and monopolization. After seven years (1967 to 1973) of search and discovery, of investigation, contemplation, and rumination, the Department is still unable to specify the criminal acts of which the company stands accused, to define what has been monopolized when and where, or to state the monopolizing malfeasances so as to bring the case to trial. Surely that gives witness to the emptiness of their criterion.

2. During the whole period of investigation and prosecution, there appears to have been no interest in and certainly no effort on the part of the Justice Department to take into account IBM's performance as a producer of good, as a creator of technologies, and as a generator of income. The antitrust prosecution has buried itself in a mountain of documents searching for the words or phrases from which some

---

[38]*Ibid.*

[39]"Judge in IBM Telex Case Concedes Error in His Damage Assessment," *Wall Street Journal* (October 10, 1973), p. 3.

[40]"Potter Instruments Decides Against Suing IBM After Winning Work from Big Firm," *Wall Street Journal* (October 15, 1973), p. 8.

malevolent intent could be inferred, and has never lifted its head to look at events and results in the open air of fact and practice where efficiency, productivity, innovation, and benefits to consumers and to labor could be at issue.

3. Under the shadow of the undefined and indefinable crime of monopoly and monopolization, the great company is perpetually vulnerable to antitrust attack in the courts by its debtors and rivals. From 1968 to 1973 there have been a dozen such attacks. In purpose and effect these have been a kind of legalized blackmail, shakedowns in which the net result has been that IBM has paid off in cash and contracts and other forms of giveaway so that it would be left in peace. "One of the best management decisions in our history," said the president of Control Data as he gloated over the spoils of their settlement. And indeed it has become a sort of management decision in the business of extortion to accuse IBM of "monopoly and monopolization," weighing the cost of the lawsuit against the possibility of shaking down the frightened giant for some enormous sum. To bleed the giant has become a profitable game, but what the giant bleeds is competitive élan and technological force; and for that society will pay the price.

4. It may be that, in Judge Christensen's words, IBM's actions were directed "not at competition in an appropriate competitive sense but at competitors . . ." but I suggest that the notion of action directed "at competition in an appropriate competitive sense" is senseless, that in the market for computers it remains to be shown that there can be any meaningful competition except vis-à-vis competitors, or that there can exist a state of rigorous competition that does not drive some competitors out of business.

   All the practices that the Department of Justice in its antitrust suit and that the IBM competitors in their antitrust suits would enjoin are *competitive* practices; and the effect of the injunctions sought and the remedies asked for must be to soften competition, to raise the prices the customer pays, and to reduce the services, concessions, and benefits the customer receives. The force of the antitrust law, whether wielded by the Department of Justice or by IBM competitors, drives IBM to become (as so many dominant firms in so many failing industries already have) passive and acquiescent, taking the lead in muffling competition, in sharing markets, and in holding up the price umbrella for the benefit of the community of firms and at the expense of the economy.

Chapter 12

Restructuring
the Pricing Context

Perhaps in any market, either through the conscious design of those who participate and/or those who exercise the relevant power or through accumulating incident and a train of unintended trials and errors, there evolves conventional practices and procedures — norms of behavior, boundaries and barriers to the exercise of aggression and competition, and a system of communication that becomes habituated, accepted, and institutionalized (and which often attains the inertial force that preserves practices and institutions beyond their time). Certainly such practices and institutions may run counter to the public interest. They can generate waste. They can misdirect competitive efforts into channels that are not conducive to efficiency or technical advance. They can work to the detriment of consumers, potential entrants into the industry, and other social groups. Hence, there may be good reason why the public authority should want to eliminate or change them. This is not to say that the framework of practices and institutions within which a market operates can be hacked down with impunity on the naive grounds that it does not approximate that of the neoclassical model. Rather, the elements and the whole must be examined and evaluated in terms of their function, their costs, and their alternatives.

Perhaps the most formidable and nominally the most successful attack on the institutional framework of a set of markets was against the system of basing points specifically, and delivered pricing generally, in the United States.

SYSTEMS OF DELIVERED PRICING

In any scheme of delivered pricing all sellers who are willing to enter the market quote price by reference to the geographic point to which the product will be delivered. With a single price prevailing at that point of delivery and with sellers differently located, the price paid will not reflect the transportation cost differences related to specific shipments made to that point of delivery. Hence, a different net return will be realized by sellers on different shipments of the same item. Or if a single price prevails for numerous points of delivery, i.e., with a system of zone pricing, there will be different net returns on shipments made from the same mill. If, for example, there is a single wholesale price for Kellogg's Corn Flakes in the United States but in fact it is cheaper to ship corn flakes from the plant in Grand Rapids to Detroit rather than to New York, then Kellogg's will realize a higher mill net on shipments to and sales in Detroit than on shipments to and sales in New York.

Basing points are a form of delivered pricing. In a basing-point system price at any point N in geographic area X is determined by the price at basing point D plus transportation costs from D to N. Sellers delivering goods to N need not have produced those goods at D, hence, their transportation cost may be greater or less than that reckoned from basing point D to N.

There may be numerous basing points in an industry; e.g., in the cement industry there were 86 different basing points at the time of the antitrust attack. The offering price plus transportation costs at basing points D, D^1, D^2, D^3, . . . D^n determines the delivered price within corresponding geographic areas X, X^1, X^2, X^3, . . . X^n. In each case the territory where a particular basing point prevails is simply that area wherein delivered cost reckoned from that basing point is less than delivered cost reckoned from any other. Indeed, every mill can be a basing point with its mill price plus transportation determining delivered prices in an area contiguous to itself; but if a mill D^1 that is the basing point for X^1 should attempt to sell in X^2, it would quote the price at mill D^2 plus transportation costs to the point of delivery within X^2.

Does the basing-point system require some sort of premeditated arrangement between competitors so that it must be considered as the consequence of conspiracy?

Chapter 12

The Single Basing Point

Under the circumstances of modern organizational enterprise where producers have the power to and do set prices independently, it is quite possible that a system of basing points could develop spontaneously *without* plan or agreement. Suppose that all those producing a particular output are concentrated in a certain geographical locale; e.g., that the makers of steel are (as once they were) all located around Pittsburgh where iron ore and coal are both available and where the mills have easy access to major consumers on the Eastern seaboard. What will be the price of steel in Philadelphia? Quite properly it will be the Pittsburgh steel price plus the cost of shipping the steel to Philadelphia, and the price in Detroit will be the Pittsburgh price plus the cost of shipping to Detroit; the price in Miami, Florida, will be the Pittsburgh price plus the cost of transporting steel to Miami. But now suppose that a small steel mill is established in Detroit and that mill decides, cautiously, not to disturb the pattern of prices but to accept them as they are. Then, of course, when it sold its product in Philadelphia, it would sell at the Pittsburgh price plus the cost of transportation from Pittsburgh to Philadelphia. When the mill sold in Pittsburgh it would sell at the price prevailing in Pittsburgh. In Chicago it would sell at the Pittsburgh price plus the transportation costs from Pittsburgh to Chicago. When the Detroit mill sold in Detroit it would sell at the Pittsburgh price plus transport costs to Detroit.

Under these circumstances, while the Pittsburgh mills (basing point) would always make the same net yield on a ton of steel no matter where they sold it, the Detroit mill would make a different net yield depending upon where it sold its product. If it sold steel in Detroit it would *add* to its yield the calculated but unpaid "phantom freight" of shipping steel from Pittsburgh to Detroit. But when it sold its steel in Pittsburgh it would *absorb* the costs of shipping steel from Detroit to Pittsburgh. If transport costs from Pittsburgh to Detroit were, say, $10 a ton, then the Detroit mill would make $20 more on a ton of steel that it sold in Detroit than it would on the sale of a ton of steel in Pittsburgh.

If this practice should become institutionalized, with mills throughout the country accepting the Pittsburgh price plus the cost of transportation from Pittsburgh to the point of delivery, then a *single basing-point system* would have emerged. For many years such a single basing-point system in fact operated in the steel industry.

Multiple Basing Points

Returning to our hypothetical example, suppose now that the Detroit mill should decide to reduce the price at which it offered its steel in Detroit to below the cost of buying it in Pittsburgh and shipping it to Detroit. Then, if any of the Pittsburgh mills wanted to sell steel in Detroit, they would have to offer their steel at the price set there by the Detroit mill. In fact, for any locale where the Detroit price plus transportation from Detroit was lower than the Pittsburgh price plus transportation from Pittsburgh, the Detroit price would prevail for all sellers no matter where they produced their steel or from where they shipped it. Detroit would have become a second basing point.

If the Detroit mill sold its steel in Pittsburgh, it would have to meet the price set by the mills in Pittsburgh; hence, it would make a lower net yield on the steel that it sold in Pittsburgh than it would on the steel that it sold in Detroit. The opposite would be true for a Pittsburgh mill selling its steel in Detroit. In both cases the mills would be absorbing freight costs. The movement of steel from Pittsburgh to Detroit simultaneously with the movement of steel from Detroit to Pittsburgh can readily take place under such a pricing arrangement especially where marginal costs are below the net yields. Such "cross-hauling" constitutes an economic waste.

The mechanism of basing points is illustrated in Figure 12-1. The mill price at Pittsburgh is shown as $100 and at Detroit as $120, with the scale of transportation costs shown in the center line. Total transportation costs between the two cities is given as $60. Hence, the net realized by Pittsburgh mills from sales in Detroit is $60 ($120–$60) and by the Detroit Mills selling in Pittsburgh the mill net is $40 ($100–$60). Prices prevailing for points between the two cities is shown on the bottom line (the lowest price is calculated on a basis of either mill price plus transportation costs).

Thus, there can be two, three, or three hundred basing points in an industry. Indeed, every mill can be a basing point providing the price at which it offers its product at the locale of its mill is lower than it would be if purchased and shipped to that locale from any other mill.

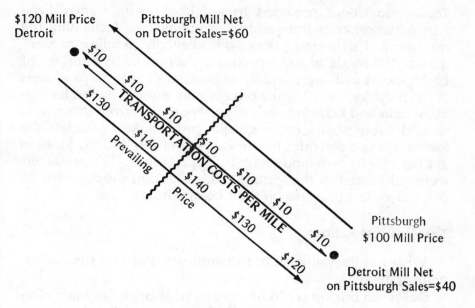

Figure 12-1
Basing-Point System of Pricing

Where every mill is a basing point, what would be the difference between a basing-point system and a nonbasing-point or FOB mill price system? Simply this. In the latter case no mill would absorb freight in order to sell in another mill's territory. For every producer there would be only one net yield on the sale of its product, regardless of the geographical location to which that product was delivered.

THE ANTITRUST ATTACK

After the turning of the 1940's, with the sanction of the Supreme Court, the Department of Justice and the Federal Trade Commission attacked the various forms of delivered pricing. Single basing-point systems were attacked as in the *Corn Products* case.[1] Multiple basing-point systems were attacked as in the *Cement Institute* case.[2] The institutionalized supports given through trade associations to basing-point pricing were attacked.

---

[1]*Corn Products Refining Company v. FTC*, 324 U.S. 726 (1945).
[2]*FTC v. Cement Institute*, 333 U.S. 683 (1948).

Trade associations provided freight books with standardized transportation costs from all basing points, thus facilitating the quotation of delivered prices and, allegedly, tending to standardize the mode of transportation. Current price offerings of basing-point mills were widely publicized so that all producers in the industry, knowing the prices being quoted by the basing-point mills and knowing costs of transportation from those mills to all delivery points, could quickly and precisely calculate the lowest basing-point price for any output delivered to any location as a basis for its own bidding or price quotations. The producers were habituated to the system and, no doubt, supported it by overt or covert pressure on their competitors.

The Antitrust Rationale

What was the rationale of this antitrust attack on the basing-point system?

Delivered pricing could be conceived as price discrimination in the sense that the seller made less money (absorbed more freight cost) on certain sales than on others, which was the legal rationale of the attack. Hence, the antitrust attack could be understood as a blow against price discrimination. But such discrimination as this was certainly not a means of selective coercion such as the Clayton Act sought to forbid, nor was it the consequence of the superior bargaining power of large buyers that the Robinson-Patman Act tried to prevent.

Then what was the idea behind the prosecution? For what purpose was it intended?

In procuring materials for government work, the political authority customarily asks for bids from several firms and purchases from the lowest bidder. In their vast construction and road building programs, government agencies need lots and lots of cement. And a major item of evidence in the key government briefs was the fact that no matter how many independent firms were brought into the bidding and no matter where the cement was to be delivered, when the sealed bids were opened, they all quoted exactly the same price down to the tenth of a cent.

Naturally so. Given the basing-point system of pricing, barring clerical errors, that had to be the case. It said nothing at all about whether or not basing-point prices were themselves competitively determined. But to the ideologists of liberalism, the picture rankled. In their conception of properly competitive behavior, it didn't happen that way. There was supposed to be bargaining, higgling, and haggling. That's what the ceremony of the sealed bids was all about. They saw conspiracy and the lawyers saw sin; hence, the attack.

It is possible to formulate a more sophisticated justification. Consider, for example, Professor Edward H. Chamberlin's theory of oligopoly developed early in his famous work on monopolistic competition.[3] He concludes that where sellers can and do anticipate the behavior of their competitors, i.e., with "mutual dependence recognized," the rational pursuit of each firm of its self-interest will lead the whole industry to act as a monopoly.

> If sellers have regard for their *total* influence upon price, the price will be a monopoly one. Independence of the producers and the pursuit of their self-interest is not sufficient to lower it.[4]

To the extent that they *cannot anticipate* their competitor's behavior or are *uncertain as to the effects* of their own decisions, and inasmuch as there are imperfections in the market that retard the movement of information and the consequent reaction to their actions, the possibility that numerous sellers can in toto approximate the monopolist's behavior in exploiting a market position is correspondingly reduced.

> . . . If the market is imperfect, however, true self-interest requires the neglect of indirect influence to a degree depending upon the degree of imperfection.
>
> If sellers neglect their indirect influence on price . . . [this leads towards a situation where] price will oscillate over an area which becomes narrower and approaches . . . the purely competitive figure.
>
> . . . Uncertainty, where present, as to (a) whether other competitors will hold their amounts or their prices constant, (b) whether they are far sighted, (c) the extent of the possible incursion upon their markets and (d) in case of a time lag, its length, renders the outcome indeterminant.[5]

Hence, more uncertainty as to competitive response, more friction, greater lags, and market imperfection would correspondingly make it more difficult for entrepreneurs pursuing their self-interest to act in concert as a rational monopolist,

---

[3]E. H. Chamberlin, *The Theory of Monopolistic Competition* (Cambridge: Harvard University Press, 1936).

[4]*Ibid.*, p. 54.

[5]*Ibid.*, p. 54.

would reduce their capacity to take the direct and indirect influences into account, and allegedly would produce more purely competitive behavior. It could be argued, therefore, that to break up the basing-point system would increase uncertainties, lags, and imperfections. Hence, this would encourage the price cutter, generate competitive behavior, and upset the oligopoly apple cart.

The Strategy of Oligopoly

Consider the matter from the industry point of view. Why should an industry be firmly wedded to a system of basing-point prices?

1. It served to bring price competition into the open and to regularize pricing practices. As with any system of open pricing, each producer knows where he stands in respect to the price offerings of his competitors.

2. A system of open prices not only reduces uncertainty but also eliminates or at least considerably reduces the possibility that one producer might grab without retaliation a big portion of his competitor's business through unnoticed or hidden price concessions. By eliminating the temptation to make such price concessions the system presumably stabilized prices upward and prevented price wars.

3. But while it thus muffled price competition, the basing-point system provided an outlet for the ambition and aggressive competitiveness of some members of the industry, enabling them to promote and to expand the sale of their product within the existing frame of basing-point prices.

4. In diverting the aggressions of firms into other selling and promotional channels, the basing-point system not only reduced the pressure for price competition but also probably tended to stabilize and to preserve the existing geographical pattern of pricing, inasmuch as firms could expand sales without lowering their mill price. Under an alternative system where they had to lower their mill price in order to expand sales, a comparative locational advantage might have induced them to do so.

The preservation of a geographical pattern of prices safeguarded the existing organization and accumulated the investment not only of the sellers but also of the secondary producers who were buyers of the product; i.e., the system presumably protected the capital investment and organization not only of the corn syrup producers but also of the fabricators of products made of steel, and of the candy makers using corn syrup.

VICTORY

The Supreme Court reversed its prior position and accepted the indictment of delivered pricing.[6] Victory. But what were its fruits?

The agencies of enforcement won, but what did they win? What was it that the Supreme Court, in fact, enjoined? Was it "all delivered pricing" or simply "*systematic* delivered pricing?" Since the conviction was on the basis of price discrimination, and delivered pricing in any form must lead to price discrimination (as indicated by variation in net returns on sales), from the viewpoint of the firm the only "safe" conduct would be to cease any form of delivered prices and, henceforth, to quote all prices FOB mill adding the cost of freight to the point of delivery with any absorption of freight costs considered taboo.

The elimination of the established format based on clearly defined practice and on precise and uniform information on transportation costs might indeed produce less systematic, less regularized, and less aboveboard pricing. Presumably, this would introduce new uncertainties into business calculation and would sweeten the bait for the secret price concessionaire. In so doing, there would be interference with the signals between competitors. It would become more difficult to achieve tacit price agreements. Correspondingly, price would tend to be de-stabilized and price wars would be encouraged. To achieve such a state of affairs might be the antitrust objective.

One cannot be certain that this would, in fact, occur. Or, if it did, it would not be certain that favorable consequences would follow. The instabilities and uncertainties introduced could be detrimental to efficient organization, to foresightful planning, to investment, and to technical progress; and hence, in the long run, to costs and prices.

If the government attack, rather than simply bringing less systematic pricing, resulted in a different system of pricing (i.e.,

---

[6]*Cement Manufacturers Protective Association* v. *U.S.*, 268 U.S. 588 (1925).

FOB mill net with uniform yields on all sales), then the following might result.

1. There might conceivably be more price competition and lower prices, not because of greater uncertainty, but because aggressive management would have no way of expanding sales other than by lowering their price at the mill. If this was the consequence, then prices would not only be lower but a pattern of relative prices might be expected to emerge which would more nearly reflect regional cost variation and comparative production costs. Presumably, this would lead to a more rational location of industrial capacity.

2. Certainly FOB mill pricing would eliminate cross-hauling (just how important cross-hauling is as an economic waste has not been established) and, hence, would result in the more rational use of transportation facilities and in a more economic allocation of work loads between producing centers.

3. It is also conceivable that FOB mill pricing might reduce price competition and bring about higher, more monopolistic prices. FOB mill pricing could segment and insulate from competitive incursions the markets of particular producers, enabling them to raise prices in the face of intense localized demand (for example, a cement mill selling in close proximity to the building of a hydro-electric project) without the fear that competitors attracted by its high prices and large profits would be drawn in to fight for a share of a lush but transitory market. This effect is illustrated in Figure 12-2 on the next page.

In Figure 12-2, under a system of FOB mill pricing, the only way that Mill B can attempt to compete for the business of User X is to lower its own mill price sufficiently so that the Mill B price plus transportation to X will equal the price at Mill A plus transportation from Mill A to X. In so doing, Mill B must drastically reduce its income from business in its own area. Under these circumstances it is not likely that Mill B would compete for X's business no matter what Mill A chose to charge. Mill A, then, could squeeze X to the limit without fear that higher prices and profits would "bring in the wolves" to cut down on its volume of sales. In Chamberlinian terms high profits would not cause a leftward shift of the demand curve of the firm and, hence, the fear of such a leftward shifting of demand would not deter the fullest exploitation of localized monopoly power.

4. Given this latter effect, FOB mill pricing would lead to a regional pattern of prices reflecting less of the comparative production advantages and more of the comparative bargaining

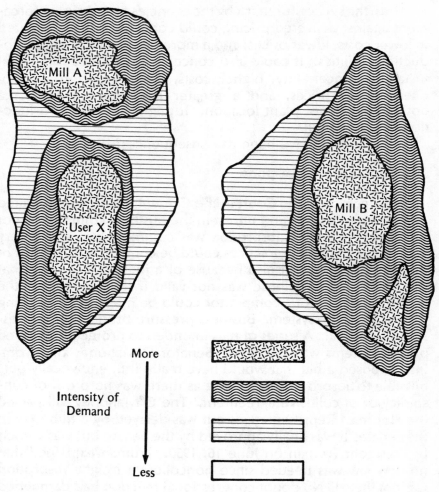

Figure 12-2

Mill Pricing System

Intensity of
Demand

More

Less

power of local monopolies. Thus, the consequent location of productive capacity might be even more irrational than with delivered prices.

5. An enforced FOB mill pricing system would uneconomically constrain plants from establishing operations in those areas where there are advantages on the side of production costs but where the local market is so thin that firms could not cover their low average cost unless they were permitted to sell in different geographical areas at different net yields.

Thus, the successful attack by the agencies of antitrust enforcement against delivered pricing could conceivably have resulted in lower costs, lower prices, and a more rational location of production facilities. It could also conceivably produce functional instability, uncertainty, higher costs, more localized monopolies, higher prices, and a greater derangement from the optimal pattern of plant location. It might have had no functional impact at all.

What, in fact, have been its consequences?

The Congressional Response

The decision of the Court in the *Cement Institute* and related cases created a profound unrest in the business community, not only because freight absorption was commonplace and a very wide range of pricing practices could be condemned as forms of delivered pricing, but also because of a judicial inference that the "good faith" defense was not valid if the meeting of the equally low price of a competitor could be interpreted as being part of a pricing system. Business pressure produced Congressional upheaval. A series of bills intended to protect established pricing systems was prepared. Senator O'Mahoney of Wyoming proposed a bill that would have made it unequivocally permissible to absorb freight so long as there was no proof of conspiracy or of collusive agreement. The O'Mahoney Bill passed the House of Representatives but was delayed by a filibuster in the Senate. It was finally approved by the Senate but was vetoed by President Truman on June 16, 1950. Truman explained that no new law was needed since noncollusive freight absorption was not illegal. No doubt congressional reaction had dampened the FTC's crusading fervor.[7] When the American Iron and Steel Institute and its members accepted an order in 1951, based on a 1947 complaint, to refrain from *agreements* to eliminate or forbid FOB pricing, or to exchange information to be used in computing basing point and delivered prices, or agreements to fix prices according to a formula that would produce identical bids, the Commission was careful to specify that freight absorption was permissible "when innocently and independently pursued, regularly or otherwise, with the result of producing competition." It was also specified that the identity of delivered prices

---

[7]Earl Latham, *The Group Basis of Politics* (Ithaca: Cornell University Press, 1952).

at any destination afforded no proof of a violation of the law.[8] There were no further prosecutions against the use of basing points and delivered pricing.

The Effect on Industry

In the industries directly affected the specific, immediate, and unequivocal result of the basing-point decisions was a sharp, rapid rise in prices and an increase in profits. The basing-point decisions freed sellers from constraints on individual price manipulations (downward or upward). Those constraints, hangovers from the long years of depression, reflected the obsessive fear of price cutting. Producers responded by taking full advantage of the seller's market in construction goods. They also took advantage of the legally sanctioned occasion to disengage themselves from less profitable relationships with distant customers. They were more anxious to do this in the light of rising freight costs.

Presumably cross-hauling decreased. In line with a universal trend (and responsive to rising railroad rates) more cement was shipped by truck. When demand slackened during the 1953–54 recession, most if not all of the cement, steel, and other affected producers were absorbing freight with consequent cross-hauling. Freight-rate books permitting the quick calculation of any competitor's delivered prices, forbidden to the trade associations, were now published by independent transportation consultants. With rare exceptions customers preferred delivered prices to FOB price quoting. In effect, a defacto basing-point system remained, or at least returned, very quickly.

Were there any benefits to the consumers and the public from the attack on delivered pricing? There is no hard evidence of any gains. Intuitively one might suppose that the attack cracked open certain depression-based practices that had served to forestall price cutting and to rigidify prices, and that thereby individual firms were encouraged to take (from their point of view) a more independent approach, capitalizing upon an era of rising demand and wide open business opportunity. A general consequence of discarding the old rigidifying inhibitions is surely the continual, self-renewing inflationary pressure that characterizes the American economy today.

---

[8]*FTC Order 5508*, issued August 16, 1951.

THE BASING-POINT CASES IN RETROSPECT

The basing-point cases have faded into oblivion which, in the light of their effect upon the American economy, is the fate they deserve. Nevertheless, in studying them the following may be learned about economic policy in the United States.

1. The antitrust agencies intended to impose, and in the first instance succeeded in imposing for the first time in American history, a radical reconstruction of the institutional format of important market systems.

2. That change was not the Court's design. The significance of the Court's decisions in this instance and over the whole range of antitrust action was that it relinquished its powers of censure and allowed administrative agencies full discretion in the interpretation and application of the law.

3. That the Court allowed these agencies full discretion in the interpretation of the law did not mean that the affected interests were without defense. Their opposition shifted to the legislative process and executive rule. Instead of the Court, Congress and the President assumed control and responsibility.

4. Because this attempt to reconstruct the organization of industrial markets was rooted in the pragmatic interests of no group in the American economy, and because it followed as its ideal and norm that flimsiest of blueprints—an anachronistic image of price competition in a peddlers market—it collapsed and dissolved as soon as business resistance was transmitted into Congressional pressure and Presidential scrutiny.

Chapter 13

The Merger Movement

An attack on monopoly faces the problem of unscrambling the egg. To break up an integral operation may cost heavily in a loss of technological advantages, while benefits, anticipated through increased competition are always uncertain. But to prevent independent companies from combining poses no analogous risk. The prevention of merger threatens neither operating efficiency nor technical progress. Economies of scale, if there are such, could be gained (though at a different pace) through internal growth even if mergers were unequivocally forbidden.

Therefore, if the criterion of economic policy and control is economic performance and, other things being equal, it is supposed that a greater number of independent competitors will improve the level of economic performance, it follows logically that the government should stringently constrain mergers. Section 7 of the Clayton Act does forbid one corporation from acquiring the shares of a competing corporation or from buying the stock of two or more corporations that were competitors where such action might substantially lessen competition or tend toward monopoly.

THE COURT AND MERGERS

In the days before the turning the Supreme Court allowed no antitrust constraint on mergers. In the *Thatcher* and *Swift* cases in 1926 the Court decided that once a company acquired the controlling shares of a competitor and used its control to procure its competitor's assets, it automatically removed itself from prosecution under the Clayton Act.[1] In the *International Shoe* case in 1930 the Court refused to allow a merger to be attacked under the Clayton Act where the merged companies were both in the same market (shoes) but did not produce identical lines. Hence, by the logic of the Court these companies were not considered to be "competing corporations."[2] In the 1934 *Arrow-Hart and Hegeman* case the Court exempted from prosecution under the Clayton Act a holding company that used the shares under its control to effectuate a merger between competitors.[3] As a consequence, the political authority was unable to apply the Clayton Act with its less stringent criterion of illegality to the prevention of monopoly, while the surgical cure for monopoly under the Sherman Act was virtually forbidden. After World War II all this was changed both by greater permissiveness of the Court and by new legislative enactment. The power of the political authority to act against mergers under the antitrust laws was firmly established.

The Celler Antimerger Act of 1950 extended the prohibitions of the Clayton Act to include not only the acquisition of stock but also its use in "voting or granting proxies or otherwise," or in acquiring "the whole or any part of the assets" of the competing corporation where the effect may be "substantially to lessen competition or tend to create a monopoly."

Consider some of the merger cases that came before the Court under the Clayton Act during the postwar period.[4]

The Bethlehem Steel Case

Bethlehem Steel Corporation, the second largest producer of steel, announced its intention of merging with Youngstown Sheet and Tube Company, the sixth largest steel producer. The merger would have increased Bethlehem's share of the steel

---

[1]*Thatcher Manufacturing Company v. FTC*, 272 U.S. 554 (1926); and *Swift and Co. v. FTC*, 272 U.S. 544 (1926).

[2]*International Shoe Co. v. FTC*, 280 U.S. 291 (1930).

[3]*Arrow-Hart & Hegeman Electric Co. v. FTC*, 291 U.S. 587 (1934).

[4]The Sherman Act also has been used to block mergers; e.g., *U.S. v. First National Bank and Trust Co. of Lexington*, 376 U.S. 935 (1964) in which the "railroad doctrine" established in the early 1900's "where merging companies are major competitive factors in a relevant market, the elimination of significant operation between them, by merger, itself constitutes a violation of Section 1 of the Sherman Act" was reinstated to prevent the consolidation of the first and fourth largest banks in Kentucky. David Orrick, then antitrust chief in the Department of Justice, found it impossible "to overestimate the importance" of the decision.

market from 15 percent to 20 percent. Bethlehem argued that Youngstown's facilities were complementary to her own, and that the combination would enable Bethlehem to compete more effectively with United States Steel, particularly in the Chicago region. The Justice Department attacked the merger. Judge Weinfeld, trying the case in a federal district court, did not reject Bethlehem's claim that the merger would make competition more effective.[5] He simply noted the danger of a trend toward increasing concentration in an already highly concentrated industry and ruled that this sufficed to support the government's case against Bethlehem. As Justice Brennan would rule in a later case, "A merger the effect of which may be substantially to lessen competition is not saved because on some ultimate reckoning of social or economic debits and credits, it may be deemed beneficial. A value choice of such magnitude is beyond the ordinary limits of judicial competence. . . . Congress . . . proscribed anti-competitive mergers, the benign and the malignant alike, fully aware we must assume, that some price might have to be paid."[6]

The duPont Case

DuPont, through a holding-company arrangement, had purchased a dominant share in General Motors stock in 1917. It was inferred that the possession of this block of General Motors stock had been used to give duPont a favored position in the sale of paint products and imitation leather fabrics to General Motors. The Court agreed that this cross-corporation stockholding, entered into more than a generation before, constituted an illegal constraint on competition under Section 7 of the Clayton Act and required the divestiture by duPont of its shareholding in General Motors.[7] In this case the Court reversed its former narrow interpretation of the Clayton Act, allowing the prohibitions of the act to apply to the foreclosure of markets through vertical integration (or through influence extended vertically through the ownership of shares) and requiring the divestiture of shares acquired in the distant past whenever the time arose that such ownership posed a threat to competition.

---

[5]U.S. v. Bethlehem Steel Corp., 168 F. Supp. 576 (1958).
[6]U.S. v. Philadelphia National Bank, 374 U.S. 321 (1963).
[7]U.S. v. E. I. duPont de Nemours & Co. et al., 353 U.S. 586 (1957).

The Brown Shoe Case

This case involved a merger between the Brown Shoe Company, Inc., and the G. R. Kinney Company, Inc. Brown was a leading manufacturer of men's, women's, and children's shoes and also had the third largest dollar volume of shoe sales in the United States. Kinney was the eighth largest company by dollar volume among those primarily engaged in selling shoes. While these were both very large firms, they were part of an enormous market so that their combined share of industry production could not be considered as remotely approximating monopoly control; i.e., Brown had 4 percent and Kinney had 0.5 percent of the national output of shoes. Nevertheless, the Supreme Court ruled the merger illegal.[8] It was willing to curb "tendencies toward concentration in their incipiency" holding that "this is an appropriate place to call a halt."[9]

What is most interesting about this case is the intense effort of the Federal Trade Commission to analyze the circumstances of the merger and to attempt to measure its probable effects above and beyond that which would have been necessary for or relevant to the Commission's case before the bar, suggesting a hopeful change in the Federal Trade Commission's conception of its role as no longer a creature of the Court but rather an agency responsible for and answerable to Congress and to the public for the long-run evolution of market structures.

The Court joined in the complex task of evolving guidelines for public control. In the words of the Court a merger was to be "functionally viewed in the context of its particular industry." It was to be approved or disapproved depending upon whether that *industry* "was fragmented rather than concentrated," on whether it "had seen a recent trend toward domination by a few leaders or remained fairly constant in its distribution of market shares among participating companies," on whether participating companies "had experienced long access to markets and easy access to suppliers by buyers or (rather) had witnessed the foreclosure of business," and on whether there had been "the ready entry of new competition or the erection

---

[8]*Brown Shoe Company* v. *U.S.*, 370 U.S. 294 (1962).

[9]*U.S.* v. *Von's Grocery Co.*, 384 U.S. 270 (1966). In this case the Court permitted a merger between the third and the sixth largest grocery chains doing business in Los Angeles to be enjoined on showing a tendency for small independents to be swallowed by the chain stores.

of barriers to prospective entrance." Account must be taken of countervailing power, permitting, for example, a merger between small companies "to enable them in combination to compete with larger corporations dominating the relevant market." Account must also be taken of the value of mergers that "might save failing firms and thus salvage a competitive force as well as an economic asset."[10]

The Continental Can Case

The Federal Trade Commission attacked the merger of the second largest producer of metal containers, the Continental Can Corporation, with the third largest producer of glass containers, the Hazel Atlas Glass Company. Was the effect to reinforce competition? It could be argued that Hazel Glass, accounting for 9.6 percent of total output, thus would be strengthened against the leading firm, the Owen Illinois Glass Company, which produced 34.2 percent of total glass container output. That argument depended on the assumption that the market for glass containers and the market for metal containers were separate and distinct. The Commission took the position, and the Court agreed, that the market for containers (both glass and metal) was the relevant one. Competition between different types of containers as well as between the same type of container was held to be vigorous, technologically fruitful, and worth preserving. Hence, the public authority was justified in forbidding mergers that might lessen such competition. The merger of Continental Can and the Hazel Atlas Glass Company was ruled illegal. In a bitter dissent Justice Harlan attacked his fellow justices for failing to provide clear-cut standards for corporate choice in the decision to merge or to refrain from merger. "The Court's spurious market-sharing analysis should not obscure the fact that the Court is, in effect, laying down a per se rule that mergers between two large companies in related markets are presumptively unlawful under Section 7."[11]

If that were indeed the case, then the appropriate answer to Justice Harlan might have been, "Perhaps so, but why not?" What will the economy lose and what will society be denied if large companies in related industries are obliged to prove

---

[10]*Op. cit.*, *Brown Shoe Co.* v. *U.S.*

[11]*U.S.* v. *Continental Can Company*, 378 U.S. 441 (1964).

that their mergers will be without negative effects on competition, or even if they are obliged to establish the presumption that the mergers they propose are likely to be of positive value to the economy?

The Penn-Olin Chemical Company Case

Sodium chloride is an important bleach for the manufacture of paper from wood pulp. Two large companies organized a third company to produce and sell sodium chloride to the burgeoning paper industry in the southeastern part of the United States. This "joint venture," having the effect of introducing a new competitor into the market, was opposed by the Department of Justice. The Supreme Court had to decide whether such a joint venture came within the purview of Section 7 of the Clayton Act.

The Court ruled that the joint venture in the organization of a new company precluded potential competition between those who had entered into the joint venture who otherwise might have entered the market and competed separately. A competitor need not be eliminated in order to establish that competition would be substantially lessened. It sufficed that a viable threat of entry was removed. If only one of the two participants had entered the market, the one remaining uncommitted would have constituted a threat to enter as well, should prices and profits warrant. Such a threat constituted a competitive pressure on those who were already in the market.

Thus, the Court decided that joint ventures, like mergers, could be prevented under Section 7 of the Clayton Act where it was established that such joint action might preclude competition between potential competitors.[12]

In other cases also the agencies of enforcement relied upon, and the Court developed the conception of, the potential competitor (a doctrine to become important in the effort to constrain conglomerate mergers). Thus, the Aluminum Company of America was forbidden to acquire the Rome Cable corporation though Rome produced only 1.3 percent while the Aluminum Company produced 27.8 percent of the aluminum conductor cable. It was held that in spite of its small size Rome was an aggressive, successful competitor with a potential for growth

---

[12]*U.S. v. Penn-Olin Chemical Co. et al.*, 378 U.S. 158 (1964).

that should not be ignored and that on those grounds it was important to preserve Rome's independence.[13] In 1964 the El Paso Natural Gas Company was forbidden by the Court from acquiring the Pacific Northwest Pipeline Company. El Paso was the only firm bringing natural gas into California. Pacific Northwest was located 500 miles away and had failed to obtain the natural gas source or the requisite financing to enter the California market. The Court held that Pacific Northwest was a potential competitor nevertheless and its efforts had already influenced El Paso's business attitudes and behavior.[14]

The Consolidated Foods Corporation Case

Consolidated Foods, owning food processing plants and a network of wholesale and retail food stores, acquired Gentry's, the second largest producer of dehydrated onions and garlic. The merger brought Consolidated into the garlic and onion dehydration business but, on the face of it, neither removed a competitor from any relevant market nor reduced threat of entry as a competitive force. The Federal Trade Commission, nevertheless, demanded that the merger be dissolved.[15]

The Supreme Court took note that numerous small processors sold to Consolidated Foods and even depended upon the procurement policies of Consolidated Foods for their survival. These processors used dehydrated garlic and onions. Hence, Consolidated Foods was in a position to pressure these processors to use the Gentry line. The force of reciprocal buying in this instance, the Court held, might substantially reduce competition. Therefore, the Supreme Court, overruling a lower court decision required divestiture.

THE POSITION OF THE COURT

The Supreme Court has opened the door to antimerger prosecution. It has been thoroughly permissive, supporting the position of the prosecuting authorities in every case that has come before it. It has spurred the antitrust agencies to base their policies not on judicial precedent but on the study of industrial structure and on the functional impacts of structural

---

[13]*U.S.* v. *Aluminum Company of America,* 377 U.S. 271 (1964).
[14]*U.S.* v. *El Paso Natural Gas Co.,* 376 U.S. 651, 659 (1964).
[15]*FTC* v. *Consolidated Foods Corporation,* 380 U.S. 592 (1965).

change. What explains the willingness of the Court to support so broad a range of antimerger enforcement?

To check and frustrate mergers through antitrust action poses few if any *social risks*.[16] The technological and organizational advantages of vertical, horizontal, or diversified extension of a corporation's activities are not precluded by the most rigorous antimerger enforcement. All these can be brought about through the internally generated growth of existing companies or through the activation of new enterprises. The extension of business activity through internally generated growth, moreover, constitutes a positive force for competition.

What then have been the consequences of the permissiveness of the Court and the rigor with which the antitrust laws have been enforced by the Federal Trade Commission and the Department of Justice?

ENFORCEMENT AND ITS EFFECTS

From 1940 to 1947 some 2,500 firms disappeared through mergers, constituting 5 percent of the assets invested in manufacturing and mining. It was this frightening phenomenon that brought about the passage of the Celler Antimerger Act in 1950. As we have seen, the Supreme Court subsequently sanctioned the most vigorous prosecution of mergers. In his dissent in the *Von's Grocery* case Justice Stewart remarked, quite rightly, "The sole consistency that I can find is that in litigation under Section 7, the Government always wins." In consequence the Department of Justice and the Federal Trade Commission have both racked up a long series of antimerger victories. In spite of these victories the merging of independent companies accelerated (at least until the recession of 1970). As shown in Table 13-1 the number of firms disappearing through merger increased at an unparalled rate.

Mergers among large companies increased at an unprecedented rate during the latter part of the 1960's. Table 13-2 on page 268 shows the mergers in manufacturing and mining

---

[16]Different positions are taken by Robert Bork, "The Goals of Antitrust Policy," *American Economic Review* (May, 1967), pp. 242–253; William Comanor, "Vertical Merger, Market Power, and the Antitrust Laws," *American Economic Review* (May, 1967), pp. 254–265, 269–272; Louis B. Schwartz, "Monopoly, Monopolizing, and the Concentration of Market Power: A Proposal," in Almarin Phillips (ed.), *Perspectives on Antitrust Policy* (Princeton: Princeton University Press, 1965); and John C. Narver, *Conglomerate Mergers and Market Competition* (Berkeley: University of California Press, 1967), containing an extensive bibliography.

Table 13-1
INDEPENDENT COMPANY MERGERS, 1950-1969

Year	Total Acquisitions		
1950	219		
1951	235		
1952	288		
1953	295		
1954	387		
1955	683		
1956	673		
1957	585		
1958	589		
1959	835		
1960	844		
1961	954		
1962	853		
1963	861		
1964	854		
1965	1,008		
1966	995	1,746	
1967	1,496[1]	2,384	
1968		4,003[2]	4,462
1969			5,400–5,800[3]

[1]Figures in this column from *Moody's Investor Service* and *Standard and Poor's Corporations* and reproduced in *Statistical Abstract of the United States, 1968.*
[2]Figures in this column are FTC data from *Business Week* (April 19, 1969), p. 36.
[3]Data in this column are from W. T. Grimm and Co., reported in *Business Week* (June 21, 1969), p. 35.

companies with assets of over $10 million.[17]   Table 13-3, page 268, shows acquisitions of the 200 largest companies in the United States during this same time period.[18] Acquisitions by these companies increased their share of total U.S. industrial assets to 60 percent, compared to 48 percent two decades before.

The merger movement of the 1940's that produced the Celler Act is dimmed by the magnitude of the merger movement of the 1960's. Is this to say that the antitrust attack on mergers has had only a symbolic significance, sacrificing the blood of a few unfortunate fatted calves on the altar of antimonopoly while the massive movement of event was rapidly transforming the industrial economy? Certainly the organization of the economy has been transformed at a rate that seems to have been wholly unaffected by the prosecutions and pronouncements of the FTC, the Department of Justice, and the Supreme Court decisions.

Yet there has been one striking change in the nature of the merger movement that in large part must be attributable to

[17]*Business Week* (April 19, 1969).
[18]*Ibid.*

Table 13-2

MERGERS IN MANUFACTURING AND MINING COMPANIES

Year	Companies Acquired	Assets (in Millions of Dollars)
1966	101	4,100
1967	169	8,222
1968	192	12,616

Table 13-3

MERGERS IN 200 LARGEST COMPANIES

Year	Companies Acquired	Assets (in Millions of Dollars)
1966	33	2,385
1967	67	5,417
1968	74	6,890

antitrust action. This is in the characteristic form of the merger. Before, mergers mostly brought together firms producing for the same market (horizontal mergers) or firms whose outputs were linked in an integral raw-materials-to-end-product chain (vertical mergers). Now, nearly all mergers are between firms that have neither vertical nor horizontal ties. These are the so-called conglomerates in which companies are merged without having any common technological or functional basis. Of the mergers that took place from 1948 to 1951, some 62 percent were horizontal or vertical integrations; the rest could be rationalized as product extensions. In 1968, 90 percent of the mergers were conglomerates; of these 57 percent could not even be rationalized as product or market extensions. What then is the meaning and significance of the new "conglomerate takeover"?

It is hard to condemn conglomerates within the frame of antitrust ideology because in the neoclassical conception the conglomerate poses no threat to competition. Bringing together firms producing different products for different markets does not increase concentration in any of the affected markets. If Swift should acquire Armour, then concentration would increase in the meat-packing business and the alarm bell would go off for the antitruster. But what happens if Greyhound Bus acquires Armour meats? Competition, as measured by the number and strength of the individual competitors in each of the two markets, would remain the same as before. Also, when a firm integrates vertically, it might use its power in one market as leverage to secure an advantage in another. But when merger incorporates wholly disassociated businesses, then where is the danger of cross-market leverage? Hence, the conglomerate offers a way of merging without violating antitrust rules or risking the admonitions of the agencies of antitrust enforcement.

This was the dilemma facing the agencies of enforcement. They saw the fearsome thing occurring, but couldn't find a basis for objection. They were caught in a hurricane, but their barometer showed no threat of rain. Various rationalizations for attacking mergers were pulled out of the antitrust hat. One such rationale was that potential competitors might be eliminated. For example, if Greyhound Bus does not acquire Armour, it might some day decide to set up its own meat-packing plant or there might be cross-market leverage. Thus, if Greyhound Bus does acquire Armour, then Armour personnel might be required to ride Greyhound buses. These arguments did not carry the antitrusters very far.

In the Johnson administration the Department of Justice set up guidelines for allowable *vertical* and *horizontal* mergers. Those guidelines ignored conglomerate mergers, as did the Department of Justice. When the new administration came into office, President Nixon set up a task force on "Productivity and Competition," chaired by Professor George Stigler of the University of Chicago who in his antitrust orthodoxy had in earlier years used *Fortune* itself as a platform to demand that all big business be chopped up ruthlessly into many little pieces. The task force declared itself "opposed to any policy move against conglomerates"[19] and antitrust chief McLaren invited conglomerates to make "foothold acquisitions . . . in the concentrated industries."[20] Nevertheless, under the Nixon administration the Department of Justice changed the merger guidelines to emphasize opposition to sheer size,[21] and the FTC set up an "early warning system" requiring very large companies to notify that agency of their intention to merge.[22]

No doubt a conglomerate merge can sometimes be opposed on grounds of antimonopoly or antibigness. But there is another more ominous and fundamental issue that escapes the rationale of antitrust proponents entirely.

---

[19]*Business Week* (January 21, 1969).
[20]*Business Week* (June 21, 1969).
[21]*Business Week* (June 14, 1969).
[22]*Business Week* (April 19, 1969).

What accounts for mergers? Why have companies merged? What are the advantages sought? What weight can be given to the diverse motivations and objectives that are conceivable and possible? These are important questions. They have not been answered, nor are they answerable with the data at hand.

It is surely conceivable that mergers take place in the expectation of attaining some technological or organizational advantage; to exploit more fully an imperfectly divisible resource, for example an R&D operation, a distribution network, or a highly evolved managerial skill; or in order to pool resources for some complex venture beyond the capabilities of either partner alone. As was noted earlier, all such advantages can as well be achieved through growth and extension of an individual firm's activities. When firms seek advantages in that fashion, they do so through aggressive competition which is presumably a social advantage.

Nevertheless, it is arguable that those technological and organizational advantages, and the positive benefits they bring to society in the form of rising productivity and the opening of new avenues of innovation, can at least in specific instances be achieved at less cost and with less disruption (or even perhaps only be achieved at all) through merger. What is *not* conceivable is that conglomerate mergers bringing together companies that have no technological link or any organizational complementarity (such as cosmetic plants, lumber yards, steamship lines, billboard advertisers, supersonic aircraft manufacturers, auto and truck tire producers, and food stores under the same corporate umbrella), can have any relationship to the attainment of technological or organizational advantages or yield any corresponding social benefits.

If these industrial-cum-mercantile potpourri have no technological or organizational rationale, and if they are not a means of acquiring greater market control (and antitrust economists and officials search in vain for any links that might increase market control), then what can account for such mergers?

They may be the means of satisfying the megalomania of empire builders. They may take place as the easiest means of unloading capital assets and realizing on accumulated profits with the minimum of taxation. But especially they are an instrument for stock promotion and financial manipulation, grinding out profit for security mills. Consider that peculiar institution, the stock market, where millions of persons and firms engage in the purchase and sale of the securities, common stock, and debentures of a great number of industrial, mercantile, mining, and other corporations. The number of traders swells continually and the demand for the possession of securities rises continually as a consequence of increasing affluence. These traders on the stock market are characterized by (1) an immense number; (2) a vastness in the aggregation of their accumulated wealth; (3) a virtually absolute ignorance of the technology, the organizational quality, and the market circumstances of the corporations whose securities they buy, sell, ignore, or hold; (4) the shortness or nonexistence of their collective memory; and (5) the mob-like panic and faddism of their responses. This mass of traders and security holders are serviced and provoked into action by an army of brokers and brokers' agents. As a consequence of the process of career selection and market operation, these operators are likely to be glib and shallow, and as ignorant of the technology, operating circumstances, and organizational quality of the corporations in whose securities they deal as their customers. Working from poop sheets and the crudest of statistical indicators they live by generating instabilities through the backward-forward, sale-resale of shares and the up-down movement of security prices.

Behind them are the grand ringmasters, the insiders and experts who know how things work from within, who ride herd on the panicky mass, pull new companies out of top hats, and whip up security concoctions to please the passing whim and fancy of the crowd. These are the master bunko artists and con men of our age — secure in the inborn knowledge that a sucker is born every minute. They are often highly skilled at skimming the affluence of the mass investor and slicing down the revenue claims of government. Their skills produce more millionaires and billionaires than all the oil in Texas and Arabia, but aside from the fortunes they amass for themselves they produce nothing. Their manipulations contribute nothing to technology, nothing to organization, nothing to the efficiency of operations, and nothing whatsoever to the social weal.

The enormous, turbulent security-trading operation does have a certain social value. Through the sale of securities, actual operating and producing corporations can sometimes finance business expansions or technological transformations. While such financing may be all or the best that is available, as a system for the allocation of investable resources it is nevertheless irrational and capricious, permitting wholesale siphoning off of financial inputs by insiders and middlemen. It must be insisted upon, moreover, that the real investment function that actually channels funds into business operations is entirely peripheral to the activities of the stock market as a whole. Indeed, it is lost in the back-and-forth trading and price manipulation of the already existing mass of securities whose purchase and sale has no effect upon the funds available for business expenditure. Nevertheless, the rapid and random fluctuations in the value of those securities produce as rapid and random fluctuations in the nominal wealth of the community; hence, in the magnitude of consumer expenditures and in employment and prices. Windfall gains and losses continuously generated randomly redistribute wealth without relation to equity or social contribution, and in no way motivate socially valued behavior.

The organization and operation of the modern stock market is *in itself* immensely wasteful, destabilizing, and dangerous. But after all, the stock market is only a sideshow, a great floating crap game that through waste and maldistribution lives off the real output of the producing economy. We can afford this so long as the real output of the producing economy is forthcoming, and so long as the activities of the stock market do not disturb, diminish, or destroy the effective functioning of the producing economy. And there precisely is the new danger, the threat of the modern merger movement manifested and made uniquely clear in the burgeoning of conglomerates — that con men and bunko artists will take over the complex apparatus of the producing economy and do it irreparable harm. These masters of security manipulation have now discovered that they can use their positions, power, and expertise in the stock market as leverage to seize control of industrial, mercantile, and other corporations. In turn, by grabbing off the accumulated cash reserves of the acquired companies and using this cash for new acquisitions and for security manipulation (thus tickling the palates of mass investors and gimmick-hungry brokers with an illusion of growth), and through inflating earning ratios by the tradeoff of equities for debt and otherwise giving an illusion of profits and progress, they can use their control of producing corporations as a form of leverage to gain advantages in the stock market. Thus, they catapult themselves and their cliques into power and fortune, pasting together organizational monstrosities in the process.

The threat is not of bigness and not of monopoly. The recent outcry has not been the protests of consumers who are exploited by monopolists, nor of little business pushed aside by the large business. It has a different source and there is a different meaning in complaints like these:

> A market-entry decision is pure hell. We're only a medium-sized company, and if we do well in a new market, some corporate raider might gobble us up just for our market.

> Our management is old, and we're trying to bring in new blood to pep the company up. Now we don't know if its worth trying to save. No matter what we try to do to preserve our family-run business . . . some outsider can take over.

> We can't even make an intelligent business decision without worrying whether it will leave us more vulnerable to a takeover.[23]

The threat is the takeover of the technologically complex organizations at the heart of the economy by the con men and bunko artists and by the wheeler-dealers and stock manipulators who will distort organization and destroy slowly-wrought management capabilities, all for a quick buck's sake.

The strength of the American industrial economy inheres in the accumulated capabilities for efficient management and progressive technology developed within its many business organizations. In the case of any business organization, those capabilities inhere in the subtle interactions and interdependence of a core of technologists and managers, expressing their motivation and loyalties and reflecting their collective know-how and the knowledge they have developed as a riposte of decades and generations of experience in the particular market and technology. That core self-perpetuates, self-renews, and develops with or without a link to some dynastic ownership power. It is perfectly certain that the perpetual threat of the corporate raider and the conglomerate takeover having no rational relationship to the quality of the firm's performance nor to the motivation and capabilities of its core group *must* debilitate managerial motivation, *must* introduce uncertainties which are costly and disturbing, *must* constrain rational planning, and *must* erode organizational cohesion. Nor can there be any doubt that the efforts made to raise barriers and to produce

---

[23]*Business Week* (March 8, 1969). This article further states that an "increasing number of businessmen are writing to congressmen of their fears about threatened takeovers of their companies by conglomerate corporations. They are calling for government measures to deter such attempts."

defenses against raiding and takeover are costly, requiring the diversion of managerial energy and ingenuity from the socially-valued tasks of production and innovation. Imagine the outcry that would arise if it were proposed that operating control of a great block of established and successful corporate enterprise be turned over to politicians, soldiers, or college professors. Yet a seizure of control by politicians, by soldiers, or by academics would be less dangerous and less certain to result in destructive consequences than the recent takeover by con men and bunko artists, stock manipulators and tax-law shysters, wheeler-dealers, and diversifiers who have never mastered the technology nor participated in creating the operating organizations which they now control. The organizational crazy quilt they have produced is bound to be a burden on effective management in the years and generations ahead.

There is nothing inherently wrong in grouping a variety of activities under one corporate umbrella. Diversification can have a positive value in balancing the sources of corporate income, in promoting the interindustry transfers of technology, in creating synergistic stimuli, in more fully utilizing managerial skills, or in exploiting R&D outputs. But that is not the issue. The issue is merger as a technique of corporate takeover used on a massive scale in conjunction with manipulated gain through security floatation and the realization of tax benefits. This is a real and present danger. What is to be done about it?

Congress has occasionally threatened to reduce tax benefits that serve as merger bait though no action has as yet been forthcoming on that score. Indeed, it is a scandal that there should be any tax incentive whatsoever to merge. The tax system, on the contrary, should be designed as a merger deterrent.

The Securities and Exchange Commission intends to require a finer breakdown in corporate reporting presumably to expose to public view the actual performance of corporate acquisitions. This is commendable but trivial, a thimble to bail out an ocean. More to the point would be a flat refusal to allow any new stock flotations based on merger and acquisition.

The modern merger movement threatens basic managerial and technological capabilities and the organizational rationale of corporate economy. From society's viewpoint there is nothing to be lost and perhaps everything to be gained by stopping that movement completely and with no equivocation.

Chapter 14

Internal Structure and Control of Organization and Public Policy

Liberalism supposed that there was an economic universe where an infinite number of individuals competed as entrepreneurs, laborers, and consumers; and where a free-moving, flexible price could be relied upon to direct their activities and to allocate resources optimally. This book has tried to show the irrelevance of that conception to the actualities of the organizational (big business) sector; to explore the incongruities of the antitrust laws inasmuch as they postulate the fragmented, price-competitive economy as an ideological norm; and to suggest alternatively the need for a system of control that would monitor, evaluate, influence, or control the specific performance of firms and industries.

The liberal conception of the economy contained two fundamental assumptions: (1) a large number of competitors, (2) who choose and compete *as individuals* in the rational pursuits of individual goals. The emphasis so far has been on the fallacy and malconsequence of the first assumption. However, the second assumption of individualized choice is also false, and its malconsequence for the development of policy will be analyzed in this chapter, using as a point of reference the development, and later the virtual abandonment by the agencies of enforcement, of the Supreme Court's "Doctrine of Intraenterprise Conspiracy."

THE DOCTRINE OF INTRAENTERPRISE CONSPIRACY

Section I of the Sherman Act forbids "contract, combination . . . and conspiracy in restraint of trade." A contract is an agreement between those who enter into it; a combination makes one of what had formerly been more than one; and conspiracy is the design of conspirators—the terms are always plural. The condemned action is between separate entities, each with the power of independent choice, who have chosen to combine, to conspire, or to enter into contract. It might seem that a single enterprise, acting by itself, which neither conspired with, contracted with, nor combined with any other could not be prosecuted under this section of the Sherman Act. Nevertheless, the Supreme Court has found that conspiracy may exist *within* a single enterprise, enunciating the Doctrine of Intraenterprise Conspiracy, that is, conspiracy within the firm to restrain trade with respect to the corporation's control of its own parts. Thus, General Motors required GM dealers to finance auto sales through a GM subsidiary, the General Motors Acceptance Corporation. In 1941 the Court found that General Motors had conspired with its own subsidiary to restrain trade.[1]

In 1947 the Yellow Cab Company, a manufacturer of taxicabs, acquired control over cab companies operating in several cities. Operating companies were required to buy cabs only from the manufacturing company. In response to the argument of the defendants that sales within the corporate family cannot involve conspiracy, the Court replied that

> . . . the test of illegality under the Act is the presence or absence of an unreasonable restraint of interstate commerce. Such a restraint may result as readily from among those affiliated or integrated among common ownership as from a conspiracy among those who are otherwise independent. . . . The corporate interrelationships of the conspirators, in other words, are not determinative of the applicability of the Sherman Act. That statute was aimed at substance rather than form.[2]

Kiefer-Stewart, a wholesale liquor distributor apparently being able to control prices in a part of Indiana, charged *higher*

---

[1]*U.S. v. General Motors Corporation,* 121 F. 2d 376 (1941); certiorari denied.
[2]*U.S. v. Yellow Cab Co.,* 332 U.S. 218, 227 (1947).

resale prices than those fixed by Joseph E. Seagram and Company for its branded whiskies. Seagram refused to sell to the offending wholesaler. Later the Calvert Distilling Company also refused to sell to Kiefer-Stewart, indicating that it "had to go along with Seagram." Seagram and Calvert were affiliated companies under a common ownership; Distillers Corporation-Seagrams, Ltd., the largest distilling enterprise in the United States and Canada. Kiefer-Stewart sued for triple damages on the grounds that Calvert and Seagram had conspired together to fix resale prices. The Court in 1951 decided for Kiefer-Stewart. Justice Black, speaking for the Court, said:

> Seagram and Calvert acting individually perhaps might have refused to deal with petitioner or with any or all of the Indiana wholesalers. But the Sherman Act makes it an offense for respondents to agree among themselves to stop selling to particular customers. . . .

> Respondents next suggest that their status as "mere instrumentalities for a single manufacturing unit" makes it impossible for them to have conspired in the manner forbidden by the Sherman Act. But this suggestion runs counter to our past decisions that common ownership and control does not liberate corporations from the impact of the antitrust laws. . . . The rule is especially applicable where, as here, respondents hold themselves out as competitors.[3]

Three corporations under common ownership but operating in different countries—the Timken Roller Bearing Company, British Timken Ltd., and the Societe Anonyme Francaise Timken—were accused by the Department of Justice of conspiring together to restrain trade in the manufacture and sale of antifriction bearings. It was alleged that in certain business agreements the contracting parties had (1) allocated trade territories among themselves; (2) fixed prices on products of one sold in the territories of the others; (3) cooperated to protect each other's market and to eliminate outside competition; and (4) participated in cartels to restrict imports to and exports from the United States.[4]

In the 1951 Supreme Court decision on the Timken Case, it was the opinion of the majority that

---

[3]*Kiefer-Stewart Co. v. Joseph E. Seagram & Sons, Inc.,* 340 U.S. 211 (1951).
[4]*Timken Roller Bearing Company v. U.S.,* 341 U.S. 593 (1951).

We cannot accept the "joint venture contention." . . . The dominant purpose of the restrictive agreements . . . was to avoid all competition, either among themselves, or with others. Regardless of this, however, appellants' argument must be rejected. Our prior decisions plainly established that agreements providing for such an aggregation of trade restraints such as those existing in this case are illegal under the Act. . . . The fact that there is common ownership or control of the contracting parties does not liberate them from the antitrust laws.[5]

Thus, the Supreme Court has enjoined as conspiracy types of joint action by agencies of a single enterprise.

Critics of the Doctrine

Almost as interesting as the Doctrine of Intraenterprise Conspiracy itself was the response of the professional community to the Court's enunciation of the Doctrine. There was hue and cry from all fronts — from those who were professionally committed to the antitrust attack against business; from those professionally committed to defending business from antitrust attack; from lawyers and economists; from the ivied halls of Harvard, MIT, Cornell, University of Pennsylvania, Michigan State, Columbia University, the University of California, Yale University, etc. The Court's reasoning was denounced as preposterous and its Doctrine as inconceivable. Academic economists found in the Doctrine still another proof of how little the judges understood economics. And the lawyers stood aghast at how little the judges understood of the fundamentals of the law. It will here be suggested that the reaction to the Supreme Court's Doctrine of Intraenterprise Conspiracy illustrates rather how little the economists and lawyers really comprehend of the basic nature of corporate enterprise in the organizational sector.

Consider, for example, the Attorney General's Committee to Study the Antitrust Laws. This committee, appointed by the Eisenhower administration, consisted of 60 economists and lawyers representing a wide range of political views but including those with the highest professional reputations. In 1955, after two years of deliberation, the Committee published a long report. This report was generally favorable to the positions taken by the Supreme Court, but it condemned the

---

[5]*Ibid.*

Doctrine of Intraenterprise Conspiracy unanimously. The Doctrine was found to be "inconceivable." It held that "to demand internal competition within and between members of a single business unit is to invite chaos without the promotion of the public welfare."[6]

While they condemned the logic behind the Court's action, the critics did not find the practical effects of the action itself, in the specific cases under review, to be against the public interest. Some of the committee members looked for an alternative rationale by which to justify the Court's injunctions. Others suggested that the Court should have gone further and rather than enjoining conspiracy under Section 1 of the Sherman Act, they should have found monopoly and forced a breakup of the enterprise under Section 2.

By way of delivering a coup de grace to the Doctrine of Intraenterprise Conspiracy, the Committee reported that while in fact the alleged conspiracy had been between subsidiary companies, logically it might just as well have been between branches or divisions of a single company. That the so-called conspirators were subsidiary companies rather than branches or divisions of a single corporation was a matter of mere organizational convenience or tax advantage. Hence, since there obviously could be no conspiracy between the branches or divisions of a single company, it was equally absurd to suppose that a conspiracy could exist between subsidiaries under the same ownership. To do so would merely penalize the use of a particular organizational technique; that is, the use of subsidiaries rather than, say, divisions as a building block of organization. The Court had evidently been misled by a trick of semantics into condemning as conspiracy relationships between integral parts of a single enterprise.

The strictures of the Attorney General's Committee so impressed the agencies of enforcement that, subsequent to their report, neither the Department of Justice nor the Federal Trade Commission dared bring another case of intraenterprise conspiracy before the Court. The several cases pending at the time were evidently dropped.

The critics were certainly right in saying that between subsidiary companies and branches or divisions of a single company

---

[6]*Report of the Attorney General's National Committee to Study the Antitrust Laws* (Washington: Government Printing Office, 1955).

the difference is merely formal. They were right in asserting that the condemned conspirators might just as well have been branches or divisions of a single company as subsidiary companies. General Motors Acceptance Corporation might just as well have been a branch as a subsidiary of General Motors; United States, British, and French Timken might just as well have been parts of one company as affiliated subsidiaries. Indeed, subsequent to the Attorney General's report, the Timken subsidiaries were dissolved and reorganized as the parts of a single company in the hopes of stepping beyond the reach of the law.

But were the critics right to assume that the Court was deluded by mere words, fooled by the fact that the operating units were called "subsidiaries" rather than "divisions" or "branches?" Were they right to suppose that the Court would find it "obvious" that branches or divisions of a single corporation cannot conspire together? Here the critics were wrong.

It is true that the Court has not condemned branches or divisions for conspiracy, since no case alleging such conspiracy has been brought before it. But nothing in the Court's Doctrine immunized relationships between branches or divisions from condemnation. The Justices, in formulating the Doctrine, seemed entirely aware that their rule could apply to branches and divisions, as well as to subsidiaries. The corporate relationship of the conspiring entities was called irrelevant. The Court was not dissuaded by Justice Jackson, whose dissent in the *Timken* Case insisted most explicitly that the Doctrine was incongruous if one accepted the notion that "a corporation cannot conspire with itself." The majority drew no line with respect to the formal nature of control. Their Doctrine held, quite without equivocation, that parts of a single enterprise (without verbal distinction) can be conceived as conspiring to restrain trade in a manner inconsistent with the public interest and can be enjoined from doing so.

To recall the words of the Court, "Such a restraint may result as readily from among those affiliated or integrated under common ownership as from a conspiracy among those who are otherwise independent. The corporate interrelationships of the conspirators, in other words, are not determinative of the applicability of the Sherman Act;[7] . . . common ownership or

---

[7]*U.S.* v. *Yellow Cab Co., op. cit.*

control of the contracting parties does not liberate . . . from the antitrust laws."[8] The hand of the law could break through the corporate veil to reach and punish arrangements to restrain trade within a single enterprise.

Evidently the Court knew what it said and said what it meant. It meant that parts of a single enterprise could be enjoined from conspiring together. The Court was not deceived by mere words. If it erred, its error was deeper.

The Obsolete Notion of Entrepreneurial Choice

Let us put aside the question as to why the Supreme Court enunciated the Doctrine of Intraenterprise Conspiracy and consider rather why the critics rejected that Doctrine. At the root of their condemnation is a conception of enterprise and entrepreneurial choice which needs to be reexamined.

The Doctrine appeared absurd because its critics perceived the enterprise as a person. This has been the traditional, and very nearly universal, way of perceiving the firm. For the lawyer the corporation has the formal status of a person, is entitled to the constitutional prerogatives of a person, and is fitted into the apparatus of the law as a person. For the economist the firm has been understood as the instrument of the entrepreneurial person, the instrument of an individual will, shaped to the pursuit of an individual self-interest. If the enterprise is a person, or may properly be conceived by analogy to a person, then the Doctrine of Intraenterprise Conspiracy is indeed an absurdity. A person cannot be made to compete with himself. Short of schizophrenia, the individual cannot conspire with himself.

But a great modern enterprise, such as General Motors, Timken, or the Distillers Corporation-Seagram, Ltd., is not a person. Great organizations such as these can no more be understood as persons than nations can be so understood. Large organizations must be conceived and treated differently.

It is generally accepted among those who consider themselves advanced thinkers that the great corporation or trade union cannot be understood as an individual. Boulding's term "organizational revolution" is in common usage. Everyone nods, everyone agrees, and everyone seems to understand. But,

---

[8]*Timken Roller Bearing Co. v. U.S., op. cit.*

alas, once the economist and the lawyer reenter their professional paradigm and bring to bear the tools and concepts that are their professional stock-in-trade, all the talk of "organization" is forgotten. Its implications are ignored. The firm is understood specifically as the profit-seeking individual. The corporation is understood as a legal person. The concept of organization has not yet permeated their way of thinking.

THE ENTERPRISE AS AN ORGANIZATION

Is "conspiracy to restrain competition," i.e., the imposition of an overt and functionally unnecessary constraint upon the spontaneous tendency of the parts of a single enterprise to compete, *conceivable* where enterprise is understood not as a person but as an organization? Consider the characteristics of the organizational enterprise which distinguish it from the entrepreneurial firm.

Sheer number introduces qualitative changes into the relationships between participants. Organizational enterprise includes the activities and involves the interest of very large numbers. Rights of ownership are possessed by thousands of shareholders. Thousands of officials, managers, and experts participate in operations. The large numbers of its participants introduce qualitative differences into the nature of the entity, thereby creating within the enterprise problems in communication and in the formulation, unification, and execution of policy. A familiar case, not unique but one of a larger genre, is the "separation of ownership from control" and the alleged inability of shareholders to exercise the rights of possession to which legal status entitles them.

The powers of decision-making, action-taking, censure, and veto are widely dispersed for several other reasons as well. *Complexity of functions proliferates specialists whose positions are rendered quasi-autonomous by the particularity of their competencies.* The modern organizational enterprise performs not a few but a very large number of functions, each of which may be carried to a point of great complexity. The adequate understanding and performance of these functions requires the knowledge of experts. In many instances the expertise called for evolves only out of long experience in one of the multiple functions of a given organization itself. Nor is this proliferation of experts due only to the greater diversity of activities carried on by a single enterprise. The sheer volume of business makes it possible to subdivide the management and control function itself into specialities and, thereby, to reap the benefits of a greater division of labor. What in the small firm is the domain of a single entrepreneurial jack-of-all-choices becomes in organizational enterprise the separate provinces of "personnel management," "public relations," "design engineering," "operations research," "investment analysis," etc. The expert and specialized groups become something of worlds unto themselves, self-contained and shielded from external surveillance and direction by the incapacity of the uninitiated to evaluate their activities.

The scale and diversity of an enterprise's activity goes beyond the individual's powers of comprehension. Control cannot be extended beyond the capacities of that which controls, and the limits of control by one or a few at a single locus of power is ultimately the capacity of an individual to comprehend and to act. The range and diversity of phenomena embodied in the modern organizational enterprise go beyond the capacities even of the most gifted individual, and what cannot be comprehended by a single one cannot be comprehended by a group of persons acting as one. The task of control must be divided.

Optimal adaptation, and sometimes competitive necessity, requires that operations be decentralized and authority delegated. Decentralization is often a preferred technique of organization for several reasons: (1) to add flexibility and adaptability to specified operations; (2) to provide a training ground for leadership and a system for the selection and upward recruitment of personnel; (3) to enable a more rapid on-the-spot business response to problems and opportunities; (4) to tap managerial creativity; and (5) to spur managerial efforts.

Hence, the powers of decision, action, and resistance are widely dispersed within the organizational enterprise. Consequently, the following second-degree characteristics of organizational enterprise arise.

Participants in decision-making will be characterized by disparities in outlook and goals. The orientations of those who participate in control are shaped by different functional experiences and responsibilities and are identified with a self-interest in different aspects of the operation of an enterprise. These divergencies of opinion, outlook, and interest within the organization will lead to conflict and competition.

Organizational objectives, functional objectives, and individual objectives will conflict. Enterprise has its functional objectives (in a steel company, for example, the low-cost production of steel products and their sale at a profit) and the powers of control will be directed toward these objectives. The powers of control, however, will also be directed to maintaining and strengthening the organization qua organization. Moreover, the control powers will be used to benefit and to strengthen the position of individuals or groups within the organization. These various objectives of control will sometimes conflict.

What then is the upshot of all this for the Doctrine of Intraenterprise Conspiracy? Simply that as a matter of necessity, survival, and convenience, there are self-directing groups within the corporate entity. The values, orientation, and interests of these groups will differ and may conflict. They will "naturally" compete, and they may work at cross purposes. What then will hold them together, counteract their contradictions, and resolve their conflicts? In part they are held together by a shared image of the company as a functioning whole, wherein they play a part, in which they interdepend, and upon which they depend. Hence, they are bound by a shared and general interest, and by an ideology of sorts. The parts are held together, their conflicts are resolved, and their contradictions are countermanded through a system of government — the intracorporate government. For the parts are governed, liberally or tyrannically, autocratically, democratically, by hereditary domain, by shifting oligarchies, or by powers that represent the special or the general interest. Such intracorporate government operates always under constraints imposed through the strength and power of the groups within or imposed from the outside by the technological and competitive imperatives of growth and survival; by the demands, pressures, and expectations of bankers, trade associations, the "industry," trade unions, and public opinion; and by the impositions of the political authority. The law, as we have seen, makes many such impositions, and whenever it does there is always the question as to what constraints (and what degree of constraint) can be imposed by the political authority on the corporate government without preventing the latter from performing its functionally necessary tasks. The Doctrine of Intraenterprise Conspiracy would have imposed another sort of constraint upon corporate government and here, as in all the impositions of the political authority a rational choice would balance the costs against the benefits thereof.

Corporate Organization as Part of a General System of Government

In the modern nation the exercise of political authority is not, and can never be, concentrated in one man or in one focal group. In this sense there can never be absolute centralization, simply because there are too many decisions to be made and too many that can only be made competently in the framework of a painfully acquired expertise or on the basis of knowledge acquired on the spot. In the United States the courts, the police, the Army, the Navy, the Air Force, the executive departments, the public corporations, the science councils and scientific foundations, the executive agencies of the state, the counties, the municipalities, the school boards, the water authorities, the city managers, etc., together constitute a mass of separate governing institutions sharing the decision-making function. Authority is segmented and decentralized as a matter of necessity. Otherwise, particular activities could not be rationally organized or efficiently performed. This decentralization creates problems producing conflicting interests and powers that are exercised at cross-purposes. Hence, the degree to which political authority should be centralized or decentralized is perennially subject to dispute and, indeed, is at the heart of the controversy over alternative political systems. It is at the heart of the controversy over alternative economic systems too.

The intracorporate government has a relationship to national (political) government akin to that which exists between city and state government or between state and federal government. Intracorporate governments exist by permission of the political sovereign. The rights and prerogatives of its participants — shareholders, bondholders, and wage-earners, for example — are assured and protected by instruments of the "higher" political authority. In important respects the intracorporate government's system for the resolution of its internal disputes is determined by the decisions of the higher political authority, for example, the prerogatives granted to the parties and the procedures required in collective bargaining. And where the conflicts that arise in the bargaining between the managerial and labor echelons of the corporate entity seem internally irresolvable, the political sovereign stands ready to intervene. The actions of the corporate governments are shaped to fit the policies of the higher political government, sometimes by the lures of promised advantages (fair employment practices and access to public works or defense contracts), sometimes through direct incentives and disincentives to action (higher and lower interest rates), and sometimes by the demands and penalties of the law (the Sherman Act). In quite the same way the federal government acts to control the activities of the lesser state and local authorities by taxes and grants, by the lures of partial financing, and by direct demands imposed by law.

In this sense the corporation is one of the decentralized elements of an encompassing system of government. It is a governing organization whose authority is subordinate to other authorities. (The equivalent of the corporation in a more rigidly hierarchical order is the Soviet Trust.) The degree in modern capitalism to which political government allows the large private company to be separate and autonomous is again to be justified (if it is to be justified) as a matter of functional advantage. By the same rationale the Soviets have introduced a higher degree of industrial decentralization; that is, they have extended a greater governing autonomy to certain operating entities.

Political or corporate power is fragmented and decision-making is decentralized in order that particular functions might be performed efficiently. Decentralized functional entities within markets, within the corporate organization, or within a political system will compete. Members of the same corporate "family" will compete (for example, with other branches of the same bank, with other autos of the same maker, with other whiskies of the same distiller) just as they would compete with entities outside the company orbit. Similarly, decentralized political agents (for example, the Army, the Navy, and the Air Force within the Department of Defense) will compete when their paths cross and their interests converge on some common objective. And why not? What characterizes the concern of the individual within the particular decision-making agency is his own record and, hence the record of the operation most closely associated with his own activity and responsibility. These are the purchase price of advancement and it does not disturb him that his advance is in place of other agents and that his record was achieved at the expense of other agencies within the same organization. Such intraorganizational competition is not only something that exists and that the governing authority must "live with," but also is a force of inestimable value that is normally encouraged, organized, and utilized in generating efficiency and innovation and as a proving ground for the recruitment of effective leadership. The force of intraorganizational competition is probably so used in every dynamic corporate organization and in every dynamic political organization. During the McNamara years, for example, the Pentagon organized and harnessed the interservice rivalry of the Air Force, the Army, the Navy, and their branches into a formal advocacy system. Through the installation of Planning, Programming, Budgeting Systems (PPBS) this became under the Johnson administration the model for the general reform of agencies throughout the executive branch of the federal government. If intraorganizational rivalry and competition is inevitable and if it may be of inestimable value, it can also be detrimental. It must be allowed, yet constrained. And in the complex and delicate decision as to where and how much to allow and where and how much to constrain, the lower echelons of the governing system (whether these are political or corporate agencies) are properly subject to the decisions of higher governing authorities since the latter presumably are concerned with the more general interest and are obliged to take into account a wider range of consequences and effects.

INTRAENTERPRISE CONSPIRACY RECONSIDERED

In the light of what has now been said, the following argument could be made in respect to the Supreme Court's Doctrine of Intraenterprise Conspiracy.

In order to survive under competitive pressure and to grow, the modern corporate organization must decentralize many of its functions. Given functional decentralization, a spontaneous competition between independent, decision-making, action-taking agencies within the organization will be normal. This competition within the enterprise will sometimes conflict with other goals of the organization, possibly with the pursuit of monopoly gain. When this occurs, the governing apparatus of the corporate organization may seek to check such competition. Decentralized functional agencies submit to the demands of the intracorporate governing authority (if they do) because they accept it as higher power expressing the *general* company interest. But company government, in turn, acknowledges the authority of the national government. The company government says to its subordinate agencies, "Don't compete. Your competition runs counter to the company interest." Can the political authority then command the corporate government, "Impose no restraints on the competition of your decentralized agencies, whenever such restraints have the effect of fixing prices in an industry or of penalizing competitors or excluding external competition"? Can the national government constrain the corporate authority from eliminating competition between its functionally decentralized operating agencies? In its Doctrine of Intraenterprise Conspiracy, the Supreme Court answered, "Yes. It can. It should."

Whether or not the Doctrine of Intraenterprise Conspiracy is a desirable social policy, it is at least clear that one can conceive of certain sorts of intraenterprise competition as something that should be encouraged and protected. If this is so, it follows that a social policy of encouraging such competition is also conceivable. If we accept organizational enterprise as a fact of life and are aware of the nature of decision-making within its framework, the Doctrine of Intraenterprise Conspiracy becomes, at least, a possible social choice. And if we believe that certain sorts of intraenterprise competition are in the public interest (even though to allow them might eliminate particular profit opportunities for the company) and, hence, believe that such intraenterprise competition should be encouraged and protected, then the Doctrine of Intraenterprise Conspiracy becomes not merely conceivable but desirable as a rule of law as well. The danger is that to apply the Doctrine might debilitate the effective powers of corporate government so as to limit the effective performance of its functional responsibilities. But such is precisely the danger of wrongly applying every phase of the law. If, in fact, the injunction written into the Sherman Act against combined action in restraint of trade or against monopoly (as the neoclassical economist conceives it) were rigidly and absolutely applied, the whole structure of the modern economy would be shattered.

The corporate entity must be in a position to manage activities and to govern its parts. But its power cannot be absolute or complete. It is always under the curb of social expectation and legal demand. How far its power can be so constrained without an offsetting loss in operating effectiveness is a difficult question that must be faced by the political authority in imposing any form of corporate restraint. And it is precisely a task of social engineering to determine how far enforcement in the public interest can be carried without an overbalancing damage to operational needs.

The importance of antitrust laws is not only in their threat and sting but also in the sanctity which they give to the competitive image. Hence, the law shapes corporate action not only by restraints imposed from without, but also by its impact on ideas of the acceptable and the proper by those who exercise authority from within. As an expression of opinion and a guide to opinion, influencing the exercise of judgment, it is one of society's techniques for reshaping or reenforcing its dominant images, a signal and a guideline for the individual and for the group. The Doctrine signalled encouragement to intraenterprise competition and demanded that corporate authority think twice about constraining it.

The Doctrine gave the courts and the agencies of enforcement a greater flexibility and facility in achieving the values of competition *without* destroying the values of technical and organizational integration. "You can have your centralized financing, research, promotion, and investment. You can preserve your hierarchy of organization and your powers of control over decentralized operating units, *provided* you do not use these powers to coordinate action against a particular buyer or seller (as Schenley did), or to oblige operating units to give special preference to products or services arising within the corporate family (as General Motors did), or to force operating entities into price-fixing and market-sharing agreements (as Timken did), or to pursue (what might come to be) other specifically forbidden practices." The agencies of enforcement would not be obliged to choose between all or nothing—between either the values and abuses of concentration or competitive values and the detriments of fragmentation. They might even succeed in having their cake and eating it too.

CONTROL OF THE INTERNAL AND EXTERNAL POLICIES OF AUTONOMOUS ORGANIZATIONS

The regulation of internal relationships is the key, and to far more than simply more effective antitrust enforcement. Rather, the regulation of the internal relationships is required around the whole circle as a necessary phase in the future development of the law. This is so because an economy which was once essentially entrepreneurial is now increasingly organizational. When the actors on the economic stage were individuals or instruments of the self-interested will of the individual, then the actor could himself be considered self-governing; and it was necessary only to regulate the (external) relationships between the one entity and the other. But when the agencies of action become not individuals but organizations (and not a laborer but a great trade union, not an entrepreneur but a great corporation), then the public interest requires that their internal structuring, their internal protections, and the internal exercise of their governing powers also be subject to social control.

Given the realities of the organizational sector, should the political sovereign, responsible for the general welfare, concern itself with the *policy* of the great autonomous organizations both in respect to their external activities vis-à-vis other organizations and entities, and in respect to the regulation of internal relationships within the organizations themselves? Certainly the political authority has already taken many steps in that direction, but it still has a very long way to go.

Chapter 15

A Policy for
the Organizational Sector

During the period of ideological liberalism the political authority in the United States accumulated, piecemeal and organically, a host of residual economic functions and protective tasks. However, its only coherent economic policy, other than protecting property and upholding the institutions of the market, was that of antitrust. The antitrust laws themselves can be understood as part of the task of upholding the market institutions, since in liberal conception price competition is as central to the market function as is contract. They are part of the task of protecting property since the protection of property means not merely the protection of objects but, more essentially, of values that are determined in the market and that can be despoiled through the exercise of untoward powers in the market.

The antitrust laws were indeed an appropriate policy blueprint for ideological liberalism but, paradoxically, it was only after the turning away from that ideology that antitrust enforcement had its heyday. This is curious but understandable. The time of the turning signalled a loss of faith in the beneficient self-equilibrating, self-renewing forces of the market. Conversely, it signalled an increase in the demands on government and in the power accorded to government. Reflecting this change in outlook, the Supreme Court took off the judicial leash that hitherto had constrained the agencies of political action; and those agencies, created in another age, carried through the purposes (now obsolete) for which they had been designed initially. For the first time antitrust policy was put to the test.

The analysis of that policy and of its consequences during the postwar decades made in preceding chapters suggests the following conclusions:

1. The functions of antitrust policy that were operative before the turning of the 1940's (namely, to defend against fraud, deceit, and discrimination, and against anticompetitive arrangements between independent firms) remain viable. At least my observations of the antitrust experience gives me no reason to suppose the contrary.

2. Evidently, every strong action in the organizational sector undertaken for the purpose of promoting competition by restructuring firms, markets, or pricing systems, has been socially detrimental. Positive benefits cannot be identified in a single instance.

3. Antitrust policy has been entirely impotent in dealing with industrial decline, with organizational distortion (such as that caused by the conglomerate merger movement), or with any other matter that should properly be of public concern in the organizational sector.

So far as that crucial sector of the modern economy dominated by large corporations is concerned, antitrust policy is a failure and a positive social detriment. This is so because the ideological understructure of the antitrust laws is wholly inappropriate as a means of conceptualizing, comprehending, and acting responsibly with respect to the organizational sector of the economy. For that sector a different economic policy is needed. This chapter will suggest the elements of one. But first let us consider (1) the demands for a radical increase in the scope and force of antitrust enforcement; (2) the role of the antitrust agencies in the future development and administration of a policy for the organizational sector; and (3) the audience to whom this chapter is addressed.

A new chorus of voices calls for drastic action against big business, demanding the radical fragmentation of some of the most successful and technologically progressive large American corporations, such as International Business Machines, General Motors, and American Telephone and Telegraph. How is this to be explained?

This attitude reflects, of course, an almost complete ignorance as to the past effects of strong antitrust decrees. Indeed, the *question* as to what have been the effects of antitrust action has not yet risen to the surface of public consciousness. It reflects more than this; it reflects a bitter mood. There are those, forced to swallow the flat failure of Nixon's initial efforts to institute a policy shaped in the image of ideological liberalism, who are turning their frustration against the great corporation. Their theory doesn't fit the world, so they want the world changed to fit that theory. They want to break up the big companies that act in defiance of the sacrosanct laws of the price-competitive market.

Then, too, there are the alienated, those who are crushed and confused by the impersonality, the anomie, and the complexity of modern organization. They yearn for intimate human contact and for a purposeful existence. They easily turn their frustration against the corporation as the symbol of organizational life.

There are those who find the pace of change unbearable. In their view technology is the enemy. It seems to race ahead without direction, its power out of control, spewing unforseen ills as black bile from its underside. More and more seems to them to equal less and less. And well-being eludes them as the will-o'-the-wisp. In the great corporation they see incarnate this demon technology.

There are those who, uncertain of their values and without a coherent image of their world and seeking simple answers for common travail, have been persuaded that the race of corporate monsters, soulless superpowers without a vote, are the enemies who have caused their troubles and who must be stricken down.

As for the future role of the established antitrust agencies, it is to be supposed that the leopard will not change his spots; an institution will not abandon the ideology out of which it was created; and Jack the Giant Killer will not become Jack the Social Engineer. The antitrust division of the Department of Justice cannot undertake the new function of control to be proposed in this chapter. Not only is the task outside its organizational design, but also it goes against the lawyer's grain. The rationale systematically inculcated in the study of the law lays it down as the lawyer's purpose to locate wrongdoers and to prosecute the wicked so that punishment strikes fear into others who might transgress and so that forbidden conspiracies can be undone. The lawyer measures his worth by the number of convictions or acquittals he obtains. The social effect of those convictions or acquittals is of no concern to him. The Department of Justice will not perform the task of social engineering. A new actor is needed for a new role.

Finally, it should be understood that the policy suggestions made in this chapter are not intended for government alone. In modern society government is an organization among organizations. Along with other organizations, it operates from an ideological base and its policies change as a function of change in concept and values. Likewise, the policies of other organizations change, their behavioral patterns change, their structure of internal relationships change, and their purposes and functions change as well. Hence, this chapter is addressed not only to government and those who elect and control its agencies, but also to corporations, trade unions, foundations, universities, Nader's Raiders, and organizations incipient and yet to be formed. It speaks to their guiding ideology and, hence, to their policies, purposes, functions, and strategies as well as to those of the political authority.

A POLICY FOR MERGERS

Before proceeding to more general issues, permit me a concrete recommendation based on an analysis already made. Mergers, particularly conglomerates, have already distorted and threaten further to distort structural rationale in the organizational sector. They have already subverted and threaten further to subvert the recruitment and selection of leadership in the corporate sector on the basis of capabilities relevant to efficient operations and technological advance. What should be sought is to keep the control of corporate operations and the recruitment and selection of corporate management outside the reach of stock market manipulators and from being subordinated to the purposes of wheeling-dealing on the securities exchange. What is certainly ultimately required and long overdue is a fundamental change in the system for channeling resources into industrial investment. But immediately there is the need to control the right to merge. The onus of proof must be shifted. It should be for those who wish to merge to establish that the merger will benefit the public. The following might be the sequence of reform.

1. Change the tax laws, not simply to offset the tax advantages of merging, but to penalize mergers. Those who would merge should pay a stiff price for the privilege.

2. Allow no mergers except on petition to a designated agency. Parties to the merger would be required to establish that significant organizational or technological advantages could be anticipated through the merger and that no significant countervailing danger to the public interest would exist. This same recommendation was made by the Temporary National Economic Committee (TNEC) in 1941.[1] Action is long overdue.

3. Following precedents and procedures established in restructuring the utility holding companies after their financial collapse in the 1930's, all major conglomerates should be deconglomerated into technologically integral and/or organizationally rational entities.

PRICE-WAGE CONTROL IN THE ORGANIZATIONAL SECTOR

Having come to the end of its conceptual tether and being threatened with electoral defeat, the Nixon administration threw aside its ideological blueprints and for the first time except under conditions of a major war, imposed general wage and price controls more or less specific to the organizational sector. That this was done by an administration more committed to ideological liberalism than any since that of Herbert Hoover, and by a President for whom all the cliches of free enterprise are oratorical stock-in-trade, demonstrates the blind pragmatism that must follow a breakdown in the guiding ideology. Those controls, imposed without any forethought or rationale, were at once denounced by the Democrats and disclaimed by the Republicans as a temporary aberration and a unique exception to the rule. And once safely elected, President Nixon announced their dismantling. Shortly thereafter they were reimposed and, at this writing, again dismantled.

---

[1]Temporary National Economic Committee, *Final Report*, S. Doc. No. 35, 1st Session 77th Congress (1941), pp. 38–39.

Why should wage-price controls be an aberration and exception rather than the rule? What brought those controls about was neither transitory nor accidental. They were imposed to stem an inflation that accelerated, even as the monetary and fiscal palliatives prescribed by the doctors of the academic establishment only regressed productivity and produced unemployment. Nothing has changed in the condition that required the imposition of wage-price controls, nor has any other cure for it been found.

Inflation is the modern malaise of all affluent Western societies. It is a disease that can only become more devastating with the passage of time. As price-rigidifying inhibitions fade and as those groups with the power to do so learn to respond more quickly in exploiting their bargaining advantage or to insulate more effectively the values of their own income and possessions from erosion, the pace of inflation must become swifter and its depredations upon those who cannot resist its force must become more terrible.

"Controls have failed," they say. But what has hitherto been imposed is not in any rational sense "control," but a mere wage-price "freeze" without any basis for reasoned judgment nor any idea of how, what, or wherefore; and with no command other than, "Hold fast! Sit tight." Of course such controls must fail. And when they do and are dismantled, the fiscal bleeding and monetary purging must start again, while inflation continues, accelerates, gallops, and becomes finally unbearable, producing the threat of an electoral revolt. In the name of control, politicians panic and impose another freeze on wages and prices. And so we shall go, between the frying pan and the fire, until in the years ahead we learn to develop an acceptable and workable system. For wage-price controls are necessary and ultimately inevitable in an economy dominated by an organizational sector where wages and prices are determined by trade unions and corporate policy.

The more so because it was done reluctantly, in contradiction to its professed ideology and cultivated public image, the imposition of wage-price controls by the Nixon administration marks a crucial turning point in the development of a policy for the organizational sector. To foresee what that policy should be, and indeed what it must come to be, it is only necessary to consider what is required for a wage-price control system to be effective and acceptable.

To control wages and prices is to control, in great part, the distribution of income. To decide what wages and prices shall be is to decide who gets what and how real income is to be divided among wage earners, dividend receivers, profit takers, and consumers. When the shoring up of things ceases to be a function of the autonomous forces of the market and becomes instead a matter of public decision, as it does in any rational system of wage-price control, then that decision must in the long run be based upon accepted criteria of justice, equity, or fairness — or at least the allowable limits of injustice, inequity, or unfairness. It is not conceivable that wages could for long be controlled but not profits, or that income could for long be controlled but not capital gains and the distribution of wealth, or that income and wealth could for long be controlled in one sector and not for the whole society and economy. A settled position with respect to the distribution of income and wealth, an *income policy*, is absolutely necessary as a basis for any coherent and workable system of wage-price control. But to have such a policy, American society must come to terms with conflicts and resolve issues that have never been permitted within the realm of conscious choice before. The great task is not to formulate an income policy, but is rather to hammer out the ideological groundwork for this and other aspects of social choice in an economy of large organizations.

To control wages and prices is to control not only who gets what, but also who does what and what is done; for these are the throttles of incentive and to control them is to open and close the sluices of the economy for the cross-flow of resources. Wage-price control cannot be detached from considerations of work incentive, operating efficiency, and resource allocation. And if the reconciliation of these operating considerations with criteria of justice and equity into a reasonable policy of control seems too formidable a task to be engaged in, it is perhaps helpful to recall that there is already a network of such policies shaping the behavior of each of the giant entities of the organizational sector; and our task is only to infiltrate those policies with elements of a social rationale, and to find the means of giving new weight to the purposes and responsibilities of the political authority in the processes of organizational policy formulation and choice.

The primitive and pragmatic wage-price freeze is only a first step on a long path of learning that surely will be strewn with failures and disappointments. That first step, nevertheless, is of great importance if only because it asserts the answerability of the trade union and the corporate enterprise concerning the social consequences of their wage and price policies and, in the instance of the industrial corporation, concerning the quality of its technological performance as measured by its achieved increase in productivity as the basis on which its normal rise in wages was to be allowed. Whatever institutionalizes corporate and trade union answerability to society at large for their policies and performance cannot but affect the image and outlook that underlies organizational behavior and reflect the emerging ideology that will underlie social choice.

All this has consequence for the corollary development of a system for monitoring industrial performance and for the promotion of technological advance in the organizational sector.

A POLICY FOR TECHNOLOGY

The wage-price controls imposed by the Nixon administration were based on the expectation of an annual rise in productivity sufficient to allow an automatically sanctioned increase in wages without the necessity of any offsetting increase in price. When productivity gains were not sufficient to cover that normal wage increase or when wage demands were in excess of the sanctioned norm, then the case was brought before the control agency for administrative action. Inasmuch as the annual gain in productivity lagged behind the norm, or inasmuch as the norm itself failed to satisfy expectations for a rising standard of life, the system was bound to fail. The system followed directly from and, in effect, institutionalized the wage-price guidelines and the ad hoc presidential pressures established by earlier administrations. What should be insisted upon is that this genre of control eventually requires the installation of a corollary system for the monitoring of industrial performance and of a complementary policy for promoting technological advance. How else can it be insured that productivity will rise enough to satisfy the normal wage increase or that the wage increase based on the rise in productivity will satisfy built-in expectations for social betterment except through a policy that insures and promotes technological advance? How else can one anticipate a disaccord between wage demands and the productivity needed to satisfy those demands, or to discern those areas where a downward pressure on prices is in order other than through the continuous monitoring and evaluation of technological performance, industry by industry, major firm by major firm? To monitor, compare, and evaluate industrial performance, new skills and competencies must evolve and a new system of surveillance and measurement must develop within the frame of the political authority. The information produced through that system plus the competencies developed by those who design and operate it, hopefully will enable us to understand why firms and industries lag, advance, fail, or succeed in the transformation of technology, thus providing the basis for an informed policy and a rational plan in promoting technological advance.

Aside from the deliberated development of the general process of technological advance (a process that transcends the firm, the industry, and the sector, and that must take into account the prevailing values, the range of learning opportunities, the organization of scientific inquiry, the transmission of information and the dissemination of technique, and the scope and substance of education, etc.), how might a policy for the promotion of technological advance reach down to the industry and even to a particular firm? For the industries and the firms that succeed, advance, and contribute to the advance of others, such a policy might follow a simple rule. Call it the "Goosian Law;" namely, don't kill the goose that lays the golden egg. Too often this has been done. But what of the others — the sterile, the eggless? Public policy might reach those firms and industries that lag and fall behind in several ways.

It could reach them *through a change in management and a restructuring of the firm.* At the present time, through the process of corporate takeover and the strategies of conglomerate merger, management is subject to disruption and displacement without technological rationale and regardless of their record of performance. That must be stopped. There is nevertheless the need to displace, systematically, entrenched managements and to restructure firms or industries that fail to meet the requisite pace of technological advance. Wage-price controls can provide the means, for when the firm or the industry cannot meet the sanctioned level of wage increase without an increase in price, the public agency might then have the option of negotiating (or requiring) the replacement of management and/or the restructuring of the firm or the industry as a precondition for allowing prices to rise and the margin of profit to be maintained.

Public policy might accelerate technological advance *through filling of the R&D lacuna.* Over the range of technological endeavor there are continuously appearing lacuna in research orientation and in the organizational capabilities and powers to innovate and to transform technology. That is to say, there are avenues of potential technological advance for which there exists no significant research effort and no agency with the motivation and power even to exploit existing information in developing new or in upgrading existing technology. Such has been the case, for example, for the technologies of urban waste disposal, underground tunneling and construction, urban transportation, and economic utilization of aqueous growth that today chokes our rivers and lakes.

As will be seen in later chapters, there has already been developed under the aegis of the political authority a most formidable capability for R&D and for the development and installation of new technology. What is needed is to integrate this capability into the systematic survey of industrial performance and the promotion of technological advance where it lags.

Public policy would also reach firms *through public investment in the transformation of technology.* It frequently seems that the gains which accrue through the installation of new technology (and very great gains they may be) are so disproportionately externalized that there is no motivation for the corporate entity to undertake them. Under those circumstances the political authority must be prepared to bear the cost of such technological transformation. Moreover, an effective system of wage-price control must increase very considerably the need for public investment in the transformation of industrial technology for the following reason.

Wage-price control makes explicit what for a long time has been implicit, in some industries at least, in the expectations of management; namely, that price in the industry will stabilize at a level that allows a "normal" rate of return on the investment required to install the existing and prevailing technology. Anything above that return will bring outsiders into the industry or will be eaten up by an accelerated rate of wage increase and now, under a system of wage-price control, will not be permitted by the political authority. Suppose then that this constraint upon future pricing exists in actuality or in management's expectations; i.e., that management does not expect that future prices will allow any more than a "fair return" on the investment required to install the existing technology. Suppose there arises the opportunity for a major transformation of technology that will greatly increase productivity and reduce operating costs, but such a transformation would require a massive influx of new investment and would render obsolete and displace the existing capital structure. Then, under the assumption of "fair return" who will lose and who will gain by this transformation of technology? Consumers will certainly gain through the lowering of prices. Workers may gain through higher wages. But ownership, those who have invested in or have a claim upon the yields allowed on the existing and installed technology, have everything to lose and nothing to gain. Given "fair return," no matter how much the new technology reduces real costs and no matter how great are its social values, the transformation of technology can only spell losses for them. Schumpeter assumed that regardless of the interests of existing ownership, innovators would infiltrate with the new technology and existing equities would be swept into oblivion by the "gales of creative destruction." But in the modern organizational sector the significant influx of new firms is very rare, and generally the transformation to technology must occur from within an existing framework of industrial control. In such industries management can resist the "gales of creative destruction" and, solicitous of the interests of existing ownership, it does so by avoiding innovation, by stalling transformation, or by only very slowly installing new technology through the process of "normal replacement" thereby denying society the gains of higher productivity. I believe that this is the reason why the great, established, capital-intensive industries in the United States (such as the steel industry) have been technologically outpaced by competitors in Germany and Japan, whose capital structures were destroyed or depleted during the war and, therefore, had no ownership interest threatened by the installation of a new technology.

Wage-price control cannot help but institutionalize and give new force to "fair return" as an operating principle in pricing, and thereby generalize and strongly reenforce the resistance to investment in the transformation of technology. Nor is management morally culpable, particularly under a system of price control based on the conception of "fair return," in attempting to protect the interests of ownership. If it is the public (and not ownership) that will benefit from a technological transformation, then surely it is not unreasonable that the public should pay for that transformation. Therefore, as a necessary complement of the system of wage-price control, the political authority must develop the capacity to assess technological opportunities in the offing, industry by industry, and be willing and able to initiate negotiations and finance warranted technological transformation, given the assurance through wage-price control that the gains consequent upon such transformation will be passed on in the form of lower prices or higher wages. In that way society would benefit, the competitive position of the firm and the industry in world trade would be protected, and the "legitimate" interests of ownership would not be jeopardized.

THE POSSIBILITY OF POLICY

To speak of public policy is to speak of a complex decision encompassing ends and means, based on settled objectives and framed in a coherent conception of circumstances. Policy is an idea as to what to do with respect to purposes and responsibilities, i.e., *functions* of the political authority. This book has been about the emerging functions of the political authority in the United States, i.e., its new purposes and responsibilities, and the implications of these for policy.

Function Competence and Power

There remains this question. Has the political authority the competence and the power that is needed rationally to formulate and effectively to implement a policy appropriate for the organizational sector? And if it does not, what is necessary so that the political authority can come to comprehend what needs to be known and to do what needs to be done in planning for, and in influencing or controlling, the choices of the powerful public agencies and the great corporations that operate in that sector? The final section of this chapter will deal with these questions.

Social Planning and Operations Management

What is required in effect is a second stratum in the decision system of the organizational sector, one that speaks for the responsibilities of the political authority in matters of general social concern, e.g., price stability and full employment; equity in income distribution; the liberties and opportunities of the individual within and vis-à-vis the organization; the conservation of resources and the preservation of the environment; the development and viability of the communications, transportation, and energy networks as integral national systems; and the maintenance of a satisfactory rate of technological advance and economic growth. What is at issue is not another form of public regulation, but the creation of two independent but co-existing and interacting power structures; that of "management" focussed on operations, and that of "planning" concerned with general effects and focussed on public objectives. The one is embedded within and skilled in dealing with the power complex of an enterprise or some other form of operating agency. The other is embedded within the political economy and is skilled in dealing with the complexities of collective choice and public responsibility. The two are drawn together by shared competencies and concerns, and by their ultimate interdependence. For management in the organizational sector has a legitimate need for sophisticated political understanding and support; while social planners, to achieve their ends, need an energetic, efficient, and innovative management in charge of operations. With overlapping competencies and different responsibilities the two power elites vector into the same set of activities. Both must seek the continuity and technological viability of those activities. Bargaining and mutual accommodation, in a quasi-collaboration toward compatible ends is to be expected. There will be conflict and controversy as well, for each would be responsive to the interests of a different clientele, and there are tensions and contradictions between those imperatives that inhere in the directions of operations and those implicit in public objectives and social priorities. Twin dangers perenially exist — that political dogmatism and ideological presumption will debilitate efficient operations, or that those responsible for the social weal will be subordinated to and made creatures of the private powers in the organizational sector. For that reason the planning stratum should possess deep and firm political roots,

clear lines of social responsibility, and technological competence of the highest order.

This may be what is needed, but it is not what now exists.
In the United States two high barriers, both essentially cultural,
stand in the way of the rational development of the capability
to control or to plan for the organizational sector.

The Myth of the Borrowed Businessman

The high echelons of the American government, its congresses and administrations, are richly endowed with the skills
of the lawyer, economist, diplomat, historian, administrator, and
professional politician. What lacks throughout is a capacity to
evaluate, question, perceive, or organize in the realm of technology. Concerning the complex, multifaceted, science-based
organization of modern technology, the lawmakers, officials,
administrators, cabinet officers, and presidents — top to bottom
— remain profoundly ignorant and in their ignorance uneasy
and indifferent, or blind and frightened, or worshipful as true
believers, or venomous as demonologists, but always naive and
incapable of rational choice and foresightful, effective action.
Faced with blowups, threatened by breakdowns, confronted by
those needs and problems for which a society in crisis must turn
to or turn upon the entities of the organizational sector, they put
their faith in the myth of the borrowed businessman.

In times of trouble when society demands action and politicians need guidance, there will always come, according to the
myth, the good dollar-a-year man to be borrowed from business
(or even the greedy million-dollar-a-year man to be hired from
business) to do the job. He knows his stuff. Only ask his advice,
or bring him in and turn him loose. Make a "czar" of him. In
his goodwill, skill, and wisdom, he is sure to put things right.

In sum, when the politicians are finally cornered and the
President is at the end of his tether, and the answers cannot be
found either in the law books or at the polls, then the "know-
how" that is required to plan for and deal with the organizational
sector can always be borrowed from or hired out of the entities
that compose that sector.

The myth is false. The skills, the competencies, the knowledge, and the orientation needed to plan for or to control the

choices of the organizational sector cannot be borrowed from or hired out of the great corporate enterprises or operating agencies of that sector. Nor is this only a matter of conflict of interests and inbred bias. Conflict of interest and bias are surely there, and are too self-evident to require comment. More fundamentally, the competence itself — the knowledge, skills, and outlook as these develop; and the strategies of action and the criteria of choice as these are learned through the experience of business management and agency operations, or ingrained through training and in the winnowing process of recruitment and promotion — is of a wholly different character and quality than that which is needed for social and economic planning and control in the public interest. Both the operations manager and the social-economic planner will require some mastery of the relevant technologies, and of the sciences related to them, but the two capabilities need to develop separately in the context of different outlooks oriented toward different purposes, drawing upon different reference values, and incorporating different criteria of evaluation. Each operates with a different sense of that which is variable and that which is inviolable, of the essential and the incidental. The forms and character of power and the constraints upon power; the imperatives of organization; the process of decision; the nature and the measures of risk; the indicators of value, motivation, incitements to action, and resistances to change will not be the same for the planner and for the manager. And all this, as much as the mastery of operating techniques and the sciences from which they might derive, is part and parcel of the body of knowledge and skill, acquired through experience and driven into instincts, that finally constitutes a competence for planning or for management.

There may be the few who can transcend the structure of cognition formed by the years of experience and the feedbacks of failure and success and slip with ease from the one form of choice and action to the other. But they must be very rare. Aside from the capacity of the rare individual to transcend and transform an acquired structure of thought, the structure of thought itself, the very capability for public affairs management and social cum economic planning must develop in its own right, independently, as a skill, a body of knowledge, an outlook, and indeed, a competence particular to itself.

The Whole and the Sum of the Parts

Besides the myth of the borrowed businessman, there is another fallacy, also culturally rooted, that blocks the path to the achievement of a social and economic planning capability. As an imperative that carries over from ideological liberalism, each individual or operating entity is constrained to fasten upon and attend to its own small, self-manageable endeavor in the confidence that if each part does its own tiny task well, the whole will take care of itself. Hence, there is no need to ask the large questions or to seek after the great goals. So long as each of us attends to his own business and endlessly and earnestly chases after his own tail, the big answers will come and the great goals will be attained of themselves.

There is a certain logic to this as an operating rule for those who participate in a competitive market economy where allegedly autonomous price coordinates and guides the multitude of individual decisions and private activity to goals that transcend the private reckoning. Alas, it is a rule that has no logic and no place in the operation of the political economy. There is no autonomous coordinator. If the large questions are not asked, they will never be answered. If the great goals are not sought deliberately and consciously, they will never be achieved. Yet this carry-over from ideological liberalism remains and pervades the organization and outlook of the political authority in the United States today. No one asks or is expected to ask the large questions. No vista is open to search for grand goals in a misted future. The tens of thousands of officials, administrators, and experts in the vast Washington bureaucracy are busy as bees with tiny tasks, yet nowhere in the immense apparatus is there a locus of power and responsibility where the fundamental questions are being asked or can be asked.

A personal experience might illustrate this point. During the Kennedy administration I was invited to attend a meeting of a policy council for science and technology set up by Dr. Jerome Wiesner, then the science advisor to President Kennedy and now president of MIT. During these meetings Dr. Wiesner evidently exchanged profundities with important business executives and well-known members of the engineering and science establishments. So far as I can discover, neither Dr. Wiesner nor the council ever accomplished anything. In the course of the particular meeting that I was attending, Dr. Wiesner paused in his discourse to ask me what was the subject of my research. I explained that I was studying the impacts of and the relationships between space and military research and development and civilian industry. I was asking what were the benefits and the detriments for civilian industry and economic growth of the enormous government program in military and space-oriented research and development, which was then employing more than two thirds of all the scientists and research engineers in the country.

Dr. Wiesner was more than annoyed with my reply. He was positively angry, for all the world like a professor exasperated that a student should dare to suggest a dissertation on a subject so broad and so fanciful. In hard words I was admonished to cut my subject down to size, to deal with a single firm perhaps in a single industry and, in effect, to avoid excursions into the clouds.[1]

There he was at the apex of power, more responsible than any other man for a comprehensive and foresightful national policy in science and technology, yet entirely unconcerned with the importance of the question, reflecting not at all that no one was asking it save this single researcher who worked with a small grant at a basement desk with the part-time use of a secretary. All that stirred him was that I had transgressed academic convention by the breadth of my inquiry.

Illustrative Cases

The following illustrative cases, drawn from the limited range of my own research and experience, may convey the gist of these arguments.

At the onset of World War II, the United States was uniquely vulnerable with respect to its supplies of rubber. All the rubber used to manufacture auto, truck, and airplane tires was imported from very distant lands; nearly all of it came from Malaysia. The capture by an enemy of those distant places or a cut-off of the sea lanes would cripple the American economy, which runs on auto and truck wheels. Yet through all the years of peace and after war broke out in Europe, and even after the Nazis had conquered the whole of Western Europe, the simple realization

---

[1]Some of the results of that study were published in Robert A. Solo, "Gearing Military R&D to Economic Growth," *Harvard Business Review* (November–December, 1962).

of that vulnerability could not find its way into public consciousness or political action. Considering the turmoil, cogitation, argumentation, political infighting and outfighting, and general controversy in the tons of newsprint and reams of reports of those years (turning upon matters trivial then and forgotten now), it is remarkable that there existed nowhere in the legislative or administrative apparatus of government any locus of competence and responsibility that could effectively take that crucial vulnerability to a cut-off in rubber imports into account. In any case when the blow did fall and the Japanese armies captured Malaysia, cutting off all imports of rubber to the United States from Southeast Asia, there were no stocks available to the American economy save normal business inventories and shipments still on the high seas; nor was there any industrial capacity able to produce a synthetic substitute for natural rubber.

Much would subsequently be made of the success of the crash program that built a synthetic rubber industry in the United States during the war. Given the veils of technological complexity, self-serving rationalizations by those who administer such programs as that one are to be expected. In fact the program, understood as an exercise in social-economic planning, was a failure. It might have been an unmeasurable tragedy. The program was geared to supply the rubber needed for a cross-channel invasion of Europe in 1943. The critical targets were never nearly met. And without the rubber, the planned attack on the Germans could not take place. What saved our skins was the improbable and unanticipated victory of the Russians at Stalingrad and the beginning of the German retreat and defeat.

From the start the government's synthetic rubber program was in the hands of borrowed bankers (Jesse Jones and his boys from the Reconstruction Finance Corporation) on the one hand, and borrowed businessmen (executives and engineers from big oil companies) on the other. In the key decision as to what technology the government should install, the borrowed businessmen, thinking like oil company executives and engineers, planned the installation of a technology that would produce synthetic rubber exclusively from petroleum. And the RFC officials, thinking like commercial bankers, gave the go ahead to the biggest companies with the best credit rating. But Congress, reflecting the rising pressure of public frustration and fears concerning rubber, threatened to set up a rubber program independent of the President and outside his authority. This revolt, the most dangerous ever experienced by the Roosevelt administration, was led by the farm bloc senators. The so-called Baruch Committee, hastily convoked to review the program, decided that a small portion of the planned synthetic rubber output should be produced from alcohol converted from surplus grain rather than entirely from petroleum. It was a concession made as a bone thrown to howling political dogs. Yet it was the alcohol-based, grain-using installations that produced virtually all the synthetic rubber made during the critical stages of the war. By the time petroleum-based rubber was available in significant quantities, it was all over but the shouting. So far as the war was concerned the petroleum-based capacity need never have been built. That capacity, which constituted the bulk of the program, was worse than a waste for it drained away vital materials and crucial skills.

My intention is not to rake up scandals nor to infer wickedness and corruption, but to show how pernicious is the myth of the borrowed businessman. Those who made the key decisions thought like sound bankers and good businessmen, and by the criteria of commercial investment they were right. They failed as public planners because the criteria they used and the outlook that served them well as bankers and businessmen were of another order than that which was needed for public management and social planning.[2]

As this is written the United States faces the energy crisis of 1974. For decades the politicians and the oilmen have been engaged in a play of maneuver and pressure, of favor and palaver, of give and get, until now, descending like a comet from outside the region of public awareness or congressional understanding — crisis.

During the Truman, Eisenhower, Kennedy, Johnson, and Nixon administrations quotas were imposed sharply closing down the importation of petroleum on grounds of national security. For decade after decade measures were deliberately taken to accelerate the depletion of our domestic oil reserves on grounds of national security. The political authority exhausted our domestic supplies of petroleum, always guided by wisdom of oil company executives and engineers, on the grounds that

---

[2]For a complete analysis of this episode, see Robert Solo, *Synthetic Rubber: A Case Study in Technological Development Under Government Direction* (Washington: Government Printing Office, 1959) and Robert Solo, "Research and Development in the Synthetic Rubber Industry," *Quarterly Journal of Economics* (February, 1954).

to do so would make the nation more secure. We are now paying the price of that stupidity. That a position so absurd as this was accepted and supported, for decade after decade, by the highest public officials from the President on down, with no sign of protest from honorable congressmen and distinguished senators of either party, nor from journalists and commentators, or from highly placed academics, is something to be explained. Granted, some politicians were influenced and some were owned by the oilmen from Oklahoma and Texas. But the rest? Theirs was the acceptance and passivity of ignorance. This strange policy could be established and work its damage unquestioned because the politicians, lawyers, economists, and administrators shied away from anything that bordered on the technological and there was no locus of authority answerable to the electorate and responsible for the public weal that was competent to take issue or at least to protest, to expose, or to inform against a policy so profoundly detrimental to the commonweal.

Suddenly the energy crisis is upon us. In haste an energy "czar" is crowned, a Colorado politician who is out before he is in. Another "czar" ascends the throne, this time a bond underwriter borrowed from Wall Street. He in turn brings in a corps of oil company officials to guide and advise him. Naturally, they advise him to raise the price of oil products rapidly and radically. And there, as this chapter goes to press, is where we stand.

Sky-high prices and huge oil company profits will be justified by the new czar on the grounds that this will induce the oil companies to search for and to discover more petroleum and to build more refineries and to produce more fuel. It need not do so. The oil companies have been making very substantial profits, leading to the present shortage at this very point of crisis. And if perchance the companies choose to use their profits to increase the search for oil and to build more refineries, they need not do so in the American domain where reserves and production can be safely geared to American needs and operations kept within reach of the American tax collector and within the scope of American public control. They may choose rather to build, as they have been building, and to search for new reserves, as they have been searching, elsewhere — in Africa, Asia, Malaysia, or Arabia — where controls perhaps are weaker and profits are higher. Alas, there exists in the political authority no locus of responsibility with the power to ask and the competence to assess the answers given to such questions as these, or with the competence to determine and the power to decide that there may be more preferred means of exploring for or promoting and guiding the exploration for oil reserves safe within the American domain, other than that of stuffing the oil companies with profits and relying on them to do the job; that there may be other preferred means of building or assuring the rapid construction of petroleum refineries than allowing this as an option to oil companies gorged with profits; that there may be other outlets for investment to the end of increasing energy supplies preferred to that of exploring for petroleum; or that there are other ways, surely to be preferred, of diverting resources away from the consumer than through the nexus of company profits.

Using a complex set of tax exemptions, tax shelters, and profit insurance schemes, for decades the American government has heavily subsidized American investment abroad, favoring those American corporations and individuals who invest or who establish operations in foreign countries as compared to American corporations and individuals who invest and who establish operations in the United States. This policy has had two effects. First, it has profoundly debilitated the bargaining strength of organized labor in the United States. American entrepreneurship, particularly in the softgoods and needlework trades, while still selling in the American market, have moved their operations abroad not by reason of absolute or comparative advantage in relative productivity but because the power to exploit labor and to escape sharing in the social burden of taxation is greater elsewhere. Secondly, it has accelerated economic growth and development in foreign countries at the expense of economic growth and development in the United States. Not only are there great external economies consequent upon such investment, i.e., economic benefits outside and beyond the measure of profits, gained by the foreign and lost to the American economy; more than that, the cream of creative entrepreneurship and innovative engineering are withdrawn from the American economy and serve to energize the process of technological advance and organizational development elsewhere rather than at home. It is not surprising that those countries that have in postwar decades consistently outpaced us in technological advance and outraced us in economic growth, have constrained (rather than subsidizing) the outflow of industrial investment. The Japanese, who grew the fastest of all, until 1973 forbade external investment entirely.

How could it be that such a policy that subsidized investment abroad, diverting real and financial resources from the process of American growth and financing the demise of the American economy, flourished for decade after decade with no sound of protest from journalists and commentators; from reigning economists and high academics; from honorable congressmen and distinguished senators of either party; from experts, officials, administrators, cabinet officers, or presidents? Some may have been more concerned with corporate profits than the national welfare. The rest were immobilized by ignorance. They shied away from the technological and they could not comprehend the complexities of the organizational sector. There existed no locus of responsibility and competence in government able to confront, comprehend, inform, sound the alarm, or take decisive action with respect to such matters as these.

In the legislative apparatus and in the high echelons of the political authority there exists no competence to comprehend the technological and science-based activities of the so-called military-industrial complex, i.e., that part of the organizational sector that works for, is dependent upon, and nominally is controlled by the military commands,[3] except in the event of extraordinary failures, actual breakdowns of equipment or a continuum of crucial scheduling shortruns and of high cost overruns. In 1962, under the Kennedy administration, a study was made of this complex, quite unique in its depth and perceptiveness, as a joint effort of the Secretary of Defense, the Administrator of NASA, the Chairman of the Civil Service Commission, the Chairman of the Atomic Energy Commission, the Director of the National Science Foundation, the Director of the Budget, and the Special Assistant to the President for Science and Technology, to comprehend an evident malaise there.[4] The study found the source of the problem in the failure of government to develop a competence sufficient to comprehend and control, able to lead and direct the powerful private contractees and the

---

[3]For an analysis of this relationship, see Chapter 24, "Research and Development in the American Political Economy," of Robert Solo, *Economic Organizations and Social Systems* (Indianapolis: Bobbs-Merrill Co., 1967).

[4]*Report to the President on Government Contracting for Research and Development* (Washington: Government Printing Office, 1962).

complex activities and crucial tasks in which they were engaged. Inasmuch as that competence did develop, it was continuously being eroded by the hiring away of the top talent in the government's contracting authority by those whom that authority nominally directed and controlled.

How To Create the Capability?

That competence that marries a mastery of technology to a mastery of political process, and is shaped to the outlook of public planning and incorporates the criteria of social choice, can only be developed through the experience of able individuals with such planning as their responsibility and task. There have been such persons, dedicated and able, through whose experience in war and crisis such a competence has developed, and has as quickly dissipated when wars ended and crisis ebbed. What lacks is an identifiable body of knowledge and skill, systematically inculcated, continuously available, cumulatively developing through time. For that there must be professional identification and career opportunity sufficient to attract the ambitious and to satisfy the dedicated, which in turn requires a public that is conscious and politics that are sensitized to the need for this competence in government. A self-image and public image that will focus collective expectation on the one side and that will guide private learning and ambition on the other must take form.

Yesterday I spoke to the Chairman of the Department of Chemical Engineering at a large midwestern university. He agreed that to deal with the energy crisis required something other and more than the knowledge of operating technology and the skills and competencies developed through the business experience of oil company executives. Because his students know that from the laboratory, the drawing board, or the drilling rig, the way up is through the executive suite, they frequently combine further graduate work in business administration with their engineering studies. "Why not," I asked, "since the task of effective public control is so crucial, have them combine their work in chemical engineering with studies in economic planning and public affairs management?" "Great idea," he replied, "but who will hire them?" I didn't answer, for I knew that the answer was, alas, "No one."

The Power Base

If one conceives of an agency that would plan for, interact with, participate in the decisions of, influence, support, constrain, and regulate some part of the activities of the organizational sector, then that agency must possess more than competence. It must have autonomous power, a capacity for independent decision based upon support from outside the sector that is charged with planning, influencing, and, to some degree, controlling. Or else that agency will be captured and itself controlled, made into a servant of and an apologist for the organizational sector. Can such a power base be created?

It can be. It has been. For good, and often for ill, agencies of the political authority have operated as an autonomous force independent of the private interests with which they dealt; e.g., the judiciary (especially the American Supreme Court), the military in nearly all countries, to some degree the State Department and its counterparts, and allegedly the elite corps of higher civil servants in Great Britain, Germany, and Scandinavia.

What then are the ingredients of this power? Evidently, they are a professional esprit, a prideful self-image, an identification with a group that stands apart. Required for and leading to all this is a system of training, of recruitment and career opportunities that beckon the ambitious and challenge the dedicated. And underlying this must be an ideology, accepted at large, that is institutionalized in the agency and expressed in the activities of its participants. Sometimes, and perhaps particularly in this instance, the agency itself must take on the role of a teacher or propagandist with the opportunity to proselytize, inform, and convince; to justify its choices; to state its case; and to seek actively a basis for support among society at large as the clientele it intends to serve.

Chapter 16

From Monopoly Regulation to Planning the Infrastructure: Energy

Ideological liberalism conceived of a universe of competitive firms whose behavior was controlled and whose efforts were directed by the autonomous force of free-moving price. In this conception there were dark corners in the economic universe that could not be reached by the salutary force of price competition and where the public authority must deal with the anomalies of monopoly. In Europe these monopolies passed into government ownership but in the United States more generally a system of regulation was developed that was intended to protect the consumer by limiting the earnings of the monopolist to the level of "fair return." During the epoch of liberalism, the solicitude of the Court for the rights of property prevented that system from ever being effectively applied. As with antitrust it was only with the turning away from the ideology of liberalism that the regulation of monopoly, as designed under the ideological blueprints of liberalism, could be put to the test. And, as with antitrust, "when it got there, the cupboard was bare." The objectives of that regulation turned out to be untenable. The theory made manifest in action and exposed to the hard light of operational realities has dissolved as a guideline to policy. The agencies of regulation are in disarray. The problems of those areas of the economy traditionally associated with "natural monopoly" have taken an entirely different form. The political authority has found itself, helter-skelter, without conscious intent, and without ideological rationale, forced by crisis and conflict to engage in organizing and planning the complex systems of the infrastructure in energy, in transportation, and in communications. Each of these is a basic constituent of the framework for industrial choice and action throughout the economy. Each is a universal resource, a cost parameter, and a binding tie for the whole society. The next three chapters will trace this road from monopoly regulation to the planning of the infrastructure, first for energy, then for transportation, and finally for communications. The purpose of these chapters is not as a complete survey or even a balanced coverage. Rather their purpose is to suggest the nature and range of public involvement; in each instance concentrating on one component element of the infrastructure (natural gas in the case of energy, railroads in the case of transportation, and the potentials offered by the conjunction of developments in computer data-processing and in techniques for the electronic transmission of data in the case of communications), in order to analyze the process by which change has come about, and to consider some of the threshold problems of planning and organization that now confront the political authority.

And finally it should be said that there is no attempt to trace this development to the end of the line. Beyond the framework of the economy there is the framework of life, the context of human living. It is in relationship to the environment that the planning of the infrastructure finds its ultimate destination. If there has been no attempt to broach the problems of environmental planning, it is because those problems call for a breadth and profundity of analysis beyond this author's present competence.

THE REGULATION OF NATURAL GAS

At the end of World War II the Federal Power Commission had jurisdiction over the regulation of the pricing of natural gas, an important new fuel carried by pipeline from the oil fields of the Southwest to urban centers throughout the nation. The FPC was a New Deal creation and, at the time, the most vigorous of the regulatory agencies. In the early 1940's in the *Hope Natural Gas* case, it assailed the reproduction costs criterion that for so long had forestalled the effective regulation of public utility rates.[1]

---

[1] *FPC v. Hope Natural Gas Co.*, 320 U.S. 591 (1944); also, *FPC v. Natural Gas Pipeline Co.*, 315 U.S. 575 (1942).

The case had to do with the price of natural gas moving by interstate pipeline. At issue was the valuation of the rate base, in relation to the expenditures made in searching for and in putting into operation the wells from which the gas was drawn, when such expenditures occurred before Congress had given the FPC jurisdiction over the industry. The Commission wanted to apply Brandeis' prudent investment criterion in computing the value of the wells. The companies, relying on long-standing precedent, demanded the use of the reproduction cost criterion. The long controversy concerning these two standards for the evaluation of the property of regulated utilities was described in Chapter 6.

Now, after the turning, the Court accepted the Commission's rate base evaluation without attempting to judge the propriety of the method used, ruling that the Commission could use whatever method of rate base evaluation it chose to so long as the effects were "just and reasonable." If the commercial integrity of the company was not threatened and if there was no financial or operational crisis in the offing, the Court would not subject the method that the Commission used in its determination of rates to judicial review.

Justice Jackson dissented. The majority opinion and Jackson's dissent were the prototype of the new norms that were to divide the Supreme Court during the postwar decades. Jackson was fully in accord with the freedom from judicial constraint that the majority opinion had given to the FPC. He accepted the need for a political authority that could exercise discretion in the administration of the law, and that would stand responsible for the effects of its actions not to the Court but to the electorate. He urged the Commission not to feel bound by any rate evaluation formula or to the choice of formulas that had hitherto been at the heart of the public utility controversy, but rather to approach the federal regulation of natural gas "from the very beginning . . . as the performance of economic functions, not as the performance of legalistic rituals." He asked whether natural gas, as a depletable and rapidly vanishing resource, ought necessarily to be subsumed under a rate-making formula developed for city street cars and the utilization of electric turbines, or whether quite another set of problems was at issue. He urged the Commission to design a system of regulation that would take into account the public's need to insure continuity in the supply of fuel for households. Beyond removing the old constraints that were designed to protect the interests of ownership, Jackson wanted to impose on the Commission full responsibility for controlling and improving the operations of a critical component of the economic infrastructure. Rather than being mere policemen with the task of holding activity within the boundaries of approved conduct, the Commission should assume the function, implicitly assigned to it by law, of planning agent and social engineer.

Speaking to his fellow justices, Jackson urged on the Supreme Court a new and positive role in seeing to it that congressional purpose was fully implemented, and that those given the task of implementing the law fulfilled its spirit as well as its letter. "This order is under judicial review not because we interpose constitutional theories between a state and the business it seeks to regulate but because Congress put upon the Federal Court a duty toward administration of a new Federal regulatory act." Regardless of its constitutional propriety, the approach of the Federal Power Commission was functionally inane; it hadn't gone far enough and it had disregarded the circumstances of the industry and the responsibilities inherent in the law. "The unfortunate effect of judicial intervention . . . is to direct the attention of those engaged in the process from what is economically wise to what is legally permissible." In its preoccupation with fair return, the Commission had lost sight of the real problems of rational utilization and optimal distribution.

BEFORE AND AFTER

Before the crucial decade of war and depression, so far as public utilities were concerned, the Court had ruled the roost. It dictated procedure, method, and judgmental criteria. It alone exercised discretion in interpreting the purpose of the law or in determining its limits. And the whole thrust of the Court was to protect private property from the incursions of the political authority. In its concern to protect private property, the Court so hobbled the commissions as to prevent any effective regulation whatsoever. In the end the commissions were reduced to positions of minor magistrates, clerks of the Court, without independence and hence without responsibility, following rules descending from on high.

But now, after the turning, the commissions were suddenly thrust into a position of independent power and responsibility. The Court, operating from a different ideological base, was no longer primarily concerned with the sacrosanct rights of private property. Rather, the Court was concerned with the responsibility of government and with the implementation of the law and with the effective fulfillment of public tasks.

Surrender of the Discretionary Authority

In the first instance the Court transferred to the commissions the discretionary authority that it had long exercised itself. This was an act of great self-discipline, reflecting the conviction that creative, effective public control was necessary and, in relation to vast and complex industrial activities, could not be performed by the judiciary but required responsible choice by an agency that had mastered the technology, learned all the ins and outs of operation, carried on research with respect to the whole, and made itself expert in respect to the parts. Control required an agency that not only laid down rules but also followed through on their application and stood responsible for their consequences. And if there were to be such agencies or if the agencies of public control were so to evolve, they must possess independent authority. They must be free to exercise discretion. They must have the capacity to make independent choices and, in turn, must be responsible for those choices. In a world of infinite complexity and perpetual change, such agencies must have the capacity to learn, which means to experiment, to err, and to improve through the process of trial and error. Therefore, the Court transferred to the commissions a power which it conceived as commensurate with their responsibilities; and it did this by a surrender of its own discretionary authority.

The traditional dispute that in the past had divided the Court in respect to the regulation of public utilities had been between the liberals asking for a prudent investment criterion in the calculation of the rate base, and the conservatives who would require the criterion of reproduction costs. Now the commissions were made free to choose and to change their methods and standards of regulation. Given the integrity of operations, the Court would remain aloof. Did this mean that the regulatory commission would no longer be answerable to anyone?

Surely not. A federal commission presumably was continuously answerable for its performance and for the consequences of its action to the President and to Congress (and a state commission to the governors and legislators). A commission could be abolished. Its personnel could be changed. Its enabling legislation could be rewritten. The funds it required could be granted or denied. And if the commission was continuously responsible to the legislative and executive branches of government, these in turn were responsible to the electorate. This was the first new norm: to render to the executive branch the responsibility and discretion required for effective control. And this norm, of itself, represented not the radical but the conservative pole in a new judicial constellation.

The Imposition of Responsibility

The conservatives supported the power of the political authority, respecting the independence of the governmental agencies and permitting the exercise of discretion within the boundaries of electoral constraint. The radicals in the judicial constellation (represented by the dissent of Justice Jackson in the *Hope Natural Gas* case) did not merely allow the public agency to act, they demanded action. Their concern was that public authority was not exercised in a manner commensurate with its task and responsibilities. They insisted that the public agency fulfill the whole purpose of the law. And indeed, in the most critical and significant decisions made by the Court during this new epoch, they would demand that Congress fulfill the whole purpose and spirit of the Constitution.

Thus, in the *Hope Natural Gas* case Justice Jackson was, in effect, saying to the commissioners, "You are acting like magistrates timidly following a prescribed ritual rather than like representatives of the public reshaping the structure of an industry and controlling its behavior in relation to some chosen social goal. Wake up. You are stunned and intimidated by constraints imposed upon you in the past. Those constraints are now done with. You are free to act, so use your freedom to do the job that Congress gave you. You have made your central concern the choice between reproduction costs and original costs in the evaluation of the rate base. While all that web of controversy spun through the last century may still be relevant when the task is to regulate a municipal electric company, it has nothing to do with the pricing of natural gas pumped from the field, which is at issue here. It has nothing to do with the question as to what degree and how rapidly the depletion of natural gas reserves should be allowed or how to apportion their use and to direct their flow. You haven't come to grips with the problems that count. What concerns me and what should concern the Court is not that you have denied property its rights but that you have failed to do the task and to fulfill the purpose assigned to you by Congress and implicit in the Act."

This then was a new double theme of the Court:

1. That Congress and the executive agencies should have the power for effective action, and

2. That the Court should undertake to demand of Congress and the executive agencies the positive fulfillment of the public purposes written into the laws, demanded by the situation, or implicit in the Constitution.

Continuing Barriers to Effective Regulation

The agencies of regulation had, for a very long time, been kept in a position of subservience. They had been shaped into minor magistracies without any creative function and responsible only for the application of principles enunciated by the true judges in the higher courts. That habit of mind, that accumulation of precedents, that established form of organization did not at once vanish because the Supreme Court had changed its tune.

Long subservient to the Court, the independent commissions and agencies of regulation were also intrinsically weak and badly placed from the viewpoint of political strategy and power. In line with a political theory popular at the turn of the century they had been made "independent" and "bipartisan." Their membership had staggered terms of office and long periods of tenure. The objective had been to remove them from political pressures. The result was to weaken their lines of political responsibility and support.

Moreover, the lower judiciary did not all share in the new dispensation, nor did they possess the technical competence of the Supreme Court. Old mossbacks on state courts, with characteristic arrogance and ignorance, reasserted themselves as guardians of property and meddled in every item of regulation. And the public utility commissioners, more secure under the familiar hand of a master and glad to be relieved of the necessity of independent choice, did not challenge the rule even where they might have done so.[2]

As will be shown in the following discussion, and as can be glimpsed already in the *Hope Natural Gas* case, the classical conception of public utility regulation was becoming irrelevant. A method intended to put the finger on monopoly and hold its net income to a norm of fair return, had little to do with the problems that now called for public intervention, or with the activities and phenomena that fell within the responsibilities of the regulatory commissions. With the demise of the classical conception of regulation the independent commissions and agencies of regulation lacked any clear idea of their proper objectives or of the appropriate means of achieving their goals. What after all were the Federal Power Commission, the Interstate Commerce Commission, the Federal Trade Commission, or the Federal Communications Commission really supposed to achieve? And by what means? Beyond the occasional prevention of quasi-criminal abuses and the maintenance of orderly procedures, if one thinks instead of the development, the improvement, or the control in the public interest of the vast national system of power supply (the Federal Power Commission), or of public communications (the Federal Communications Commission), or of air, land, and waterway transportation (the Interstate Commerce Commission and Civil Aviation Board); then in truth there was not and there is now no consensus as to ends or means.

THE UNCERTAIN PATH OF REGULATION: NATURAL GAS

The Natural Gas Act of 1935 gives the FPC authority over the *transmission* of natural gas between states, requiring the Commission to establish "just and reasonable" rates. The production and gathering of gas and its retail distribution were

---

[2]See, for example, *New England Tel. and Tel. Co.* v. *Department of Public Utilities*, 327 Mass. 81, 97 N.E. 2d 509 (1951), where Chief Justice Qua, speaking with the voice of Justices Sutherland or Reynolds of another era, makes it quite clear that he has not caught up with Brandeis' notions, let alone Jackson's.

exempted from the Act. Rates could hardly be imposed unless the costs of producing as well as transporting the gas were taken into account. With the Court's sanction the FPC extended its jurisdiction over the production of natural gas by integrated companies;[3] i.e., companies that gathered the gas from their own wells, and out of the wells of independent producers from whom the integrated companies purchased gas, and transported it by pipeline to distributors in consuming centers. But just how was the gas pumped out of their own wells to be priced for purposes of regulation? Justice Jackson was right to reprimand the FPC for failing to confront this problem. Following the *Hope* case, between 1946 and 1948 the Commission undertook a large-scale study of natural gas pricing, searching for a criterion of choice and a basis of policy. In that search the five commissioners divided into opposing blocs. Two "conservatives" were against any attempt by the Commission to set the price of natural gas. Rather, in their view the price of natural gas should be set by arm's-length bargaining between the independent gas producers and the integrated companies when the integrated companies needed to purchase additional supplies. This field price would then be allowed as the imputed value of the natural gas that the integrated companies themselves produced and distributed. Two "liberal" commissioners wanted the FPC to undertake responsibility for fixing price in relation to producer's costs, but were not able to develop the criteria by which such price would be determined.

In 1948 the FPC investigated the largest of the independent producers of natural gas, the Phillips Petroleum Company. And the natural gas industry, fearful of the action that might follow, exerted great pressure on Congress, the President, and directly on the Commission to prevent the regulation of the field price of natural gas. One of the "liberals," allegedly under industry pressure, was forced into the conservative fold. President Harry Truman replaced the other. In 1950 the FPC, on its own motion, held that it had no jurisdiction over the field pricing of natural gas and dismissed the complaint against Phillips.[4]

The pipeline and retail distribution companies had incurred obligations to supply natural gas to consumers in particular cities or regions, and there had been a rapid increase in the

---

[3]*Colorado Interstate Gas Company v. FPC*, 324 U.S. 581 (1945).
[4]*Phillips Petroleum Co. v. Wisconsin*, 347 U.S. 672 (1954).

demand for natural gas for home use. In order to fulfill their obligations, these companies were obliged to contract with independent producers for increased supplies at high prices. Following the decision of the FPC, it would be the unregulated price of these purchases that would, henceforth, determine the prices charged for all the natural gas shipped to consumers. In an attempt to force the FPC to accept jurisdiction over the prices of independents, the public utility commission of the state of Wisconsin sued Phillips Petroleum on whose field prices the rates set for its home consumers depended.

In 1954 the Supreme Court ruled that the FPC had erred, that the Natural Gas Act required that it take jurisdiction of natural gas pricing in the field and that it could not on its own motion evade the responsibilities imposed upon it by the law. Again the Supreme Court forced the hand of political authority, requiring that responsibilities written into the law be undertaken in the fact.

The Commission devised a formula again intended to evade its pricing responsibilities. This time rather than accepting whatever "field price" a company was obliged to pay, it took an average of field prices as the criterion, arguing that if this was higher than costs plus fair return on the output of particular wells, the surplus was needed to induce exploration for new reserves.[5] An appeals court rejected the Commission's rule, asking that it justify by some evidence the need to pay an excess over fair return in order to induce the exploration for new reserves.[6] It was again the Court that forced the Commission, against its intentions, to hold to the objectives of the law.

The Federal Power Commission began a company-by-company investigation that choked the Commission's dockets, allegedly stalling until Congress had had time to repeal or to amend the Natural Gas Act. In 1957 a bill exempting natural gas field pricing from the jurisdiction of the FPC was passed by both houses of Congress and was sent to the President.

But industry made one fatal error — it tried to bribe the wrong senator. Senator Case of South Dakota revealed that he had been offered a flat bribe to vote for the industry bill. The press reverberated and President Eisenhower reacted by vetoing the bill.

---

[5]*In Re Panhandle Eastern Pipeline Co.*, FPC Opinion No. 269 (1954).
[6]*City of Detroit* v. *FPC*, 230 F. 2d 810 (1955).

In 1960 the Landis Commission, investigating administrative practice in government, lambasted the Federal Power Commission as having brought about a virtual breakdown of its own administrative procedures. Under then existing practices the FPC dockets evidently would not have been cleared for a century. The Federal Power Commission was at last forced to issue an order.

Area Pricing

How should the price of natural gas be set? There were numerous companies whose original costs varied greatly, depending, for example, on their luck or prospecting skill in finding gas and oil deposits. Variations in rate bases reflecting these differences in original costs would mean corresponding variations in price and multiple pricing for the same product going to the same market. Moreover, oil and gas are ordinarily sought for and found together. The costs of producing them are joint, yet the price of only one was to be regulated. Since the allocation of joint costs is necessarily arbitrary, so too must be the calculation of an original cost rate base for pricing natural gas.

In its 1960 opinion in the *Phillips Petroleum Company* case, the Commission rejected an approach that would fix the price of gas by reference to costs independently evaluated for each producer on the grounds, first, that costing was arbitrary

> . . . the traditional orginal cost, prudent investment rate base method of regulating utilities is not a sensible or even workable method of fixing the rates of independent producers of natural gas. . . . The calculation of the unit cost of gas is, and will be, an inexact, complex, unsatisfactory, and time consuming process, fraught with controversy. . . . "To let rate-base figures, compiled on any of the conventional theories of rate making govern a rate for natural gas seems to me little better than to draw figures out of a hat. . . . These cases vividly demonstrate the delirious results . . . in three different prices for gas from the same well." [Quoted by the Commission from Justice Jackson in his concurring opinion in the *Colorado Interstate* case.]

and, second, on the grounds that the process of rate making based on the independent evaluation of each individual producer's costs would be unduly burdensome from the point of view of administration.

Thus, if our present staff were immediately tripled, and if all new employees would be as competent as those we now have, we would not reach a current status in our independent producer work until 2043 A.D. — eighty-two and one half years from now.[7]

But if the Commission rejected a company-by company cost-based rate determination, what alternative was left it? In fact the Commission decided that it would set two price schedules to cover the outputs of particular producing areas. One price schedule was to be "applicable to new contracts above which we will not certificate new sales without justification of the price," while the other was "a price pertaining to existing contracts, above which we will suspend price escalations." These price schedules were set out "only for guidance" and not intended to "constitute a determination of just and reasonable rates."

The state of Wisconsin was not satisfied and challenged the proposed method for rate setting. It appealed the FPC order, and the case was taken to the Supreme Court. In its ruling the Court upheld the Commission, expressing no opinion on the value or validity of the procedure but refusing to prejudge the results and joining the Commission in hoping for the best.

> We recognize the unusual difficulties. . . . We respect the Commission's considered judgment. . . . We share the Commission's hopes. . . .[8]

Justice Clark, with Justices Warren, Black, and Brennan concurring, wrote a bitter dissent, arguing that the difficulties of producer cost determinations were greatly overstated by the Commission and that its scheme for area pricing was unwise, unworkable, and of doubtful legality.

> . . . It can hardly be denied that the Commission's action will leave producers for a number of years — estimated by the Court of Appeals at up to 14 — without effective regulation and will result in an irreparable injury to the consumer of gas. The only brakes on the spiraling producer prices are the "guide prices." . . . They have no binding effect. Indeed they may establish a floor rather than a ceiling. . . . Inevitably the area average will be lower than the high cost producer. Hence the

---

[7]*Phillips Petroleum Co.,* 24 FPC 537 (1960).
[8]*Wisconsin v. FPC,* 373 U.S. 294 (1963).

"financial requirement of the industry" will not satisfy him. If the rate is set by the "financial requirements" of the higher cost producer it will be higher than necessary to make it just and reasonable to the lower cost producer. . . . If the "financial requirements" of the lower cost producer are used it will result in a rate that will confiscate the gas of the higher cost producer. If the higher and the lower costs are averaged, as the Commission indicates it intends to do, then the higher cost producer will not recover his costs and the rate will be confiscatory . . . any criteria the Commission uses will not reflect individual just and reasonable rates . . . after all of its area pricing investigations, . . . the producer aggrieved . . . may demand and be entitled to a full hearing on his cost. The result is additional delay, delay and delay until the inevitable day when there is no more gas to regulate.[9]

President Kennedy came into office. The personnel of the Commission were changed, but not its outlook. The new chief economist of the FPC, Dr. Harold Wein, did ask one essential question: What determines the rate of exploration and the development of new reserves? He demonstrated that the key determinant was not wellhead price but demand volume and, hence, that higher contract prices "would not result in the long run in additional reserves and indeed would depress total exploration by reducing total demand and sales, particularly the significant and relatively flexible industrial demand."[10] This answer enraged the producer and brought cold comfort to the commissioners. Dr. Wein's tenure at the FPC was destined to be a short one.

The Permian Basin Area Gas Price hearings continued. The commissioners wanted the two-price formula. It was pitched at keeping things pretty much as they were, and it provided the basis for the sort of "deal" between producing and consuming interests that "practical men" like themselves might negotiate. In 1965 the Commission laid down the first area price schedule for the Permian Basin of Texas and New Mexico, allowing as a price 16.5 cents per thousand cubic feet for new gas wells, and 14.5 cents for gas from oil wells and from old gas wells.

If equity is the criterion or if the objective is to maximize exploration at minimal cost to the public, there is no rational

---

[9]*Ibid.*

[10]Leventhal "Reviewing the Permian Basin Area Gas Price Hearings," 73 *Public Utilities Fortnightly* 19 (1964).

justification for the system of price regulation chosen. The "system" of regulation makes sense only if regulation is conceived as a kind of compulsory arbitration where the Commission guides negotiations between producers and consumers toward some sort of settlement where political forces are in balance and there is not too much squawking by those who feel the pinch. Certainly nothing has yet been settled. A resolution of the natural gas pricing controversy is not in sight.

The Dilemma of Regulation

On the face of it, the performance of the Federal Power Commission might seem an extended exercise in futility, an unhappy tale of confusion, stalemate, and backstairs maneuvers. If there had been no enabling Act, no regulation, and no Commission, but competition with no holds barred between the suppliers of natural gas and between electric power companies and those supplying natural gas (with distributors and cooperating utilities integrating backward into the fields as pipeline owners and producers of the fuel), might there not now be lower prices and a wider utilization of natural gas with larger reserves in readiness?

On the other hand these events might also be seen as the first painful effort in the United States to confront a complex, dynamic industry whose integrated web of activities covering the entire space of the nation and beyond are essential to the entire producing and consuming economy, and through regulation to bring those activities and drives into harmony with the public interest. Understood as a step in the transition from a weak to a strong political system and from a political authority whose role was peripheral to one whose responsibilities are sovereign and whose functions are central, natural gas regulation reveals in microcosm something of the emerging political role and responsibility with respect to the basic systems of the economic infrastructure.

Congress passed the Natural Gas Act of 1935 with no clear idea of what the FPC was supposed to do or what ought to be done in regulating the new industry. The purposes written into the Act were the usual declamatory legalisms. The provisions of the Act, which at once required that prices be controlled to protect consumers and yet exempted the production and the gathering of the fuel, were inherently unworkable. Presumably,

Congress was reasonably apprehensive that consumers might be victimized and resources misused, and hoped that the Commission with its general powers and the large, indefinite objectives of the law might somehow make things right. What more could have been expected of any legislative body at that juncture?

The Commission initially conceived of its task in the classical mode. The thing was to overcome the opposition of the Court. The Court, however, proved not a barrier but an open door.

After so many frustrated decades, the FPC marched victorious under the prudent investment banner of Brandeis and Bauer. The victory was easy, but the payoff, alas, was meager. The major problems of purposeful control remained unresolved. Feeding pipeline companies, distributors, and consumers over the face of the nation were thousands of wells owned by competing producers, both integrated and independent. There were great variations in the costs of producing regulated natural gas jointly with the production of unregulated petroleum. And not only must these producers gather the fuel, they must also be relied upon to explore and discover new resources of natural gas. And there were the questions of resource waste, depletion rates, conservation, optimal utilization, and a rational national system of fuel distribution. To these questions the prudent investment rate-making criterion gave no answer.

In the blind alley of their technique, the Commission was faced with the suspicion and ire of the producers (great oil companies and billionaire oilmen whose political muscle is evidenced by the favored position they have garnered for themselves on the tax rolls through oil depletion allowances, the protections they secured for themselves in a ludicrous oil quota system where the national security was for decades allegedly served by accelerating the depletion of domestic reserves, and in the grants they have secured for themselves in drilling rights in the national domain). Pressured by the cronies and cohorts of the little man from Missouri, the Commission surrendered effective jurisdiction. But urban consumers who also carried political weight demanded protection, and the Supreme Court held the Commission to its responsibilities under the law. Congress, alarmed that the Act they had passed might actually be enforced and also feeling the elbows of the billionaires from Texas, prepared to repeal it. All this is a tale twice told, but the point is this. The transfer of real authority to an agency of administration and the demand by the Court that that agency adhere to the declared purposes of the law, served only as the start of a whole process of political transition and transformation. The agency itself now had to acquire the will and capability to act, and new lines of accountability and responsibility had to be developed vis-à-vis the agency's action. Regulation needs not mere exhortation, but a clear purpose and a coherent theory. Neither the Commission, nor Congress, nor the public had either clear purpose or coherent theory.

What should the purpose of regulation be? Consider, without attempting to judge their validity, some alternative conceptions of the purpose of price regulation in the natural gas industry.

The Commission might be conceived as an arbitrator between consumers and producers, negotiating an acceptable price schedule on a balance-of-power basis, or at least preserving some decent time interim between periodic price jumps. This probably describes the self-conception and outlook of recent commissioners.

The Commission might act as a representative of consumer interests, with its objective to reduce natural gas prices as low as is consistent with the continuing production and transmission of adequate supplies. Here the key question is who gets the rents attributable to productivity above that of the marginal wells. Serving the consumer interest, a regulatory agency might appropriate these rents in whole or in part and have them passed on as lower product prices. It is the nature of rents (in this case any income on the market sale of natural gas above operating costs including the cost of inducing the necessary investment) that they can be siphoned off by the political authority without affecting entrepreneurial motivation or output. If this was done so that rates permitted producers to receive no more on specific sales than operating costs plus a fair return on actual investment and on the extra mineral value of the land (i.e., allowing no capitalization of the productivity of nonmarginal wells), then there could be no uniformity in consumer pricing. Consumers buying from different sellers, even in the same market, would be charged quite different prices. This raises questions. Should the consumers rather than the producers of natural gas benefit from the rents on wells of a higher-than-marginal productivity? If consumers are to benefit, why should consumers in certain localities or buying from certain sellers benefit more than other consumers?

If rents are expropriatable, why should this be for the benefit of consumers of natural gas rather than consumers generally, or (through taxation) for the benefit of the public at large? And why expropriate these rents and not other sorts of rent? The question is not only one of who gets what. There is also the matter of pricing outputs so that something approximating optimal use is made of this as compared to substitute resources. And for this to happen, prices must provide an index of relative scarcities; i.e., they must reflect real cost differences. For the production of natural gas, is it the cost of producing and gathering from the marginal well in the area from which gas is being transported that counts as an allocation criterion? Or should current prices reflect as well the expectation of increasing future scarcities? If prices to consumers were reduced to an average, below-marginal cost by some kind of rent sharing on more productive wells, then price would not serve as a guide for the rational allocation of this as compared to substitute fuels otherwise priced. Alternatively, these rents could be siphoned into a general fund allowing producers no more than a fair return on real investment, excluding any capitalized rents. Prices then could be separately determined by marginal costs discounted for future scarcities. But this presupposes, beyond keeping prices down for the benefit of one set of consumers, a responsibility for the sensible allocation and utilization of a limited resource over the years.

If fair return does not suffice to induce the requisite exploration for new wells, the costs of exploration might be reduced through subsidy or other measures taken separately to encourage exploration. If its present organization makes the industry difficult to regulate, there is no inherent reason why the industry should not be reorganized to facilitate regulation; integrating or separating the functions of exploration, well operation, transmission, and distribution.

Regulation also might be conceived as having another and quite a different focus than price control. A major objective might be to rationalize the national system for natural gas transmission. For when transmission systems develop as the consequence of piecemeal decisions by many independent producers, distributors, and consumers — no matter how logical each might be within his particular parameters of choice — the consequent pattern of transmission facilities cannot be the same as that which would have been designed where planning was at the national level and was intended to link the producing and consuming centers of the nation with a minimal fuel gathering and transportation cost. Nor will an optimal pattern for the gathering and transmission of fuel emerge spontaneously and autonomously under the principle of the survival of the fittest, for in an industry such as this there are no second guesses, no chance to rethrow the dice. When a pipeline has been laid, that decision is not reversible. No matter how wrong it might have been, no matter how misplaced and mistaken, the decision henceforth becomes a fixed parameter for all subsequent choice. With its objective to rationalize the national system of natural gas production and distribution, the Commission might produce national or regional plans to serve as guidelines for requiring interconnections and transmission patterns as a basis for approving or disapproving privately sponsored interstate projects. Moreover, as part of such planning, differential pricing or other promotional methods might be used to encourage industrial development in areas where unexploited fuels are available or when low-cost transmission of fuel is possible.

Power, the nation's energy resource, has for decades been the charge of the FPC (Federal Power Commission). It's initial concern was with the interstate transmission of electricity. Here also, as much as with natural gas, the FPC has wandered purposelessly in a morass, unable to comprehend and incompetent to deal with national power needs or even with the scandalous performances of particular electric utility companies. For example, the Commonwealth Edison Company of New York City, with unsurpassed technical advantages in low cost fuel transportation at the nation's greatest transportation hub and perhaps the largest contiguous mass market in the world, charges the highest rates of any major utility in the nation, operates continuously on the edge (and repeatedly tumbles over the edge) of breakdown and blackout.[11]

THE RATIONALE OF REGULATION

In the traditional view "regulation" was required to protect the consumer against exploitation by an unregulated monopolist.

---

[11]See "Con Ed Runs Out of 'Clean Energy'," *Business Week* (August 16, 1969).

That rationale has changed. One no longer conceives of a few natural monopolies as monsters in a world of small competitive enterprise that must be chained and guarded against through regulation. Elements of monopoly power, i.e., the power independently and autonomously to influence price and outputs, is pervasive throughout modern enterprise. And no industry or sector is to be considered as being beyond the need for public surveillance nor immune from some form of public control. Then why set a few industries apart and put these under public regulation with the directives of public authority substituting for the autonomous force of market competition? The division between the regulated and the nonregulated remains traditional and its rationale obscure. It is by no means clear, by reference to this or to any other functional criterion, as to which industries ought to be and which ought not to be in the category of the "regulated." If the price of natural gas should be regulated, then why should the price of petroleum, its joint product, be left to market determination? And if the price of petroleum is left to the company's determination, then why should the price of natural gas, its joint product, be fixed by a public commission?

Rather, there is a different rationale emerging through the force of pressure and crisis. It is this. The provision of power is so basic as the precondition and context of all economic choice that the political authority must be involved in, and ultimately must share the responsibility for performance. And in this respect the task of insuring equitable distribution of income between consumers and dividend receivers is a matter of relatively minor importance. Nor can public concern and social responsibility be focussed only on the efficiency of operations and the acceleration of technological advance, leading to higher productivity, lower costs, improved quality, and the extended use of a particular resource. They must also be concerned with *power* from all sources, as much through water power, atomic energy, solar energy, or fossil fuels as from the use of natural gas.

For generations the Army Corps of Engineers has been damming rivers and creating hydroelectric sites. The TVA has provided the energy base for a major regional development. Atomic energy is entirely a product of government R&D and the development and use of nuclear reactors has been through government initiative and subsidy. The development of solar energy is under public aegis. The government is heavily engaged in protecting the coal industry and in developing new product outlets and a lower cost transmission system to extend the use of coal as energy resource. For better or worse, government has been continuously involved in the control of petroleum output and in the exploitation of domestic vis-à-vis foreign oil reserves. This multiple involvement has been piecemeal, entirely uncoordinated, and without any coherent rationale.

If the social objective is indeed to promote or to insure the optimal provisions of fuel and power sources to the economy at large, then the present crazy quilt of public responsibility and intervention provides no rational apparatus for surveillance, for the formulation of policy, or for the exercise of control.

Since this chapter was written a major energy crisis has accelerated the movement toward a recognition of the political responsibility for the viability and development of the energy infrastructure.

Chapter 17

From Monopoly Regulation to Planning the Infrastructure: Transportation

In all developed economies the political authority has directly engaged in planning, providing, and managing the operation of transportation facilities. Government builds roads and bridges, creates ports and harbors, builds and operates wharves, dredges streams and rivers to make them navigable for shipping, and builds and operates canals and seaways. When roads, bridges, canals, and wharves and warehouses have been built and operated privately, government has intervened to regulate the terms, conditions, and charges imposed. In most Western societies the railroads also have been built and operated by government. Not so in the United States. Here railroading has been a private operation, although the government has had its hand in from the beginning.

THE RAILROADS

The railroad companies and their many supporters have complained that other forms of transportation are subsidized while the railroads are not. But the railroads were recipients of a vast subsidy in aids and concessions of all sorts. From the federal government they received grants in excess of 130 million acres of land, much of which was of prime value *because* it was contiguous to the railroads. Moreover the railroads were "subsidized" by shippers during the decades in which they epitomized ruthless and exploitative monopoly. At a time when the

Americans were poor and the nation was backward, the railroads spawned the fabulous fortunes and the prodigal, even mythical, luxury and waste of such families as the Vanderbilts, Harrimans, and Goulds. That the land grants and the monopoly profits were capitalized so that a few could skim off the loot and the many be left without, does not change the fact that the costs were paid and the burden borne by shippers and citizens at large. Indeed, that those costs were borne by citizens through the surrender of the public domain and by shippers through the payment of monopoly prices is almost irrelevant. What is essential is that the railroads entered the era of competition in possession of a great quantity of producer durables — roadbeds and the railways, freight yards and switching yards, tunnels and bridges, coaches and pullman cars, and freight cars and locomotives. All these had been acquired in the past and all the real costs had already been borne, whereas the competing forms of transportation had no such cumulated possessions. In addition to the cost of operation, the competing forms of transportation had currently to bear at least a part of the cost of creating the infrastructure and the capital goods margin required for operations. But this is to get ahead of our story. In the 1870's, 1880's, and 1890's there was no outside competition and none on the horizon. The railroads were astride all commerce. The farmer shipping his grain and livestock from the West to the urban markets in the East or to Europe, the miners shipping coal to the factories and homes in the cities, and the manufacturer shipping inland for distribution and sale all depended entirely on the railroads. There was no competitive escape. And the railroads pooled their power to squeeze the shipper dry, or so it seemed to the shippers.

Farm associations forced the enactment of the so-called Granger laws, fixing maximum railroad rates or setting up commissions to control rates. Between 1871 and 1874 such laws were enacted in Illinois, Wisconsin, Iowa, and Minnesota. By 1887 commissions to control railway rates were operating in 25 states. The states were constrained by the Supreme Court from fixing rates in interstate commerce and the pressure was shifted to Congress.[1] In 1887 Congress passed the Interstate Commerce Act requiring that railway rates be "reasonable" and "just," forbidding pooling of traffic or earnings and discrimination of

---

[1]*Wabash, St. Louis and Pacific Railway Co. v. Illinois*, 118 U.S. 557 (1886).

various sorts, and setting up the Interstate Commerce Commission (ICC) to enforce the provisions of the Act. Almost at once the Supreme Court emasculated the Act and foreclosed the possibility of effective regulation.[2]

The Classical Regulation of Fair Return

The Hepburn Act of 1906 and the Mann-Elkins Act of 1910 finally gave the ICC the legislative basis it required to attempt effectively to regulate railroad rates; i.e., to fix rates that were, according to the classic conception, "reasonable" and "just" for each railroad, allowing no more and requiring it to accept no less than a fair return on its investment. This required that the rate base be determined for each railroad following the criteria laid down in *Smyth* v. *Ames* (discussed in Chapter 6). Hence, the Valuation Act of 1913 directed the ICC to ascertain the original costs, reproduction costs, land values, and intangible values for every railroad in the United States and, giving a just and proper weight to each, to propose a tentative valuation for each railroad as of 1913. After offering the opportunity for protest at public hearings, these valuations were to be pronounced as final, kept up-to-date thereafter, and used henceforth as the rate base for the determination of fair return. The process of evaluation was supposed to take three years. It took almost twenty years and cost $50 million; and in 1933 when the tentative 1913 figures were ready, the whole notion of using a rate base for the determination of fair return had lost its relevance. Concern was no longer with holding in check the power of a rapacious monopoly, but with getting the railroads out of hock.

The idea, underlying the formation of the ICC and expressed in its enabling legislation, of setting rates for each railroad separately by reference to that railroad's costs and the value of its rate base, according to the criterion of fair return was inherently incongruous and impossible of application. It was unworkable inasmuch as railways in the same region have myriad operating costs and different capital structures, but rates must be competitive inasmuch as shipments are parallel

---

[2]*Counselman v. Hitchcock*, 142 U.S. 547 (1892); *I.C.C.* v. *Cincinnati, New Orleans and Texas Pacific Railway Co.* 167 U.S. 479 (1897); and *I.C.C.* v. *Alabama Midland Railway Co.*, 168 U.S. 144 (1897).

or serve the same market. Railroads taking quite different routes may be nevertheless competitors with respect to shipments between principal shipping points, as from Baltimore to San Francisco via routes A, B, or C, or from Chicago to various east coast ports for shipment to Le Havre in France. And it was unacceptable as a form of regulation inasmuch as shippers over different lines are not to be given a competitive advantage in transportation costs, but rather where some general cost-mileage relationship in rates is required for the system as a whole so that the development of one region will not be favored at the expense of another. This was recognized in the Transportation Act of 1920 before the computations of the Valuation Act of 1913 had been made. This Act recognized that since the rates of different railroads presenting alternative routes to the same markets compete for the same business, their rates must be competitive; and unless each line was to have its unique rate schedule, the fair return criterion was an absurdity. Hence, it proposed a different rule for rate regulation. Rates were to be set for such "rate groups or territories" as the Commission designated, "so that carriers as a whole . . . will under honest, efficient, economic management . . . earn an aggregate annual net railway operating income equal, as nearly as may be, to a fair return upon the aggregate value of the railway property of such carriers." Some roads presumably would make large profits, and others great losses according to the efficiency of management, the character of the capital structure, and the happenstance of its routing.

Railroad Systems

Within the very year of the American entree into World War I, the privately owned and operated railway system in the United States broke down under the urgent need and massive effort to deploy railroad resources. In 1918 the government took over the railways and during the war controlled their operations as a single system, allegedly with great success. The Transportation Act of 1920 was designed in part to facilitate the return of the railways to private ownership. Reflecting the more technically sophisticated outlook of an officialdom that had not yet forgotten the experience of the war, the Act gave the ICC a new role: to effectuate a degree of technological coordination in railroad operation and development. The ICC was given the power to require the joint use of terminals, to establish rules relating to the shared use of freight cars and locomotives, and to impose unification under emergency conditions. Particularly, the Commission was given the right to allow or to disallow railroad pools, mergers, and combinations accordingly as these might serve to rationalize organization, advance technology, and reduce costs, and to reduce or improve service. The Act instructed the Commission to prepare plans for a number of consolidated railroad systems, each to be organizationally strong and technologically rational, able to compete together effectively. Thenceforth, the ICC would favor those mergers and acquisitions that followed the lines of the proposed systems and would disapprove those that did not. In this way it would promote the actual formation of the planned systems and, hence, the gradual rationalization of railroad organization. By this time automotive transportation was already battering the vested power of the railroads.

Under the Act the permission of the ICC was required before a railroad could abandon or add to any of its established lines or services, or before it could attempt to obtain new capital by offering its securities for sale.

The ICC did prepare consolidation plans for nineteen model systems. However, in neither this respect nor any other was the ICC able to impose a positive change in railroad organization or technology. The railroads chose not to combine according to the plan. Until 1933 they followed their own paths of combination, evading the authority of the ICC through the use of holding companies. In 1940 the model systems scheme was abandoned.

Bankruptcy

The railroads were hit hard by depression. In 1932 their gross revenues were down by half from what they had been in 1929. Besides the effects of depression, they were losing a major share of the passenger and freight traffic to automobiles, trucks, buses, and airlines. By 1938 more than a hundred railroads, including almost a third of the national railway mileage, were in receivership. The bankruptcy of the railroads hit saving banks, insurance companies, and other institutional investors in blue chip shares. The pressure was not to save the shipper from monopoly, but to salvage the financial underpinnings of the institutional investor. The RFC bailed out railroads with loans totalling $850 million. The Emergency Transportation Act of 1933 directed an effort, abortive of course, by the ICC to form management committees that would stimulate cost reductions through greater efficiency. And again Congress changed the rate-making rule. The notion of rate making by reference to fair return, calculated from a value-of-property rate base for each railroad or for the roads as a whole, vanished in a cloud of hortatory cliches. Now rates were to "give due consideration among other factors, to the effect . . . on the movement of traffic, to the need, in the public interest, of adequate and efficient transportation service at the lowest cost consistent with the furnishing of such service; and to the need of revenues sufficient to enable the carriers, under honest, economical and efficient management to provide such service." Instead of any administrable rule there is an expression of hope and good intentions. But after all, what else could be expected? The railroads were no longer the giants of old, astride all commerce and from whom there was no competitive escape. In 1933 they were beaten, broken, and gasping to survive.

Policy and Practice

It is of some interest to contemplate the changes in congressional intent expressed by its laws over these years. From the initial Interstate Commerce Act in 1887 until 1913, the prevailing conception and the legislated intent was simply and specifically to keep the rates of each and every railroad down to its level of fair return. In 1913 the massive effort to evaluate the rate base of every railroad was begun following the rule of *Smyth* v. *Ames*.

In 1920, after the experience of World War I and the public knowledge and official exposure of the great technical deficiencies of railroad organization and management under corporate ownership, the prevailing conception of an appropriate role for public regulation and the focus of legislative intent shifted, proposing intervention to achieve technical coordination, to establish strong, balanced, rationally organized railroad systems, and to build in incentives for efficient, economical management. In 1933 intervention became a salvage operation.

Such were the shifts in legislative intent, but never at any point or at any level was congressional purpose achieved. Blocked by the Court, denied the required authority, because intent itself was out of line with reality, or for whatever other reasons, the ICC never regulated rates and never coordinated operations, rationalized technology, created consolidated systems, or raised the railroads from their path of decline. Then what has the ICC done in its long years of existence?

ROLE OF THE ICC

It has become a quasi-official appendage of a self-regulating cartel, for the railroads set their own rates through their own rate bureaus. Over these rate bureaus the ICC exercises only the most nominal authority, but it lends them its official sanction. The ICC is the industry's board. It owes its existence and gives its allegiance to the industry; and in turn, it is stoutly supported by the industry. The commissioners service the industry and play roles not unlike those of Czars of motion pictures or professional baseball or football, setting rules of fair play and concerning themselves that the industry retains a respectable image in the eyes of its patrons and clients. In its hearings and rulings the Commission arbitrates disputes. It provides an outlet for the expression and a means of settling some of the grievances of shippers who consider themselves discriminated against, arbitarily dealt with, or otherwise abused; which is all useful enough. With its caution, uncertainty, and the slow grinding wheels of its procedure, the ICC has been a price-stabilizing, change-moderating force, holding practice to precedented boundaries and slowing down the extension or contraction of service.

By the mid 1930's the railroads were in heavy competition with autos, buses, and airlines. The automobile and the airplane had intrinsic technological advantages as transport media for traffic of certain sorts, and it was to be expected in any competitive shakedown that they would emerge with a substantial share of the passenger and freight traffic that had once belonged to the railroads. Each of the media had intrinsic advantages, and the aggregate increase in traffic would seem to have provided a basis for their prosperous coexistence. Yet, except in the stress of war, the railroads have been in continuous trouble. They have blamed this on the subsidies received by competing forms of transportation, but in fact they had a great headstart on all the others in an infrastructure already created and a vast plant already possessed. They have blamed organized labor and rising labor costs. Of course wages have gone up and up, in railroads as everywhere else. However, the trouble was *not* that wages went up and competition with truck and aircraft would not permit higher labor costs to be shifted into higher rates and revenues, but rather that railroads failed to increase productivity fast enough to offset or more than offset (as elsewhere) the rise in wages. And if the practices of organized labor in railroads are hide-bound and their demands are rigid, this is part and parcel with and a reflex and reflection of the structure, organization, and management of the industry. If not creating, then certainly compounding the problem are the unprogressive quality of railroad management and the archaic structure of industry pasted together as the random consequence of financial manipulation and never rationalized through public planning or private intent into technologically viable systems. The railroads were pressed to the wall because the competition was more flexible, more adaptive, and better able to reduce costs and increase its service through organizational innovation and technological advance. The railroads are living proof that there is no necessary relationship between scale of operations and investment in R&D. They have never developed the internal capability to produce technological advance, and they have been indifferent to the opportunities implicit in and resistant to the infiltration of new technology (like dieselization) that has had its origin elsewhere. Nor did the ICC bother with these questions. Its concern was not to speed up the advance of technology in the railroads but to slow it down elsewhere. For now government regulation extended itself to the other carriers as well. In the Motor Act of 1935 all interstate motor carriers were brought within the jurisdiction of the ICC. In 1940 ICC control was extended over all interstate water carriers. In 1938 the Civil Aeronautics Board (CAB) was established to regulate the airlines.

The Transportation Act of 1940 expressed another qualitative change in legislative intent. Long gone was the notion of controlling rapacious monopoly. Gone also was the notion of simple salvage. Now Congress asked the political authority to create a general transportation system, rationally organized, where each of the available techniques of transportation would realize upon its functional advantages and have its proper role and place with ". . . fair and impartial regulation of all modes of transportation . . . so administered to recognize and preserve the inherent advantages of each; to promote safe, adequate, economical and efficient service . . . developing, coordinating, and preserving a national transportation system by water, highways, and rail as well as other means . . . to meet the needs of commerce in the United States. . . ."

But whatever congressional intent it was not to be for the ICC, atrophied as an appendage of the railroad industry, to rationalize and develop an integral national transportation system. The purpose of the ICC, pure and simple, was to protect the railways from competition by imposing on all the carriers the quietude of a cartel. To this end it set minimum rates on contract motor carriers (working under contract for a limited number of shippers) and minimum and maximum rates for common carriers (offering their services to the public at large). Motor carrier rates were based on those charged for analogous services by the railroads. Motor carrier, like railroad, rate adjustments were made subsequently through rate bureaus.[3] Controverted rates and disputes between the carriers came before the Commission. The normal effect of ICC rate rule was to prevent undercutting and to limit competitive incursions from any side. To keep down the competitive pressure, formidable barriers were placed on entry into the trucking business.[4] Regulation was geared to accelerate the concentration of control in that industry.[5] Thus, with all the expansion of traffic and even though a relatively small investment is required to operate as a trucker, the numbers of certified motor carriers has steadily declined. What remains to keep the situation in flux and motion are the private carriers. Companies can still use their own trucks to ship their own goods without regulation. Inasmuch as this is the only way around cartel pricing, its advantages are confined to those producers and shippers who are large enough to own and operate a fleet of trucks.

Since 1940 there has been a substantial increase in the gross revenues of carriers of all types. Between 1940 and 1966, with revenues shown as a percentage of the 1957–59 receipts, the

---

[3]After a case had been brought against them by the Department of Justice in 1944, the rate bureaus asked for congressional relief. In 1948 the Reed-Bulwinkle Act exempted them from antitrust prosecution.

[4]See *Competition, Regulation, and the Public Interest in the Motor Carrier Industry,* Report of the Select Committee on Small Business. U.S. Senate (84th Congress, 2d Session, Senate Report No. 1693, 1956).

[5]See Walter Adams, "The Role of Competition in the Regulated Industries," *American Economic Review,* Vol. XLVIII, No. 2 (1958).

index for railroads increased from 43 to 108, from 4 to 234 for air carriers, from 14 to 168 for motor carriers of property, and from 29 to 148 for motor carriers of passengers. Nevertheless, net operating income for railroads declined substantially, from $1,040 million in 1950 to $677 million in 1967 for Class 1 railroads.[6]

THE AIRLINES

The airlines have developed under the aegis of two quite different types of regulatory bodies. The Civil Aeronautics Board (CAB) and the Federal Aviation Agency (FAA) were both initially created by the Civil Aeronautics Act of 1938. The CAB controls entry into the industry, rates, routes, and subsidies. The FAA is charged with the control of air traffic, air safety, and the federal airport program. In 1967 these two agencies were incorporated into the new Department of Transportation.

Like the ICC, the CAB and the FAA have been quasi-official appendages of their industry, serving the industry and relying upon its support. Unlike the ICC and its congressional supporters, however, the CAB and the FAA and their sponsors have never considered their role as that of constraining a monopoly power. These agencies rather have been developmental and promotional in purpose, embodying the drive of the airlines to establish a powerful and profitable new industry. In the background to governmental choice has always been the close association of civilian and military aircraft technology, and the bulk of technological advance in modern aircraft and air safety devices has been a spillover from government-supported R&D related to military aircraft. It is in these terms that regulation by the CAB must be understood. In the earlier days rates were set not by reference to cost, but by reference to the price of first-class railroad accommodations, which were considered as the competition that must be met. The CAB made up the airlines' losses through subsidy. The Board tried to get the maximum promotional impact from the funds made available to it as subsidy and eventually to eliminate the need for subsidy entirely. And indeed, while the absolute amount of subsidy

---

[6]U.S. Bureau of the Census, *Statistical Abstract of the United States, 1968* (Washington: U.S. Government Printing Office, 1968), pp. 540–564.

increased from $10 million in 1938 to $84 million in 1965, as a proportion of gross revenues the significance of subsidies declined from 25% in 1938 to less than 3% in 1965. The major "trunk" lines have been unsubsidized since 1957. In 1960 the CAB established a "reasonable" level of earnings calculated as a return to investment, and subsequently refused to allow rate increases when airline earnings were above that level. In general the rule of the CAB has been pragmatic, accommodating airline initiatives, promoting the extension of service, and encouraging successive technological transformations. It has permitted no new trunk lines to enter the industry, and since 1938 the number of trunk lines has been reduced from sixteen to eleven through merger and bankruptcy. A substantial entry of local and feeder lines, and "nonskeds" for charter flights, has been allowed. As the smaller cities grow in population and as technological and business linkages with metropolitan centers increase, the small lines have ceased to merely "feed" the trunks. As the traffic warrants, they have been allowed by the CAB to schedule direct flights to metropolitan centers.

From 1940 to 1967 the domestic "revenue passenger miles" flown increased from 1,052 million to 75,487 million (the numbers of passengers flown domestically increased from 25 million to 129 million).[7] The response of the railroads was not to fight back for passenger business, not even in those areas such as the intercity connections of the East where they operated from a position of technical advantage. Rather, they met the challenge by reducing the quality or availability of passenger services and sometimes eliminating the service entirely, thus "cutting cost." Correspondingly, the shift of passenger demand to the airlines accelerated.

Air Traffic Control and Airport Congestion

By 1969 increasing air flight demands, particularly in areas of great urban concentration, had produced a crisis in air traffic control and in airport congestion. A major overhaul of the very complex system of traffic control, automating guidance and more fully utilizing the air space for traffic lanes as well as a major air-

---

[7]*Ibid.*, p. 573.

port construction program, was called for. Hitherto, airports had been built as the ad hoc response to local pressure and crisis, relying on the foresight and guesswork of city officials. There has been no planning of a national airport layout developed in relation to projected services and airline extension plans and taking into account land availability and highway (access route) design.

At the request of the Department of Transportation, Congress passed the Airport and Airway Development Act of 1970 which established a trust fund (modeled after the much-criticized Highway Trust Fund) in which revenues from user taxes were to be earmarked exclusively for airport and airway development. The Act assured that at least $11 billion would be spent for these purposes over a ten-year period. From 1971 to 1976 an annual expenditure of at least $250 million would go to modernization of airway traffic control systems. For the full ten-year period at least $250 million would be made available each year to be matched by the states for airports serving CAB certified aircraft. Airports would be constructed or developed under a coordinated federal-local planning system in which the Secretary of Transportation would wield a power commensurate with his considerable discretion in the allocation of funds.[8]

A national ten-year plan for airport construction and development was published in 1971 that surely transcends the piecemeal decisions of local authorities that formerly prevailed, basing itself on long-term estimates of volume and flow at the national level and taking some account of airport-urban transit facilities and intercity access as well as of the environmental effects of airport location and development. However, it is not yet in any sense an element within an integrated, intermodal transport plan.[9]

Interesting in relation to the development of an ideological basis for public choice was the refusal of Congress to continue a heavy subsidy in support of the development of a supersonic transport plane (the SST) in the spring of 1971, in spite of strong Presidential pressure to the contrary.

---

[8]Department of Transportation, *Fourth Annual Report, Fiscal Year 1970* (Washington: Government Printing Office, 1970), pp. 51–58.

[9]Department of Transportation, FAA, *The National Aviation System Ten-Year Plan, 1972–1981* (Washington: Government Printing Office, 1971).

In the nature of the case, there was nothing new about the subsidy. It was one with a stream of support and subsidies to river-damming, road-building, railroading, airlining, and to hosts of analogous R&D projects flowing out of the national treasury for nearly two centuries in blind political response to the demands of vested interest and manifesting a national pride and an intuitive faith (without coherence or foresight, but not always unwarranted) in whatever gives promise of accelerating the pace of technological advance. The novelty was that those who opposed the SST demanded a justification for the new technology in relation to its contribution to and its effect not only on the national transportation system but also on a system of life, taking into account the spoilage of living space with noise and the unforetold dangers of polluting the biosphere with fumes.

The recurrent crisis of air travel congestion should be resolved in terms not only of the air transport system, but of the transport system as a whole. Important in this instance is the use by passengers of (or rather their failure to use) intercity rail connections, particularly in the densely populated Northeast Corridor. Railroads could offer high-speed, safe, intercity travel that would be cheaper, more comfortable, much easier of access, more certain, and almost as fast as that offered by the airlines between major eastern cities if there was the upgrading of organization and technology to the level currently achieved in Japan or Germany.

In the High-Speed Ground Transportation Act of 1965, Congress appropriated $20 million to support the development and demonstration of high speed intercity railroads on the model of the well-established 320 mile run on the Tokaido line between Tokyo and Osaka. In January, 1969, the demonstration started with the once-a-day run of the Metroliner between New York and Washington, cannonballing down the track at the speed of 75 miles an hour, a pathetic commentary on the state of American railroading. It was, at least, a beginning.

TRANSPORTATION AND LOCATION

Beyond the planning and development of the transport function, which must embody railroad and road, auto and truck, airports, air routes, water routes, pipelines, and the control of air traffic, is the basic and very urgent question of urban reconstruction and location of population and industry. Transportation is the functional link between populations and organized activities dispersed in geographical space. The link depends on the pattern of dispersion; but, in turn, the distribution of populations and activities is significantly determined by the existing transportation complex. Both the population-activity patterns of dispersion and the transportation link are variable, and a policy, that seeks to produce a preferred pattern of living and a more effective use of resources should take both (and their interaction) into account.

The Department of Transportation, which came into operation in 1967, is the first administrative instrument of the American government to reflect an intent and to be designed for the purpose of supporting and guiding the development of the transportation function per se. It is one of the new genre of functionally oriented federal agencies, expressing the emerging responsibility of the political authority for the development of the systems of the infrastructure. Its own road to coherence and effectiveness will not be an easy one, for it encompasses a number of diverse and sometimes competitive and conflicting interests and outlooks. It incorporates preexisting federal agencies that have long been engaged in highway planning and aviation development whose prior affiliations and specialized focus will be hard to change. In the few years of its existence the pressing problems and sensitivities particular to the times—the epidemic of skyjacking, the new concern for the environment, the demands for greater highway safety, the urban crisis and the sheer need to salvage through subsidy the urban and suburban public transit facilities—have swept like waves through the new organization and shaped its endeavors. Because of the deterioration and virtual discard of passenger service by the railroads, the Department of Transportation picked up that responsibility and established Amtrak, a national railway passenger service, through a set of highly equivocal arrangements with the privately owned railroads. It is doubtful that Amtrak has the powers commensurate with its responsibilities or the scope for the changes and innovations that are needed.

Caught in the treadmill of pragmatic response to crisis and pressure, the DOT seems nevertheless not to have lost the commitment eventually to provide an integrally planned, balanced, intermodal, national transportation system. Under its aegis a national plan for airway and airport development is evolving. It has supported transport-related research and development projects that range from taxation to tunneling, but a continuous emphasis has been given to the development of techniques for the evaluation on intermodal transportation alternatives.[10] The Northeast Corridor Transportation Project, reported on in 1970, was intended as a case study in intermodal regional transportation planning. The first *National Transportation Report*, published by the DOT in 1972, attempts an overview of the key elements in the national transportation system as a basis for planning federal aid programs, and the *National Transportation Report* scheduled for publication in 1974 will survey the system's performance.

Thus, the public regulation of transportation parallels the public regulation of power. In both instances regulation has been piecemeal and partial, with authority fragmented. In both there at first prevailed among regulators the classical conception of a monopoly running amok, and which must be constrained to earning no more than fair return. For both, the attempt at such regulation was forestalled by the Court. And for both, by the time the judicial barriers had been lifted and the regulatory agency possessed the authority it required, the day of the rapacious monopolist had gone and the classical model of regulation had lost its relevance. Classical regulation never existed in fact. It hardly now exists in fancy.[11] It has been replaced by an entirely different dimension of responsibility, namely for the progressive development of an integral yet multifaceted transportation system as a component of the economic infrastructure.

---

[10]"Computerized models were developed to analyze transportation systems, to calculate the impact of pricing, service, and system changes on road and rail freight traffic, and on passenger traffic by various modes, to analyze the interface between intercity and urban transportation." Department of Transportation, *Fifth Annual Report, Fiscal Year 1971* (Washington: Government Printing Office, 1971), p. 52. See also the discussions on intermodal planning in the Department of Transportation, *Sixth Annual Report, Fiscal Year 1972* (Washington: Government Printing Office, 1972), p. 61.

[11]In the light of the analysis offered in this chapter, it is of some interest to note the report of the Center for the Study of Responsive Law, written under the direction of Ralph Nader and released on March 16, 1970, that demands the abolition of the ICC and calls it "an elephant's graveyard of political hacks" designed and administered to protect the transportation industry from the demands of consumers. In its summary charge the report states that "the Commission should clearly identify the nation's surface transportation needs and compel the several industries to serve those needs. Instead the ICC responds to the demands of the industry, and only if satisfaction of those demands complements the needs of the transportation public is the public interest served."

Chapter 18

From Monopoly Regulation to Planning the Infrastructure: Communications

Adam Smith called the post office "the only mercantile project which has been successfully managed by, I believe, every sort of government. The capital to be advanced is not very considerable. There is no mystery to the business. The returns are not only certain but immediate." Today there is considerable mystery, enormous expenditure, uncertain returns, and retrograde performance in that ancient public endeavor. And the mode of managing the post office, reestablished in the United States as a "public corporation," is very much at issue. At an earlier time the post office was universally *the national system* of communications, an element of the infrastructure and a sinew of nationalism that no government dared neglect.

Later the national system of communication took on a new dimension with the telegraph and then the telephone carrying messages by wire. In most Western countries the telephone system was developed and is operated by the government. In the United States it is essentially in the hands of a single regulated holding company, the American Telephone and Telegraph Company (AT&T), which has twenty-three state and regional subsidiaries; a manufacturing subsidiary, the Western Electric Company, which produces telephone equipment and sells the same to AT&T operating companies; and Bell Laboratories engaged in communications-related research and development.[1]

---

[1]In 1964 a smaller holding company, General Telephone and Electronics Corporation, was serving about 6 million phones and independent companies were serving about 8 million phones, while AT&T and its subsidiaries provided local service to some 70 million phones and long-distance service to 84 million phones.

AT&T itself operates the interstate and international telephone connections and acts as a financial agent and central manager for the system.

THE REGULATION OF THE TELEPHONE

Regional subsidiaries of AT&T operating intrastate services and setting intrastate charges have been regulated by state public utility commissions. Following the traditional "fair return" conception, such regulation encountered the usual judicial barriers to effective control. To these were added, as an additional constraint on systematic regulation, a set of charges that were outside the jurisdiction of state commissions; namely, the holding company's charges for management and financial servicing and the pricing of the equipment procured by the subsidiaries from Western Electric.

In 1934 the Federal Communications Commission (FCC) was given the task of regulating interstate telephone charges.[2] Between 1935 and 1939 the FCC conducted an exhaustive investigation of the telephone industry and subsequently negotiated changes in AT&T's accounting practices that were intended to tighten regulation with the effect of reducing rates.[3] Since dividends remained at a virtually fixed level, this was presumably at the expense of corporate saving and the company's expansion into the diverse operations in which it engages. AT&T has created and has entered into new fields of technology beyond voice communications to the communications of electronic data in computer networks and in television relays, and beyond cabled communications to the use of orbiting satellites and microwave transmissions. The political authority has generally opposed the extension of AT&T dominance into new fields of communication. Thus, control of communications satellites has been vested in Comsat, a consortium of companies including AT&T and representatives of the federal government, even though AT&T developed and built the satellite and provided the scientific-technological backbone to the consortium's operation. AT&T, in its vastness and prosperity has been and

---

[2] Formerly the ICC has had jurisdiction but its control was nominal.
[3] Federal Communications Commission, *Investigation of the Telephone Industry in the United States* (Washington: U.S. Government Printing Office, 1939).

remains an inviting target for regulators and antitrusters.[4] In 1949 the Department of Justice filed suit against AT&T under the Sherman Act to separate and fragment the manufacturing subsidiary, Western Electric. In 1956, sobered perhaps by the equivocal effects of other successful antitrust prosecutions, the Justice Department accepted a consent decree whereby AT&T would license patents to other manufacturers of telephone equipment and Western Electric would confine its sales to AT&T's operating subsidiaries.[5] This consent decree was greeted with chagrin and protest by antitrust advocates who wanted the company broken up.[6] No one seemed to notice in eliminating an innovative and effective competitor from domestic and foreign markets, that the American consumer might suffer and that American export capabilities in an area of evident comparative advantage would be debilitated. Then in 1968 in the *Carterphone* case, the FCC ruled that AT&T could not exclude equipment produced by other manufacturers from being attached to its lines.[7] And in 1969 the FCC licensed a competing intercity microwave system for the mass transmission of electronically embodied messages.

AT&T is the largest American corporation. It has more than three quarters of a million employees and more than two and a half million shareholders. It has developed its own technology. It recruits and trains its engineers, scientists, and managers. It has institutionalized its relationships with shareholders, so that its common stock has come to have the aspect of a debenture. On the face of it, compared to other telephone companies elsewhere or to other industries, its long-run performance in terms of the quality, diversity, and the prices of its services has been quite outstanding; and its contributions to world science and technology, through AT&T Bell Laboratories, has been extraordinary.

---

[4]See John Bauer, *Transforming Public Utility Regulation* (New York: Harper and Row, 1950), and Roger Cramton, "The Effectiveness of Economic Regulation: A Legal View," American Economic Review, Vol. LIV, No. 3 (1964), pp. 182–91.

[5]*U.S.* v. *Western Electric Co.*, District Court of the U.S. for the District of N.J. Civil Action No. 17–49, *Complaint* (January 14, 1949).

[6]The Antitrust Subcommittee of the Congress is reported in 1959 to have called the consent decree "a blot on the enforcement history of the antitrust law." *New York Times* (May 26, 1959).

[7]*Use of the Carterphone Device in Message Toll Service*, 13 FCC; aff'd. on rehearing, 14 FCC and 571 (1968).

Like any large organization, AT&T operates within and its policies are shaped by a complex of internal and external pressures. Surely there are many interests who, if they can, will manipulate these policies in their own favor. Hence, it is important and proper that the consumer interest has power and a voice in the formulation of policy and in the sharing of benefits. But the magnitude of benefits to be shared is a function of organizational capabilities that have been slowly and organically developed. These capabilities, developed through accumulated experience and embodied and institutionalized in an outlook and a practice; in a complex of person to person relationships; and in the traditions, morale, and self-images of those who participate, cannot be replicated but can be destroyed on the antitrust chopping block. Minuses for size in the dogma of antibigness will not do as a substitute for the systematic evaluation of performance. Nor, as we have seen, is there any reason to rely on a policy of fragmentation to promote creativity and technological advance or to upgrade efficiency or to produce a more equitable distribution of income.

THE REGULATION OF RADIO AND TELEVISION

Radio and television adds another component to the national system of communications. The regulation of the airwaves begun in 1912 in the Department of Commerce was turned over to the Federal Radio Commission in 1927, and then to the FCC in 1934.[8]

The wavelengths available in the public domain for broadcasting are relatively few and advertisers want them all. Hence, the spectrum must be divided, being made available to some and denied to others. The function of the FCC and its predecessors has been primarily to divide the airwaves among private users and to insure that no one intrudes on another's allotted space.

Space on the spectrum is scarce and it has a high market value. A license to operate granted to one broadcaster at no cost may

---

[8]See Ronald Coase, "The Federal Communications Commission," *The Journal of Law and Economics*, Vol. II (October, 1959), pp. 1–40, for a rundown on the history and functions of the agency as well as Coase's critique of its operation. Also by the same author, "The Interdepartmental Radio Advisory Committee," *The Journal of Law and Economics*, Vol. V (October, 1962), pp. 17–47, discusses the IRAC, which controls radio frequencies allocated to the federal government (constituting over half the radio spectrum), and "Public Policy Relating to Radio and Television Broadcasting," *Land Economics*, Vol. XLI, No. 2 (May, 1963), pp. 161–168, with H. H. Goldin proposing auctioned licenses and pay TV.

be resold by him for millions of dollars. If the airwaves have value and are to be used for commercial purposes, why not lease them for a price with rentals accruing to the public purse? For more than a decade Professor Harvey J. Levine has been a lonely crusader, urging that the right to use the airwaves be auctioned by government with revenues used in support of educational broadcasting.[9] Congress has been indifferent, and the public has never gotten the message. The Commission continues to give away its great prizes to a chosen few.

On what grounds? Conceivably, the Commission might grant licenses to those broadcasters most firmly committed to providing high quality programs. But that has never entered into the judgment of the Commission. Licenses have been awarded presumably on the basis of financial power, political pull, or chance. And once the Commission has given a license, it does not (hitherto, at least) take it away.

It is even possible that radio and television could be something more than a vehicle for huckstering. Potentially, radio and television are powerful instruments of mass education. They offer marvelous possibilities, not to have been dreamed of in an earlier age, of increasing society's philosophical, ideological, and political options; of widening the range of philosophical speculation and political discussion; and of introducing to the electorate, ideas and men as part of the process of political choice and recruitment of political leadership. The potentials are marvelous but the realization is minimal. The habit-forming, choice-shaping, value-creating thrust of the programs has been toward sanitized armpits and personal violence.

Then what has been the positive role of the Commission? It has had to resolve some tricky technical question in the allocations of the radio spectrum and in deciding when to "freeze" a rapidly advancing technology into operating practice. Once activated, operating practice is very hard to change despite advantages offered by an advancing technology inasmuch as doing so renders obsolete the plant and equipment in the hands

---

[9]See Harvey J. Levine, "The Radio Spectrum Resource," The Journal of Law and Economics, Vol. XI, No. 2 (October, 1968), pp. 433–501; "Federal Control of Entry in the Broadcast Industry," The Journal of Law and Economics, Vol. V (October, 1962), pp. 49–67; "Regulatory Efficiency, Reform and the FCC," Georgetown Law Journal, Vol. V, No. 1 (Fall, 1961), pp. 1–45; "Social Aspects of FCC Broadcast Licensing Standards," in Business Organization and Public Policy (New York: Holt, Rinehart and Winston, Inc., 1963), pp. 480–495.

of the broadcasters, manufacturers, and (as receiving sets) of listeners and viewers. The Commission has been involved in two such crucial decisions: (1) to license television (only World War II prevented the Commission, under great pressure from the broadcasters and manufacturers, from freezing a more primitive technology); and (2) to license color television. In October, 1950, the Commission had licensed a more primitive technique but the Korean War prevented its decision from coming into effect. In 1953 a superior technique was licensed. It is nevertheless clear to any viewer that current television in the United States is technically inferior to that which was later installed in Europe. Nor is that the end of the matter, for certainly technology can continue to improve. But the control system as it now operates fixes itself in technological grooves, closing the avenue of continuing technological advance.

In 1952 ultra high frequency (UHF) wavelengths were opened for telecasting, and 275 UHF stations were licensed. Alas, few television sets were equipped to receive the programs. Given commercial sponsorship, small audiences meant cheap, poor programming. Low-quality programs killed consumer demand for sets equipped to receive UHF programs or for remodeling their old sets for that purpose. Without an audience many UHF stations stopped broadcasting. With fewer broadcasts the value of UHF to the consumer further declined. The cycle could only be broken by enacting a law requiring that all television sets be equipped for ultra high frequency broadcasts. The law was requested by the FCC. Congress complied and this was made a requirement for all sets manufactured after 1964.

The Commission has sought to promote competition among broadcasters. It supported the development of a third national network. It has protected the options of the local stations against the networks although it is not clear who receives the benefits. In some instances surely the quality of the programs will be higher, the listener's burden of intermittent commercials will be less, and the range of political viewpoints will be wider with network rather than local station programming. The options of the local station owner may be greater, but not those of the viewer or listener. Too often the Commission and its critics forget that freedom of speech means something more than the unconstrained right of the broadcaster and the local station owner to do whatever yields the fastest buck. Freedom of speech must also be measured by the range of intellectual and political options that enter into the forum of public thought and discussion. By that measure our freedom is meager indeed.

The Commission has acted, somewhat perfunctorily, to require fairness where broadcasts treat controversial issues or criticize individuals or institutions. According to its rules, a station that allows a candidate for political office to buy time to present his views must allow the opposition to buy time also. If a station attacks an individual or an institution, it is supposed to give the individual or institution attacked an opportunity to reply. When it airs a controversial issue, it is supposed to allow the different sides of the argument to be expressed. Since 1960 the Commission has been empowered to impose fines in order to enforce its rules, but has in fact been extremely reluctant to require any clear line of conduct by broadcasters, preferring to rationalize quite extreme abuse of the broadcaster's power in order to avoid any punitive action.[10]

The Commission attempted to improve the quality of broadcasts by limiting time devoted to commercials. That effort was aborted by Congress acting under pressure of broadcasters and advertisers in 1963. The most significant action yet taken by the FCC, recognizing the responsibilities implicit in its jurisdiction over the value-shaping force of mass communications, was the decision made in 1969 to forbid cigarette advertising on television.

Role of the Private Foundation

The Commission has also reserved a small portion of broadcasting space, nearly all on the FM and UHF bands, for educational purposes. And only a small part of what is available has been used. In 1962 Congress established a matching-fund offer to build educational broadcasting facilities. It is not Congress nor any public agency or university that has taken the lead or in any significant way initiated and developed the educational potentials of telecasting; rather, it is the private foundations, particularly the Ford Foundation, that have done so.

Although they are not the subject of this study, at least a word is needed concerning these foundations as the embodied

---

[10]See, for example, "Application for Renewal of Station WLBT," *FCC Reports*, 2d Series, pp. 40–45; and Harvey Fisher and John Willis (eds.), *Pike and Fischer Radio Regulation*, 2d Series, Vol. V (1965), pp. 205–230 and (1967), pp. 1901–1947.

"conscience" of corporate enterprise. As operational entities and as a form of organization, the foundations are outside the inherited conceptual framework. They fit into none of our intellectually established categories. For that reason they have been virtually invisible as a phenomenon to the intellectual, excluded from his field of vision even when he works in their cubicles and lives upon their grants. Politicians are concerned with them only in the suspicion that somebody must be getting away with something. For the haunted underground who most recently have found voice in George Wallace, foundations loom among the spectres who conspire to frustrate and deny the little man.

And indeed these anomalous entities, some small, some vast, are a mystery. We have no notion (we have not bothered to inquire) as to their modes of operation and control, their reason for being, their answerability, their responsibility, their system of recruitment, their objectives and orientation, their wastes and inefficiences, or their function in the modern economy. Yet they have a function, surely. I would in fact suppose that they are the most important agency for promoting social innovation in American society. They have contributed to educational broadcasting and to the whole spectrum of educational development; e.g., in the basic reform of the secondary school science curriculum. And they have promoted social innovation elsewhere, for example, in the sphere of social and technological change called economic development. Thus, in 1970 the contribution of American foundations to the so-called less-developed countries was greater than that of any government in the world save that of France and the United States. While the contribution of these two governments was lower, it was also largely in the form of loans that must be repaid at interest, while the foundation contribution was in the form of grants. Nor was the foundation contribution distorted by a heavy margin of overt or covert military subsidies, diplomatic payoffs, or accommodations to domestic policy, such as the tying of grants and loans to the procurement of goods and services from the donor country, that limit the value of government aid. It is probable that the contribution of the American foundations is now the world's most effective source of support for economic development. Certainly the one and only revolutionary change in the technology of developing countries attributable to external aid, the so-called green revolution, was a foundation enterprise.

THE ELECTRONIC TRANSMISSION AND PROCESSING OF INFORMATION

We are now on the threshold of irreversible developments in the national system of communications arising out of the rapid development of technologies for the electronic transmission of sound, image, and encoded symbols; and of technologies for the independent or conjunctive electronic processing of data. These two sets of technologies, abbreviated as ETPI (*Electronic Transmission and Processing of Information*), interest as ever more powerful and versatile instruments for storing, switching, and programming the use of information inputs; and for the electronic transmission of such information by telephone, telecast, broadcast, microwave, laser, satellite, and cable.

Consider, for example, cable television. There is nothing new or technically exceptional about the CATV developed by small-time operators in out-of-the-way places to receive network telecasts not within the range of antennae set up on home roofs. But once such cable is laid in the city where nearly every household has a television and where each receiving set can be readily wired for cable telecasting, then there *could* ensue a quantum of change in the range of potential communications as a basis for social action. For then, at a small incremental cost, an unlimited number of channels can be made available for a range of purposes beyond those of commercial broadcasting, *provided* that this capacity is built in at the time the transmission lines are initially laid. But who will see to it that such potential is realized upon *now,* for now is the time when the franchises are being given and the transmission lines are being installed? Who will be concerned to insure that this opportunity to bring a full-scale system of continuing education into every home will not be lost? Who will be the gatekeepers, controlling the access to these new channels of communications? Will it be cable owners interested in operating as monopolists and in restricting use so as to maximize the rental value of their offerings? or telecasters concerned with avoiding dispersal of the audience among numerous channels? Or will the cable be regulated as a common carrier and obliged to provide a service at a fixed price to all who wish to use it as a medium of communication? And will there be an institutional base organized to utilize these new communications capacities for purposes other than as outlets for commercial huckstering?

Consider some of the issues and problems for public choice implicit in the development of ETPI as a component of the national system of communications.

The Concentration of Market Power

Facilities for the electronic transmission and processing of information may be powerful business tools, but they are very expensive and their use can be justified economically only when there are very large volumes of data to be processed and communicated.

Inasmuch as these are integral instruments or systems, available for individual lease or purchase, their use will be confined to large corporations and big public agencies. Then, since its benefits will accrue only to large organizations, the new technology must act as a force for concentration and centralization. Given that large organizations constitute the market for the technology, R&D will be oriented and the technology will develop in line with the problems, interests, competencies, and operating circumstances of these and not of some other set of possible clients. And as the benefits of a progressively more powerful technology accrue to the larger firms, the smaller ones will be less able to survive and the economies of scale will become an ever more formidable barrier to entry into industry.

Alternatively, the electronic transmission and processing of data could be developed as a utility grid, a national network organized and operated as a common carrier and offering its services and programs at a fixed price to all, with data banks and computers built into the transmission-of-information network just as electrical generators are (or rationally ought to be) built into an energy transmission grid. The technology then might be neutral as between large and small enterprises, and the capacity of the small independent to survive and prosper might be enhanced.

Thus, there are two possible avenues of technological development. Without public intervention the second of these two avenues will not be taken.

ETPI and the Political System

Where should the locus of effective political power reside? Who ought to make the decisions or participate in the processes of collective choice? Inasmuch as one believes in increasing participation and promoting grass roots creativity in the formulation of public policy, correspondingly, there is reason to develop the means of rational, political discourse among the people.

At present two major parties constitute the machinery for the recruitment of political leadership and for the formulation of the policy options open to public choice. Each of these parties is a complex of inter-connected entities manned and controlled by professional politicians. Qua organizations the parties are above all concerned with self-preservation. Like all organizations they are geared to serve the interests and to further the prerogatives of those on the inside. Qua organizations their objective is to minimize the dissonance, disturbance, and noise coming from the outside. This is done by minimizing electoral options, homogenizing issues, blocking external initiatives, and smothering the outcries of the imprudent and impatient with political pablum. What then will be the effect of ETPI on this tension between political organization and those forces and voices outside the organization that are seeking political expression?[11]

The ever-increasing coverage and encompassing scope of the televised media, infiltrating every aspect of the individual's environment, has certainly already greatly increased the power of the political establishment to mold values and influence mass opinion. But developments in ETPI, and especially in humble CATV, offer the possibility of an entirely new and radically different avenue of development. The essential *political* character of television at present inheres in the fact that the available channels are very few and, hence, are available only to those at the summit. This must have the effect of narrowing the range of opportunities open to public choice and of concentrating power in an elite group or in whosoever commands the summit. But technology now makes it economically feasible to provide an unlimited number of channels for low-cost telecasting, and

---

[11]Paul Baran, "On the Impact of New Communications Media upon Social Values," Symposium on "Communications: Part I"; Harry Trebing, "Common Carrier Regulation—The Silent Crisis"; and Manley Irwin, "Computers and Communications: The Economics of Interdependence," *Law and Contemporary Problems* (Spring, 1969).

these channels *could* be used for a continuum of discussion and debate on issues of public or special concern to numerous, relatively small audiences of common background, competencies, and interests. Such forums would enable a grass roots exposure of men and ideas, and could provide the nucleus for a manageable, direct participation by the individual in creating policy options and in influencing social change. Thus, a system for the recruitment of political leadership could develop, based not on selection from above nor accommodations to the political machine, but rather on popular response to qualities displayed in grass roots discussion and debate.

The Automated Library

ETPI's prime value as an instrument of research is through the computer's capacity to match the data seeker's objectives and the prespecified characteristics of his reference data quickly. For example, NASA has installed a system for profiling and coding the technological interests of client firms and, using encoded keys that signal the specific relevancies of research reports, matching these interests to the indicated relevancies of each of the vast incoming streams of space-related research reports. In this way they are continuously searching for and selecting R&D material that might be of interest to each client firm. Similarly, by encoding the results of a series of medical tests made upon an individual and matching these against syndrome patterns prespecified in medical analytics or abstracted from medical case histories, the automated library could pull material useful in medical diagnosis. The automated library can also be a powerful aid to the law researcher in searching through law cases for precedents and relevant decisions for building a case, or for any other sort of information retrieval.

A national ETPI network could build an automated library to provide these and other services on a national scale, with reference data centrally stored for search requests originating in schools, offices, laboratories, hospitals, production sites, factories, and homes.

ETPI and Education

ETPI's effects on the system of education can be malignant or beneficent depending upon the depth and the sophistication of public awareness and on society's capacity for foresightful action. On neither account are the prospects hopeful.

One major value of ETPI as an educational instrument is through the televised lecture and other screened programs. The possible values of the televised lecture are fourfold.

First, in reducing the teacher to student ratio, the televised lecture reduces teaching costs. Other things being equal, this increase in productivity will be offset by a deterioration in quality through the loss of personal contact, the elimination of dialogue, and the dissipation of group discipline. But while beyond a certain threshold the increasing diseconomies of scale becomes insignificant, the increasing economies of scale continues apace. For example, there is a great loss of quality in going from a teacher/student ratio of 1 to 20 in the seminar or classroom to a ratio of 1 to 200 in a lecture hall; and there is some but much less loss in going from that ratio in the lecture hall to a ratio of 1 to 2,000 by closed-circuit television; and very little if anything is lost in quality in going from the closed-circuit ratio to an open broadcast reaching an audience of 20,000, 200,000 or 2,000,000. This suggests that the economies of this form of teaching will be adequately realized upon only when carried out on a national or international scale.

Secondly, the televised lecture makes it possible to exploit rare talents and abilities more fully. Creative thinkers, teachers of insight and genius, and exciting minds are very rare, and they are a most important educational resource. Normally they can interact with only a handful in close physical proximity. Through selective telecasting on an educational network, the light of their minds, though somewhat dimmed by the screen's intercession, could reach many people separated from them in time and space.

Thirdly, the televised lecture is highly mobile in space and is flexible in time, so that it can be easily fitted into the activities of the office, the factory, the laboratory, or the home; thus providing a basis for a post-academic, multi-leveled, continuous education.

Finally, the televised educational program can reach into the home and upgrade the cultural environment, particularly of the "disadvantaged" preschool child, systematically inculcating a high order of motivation, a directed curiosity, and civilized values and intellectual awareness as surrogates for the educated parent and the cultured family.

But, alas, though the potentialities for educational advance and cultural enrichment through broadcasting and telecasting have been available for half a century, the realization of that potential has been marginal. The use of this technology has not significantly affected educational cost. It has never in the United States been used to augment the impact of the rare spirit or to carry the light of the first-class mind. Except for pilot projects under foundation aegis, there has never been any attempt to upgrade preschool or extracurricular learning.

It is likely that the very great educational potentialities of ETPI can only be achieved through the foresightful design of a national system under the auspices of the political authority. For such an enterprise there are pitfalls and problems, as well as possibilities.

A new component would be built into the educational process, namely the producers and packagers of educational programs and machines. This would introduce into the educational system skills, values, and men of a different sort than those normally associated with academia. What sort of men, skills, and values? Would they be salesmen, showmen, gadgeteers, super mechanics, promoters, producers, directors, actors, and clowns in a new species of show biz? The prospect is not enticing.

And what would happen to the pedagogical resources released by the use of the new technologies? Would they be used for more individualized instruction? Or would they be drawn with the drift into academic research and graduate training, leaving on the one hand a vast undergraduate mass subject to a depersonalized, synthetic processing organized through distant educational packaging centers, and on the other hand selected elites, intensively trained and geared into academic research.

Conceivably, a National University of the Air could be created, commanding great resources, talents, and academic respect; operating autonomously, supported by private or public funds; and having as its sole task and responsibility the gearing of ETPI into the multi-leveled processes of disciplined learning. Its research would focus on the means for achieving that end. It would develop programs for the cultural enrichment of the home and the cultural and cognitive upgrading of the preschool generations. It would serve the universities through national lectureships that could gear our greatest thinkers into the organized curricula of colleges and universities throughout the world. It would organize external degree programs using screened lectures and other teaching devices, and would administer examinations and grant degrees. It would prepare and organize the use of nondegree, postcollegiate, postgraduate programs focussed on the needs and interests of adults and working professionals, and preschool programs vectored to the interests and designed to promote the development of the child. And it would operate centralized library services linked to a large network of outlets for the request, retrieval, and reproduction of materials needed as a part of the disciplined learning function.

I can dream, can't I.

Surveillance and Privacy

ETPI as a national system could create an entirely unprecedented capacity for the low-cost, effective surveillance of natural phenomena and social event. This capacity could be used alike for purposes that are benevolent or malevolent. Hence, there is the need to be clearly aware of what is at issue in order (1) to vector R&D into the development of a technology related to objectives considered to be in the public interest and to insure that that technology and those purposes are built into the national communications system; and (2) to foresee, forewarn, and prepare institutional protections against dangers to privacy and freedom.

An ETPI network recording inputs automatically or otherwise from observation points throughout the world and in space, storing observations, and autonomously and automatically interpreting and generalizing upon the universe from which the inflowing data are drawn, could be geared to a diversity of purposes. It could be used for the world-wide recording, analysis, and reporting of temperature change and those variables related to the formation and movement of storms, hurricanes, typhoons, tornados, tidal waves, fog, and flood as a part of the system of weather forecasting. It could be used for the continuous world-wide observation and recording of soil structure and conditions, and of the institutional deficiencies of flora as a basis for conservation planning and the upgrading of soil fertilities. It could be used for continuous, coordinated observation, analysis, and reporting on pollutants in or chemical conditions of rivers, lakes, oceans, air currents, the atmosphere, and outer space, all as a means of achieving a better understanding and control of basic ecological systems. It could be used continuously to monitor the location and migration of locusts and other insects and their predators as a part of the system of pest control. Through the ETPI network there could be organized a continuous, world-wide survey of infectious disease, and of physiological and psychic syndromes as these change spatially and between population categories based on age, sex, and income, and correlated with variables conceivably related to health and mental stability, which would be useful in medical research and in disease control. This, coupled with the automated library for medical diagnosis and the provision of the health and medical care record of every individual, would provide in toto a formidable support for national health and disease prevention programs. It could be used continuously to monitor, analyze, and report on (a) employment, unemployment, and quasi-employment based on sex, race, and age; (b) on industrial outputs in relation to plant capacities; (c) on industrial investment, investment plans, and the process of technological transformations; (d) on locational shifts of economic activities and populations; (e) on intercity, interregional, and international trade flows; (f) on price and product changes; and (g) on the changing matrix of input and output coefficients, all as a useful basis for economic policy and its implementation. And, if there is foresightful planning, this could all be a simultaneous, coordinated operation based on the use of an integral capital structure.

ETPI as a national system would as well enable the creation of a universal income-expenditures, balancing and credit-clearing mechanism, with debits offset against credits continuously, thus permitting an immediate check on the liquidity condition and the credit line of any individual, business firm, or institutional entity. It could eliminate the need for cash and checks and, in large part, replace the function of the commercial bank. The credit card has carried us a considerable distance in this direction already.

As the universal mechanism for credit and exchange, monitoring every receipt and expenditure, ETPI would provide a very powerful instrument for precise tax assessment and collection on an income and/or an expenditure basis. Moreover, the continuum of recorded financial transactions, specifying sources of income; objects of expenditure; the recipients of expenditures, gifts, and transfers; and the place and time of each transaction would constitute a means of monitoring, policing, and controlling the behavior of firms and individuals.

Given the potential for such surveillance, in each instance questions remain. Who will organize it and how? From where will the technology and the design come? What will it cost and what is it worth? Who will benefit? Who will pay? How can the particular surveillance be incorporated most economically into the larger techno-system?

Given ETPI, it becomes feasible and "economic" to have immediately available the health record; the record of criminal offenses and misdemeanors; the record of earnings, other income receipts, savings, and expenditures; a work record; a record of residences; records of education and training, publication, political associations, and participation in organizations, demonstrations, and meetings; and a record of the opinions of neighbors, friends, and enemies concerning the moral character, political sympathies, associations, and activities of every American from birth until death.

Every category of event subject to surveillance will have its proponents and its social values. Health records are valuable for medical treatment and for preventive medicine. The record of the individual's financial transactions, spatial movements, and encounters with the law are all relevant to and useful for crime control. The complete income and expenditure record can provide the basis for a more equitable and efficient tax system. And so on. However, this brings up an old issue in a radically more volatile form. If surveillance extends the powers of control, how far should that extension be allowed to go? And who is to exercise those controls, under what constraints, and with what safeguards? How are the values of surveillance to be balanced against the intrinsic worth of privacy? What will be the psychological effect of coexistence with a machine that records so much and never forgets?

ETPI as a national system could enormously magnify the powers of surveillance and control. Control could be exercised by the wrong people for the wrong purposes. It could assist in tracking down ideological heresy and a cracking down on political dissent. And though we approve of an objective of surveillance and control, nevertheless, its exercise may pose some threat to the innocent. Anyhow, surveillance itself is unpleasant. We don't like to be watched, and especially not by cold strangers. We don't like to be policed. We treasure our "air of freedom."

In a society so rent with crime as ours, where dangers to person and property intensify each day, can it be doubted that there will be more policing? And policing *is* surveillance. It means watching and keeping tabs on the good as well as on the wicked. Like it or not, the increase in crime demands more control. More control means more surveillance. If ETPI increases the potentials for surveillance, this simply increases the urgency of social choice and action with respect to a power that invites application but must be used with proper safeguards.

The Need for Rational Design and Rational Designers

Clearly the design of ETPI as a component in a national system of communication, taking rational account of potential values and dangers, is not a simple matter. To engineer the system so that common facilities economically serve multiple objectives and technology gears into social purpose, with benefits overbalancing costs, is a very complex and difficult task requiring great competence and creativity, even when the applications of the technology are not controversial. But applications are controversial. Privacy, liberty, and civilized values are at stake. Hence, beyond the technological, the proper design of the system becomes an issue for reasoned collective choice.

All that has been said so far suggests the need for a blueprint for collective choice, the need for a common idea and for a clear image of what society expects, wants, doesn't want, and seeks to avoid in organizing ETPI as part of the national system of communication and more than that, as part of the national *systems* of education, political choice, health control, crime control, etc. We need to know what our essential, viable choices are. We need the cognitive base and the ideological understructure for policy and action.

In the meantime the electronic transmission network spreads rapidly over the land, linked to proliferating data-processing facilities, variously possessed and variously oriented. The pattern that emerges may be as wildly irrational and wasteful as that of the railroads or as constrained and distorted in its social utilities as those of radio and television. Whatever pattern does emerge, it will not be reversible.

Numerous problems and efforts need to be taken into account beyond those already mentioned. There are the dangers of mechanical breakdown and failure, of deliberate manipulation by those who program and control the mechanism, and of human error multiplied manifold when hidden within the vast complexity of the apparatus. There are the grave problems of confining the utilization of information inflows and programs to authorized persons and purposes. There is the danger that massive data inputs rearranged and regurgitated as massive information outputs will further pollute the intellectual atmosphere, drowning us in irrelevencies and further ruining our intellectual digestion. There is already a desperate need to develop and to institutionalize the capacity to select, to reject, and to synthesize as well as to produce, to process, to publish, and to disseminate information.

These are the tasks for which we are not prepared conceptually, and with which we are in no way organized to deal. There is no locus of power and responsibility able to exploit the potentialities of ETPI as an instrument of education. There is nothing to promote and develop its use as a means of citizen involvment and grass roots participation in collective choice. There is nowhere the required locus of responsibility and competence to evaluate and design ETPI as a component in the national system of communication, geared to a multiplicity of objectives and providing the context for public and private action and choice.

Chapter 19

Liberalism, Nationalism, and the Housekeeping Function

This book has been about social change, with emphasis on the role of ideology in the process of social change. We have seen the tension between ideology and pragmatism expressed in the interplay between the Supreme Court and its interpretation of the Constitution on one hand, and Congress and the President responding to pressures of the electorate on the other. Sometimes the Court has been the harbinger of reform, and at other times it has been the bulwark of status.

This and the following chapters will approach the matter somewhat differently, turning from the relationship between ideological change reflected in the interpretations of the Constitution and the laws, with their impact on public policy; to examine the relationship between ideological change, the reformulation of political purpose, the reorganization of the administrative structure, and the development of technologies of choice and policy implementation.

It will be shown that the political authority in the United States has three central economic functions. Named in the historical order of their appearance on the stage of ideological legitimacy and public consciousness, they are (what we will call):

1. Housekeeping
2. Offset Planning
3. Planning-Programming

The nature of these three functions and the argument to be made concerning each of them will briefly be summarized.

In western societies during the epoch before the Great Depression, the political authority was immobilized by the prevailing ideology of laissez-faire liberalism. The market system was conceived as a marvelous, delicate, and wholly self-equilibrating mechanism that must, above all, be kept free of meddlesome government intervention. Economists were the professional defenders of the market's autonomy. The legitimate role of the political authority was simply to protect property and to enforce contract. Uniquely among western societies the political authority in the United States, under its antitrust laws, undertook to keep competition pure. Furthermore, the political authority produced information for and rendered a grab bag of services to groups in the private sector. And it shared the surpluses accruing in the public domain. In effect, the political authority functioned as a housekeeper in a house of many rooms, keeping the house safe and in order, watching out for unfriendly strangers, locking up at night, keeping the hallways clean, giving information when asked, providing certain services to the boarders, and extending her special favors to a few, but so long as there was no overt hanky panky, leaving each to his own.

The Great Depression overrode the canons of liberalism. In the changed view of things, the market continued to be regarded as the primary economic mechanism alone able to capture and to convert social energies into an output uniquely adapted to the values of the consumer. But it was no longer conceived as autonomous, self-steering, or self-equilibrating. On the contrary, perennial dangers of market imbalance, misdirection, distortion, and indeed, of self-destruction were recognized. A new task was conceived for the political authority — that of compensating for and offsetting the imbalances and malfunctionings of the market system. To that of housekeeping, a new "offset function" was added.

Underlying the legitimacy of this offset function was the conviction that the market can do the job provided it is buffered, balanced, pressured, and constrained through the leverage of public expenditure or through the imperatives of law. That conviction now founders. Increasingly, under the frustrations of failure and the pressures of need, the political authority plans, programs, and manages complex activities and engages in the restructuring of institutions directly.

Thus, the functional phases in the development of the political economy are:

1. To maintain the institutional underpinnings of individualized choice and to render services to private interests: the housekeeping function.
2. To offset and counterbalance the effects of private choice in the market economy: the offset function.
3. To initiate, plan, organize, and manage complex activities in pursuit of goals selected through the process of political choice: the planning-programming function. In this development one function did not replace but was overlaid on the others. The American political economy now contains them all.

THE HOUSEKEEPING PHASE

During the period before the Great Depression, internal policy, political organization, and the interpretation of the law all reflected the prevailing ideology of laissez-faire liberalism.

Through the judiciary and the police the political authority protected property, adjudicated conflicts in the claims and prerogatives of property holders, enforced contracts, and tried to protect and promote competition. Through utility commissions it nominally "regulated," and in fact threw up a feeble defense of the consumer's interest against the pricing power of "natural monopolies."

The political authority also rendered various services to individuals and groups, partly on grounds of tradition, but more often in blind and cumulative response to pragmatic pressure and crisis. The services rendered by government can sometimes be rationalized on the grounds that they required the protection of the police and the coercion of the courts, like the granting of patents or the minting of coins, or because they were essential to the economic and social infrastructure with their benefits largely externalized; and, hence, were unlikely to be otherwise provided, as with the building of roads and bridges, the provision of mass education or postal services, or the gathering and dissemination of census data.

But there was more. During this period a vast treasure in the form of enormous territories and natural resources of inestimable value rested within the public domain. It fell to the political authority to mete out this treasure, and government was so organized that functionally important and politically potent groups had their hands in any divying up the "pork." It was thus also a "pork-barrel government" organized to divide the prizes of chance and even to redistribute a part of the economic surplus in some acceptable manner. The division took many forms: in annual appropriations to the congressional districts for roads, harbors, and public works; in land grants to homesteaders; in tariff protection for industries; in oil and mineral rights; in concessions to strip the national forests; in endowments of land to agricultural colleges; and in land grants to railroads along with rights of way. These grants and favors were normally the double reflex of pressure and ideology. Tariffs; grants to railroads, agricultural colleges, veterans, and homesteaders; and the rest were surely the result of self-interested pressures by politically powerful groups. They took place nevertheless within the constraints and boundaries and under the impetus of prevailing ideology that, for example, favored and sought to promote rapid industrialization or the mass migration into and the quick development of sparsely populated areas and frontier regions.

These then were the *housekeeping* functions of the political authority: (1) to provide a safe and settled place for individualized choice, for the exercise of property power, and for the market interplay; (2) to provide certain services that the market did not make available; and (3) to divy up a part of the economic surplus and the treasure trove in the public domain. In their classic organization the "old-line" agencies of the federal government are organized to perform such housekeeping tasks as these.

The courts and the police were there to protect property and the prerogatives of ownership, and to enforce contract. The task of enforcing competition also fell to the courts, the Department of Justice, and the Federal Trade Commission.

Three departments of government — Agriculture, Commerce, and Labor — were designed specifically to provide a miscellany of services for major producer groups in the market economy and to help assure that each got its share of the national spoils. The Department of Interior was the pork shop itself.

The Political System in the Era of Liberalism

The political authority in its housekeeping role generated no goals, exercised no initiatives, and undertook no primary responsibilities except to preserve a social framework and to serve individuals and groups within that framework. In this context what the political authority *does*, what it *achieves*, and the *quality* of the services it performs are very secondary considerations. What counts is its intrinsic value qua process, rather than any instrumental effectiveness. What is of primary importance is that the process *represents*, and that it operates through acceptance, voluntary submission, and "consent of the governed."

The political system was organized as a pressure outlet with the latent power to respond to crises. It was a forum where, through the passage of laws, widely shared moral indignations could be expressed and enshrined and where patriotic exultations could be indulged in. It was the social whole in microcosm, representative men with representative interests and representative greeds striving to better themselves or to preserve their place and grabbing what they could for themselves and their constituencies. It was where intergroup, intersectional squabbles could be dragged out and eventually exhausted; where conflict could, as they say, be "compromised" or more likely, lost in some limbo of words in the labyrinth of parliamentary manipulation. That system could not be judged by what it did for it didn't *do* anything and it didn't plan anything. It did not and was not meant to organize anything. It wasn't designed for that purpose. It was designed not to act but to preside. Its virtue was that it existed. Its achievement was in continuing to exist. It *continued*; and, hence, it promoted social continuity. As an element in the process of self-perpetuation, it helped to preserve the continuity of an infinitely larger social system. It is thus that classical political science still appraises politics and policy — not at all for the capacity of the political system to produce a measured evaluation of priorities, nor for a cost-conscious search for project alternatives, nor for an optimal use of resources, nor a capacity for foresightful planning. The criteria of the political scientist rather are universal acceptance, conflict minimization, consensus, and the muffling of dissonance. In the era of liberalism, "utility" was the byword for the market system. For the political system it was *continuity*.

That was the nature of political organization and political purpose during the era of liberalism. The purposes of that system have changed radically, but its organization remains essentially as it was. Such is a dilemma of our time.

In the frame of the housekeeping function, the classic federal agencies — Commerce, Labor, Agriculture, and Interior — were created and operated. None of them had any objective purpose nor any integral responsibilities. They "represented" important and potent groups in Washington, and rendered their clients a miscellany of services on demand.

There were a few agencies of government, anomalies in the era of ideological liberalism, that had concrete economic tasks and operating responsibilities of some importance; the post office, for example. Their organization was also affected and their operations were shaped by the ideology and the conception of the political function that then prevailed. The post office was looked upon as another prize to be shared in the public domain. It was institutionalized as a source of patronage. The primary, accepted, and legitimate concern of the political authority in the organization of the post office was to divide the pork; here there were jobs for the faithful and postmasterships for professional politicians, and there were grandiose buildings passed out as public monuments to the towns and cities. Aside from the housekeeper's virtues of neatness and honest accounts, no attention was paid to the operating technology of the post office or of any other such agency.

The Independent Commission as a Technique of Choice and Action

The political system in this era of liberalism worked through congresses, legislatures, agencies of administration, and party machines that were, in effect, quasi-mobs, heterogeneous and transitory and absolutely amateur in everything but maneuver and survival in the political free-for-all. What was to happen on such rare occasions when government was forced by circumstances and cumulating pressures to confront issues head on that required complex judgment, expert knowledge, and continuing responsibility for performance?

Usually a law was passed, like the Sherman Act, full of high-sounding moral imperatives to which the courts, hopefully, would give some substantive meaning. But judges were as amateur and as ignorant of technology as were the congressmen. Nor was the judiciary designed or in any way equipped to monitor and control performance, to design and organize complex activity, or to build up the body of knowledge required for technical choice and control. The task of the judiciary and the competence of the judges was in smiting the wicked and in setting compensation for those who had been illicitly injured, case by case. What then was to be done?

An answer was forthcoming in the invention of the so-called "Independent Commission," a great favorite of reform politicians and academic political scientists like Woodrow Wilson, in the early decades of the 20th century.

If politicians were corrupt and judges incapable, then who was left to turn to? To "experts," of course. Experts were formed into commissions so that they might be independent of politicians and outside of politics. They were "detached from" Congress and the President, and from governors and legislatures. To this end commissioners were given long-term tenure. Their appointments were spaced out or otherwise arranged to minimize political partisanship. And they were charged with carrying out some large loose imperative enunciated by the legislative branch as a law. But they had no coercive power! To protect liberty and to keep enterprise free, the law must be enforced only by the courts. The commissions were to operate through persuasion — persuading those subject to the law on the one hand and those who made or enforced the law on the other. They must go to the courts to enforce the law or to Congress to change the law. After all, they were the "experts" who had the facts and the truth. And truth prevails, or so they say.

In any case as the economy and society increased in complexity, independent commissions proliferated. Every state save Delaware had its public service or public utility commission. At the federal level there were the Interstate Commerce Commission, the Federal Trade Commission, the Civil Service Commission, the Federal Reserve Board, the Civil Aviation Board, the Federal Power Commission, the Securities and Exchange Commission, the Federal Communication Commission, and many others.

Their fates have been various. In some cases — e.g., the Atomic Energy Commission — they became absorbed into the executive arm, virtually indistinguishable from other service agencies of government. Certainly they never became what some of their sponsors envisioned. They have never been independent sources of judgment and choice, able to frame distinctive policies, organize change, and control events. There were several reasons for this.

First, the commissions had no coercive power and had to turn to the courts to enforce their rulings. During the formative years (agencies and institutions also have "formative years") in the long era of liberalism, the courts gave no special credence to the commissions' rulings but treated them simply as another prosecutor or plaintiff before the judicial bar. It was not the commission, but the courts that interpreted the large, loose imperatives of the law as it had done before, ad hoc and as amateurly as ever. The effort to create a rule of experts —based on knowledge, accumulated through the feedback of experience, and responsible for results and performance — came to nothing.

During the post-World War II decades when the prevailing ideology had changed, the court become willing to allow the commissions a broad discretion in their interpretation of the law. But by then the tasks that confronted the political authority had outgrown the competence of the commissions; and the commissions have been unable to outgrow those proclivities that generations of impotence have built into their outlook and organization.

Second, the design of the commissions was intended to make them independent of control by one political party or the other. However, it was not the political parties that itched to control the commissions. It was rather the "interests" that the commissions were intended to regulate and control. And these interests worked through both parties, year in and year out, to influence appointments and hence to insure the compliance of the commissioners to their will.

The commissions and the commissioners also sought a power base. They needed one in confronting a Congress that was indifferent to their fate, and a President soon likely to become oblivious of their existence, in requesting funds, in safeguarding themselves from arbitrary displacement, and in order to achieve anything at all. And the commissions found their power base, their constituency, in the only place where it could be found; among those who in some specific systematic way consciously depended upon them, namely those whom they were supposed to control and regulate. And when the commissioners were corrupt, to whom could they offer favors for a price? Only to those whom they were supposed to regulate and control.

For these reasons, licit and illicit, the independent commissions were never independent. Most often they have been captured by and become subservient to the private interests they were intended to regulate and control. Nor on the whole did this turn out to be a bad thing. The Interstate Commerce Commission, for example, never controlled and regulated the railroads in the public interest as it was supposed to do. Instead it served the railroads in numerous ways, and represented the interests of the industry in the processes of political choice.

But, after all, so also did the Department of Agriculture serve agriculture and represent the interests of the farmers in the process of political choice. And the Department of Labor served working people and represented organized labor interests in the process of political choice. And so on. In a word the independent commissions became "housekeepers" like the other agencies of political choice and action, dependent upon and representative of a functionally important and politically potent group (their "industry"), expressing its interests and rendering it a miscellany of services.

THE EMBODIMENTS OF NATIONALISM

During the years before World War II it was not only liberalism that stood on the ideological rostrum. Nationalism shared the stage and remains there still. The ideology of nationalism — with its pantheon of patriots, its anthems of self-glorification, its tales of victory, its flag, and its expression in LaGloire, in manifest destiny, and in imperialism — has never had the rationalization and intellectual articulation of ideological liberalism, at least not in the English-speaking countries. Like sex and religion, it is something that polite Englishmen and Americans have an interest in but prefer not to talk about.

Georg Wilhelm Friedrich Hegel's apotheosis of the nation-state gives nationalism a rationale.

What is the material in which the final end of Reason is to be realized? It is first of all the subjective agent itself. . . . In human knowledge and volition, the rational attains existence. . . . As a subjective will in limited passions, it is dependent. . . . But the subjective will has also . . . a reality where it moves in the region of essential being and has the essential itself as the object of its existence. This essential being is . . . the moral whole, the State . . . in which the individual has and enjoys his freedom, but only as knowing, believing and willing the universal. . . .

The subjective will, passion, is the force which actualizes and realizes. The Idea is the interior, the State is the externally existing, genuinely moral life. It is this union of the universal and essential with the subjective will, and as such it is Morality. The individual who lives in this unity has a moral life, a value which consists in this substantiality alone. . . . It is the end of the State to make the substantial prevail and maintain itself in the actual doings of men and their convictions. . . .

The State is the realization of Freedom, of the absolute, final purpose, and exists for its own sake. All the value man has, all spiritual reality, he has only through the State. . . . Only then is he truly a consciousness, only then does he partake in morality, in the legal and moral life of the State. For the True is the unity of the universal and particular will. And the universal in the State is in its laws, its universal and rational provisions. The State is the divine idea as it exists on earth.[1]

Thus, in Hegel's vision individuals — being born, dying, the group regenerating — are clustered around the Idea, i.e., the ideology. In sharing the Idea they acquire the quality of a community. The Idea constitutes their historical reality; it expresses their purpose; it gives them distinctness and a meaning beyond mere animal existence. In their ideology is their shared purpose, and in their shared purpose is their morality. In their morality is their link to the divine; it is their grasp upon the divine. And the nation-state is the embodiment of the Idea. It expresses the ideology, the morality. It realizes the grain of divinity. The nation-state is a people's concrete commitment, known and willed to the universe. Through the laws and institutions of the state a people's Idea, wherein is their Spirit, is made manifest. Hence, the individual who is of a people and shares in the ideology of that people can only have value, can only know a spiritual reality, can only realize himself and be free, and can only lead

---

[1]Georg Wilhelm Friedrich Hegel, *Reason in History*, trans. Robert Hartman (Indianapolis: Bobbs-Merrill Co., 1953).

a moral life inasmuch as his life expresses, wills, and is consonant with the Idea that is his essence. Since the state embodies the shared ideology, there is no personal value, no moral life, and no spiritual reality except in the state; and no freedom except in obedience to its laws and the willed and willing self-subordination to its interests and purposes.

Hegel makes the best case that can be made for nationalism. It is for him something more than a bloat of accumulated self-interests. It has a certain nobility and a basis in reason. How can one better rationalize the bowed heads and hands to the heart in a salute to the flag? How can one justify the suppression of honesty, kindness, conscience, and the laws of Moses and Christ to the absolute imperative of patriotism? "My country . . . right or wrong, my country." How else can one explain the difference between the soldier and the gangster and between arrogance and self-righteousness coupled with the absolute dishonesty of all the State Departments and Foreign Offices; except that they are the appointed oracles of the nation who can alone divine and speak for the supreme interests of the state?

Hegel's idea is a rationalization of nationalism. It is not itself the ideology of the nationalist. It does not express the Idea of a nation, nor does it say anything about the idea of nationhood. The historical origins of the ideology of nationalism and the American unfolding of that ideology in the law and in the development of the federal power, was the subject of discourse earlier in this book. The following paragraphs will take a final look at American nationalism and its embodiment in agencies and policies in today's world.

The State Department as the Temple of Nationalism

Ideologies as they prevail in a society at a particular time become embodied in agencies of choice and action. Conceptions of a universe to be acted upon, the objectives of action, and the appropriate strategies and means for the achievement of these objectives, as these once prevailed are fixed and frozen into the operational design of those agencies. An ideology is preserved and propagated there beyond its time. And even when the underlying conceptions are no longer believed, the grooved patterns of habit remain, the organizational apparatus remains, and the machine of choice and action grinds out action and error monotonously with the profound force of functional inertia. So it has been with the antitrust agencies and certainly with the Department of State.

The State Department is the temple of American nationalism. But the idea and the self-image of the priest is not necessarily the same as the expectations and beliefs of those who worship at the shrine, who light the candles, and make their offering. Nor are the conceptions that underlie the State Department and all the Foreign Offices of the world at all the same as the communal egoism and mass xenophobia on which those agencies feed. What then are the conceptions that underlie the organization and operation of the State Department and Foreign Offices everywhere?

It is an ideology that predates the liberal economy and the emergence of bourgeois rationality and individualism. It belongs to the era of monarchy, where all resources were harnessed to the royal interest in power and domination in a world seen as so many airtight entities; each the sovereign and admitting no interest save its own and accepting no constraint save the offsetting power of antagonists. Within, the sovereign claims the absolute allegiance and submission of all. Outside, the sovereign is hard-shelled and monolithic, speaking with a single voice for the supreme interest; that is, the royal interest, the interest of the state, which becomes the national interest.

But what interest is the national interest, and who is to identify it? Was this to be determined through the processes of democracy, emerging out of Congressional debate and composite choice? Not in the Foreign Office paradigm. In the market place the bourgeoisie might gather to itself the powers and prerogatives of property. In Congress and in Parliament, elected representatives might dispute over internal policies and play for a share in the spoils of the political game. But so far as foreign affairs were concerned, the *long-run* national interest could only be understood and must be interpreted by an aristocracy, an elect, or an elite. Epitomizing this elitism was the notion of the ambassador as plenipotentiary who represents and speaks for his sovereign in the court of another sovereign. Abroad, he alone is the voice of the nation, able to interpret and to speak for the national interest. In the councils of his own government, he is the authoritative source of knowledge and information about the foreigner. It is around this image that the State Department is organized. The ambassador supposedly represents and speaks for his nation in each foreign land, while the State Department incarnates the plenipotentiary role for the United States as a nation. The State Department and Foreign Office elites interpret the national interest in terms of three criteria: the advantage of clients, the moral message (in Hegelian terms, the national Idea), and the sovereign's power. In the American case the clients (those who depend to some degree on the services and support of the State Department and on whose support the Department, in turn, to some degree depends) have been traders, investors, property holders abroad and, more recently, international corporations seeking protection or privilege.

The moral message of the State Department has been one of ideological liberalism, conceived in stark simplicity wherein power and privilege rightfully inhere in property, and where the highest good is liberty and liberty equals free enterprise. As with the regulation of monopoly and the implementation of antitrust, so too in foreign affairs it was only after American society, in its beliefs and in the organization of its economic system, had turned decisively away from ideological liberalism that the State Department had its heyday as the priests of liberalism and the crusaders for free enterprise.

In its conception of power the world is a set of closed, hard-backed sovereign entities, allied or opposed in a perpetual struggle to survive and/or to dominate. But how can the line between friend and foe be drawn? And what meaning is given to "dominance"? For the State Department the line drawn between ally and enemy was entirely ideological. It was a universal contest between the powers of property and those of the political authority, between the communist conspiracy and the alliance of the free, etc., etc. Correspondingly, *dominance* meant to extend the boundaries of sound money, balanced budgets, laissez-faire politics, and the unbounded prerogatives of property.

As compared with other public agencies, the State Department and others involved in the conduct of foreign affairs are insulated in a particular way from the lessons of experience for the following reasons:

1. Conceiving of itself, and conceived, as being engaged in a continuous struggle against foreign enemies, the State

Department operates in a privileged position of secrecy — deciding in secret, secreting its information, revealing only what it pleases. The effect is not only to shield the agency and its ideological biases from external question, challenge, and criticism, but also to constrain internal communication, question, reflection, debate and reconsideration.

2. As true interpreters of the national interest whose decisions are based on a secret knowledge possessed by themselves alone, it becomes their task to control and to manipulate popular opinion. This posture of the know-all who cannot reveal what he knows permits no dialogue that might serve to promote public learning.

3. Above all, the State Department and the agencies of foreign affairs are kept outside the learning process because the society to whom they are answerable, and upon whose support they depend, is normally not able to observe their activities nor directly to experience the consequences and effects of their policies. For these activities and their consequences and effects take place in faraway places among foreign peoples. Congressional backing and popular support come not from a knowledge of their performance or an appreciation of their services, but are rooted rather in the imperatives of patriotism, the national egoism, dark xenophobia, and the obsessive fears of strange shapes and fearful things lurking on distant horizons.

It is time the question was raised as to whether the State Department is a useful institution and whether it has any viable function in our present society. I would answer that it is useless and worse than useless, a positive source of obscurantism and distortion in the process of political choice, and that the agency itself should be dispensed with for several reasons.

It harbors an ideology in its organization, its operating outlook, and in its criteria of decision in which we no longer believe. Indeed, it is the institutional expression of that ideology. So long as the State Department exists, it will continue to embody, to express, and to propagate that ideology.

It is organized around the notion of a plenipotentiary, the gentleman amateur who interprets and represents the totality of the interests of the nation to foreign kings and chiefs and who is at once his society's source of information concerning outlandish places and strange people. In our day the notion is grotesque. Distance is no barrier. Millions criss-cross oceans and continents and move en masse through nations. We need not, and most certainly we do not, rely for our information on the reports of the gentlemen amateurs ensconced in their embassies; and we do not need a know-all, know-nothing agency to interpret the great range of our society's interests and objectives at home and abroad.

Of course there is the continuous need for complex cross-national arrangements, organizations, and operations. And these ultimately are made and can only be made by organizations and agencies with specific competence and relevant responsibility. At issue is whether all these organizations, operations, and arrangements should be obliged to go through the thick bureaucratic apparatus of a single agency that claims omnipotence for the totality and is without competence in any of the parts.

And there is certainly the need also for policies to be formulated and decisions to be made with respect to foreign countries and international relations. But what has the State Department to do with the formulation of those policies and the making of those decisions? It is, of course, of great importance — if our policies are to be wise and foresightful — that we as a society, as participants high and low in the process of political choice, should be well-informed concerning foreign nations and societies other than our own. And for that we need honest scholarship; continuing and on-the-spot research that focuses on problems and phenomena of general interest and political relevance; a thorough, high quality journalism with full newspaper coverage; an inflowing stream of books and reports; and direct observations by many Americans through travel and person-to-person contact. The political authority, rationally, should bend every effort to promote the fullest dissemination of such information and to facilitate such learning. In fact the State Department has been an unyielding barrier to the dissemination of information and a constant enemy of such learning. Given that "know all, reveal nothing" is in the nature of its mystique and is a source of its power, an enmity to social learning is inherent in its role.

China is a good example. Surely no knowledge could be more important for political choice in our time than a knowledge of the new China. Yet for a full quarter of a century the Department of State mobilized all its forces to impose an absolute ban against any American scholar, scientist, journalist, or citizen visiting that vast and complex land under pain of imprisonment until the mid-1960's when a black journalist defied the ban, was prosecuted, was convicted, and appealed his conviction to the Supreme Court. The Court ruled the State Department's action to be unconstitutional, and thereby broke its power to stop Americans from traveling, observing, and learning in foreign lands; though that agency still forbids those whose political ideas or associations it disapproves, even the greatest scientists and men of genius, from visiting the United States. Surely if social learning is our objective, and if an understanding of realities abroad is considered to be a desirable basis for rational choice in the development of foreign policy, then we'd best be rid of that Department that persistently intervenes between ourselves and the world in which we must live and would try to understand. It should be self-evident that the Central Intelligence Agency, the most malignant element of the body politic, is the pathological expression of this same ideology and outlook.

Chapter 20

The New Deal Credo and the Offset Function

The ideological structure of liberalism, eroded by half a century of event, was finally sundered by the economic cataclysm of the Great Depression. When the old belief was shed like a dead skin, what was there beneath to replace it? An analogy will suggest my answer to that question.

Consider the Newtonian universe. It was called a clockwork that, once set in motion by the Great Clockmaker, ran perfectly and perpetually thereafter. Now suppose there was such trouble and discord in the skies that while no one doubted the clock-work of the physical universe to be a marvelous mechanism, it was conceded that it could occasionally run too fast or too slow, get out of kilter, and even break down and come to a halt entirely. Under those circumstances there had better be at least one apprentice to the Great Clockmaker, keeping an eye out standing ready to remove whatever clogged the gears, to lubricate the parts, to wind the machine, or to replace its broken springs.

A STANDBY ROLE FOR THE GREAT CLOCKMAKER'S APPRENTICE: THE SECOND PHASE

In neoclassical conception the economy also was a perfect and self-perpetuating clockwork. Before he made his own revolution, Keynes lauded Marshall's discovery of "a whole Copernican system by which all the elements of the universe are kept in place by mutual counterpoise and interaction."[1]

---

[1] John M. Keynes, *Essays in Biography* (New York: The Macmillan Co., 1933), p. 223.

After his own long draught on the bitter cup of national stagnation and decline, Keynes concluded that splendid as the clockwork was, it was not self-perfecting and self-perpetuating. It could break down; it had broken down. Hence, some surrogate for the Great Clockmaker had best stand by and be responsible for keeping the Great Clock adjusted, oiled, wound, repaired, and running right. This could be the task of none other than the political authority.

Keynes and his followers did not for an instant challenge the inner symmetries and values of the market system. They did not seek to detract from nor replace the established housekeeping functions of the government. But to these must be added another and far greater responsibility. Continuing to rely on the market system as the organizer of production and consumption, the political authority must stand outside that system; diagnosing its ills, correcting its malfunctions, offsetting its imbalances, and responsible for its performance.

The Keynesian Transition and the Offset Function

It has often been observed that during a phase of ideological change and conceptual transition, great and successful innovators (Galileo, Kepler, Bruno, for example) produce a strangely incongruous admixture of the new and the old; a melange of such incompatibles that we, looking back, wonder how such powerful minds could ever have concocted such brews. No doubt the innovator himself reflects the confusions and gropings of his time. But there is something more. If those who achieved the conceptual breakthrough had been more clear-headed and if instead of the wholly confusing mixture of the old and new that they offered, they had instead come forward with a science or ideology that was clear, internally consistent, and fully developed; they probably would have failed to lead the intellectual world down the track of change. They might then have been great heretics; they might have been anomalies of their time, like poor Mendel and his genetic laws. They would then have made interesting footnotes in the history of thought, but they would not have played a part in the process of reconceptualizing ideas that guide social decision and choice and shape man's image of the world.

The task of cognitive and ideological innovation may be less to deliver a new truth than to lead a society, a group, or a discipline out of the labyrinth of old error. And this is a delicate and difficult task. The new truths must infiltrate established belief. They must be smuggled within the gates. This would seem to require that the new be so overladen and intermingled with the old that those who accept it can do so in the illusion that in so doing they are not abandoning established conceptions nor the faith to which they are committed.

Certainly such was Keynes' achievement. He succeeded in releasing a generation of intellectuals from the rigid constraint of ideological liberalism; and he did so by *seeming* to reconcile the old cry of heretics, and the new pragmatic policy responses of political authority to a desperate crisis, with the imperatives of liberal orthodoxy.

His was a transitional theory; the theory of a man who stands between two quite incommensurable conceptions of the social universe, seeing the light of one and reaching hard toward it without ever disentangling himself from the older view into which he was born. He succeeds in obscuring incongruities by burying them in his own confusion. What are the incongruities of his theory?

Keynes had long accepted Alfred Marshall's Copernican universe where every element of the economy was guided in predestined orbit by the autonomous force of free-moving price. In that conceptual universe there was no place for mass unemployment; yet, the fact of mass unemployment could no longer be denied. In order to explain it Keynes had to postulate that price and, ultimately, the wage of labor itself was *not* a function of supply and demand in the market bargain, but rather was determined by some other process and some other set of forces.

Inasmuch as this was true, the neoclassical universe of free-moving, autonomously determined price must be false. To explain unemployment it was necessary to deny the essence of neoclassical economics. Keynes did and he didn't. It was the nature of his achievement that he abandoned yet seemed not to abandon the established theory. He did this simply by changing the viewfinder depending on what aspect of the world he was looking at; one for aggregate spending and mass unemployment, the other for individual spending and the allocation of resources. Thus, economics developed the schizoid relationship between macro and micro theory.

The primacy of the market economy of autonomous, free-moving price is proclaimed for the allocation of resources and for the organization of outputs. But that market economy, taken as a whole and disregarding its internal operation, is conceived as a sort of balloon adrift in air currents of aggregate spending. Depending on how those currents move, the balloon is driven up into the ether of inflation or down into the storm of mass employment—the thing is to control the current so that the economy is held on the perfect course of full employment and price stability. The mass flow of aggregate spending is determined by the spontaneous spending/saving decisions of individuals and firms, each blind to the totaled effect on the state of the economy. The political authority must therefore *offset* any propensities to underspend or to overspend as a consequence of private choices and maintain the volume of pressure that would permit the market to stay afloat at just the level where prices are stable and employment is full; hence, the *offset* function.

In its offset role the political authority does not replace the market. The political authority as offsetter does not plan and organize anything. It stands by and waits for trouble. And when trouble comes, or seems in prospect, the political authority compensates and adjusts; fiddling with the machinery, compensating for slack, or reducing the heat.

The charm of the government's new role was its sweet simplicity. It merely required the use of fiscal and monetary leverage. No technological competencies or institutional insights were needed. There was no complex planning, and no complex activity to be organized! No selfish interests need be subordinated. No one would be hurt. All could be kept in order by a few sophisticated officials and their statisticians working at Whitehall, or Le Ministere de Finance, or in the Treasury and the Council of Economic Advisors.

The Offset Function and the New Deal Credo

Keynes and his disciples did not create policy in the period of the depression, they rationalized it. The academic economists did not lead, they followed; and very slowly at that. And indeed Keynesian theory was encompassed by a much larger sweep of politics and policy.

In the United States the "answer" to the crisis of the Great Depression emerged through a process of composite choice, out of the ad hoc response of politicians to mass suffering and desperation and out of the experience of social workers in the forming of new political ranks against the rich and entrenched, who fought with extraordinary venom against all harbingers of change.

The Demand for "Relief"

The new outlook emerged in the process of political action; and in the first instance the purpose of political action was *relief:* relief for those in desperate need; for the workingman without work for years; for the bankrupted farmer with his land on the block; for the young without opportunity; and for the old without hope. And the government did give relief. For those times it was massive on a scale without precedent, and it was administered with exemplary honesty. It came in the form of welfare payments, public works, and social security. What Congress was asked to do and what it did was to pass laws and to appropriate large sums intended to bring relief and to ameliorate misery. No planning or social engineering, knowledge of technology or of complex organization was required. What the crisis demanded of the political authority was simple enough; the difficulty was in passing over a psychological threshold, in overcoming ingrained inhibitions and the folklore of laissez faire. Congress crossed that threshold. It appropriated the large sums and it passed the laws. Wonder of wonders, there was no retribution. The prophecies of doom and disaster did not come to pass.

For the first time the political establishment rejected the conviction that the poor are to blame for their poverty and the market punishes those who deserve to be punished. It was no longer accepted that the lash of poverty and the scourge of unemployment are needed to drive men to work. Under the new dispensation the facts had a different meaning; events had a different face. Poverty and prolonged unemployment now seemed not to motivate but to debilitate motivation. Work was needed to keep the hand skilled and the soul alive. Poverty and unemployment became signs of social and policy failure: the failure of laissez-faire liberalism. The electorate now expected and politicians accepted the obligation of the political authority to guarantee every man (1) the opportunity for gainful employment,

(2) a minimum standard of life, and (3) protection against the grand vicissitudes of age and illness in the uncertainties and instabilities of a market economy and an industrialized society. The change in popular expectation and in accepted social obligation foreshadowed policy and action.

Offsetting Corporate Power

The demand for relief came also from functional groups, particularly from farmers, industrial labor, and small business. They had something in common, complaining of comparative disadvantage in the market system. Their complaint, rising to an outcry under the hammer blows of the depression, was of long standing. It had the same root cause — the growing importance and ultimate dominance of the giant corporate organizations. They were alike victims of the organizational revolution.

For decades, indeed for generations, the terms of trade had been moving against agriculture. For the same product output the farmer took a smaller and smaller bundle of the industrially produced goods in exchange. And in the depression the price of farm goods dropped catastrophically while the prices of the industrial goods bought by the farmer held firm.

Whenever two sectors traded, where choice was decentralized and price moved autonomously in the one while in the other choice was concentrated and price was controlled, then the terms of trade tended historically to move to the advantage of the latter. The effect was universal. Indeed, its clearest manifestation was in the Soviet Union during the NEP period of free trading between 1921 and 1927 when agricultural prices were driven down and industrial prices moved rapidly upward, even at a time of severe food shortage, producing the so-called "scissors crisis" that virtually forced peasant farmers out of the system of exchange. The New Deal's response to the farmer's demands was to *offset* the effects of this bargaining imbalance by passing a new law and money bill that transferred income from the industrial worker and urban consumer to the farmer through crop restriction and price parity payments.

The industrial worker too was disadvantaged by the might of the business entities with which he bargained. As an *offset* to the bargaining power of the great corporation the political authority, through the agency of the National Labor Relations Board, guaranteed the right of industrial workers to organize into trade unions. As a consequence, powerful industrial trade unions came to countervail against industrial corporations.

Small business came before the bar of social justice claiming that it too was unfairly disadvantaged in relation to its large competitors. By its promise or threat to give or withhold its massive purchases, the large corporation was able to gain concessions from sellers not available to its smaller rivals. To offset buying power as a basis for price discrimination, the Robinson-Patman Act was passed.

Policy and the Offset Function

The central task of the time was to bring the unemployed into gainful employment in the market economy. And employment was understood as a function of aggregate expenditure. All traditional stimuli were tried. The rate of interest was driven down. Liquid surpluses were pumped into the banks. What seemed most effective was the increase in government spending over and above the level of taxation. Through deficit finance the government added to the stream of private expenditure, raising the aggregate spending to a full employment level.

Thus, the offset function became central for the political economy: offsetting the pools of poverty and the inequities produced by the market distribution of income; offsetting imbalances in the bargaining strength of parties to exchange; offsetting insecurities and vicissitudes of the aged and the sick under the remorseless rigors of the market system; and especially offsetting deviations from that volume of aggregate demand necessary to maintain a normal level of employment.

The offset function has been extended under successive administrations. Federal support to "basic" (academic) science and higher education has offset the market's neglect of those activities where a large proportion of benefits are externalized. Medicare has been added to social security, and now in the offing is a guaranteed minimum income to offset the inequities, uncertainties, and instabilities of the market economy.

THE NEW DEAL CREDO

Out of all this, and as a part of all this, came an outlook (indeed an incipient ideology) that might be called the "New Deal Credo."

1. It was above all characterized by a release from the fears and inhibitions of laissez-faire liberalism.
2. It rejected neither the centrality of the market nor the primacy of the individual. It's intention was to protect the individual and to save capitalism. For that reason the political authority had to make the market economy work, and work well. But to the free functioning of the market was left all the complexities of resource allocation, the organization of production, and the transformation of technology.
3. Within the market the political authority had to reweight the scales of power in order to offset bargaining inequities. And tapping the margin income available for redistribution, the political authority would guarantee a minimum standard of life for all.
4. To achieve its purposes the political authority would *not* attempt to plan, organize, and control complex activities but would rely on public spending, fiscal and monetary offsets, and the passage of laws that would affect the parameters of individual and business behavior. At the initial stage in the formation of the new outlook were vast reserves of unused industrial capacity and of unemployed labor. Incremental public spending drew idle resources into production so that no matter who gained, no one lost. It was possible then to pay Peter without robbing Paul. That was critical in the development of the New Deal Credo. So far as the congressman, the public official, and the man in the street were concerned, the great discovery was that government could spend and spend (and had spent and spent) more than it was before thought possible without disaster. There were deficits and debts, but no bankruptcy and no breakdown; in fact, the country was made stronger and richer. They took from this the lesson that anything could be done by passing another money bill. What distinguished reform from reaction, the warm from the cold, and the left from the right, was the willingness to appropriate new monies for worthy causes. To progress meant to raise the level of offset spending. The measure of the worth of an administration was the number and magnitude of the money bills (for good causes) it managed to get through Congress.

Such were the conceptions and the misconceptions of the New Deal, the Fair Deal, the Square Deal, the New Frontier, The New Society, and even the New Revolution.

POLITICAL ORGANIZATION AND OFFSET TECHNIQUES

The new primacy of the offset function has had little effect on the structure of the political organization. It led to the development of few major new agencies. Most of those created in the throes of depression have vanished. Nor did the offset function serve to introduce new techniques of policy implementation. In their efforts to maintain full employment, for example, officials have been content to use traditional instruments appropriate to the days of Walter Bagehot rather than those of J. M. Keynes (deficit finance, interest rate control, and open-market operations by the central bank) that have the virtue of familiarity, ill-adapted though they are to the purpose at hand. Abba Lerner's "functional finance" and Nicholas Kaldor's "expenditure tax" are among the rare efforts to invent new and more effective offset techniques; i.e., techniques that could enable a more precise control of aggregated expenditure with less costly side effects. Along a different path, however, there have been significant developments in the technology of choice and control related to the offset function. The offset task has this special character: it must respond to whatever happens in the market economy. It is a system of counter-punching and its effectiveness depends on a capacity to anticipate what is coming in a highly variable and uncertain universe of private choice, and on a capacity also to foresee the response of the private economy to corrective measures.

The offsetter is like a mechanic attending a complex engine where one mechanical failure can produce another in rapid chain reaction, leading to great damage and even absolute breakdown. He listens for knocks and rattles. He watches for any sign of trouble so that he can lubricate the gears, fill the tank, and replace the worn out parts in time. His strategy is to deflect the dislocating movement in its incipiency before it snowballs into an avalanche of disaster. Everything depends on his ability to foresee and to anticipate. It is in the development of forecasting techniques that the professional economist has contributed the most to offset technology. The proliferation and subtlety of national income and related statistics from the mid-thirties; the support to the extension of input-output studies after World War II; the Research Survey Center at Ann Arbor; and the econometric models maintained and operated as the in-house property of the University of Pennsylvania, Yale, MIT, and elsewhere, are all related to and have been subsidized as an adjunct to the offset function. Within government administration it has been the primary task of the Council of Economic Advisors to make forecasts and to peruse and evaluate the forecasts of others, and on that basis to design a continuing fiscal and monetary strategy to offset inflation and unemployment in the market economy.

It is in fact not in the United States but in the rather particular circumstances of the French economy, that the technology of offsets has been most fully developed and rationally organized.

French Planning and the Offset Technology

French indicative planning, which is in fact a system of market offsets to the end of maintaining full employment and price stability, relies on the stated plans and intentions of business and government decision makers rather than on forecasts of those plans and decisions. While the mutually desired objectives of full employment and price stability cannot be achieved except accidently when decisions are made in isolation and in the ignorance of the plans and intentions of others, they might be achieved through some mutual adjustment and a cooperative effort when the sum of effects of all the individual plans of business firms and public agencies are made explicit. To this purpose the French Planning Authority brings together representatives from:

1. Large private industrial companies whose decisions are of prime importance in determining the level of business investment expenditures.
2. The monetary and fiscal agencies of the French government.
3. The major functional agencies of the French government whose budgetary planning is of prime importance in determining the level of public expenditure.

On the basis of the stated intentions of these key decision makers, the Planning Authority anticipates (1) the level of private investment and (2) the level of public expenditure, with (3) consumption expenditures, deduced in part from anticipated wage change and anticipated change in the income level as a function of the foreseen rate of investment and government spending.

If the anticipated level of spending appears inflationary or deflationary, the French Planning Authority tries through informal persuasion and pressure to induce a modification of governmental expenditure and/or of planned business investment to the level it supposes to be required for price stability-full employment conditions.

French planning permits the offset function to be exercised ex ante rather than ex post; i.e., to permit modification of the plans and intentions of decision-makers rather than acting upon the aftereffects of decisions made and actions taken.[2]

---

[2]See John Sheahan, *Promotion and Control of Industry in Postwar France* (Cambridge: Harvard University Press, 1963); Stephen S. Cohen, *Modern Capitalist Planning: The French Model* (Cambridge: Harvard University Press, 1969); John H. McArthur and Bruce Scott, *Industrial Planning in France* (Boston: Harvard University Graduate School of Business Administration, Division of Research, 1969).

Chapter 21

Planning
and Programming
in the Political Economy

Basically, everything turns on a change in the outlook and expectations that prevail in society. During the post-depression, post-war years of ideological transformation, the governed and governors alike expected the political authority to stand responsible for the performance of the market economy. The expectation and the acceptance of the obligation is fundamental. And the responsibility of the political authority for market performance has drawn and must continue to draw the political authority into a more complex and more complete involvment with the economic system.

FROM OFFSET TO SYSTEMS PLANNING

What sort of performance was to be expected? In the first instance the political authority was confronted with a breakdown of the very capacity to utilize resources and to produce goods and services and it sufficed to overcome mass unemployment, mass bankruptcy, and desperation. Nor, in retrospect, was the political authority particularly foresightful and vigorous in that undertaking. It moved timidly, "pump priming" to tickle the economy awake rather than jerking it into harness and driving it forward. Surely there is reason for regret. Once the inhibitions of the laissez-faire ideology had been shed, the Great Depression posed a marvelous opportunity for collective achievement. Half or more of the nation's productive capacity was latent and unused. It remained so through the whole decade of the thirties.

These mighty unused productive powers could have been devoted to rebuilding America's cities. They could have upgraded and vastly expanded our educational system. They could have rearmed us for the crisis of fascism which was rapidly closing in. But nothing of the sort was done, and not until the massive public expenditures of World War II did the economy cease to crawl and become fully alive.

In the course of post-war decades, the problem of inflation became increasingly troublesome. To approach the performance criterion of full employment *and* price stability proved beyond the scope of microeconomic conceptualization and outside the range of offset techniques. Economists rationalized the failure. If the political authority couldn't have full employment and price stability, at least the offsetter could choose between combinations of more unemployment-less rapid inflation and less unemployment-more rapid inflation neatly arranged on a "Phillips Curve."

During 1968–70, confronted with accelerating price inflation, the new administration swore off "jawboning" and engaged in savagely restrictive monetary offsets, driving interest rates up to unprecedented heights, collapsing stock market values, reducing GNP, and creating a politically unacceptable level of unemployment. Inflation, nevertheless, continued. In the face of failure the administration reversed itself and attempted to stimulate aggregate expenditure; and the President began to jawbone and otherwise to exert ad hoc pressure and influence in an effort to keep wages and prices in line in the organizational sector.[1] Finally, in 1971 a system of general wage-price control was introduced.

It turns out thus not to be possible to achieve full employment and stable prices simply through the judicious withdrawal and injection of public expenditures or by any of the other offset techniques. So long as the industrial sector is dominated by great companies and trade unions who set wages and prices as a matter of organizational policy, controls of quite another order are required.

To full employment and price stability has been added the *growth* of the economy as a criterion of performance. Only through growth in labor productivity, and hence in annual output, can the rising expectations of society be satisfied. And only

---

[1]President Nixon's economic controls are discussed in Chapter 15.

through growth can a nation retain its status and power among other nations. How can a nation promote growth or deal with those great industries in which technology has lagged and productivity has sagged? This cannot be accomplished with more fiscal-monetary offsets, nor with a law, or a money bill. That task too must involve the political authority in the complex system of technological advance, especially in the organization of education, science, research and development, and investment.

After World War II, for compassionate, strategic, and economic reasons, the American political authority underwrote West European economic recovery. It did this simply through the passage of a law and money bill, the Marshall plan. Given a resource margin for maneuver, the Europeans did the rest. Following this successful venture the American political authority, for compassionate reasons and in order to "reduce the dangers of communism," undertook to raise output and income in the backward economies of India, Africa, Asia, and Latin America. It turned out that such economic development needed more than a law and a money bill. Repeated failure in efforts to promote economic development in this fashion has drawn the political authority into multifaceted planning and programming, not only at the level of economic organization and technology, but reaching down to the bowels of society to reconstitute and reconstruct culture, cognition, and the forms and distribution of power.

Initially it was supposed that the problem of race in the United States could be straightforwardly resolved by a determined enforcement of constitutional guarantees. It was also supposed that the related "crisis of the cities" required only that Congress appropriate more money to subsidize the buying up and redevelopment of "blighted areas." Alas, experience reveals that the problems of race and the problems of the cities — indeed, the problems of human relationships and human environments in modern society — will require fundamental planning and programming of institutional change and of technological organization and economic activity as well.

Responsibility for economic performance is expected and is accepted: rhetoric and the squeals of politicians to the contrary, that responsibility cannot be met by laws and money bills, by turning the deficit spigot on and off, nor by manipulating interest rates. It demands the foresightful planning of very complex systems. It requires that the political authority have a direct knowledge of technology and institutions and a high competence for organization. Consider, for example, the commitment to guarantee fundamental security and a minimum standard of life. The first step was social security, which *could* be handled by a law and a money bill and which *was* within the scope of the offset function. What happened when the commitment was extended to the provision of medical care for the aged? Through Medicaid the political authority tried to achieve this end with a law and a money bill. But given the fixed numbers of doctors, the long-standing constraints on the supply of new doctors, and the limited medical facilities, the result was that doctors became scandalously rich and the quality of health care depreciated. And in 1971 in his State of the Union address, Mr. Nixon proposed

> . . . a major increase in and redirection of aid to medical schools, to greatly increase the number of doctors and other health personnel.
> Incentives to improve the quality of health services, to get more medical care resources into those areas that have not been adequately served, to make greater use of medical assistants, and to slow the alarming rise in the costs of medical care.
> New programs to encourage better preventive medicine, by attacking the cause of disease and injury and by providing incentive to doctors to keep people well than just to treat them when they are sick.

Did Mr. Nixon understand the implications of his own proposals? Does he understand the degree of complex organization and planning that is required of the political authority for any rational implementation of any one of them? Planning and organizing are required for an increased output of doctors in relation to anticipated medical needs; hence, planning and organizing for the elimination of the institutional and monopolistic constraints and the medieval educational methods that constrain the output of doctors. Planning and organizing are needed for an increase in educational facilities, for the relocation of doctors and hospitals "to get more medical care resources into those areas that have not been adequately served," and for the planned reorganization of medical practice "to make greater use of medical assistants." Hence, planning and organizing are also needed for the mass training and placement of such medical assistants, and for controlling "the alarming rise in the costs of medical care." Above all, an immense, open-ended organization and planning under the aegis of the political authority are required to reorient research and practice toward "preventive medicine by attacking the cause of disease and injury."

Whether or not Mr. Nixon understood the implications of his proposals, in this instance he expressed if not his own logic, then the logic of events. Given the commitment to the people's health and given the failure of medicaid and the spend-spend offset technique, there is no other way for the political authority to go. It must deal with national health as the consequence of a very complex system; and the changes in that system can be successfully engineered only on the basis of forethought, organizational competence, and expert knowledge.

As with health-care programs, so go all the systems of the social and economic infrastructure. To comprehend, control, and engineer change in any of these programs — education, energy, transportation, communications — requires expert knowledge, complex organization, and planning.

Thus, one can understand the basic changes that had occurred by 1971 in the organization of the executive branch of the federal government. A new set of government departments with responsibility for integral functional systems (Health, Education, and Welfare; Housing and Urban Affairs; Transportation) have developed side by side with the classical agencies (Interior, Agriculture, Labor, Commerce), performing housekeeping tasks and representing an interest group in the process of political choice.

THE "NEW REVOLUTION"

Further changes in the organization of the executive branch of government are certainly in prospect. In the 1971 State of the Union Address, which President Nixon considered as "opening the way to a New American Revolution," it was specifically proposed

The . . . sixth great goal is a complete reform of the Federal Government itself.

Based on a long and intensive study with the aid of the best advice obtainable, I have concluded that a sweeping reorganization of the executive branch is needed if the Government is to keep up with the times and with the needs of the people.

I propose that we reduce the present 12 Cabinet departments to eight. I propose that the Departments of State, Treasury, Defense and Justice remain, but that all the other departments be consolidated into four: human resources, community development, natural resources, and economic development.

Let us look at what these would be.

First, a department dealing with the concerns of people — as individuals, as members of a family — a department focused on human needs.

Second, a department concerned with the community — rural communities and urban — and with all that it takes to make a community function as a community.

Third, a department concerned with our physical environment, and with the preservation and balanced use of those great natural resources on which our nation depends.

And, fourth, a department concerned with our prosperity — with our jobs, our businesses, and those many activities that keep our economy running smoothly and well.

It was further purposed that the "independent commissions" set up by Congress to "regulate" particular industries should be rationalized and transformed into administrative agencies of the executive branch.

All this confirms the trends that have been identified here in the changing roles and functions of the political authority. It was proposed that the independent commissions and the agencies designed to represent the interests and to render residual services to particular interest groups — alike creations of the era of ideological liberalism, designed to perform housekeeping functions — would vanish and be replaced by problem-oriented agencies with large functional responsibilities.

Certainly a major restructuring of the executive arm is required in order to bring organization into line with the radically changed roles and functions of government. And the Nixon administration is to be credited with a bold plan that has this objective in mind. Yet something is lacking. The proposal has a taxonomic rather than a functional character; i.e., it groups together activities that share some common quality rather than activities that bear upon the development and control of integral, functional systems. Thus, I would prefer the formation of a Department of Health that could undertake to plan and organize an increased output of doctors and medical assistants, the reform of medical education and the expansion of medical facilities, the deployment of doctors and medical facilities, the control of medical costs, the administration of medical aid to the needy, the determination of research priorities and the support of medical research, and the development of an effective system of disease prevention. I would favor, too, a Department of Transportation with responsibility for the railroads, airlines, roads and highways, mass transit facilities, and the organization and performance of an integral, national transportation system. A Department of Education and Science would include the function of the National Science Foundation and would be answerable for educational performance in the schools and universities; would organize a National University of the Air to promote preschool, extra academic, and post-graduate, continuous professional education; and would supply schools and universities with screened programs of a quality that could only be obtained from a national center. A Department of Energy, absorbing the functions of the Federal Power Commission and the relevant activities of the Atomic Energy Commission and of the Department of the Interior, would have the specific responsibility of researching, rationalizing, and promoting the continuous development of energy resources and energy transmission as an integral national energy system. A Department of Communication, displacing the Federal Communication Commission, would have the great task of developing the electronic transmission and processing of information as a national utility, promoting its marvelous potentials and protecting against its awesome dangers. A Department of Industries, replacing the Federal Trade Commission and the Antitrust Division of the Department of Justice, would be concerned with productivity and price and would have the task of monitoring and upgrading industry performance through manpower training, antimonopoly injunction, sponsored R&D, the support of technological transformation, and wage-price control for the organizational sector.

PLANNING AND PROGRAMMING WITHIN THE POLITICAL ECONOMY

Aside from this dialectic of tasks that drew the political authority into a position of responsibility for and a more complete and complex involvement with the private sector and the market economy, planning and programming of great significance and complexity have developed *within* the political economy that is parallel to rather than intermeshing with the market economy. In part this has been a response to war and to the cold war, where a new category of science-based weaponry has become prerequisite to power.

Technology has always been critically related to military power but before World War I, and for the most part before World War II, those avenues of technological advance most significant for war were so intertwined with and so largely identical to those of peace that industrial productivity generated in the civilian market was the direct reciprocal of military power. From the wars of Napoleon until World War II, the capacity to transport and deploy large armies rapidly by land, sea, and air— and to feed, clothe, and supply those armies—was decisive. The nation with these capabilities in peace, ipso facto could use them as well in war. It was certainly not the quality of the military elite, the ferocity of its soldiers, nor the superior design of its armaments, but rather the capacity to produce great quantities of steel and other metals; to produce vehicles and other motorized equipment; to gauge precisely and to mass produce standard engine parts; to produce great food surpluses; hence, to feed, equip, transport, and maintain great armies; that made the United States a dominant military power.

By the end of World War II there had emerged a new category of weaponry of an incredibly destructive force that belonged to a universe of technological capabilities quite different than those in the market economy. This force was of another order than that which could be expected to evolve through the competition of consumer-oriented enterprise. Such technology had to be developed through the plans and programs of the political authority. This sometimes required the development of a new science base, new educational facilities, and the training of specialists, scientists, engineers, and managers equipped with the appropriate new body of knowledge and skills; as well as the research, development, testing, production, and systematic deployment of complex outputs. And in this regard the political economy has inaugurated new fields of academic science; promoted the establishment in academia of new schools and departments, research areas, and education programs geared to its needs; has established numerous information centers and networks; and has employed off and on, directly and indirectly, some two thirds of all the trained scientists and research engineers in the United States.

Inasmuch as the political economy acquired the capacity to organize complex economic activity for public purposes, that capability will be used to achieve goals that are other than strategic. During this decade the great achievements of space exploration are the best example of this.

Three agencies have been most directly engaged in the planning-programming-management function of the political economy: namely, the Department of Defense, the Atomic Energy Commission (AEC), and the National Aeronautics and Space Administration (NASA). Of these, NASA is the most recent and the most rationally organized, being the least encumbered by an archaic and incongruous tradition and the nearest to a "pure" instrument for planning, programming, and managing virtually any technologically complex activity in pursuit of a public goal. It would have been, for example, uniquely well-equipped to plan and organize the development of electronic transmission and processing of information as a national utility. It could have been transformed into the technical arm of a Department of Communications. It might have been used to explore and to evaluate alternative avenues of research for the development of energy sources, and itself could have engaged in such research. James Webb, its former head, asked that NASA be developed as just such an all-purpose technical agency. The random debilitation of that agency and the dissipation of its competence — and not only of NASA but of a vast complex of organized talents constituting the aerospace industry, which could have been turned to vital public purposes — demonstrates that no matter how rational and sophisticated the planning and programming of specific projects might be, that competence has not infiltrated the policy making process, nor is there any planning and programming of the use of the critical organizational and manpower resources available to or utilized by the political economy.

Planning and programming in the American political economy in no sense implies a kind of centralized national plan, either for the economy as a whole or for those activities that fall within the bounds of the political economy. There has been no explicit or implicit determination of national goals and priorities. Nor has there been any attempt rationally to allocate any category of resource. Government agencies plan and program much as the large private corporation does. Both, perforce, operate through sequential choice and piecemeal decision in response to the uncontrolled action and autonomous choice of numerous governmental, corporate, and other agencies. Nevertheless, there have been advances in the planning-programming competence.

PPBS

As an example of the technologies of choice and implementation developed in relation to the planning-programming function, consider the so-called "Planning, Programming, Budgeting Systems" (PPBS).[2] This technology of choice, evaluation, and control was developed in special circumstances by the Pentagon and any evaluation of PPBS should be made by reference to that particular context.

Each of the three services — Army, Navy, and Air Force — bases itself on an ideology and a way of life inextricably related to a particular weapons technology. Each struggles to survive or grow, hence, to perpetuate and to increase the relative importance of its own weapons technology and the skills and strategies deriving from it. In the postwar decades that interservice rivalry became more intense, as a highly fluid and rapidly advancing military technology and the explosive new war potential of scientific research put traditional organization and traditional weaponry in jeopardy. These developments introduced basic uncertainties as to the relative position, function, and ultimate survival of the service arms and their constituent parts.

Hence, the three services engaged in their own cold war. With the ferocity of those who feel that their corporate survival is at stake, they advocated and fought for alternative and conflicting avenues of R&D investment and weaponry development. And there was no established competence capable of rationally evaluating and choosing among their conflicting claims by reference to a more general criterion of national power. To develop that capability it was first necessary to subordinate the three

---

[2]For additional information on PPBS, see publications of the hearings before the Subcommittee on National Security and International Operations, Committee on Government Operations, U.S. Senate, 90th Congress, 1st and 2d sessions, 1967–1968.

services to an authority that shouldered the general responsibility for the development and deployment of military power. That was done or at least substantially advanced under the stewardship of Robert McNamara as Secretary of Defense. It was under McNamara that the new PPBS technology of evaluation, choice, and control was installed. It involved:

1. The development of a new group of experts drawn in part from RAND and other bodies of captive academics, who would sit with or in proxy for the Secretary of Defense in evaluating and choosing among the alternative proposals that emanated from and were sponsored by the three military services; and
2. The formalization and institutionalization of advocacy procedures intended to facilitate the presentation of alternative proposals in terms that would permit an objective comparison of plans and projects, with long- and short-term implications fully specified.

The Pentagon PPBS brought within the range of consideration only those alternatives promoted by the services in the light of their particular and partisan interests. Hence, the system provides no way of doing more than extending and developing already entrenched technologies. PPBS was, nevertheless, a considerable advance over the blind composite choice that preceded it.

During the last years of the Johnson administration, PPBS became the "in thing" in Washington. In March, 1967, a Presidential order required that it be installed in every department and agency of the federal government.[3] By 1968 its luminosity had diminished, and during the Nixon administration the star was in rapid decline. It will no doubt rise again.

But consider what Johnson's Budget Bureau had in mind. In 1968 selected agencies were required to submit a *Program Memorandum* describing the issues that were involved in their choice, the projects chosen, the programs planned, and the alternatives that had been considered; citing the cost-effectiveness studies on which choice had been based. In addition, the agencies were required to submit *Analytic Studies* constituting a record of the detailed analysis of alternatives and other

---

[3]The President's Message to Congress, "The Quality of American Government" (March 17, 1967).

information relevant to choice. Finally, the agencies were required to present *Program and Financial Plans*, comprehensively summarizing anticipated costs of each of the projects or programs that they asked to be funded and the anticipated benefits for the budget year and for four years thereafter.

Thus, it was hoped that under the surveillance of the Budget Bureau the following would happen:

1. A systematic search for and a continuous opportunity to present project and program alternatives would be built into the process of choice and planning.
2. The choice among these alternatives would be based on the study of, and would in a significant way reflect, the considered comparison of the costs and benefits imputable to these alternatives.
3. A precise and unequivocal statement of expected costs and anticipated benefits would permit a higher authority subsequently to measure promise against performance and, thereby, to evaluate the judgment of those who made the choice and the competence of those who implemented it.
4. Congress and the higher political authorities would have a clearer and more concrete idea of what the alternatives were and what choice implied not only for the single year when the funds were appropriated, as has been customary in budgetary practice, but for the whole period of cost commitment and anticipated benefit.

This is what the PPBS is (or might be); consider what it is not (and cannot be).

1. PPBS does not generate policy goals nor determine priorities.
2. The Pentagon technique is not applicable where there does not exist intraagency rivalries that find their normal expression in the advocacy of alternative projects and programs. Where such rivalries do not exist, then some other motivating force must be built into the system to insure a genuine search for alternatives. Otherwise, the alternatives considered will be straw men, raised up only to be shot down in pro forma justification of habituated activities.

   Nor is there any assurance that such rivalries as do exist will serve to bring all or the most significant alternatives into the scope of the consideration.

   It is possible and it would be desirable to build into any agency a search function committed to the search for and the promotion of innovationary alternatives. If this could be done successfully, it would go beyond the achievement of Pentagon-style PPBS.

3. Nor is the PPBS appropriate for budgeting the reiterative activities of the housekeeping function. Is it not of any relevance where the agency has an offset task, with expenditures made sporadically in point-counterpoint response to whatever develops in the market system?

Whatever its practical significance, PPBS manifests an ideological transformation. It expresses a new consciousness of the need for foresightful, time-extended choice; i.e., for planning and for the systematic evaluation of plans and programs as a continuing process of the political economy.

Individuals are shaped by a self-image. So are institutions and public agencies. In the view that prevailed before World War II (one that is not yet dead) it was considered unnatural, even downright dangerous and subversive, for a government agency to be efficient and progressive. Efficiency and progressiveness were the qualities of private enterprise *not* of government. An efficient, progressive, creative public agency was looked upon as a threat, a wickedness to be eradicated by the right thinking. The TVA, for example, with unblemished credentials for performance, innovation, and organization, developed the backward agriculture in the Tennessee Valley; provided the power base for an industrial expansion of great magnitude; and by its example reduced power rates throughout the country. But TVA was born a few decades before its time. It was not supported by the public at large. Instead of trying to preserve and accelerate its creative momentum, successive Congresses and administrations attacked, subverted, and harrassed that poor harbinger of "creeping socialism" until it diminished into a routine bureaucracy that feared its business betters and was without drive or ambition, but was "safe." A public agency will be, indeed can be, efficient and progressive only if efficiency and progressiveness are internalized as goals by which it judges and is judged.

In an earlier era the agencies of government were operated in the mode of the "traditional" economy. Once a workable mode of operation was crystallized, it was fossilized by authoritative regulation. Thenceforth, the operation ran "by the book." The purpose of the book was to insure order, regularity, equity, and stability; to constrain arbitrary power; and to check corruption. These are all permissible values, but creative change was not among them. When the organization runs by the book the highest positions, those of nominal leadership and fundamental choice (since there can be no real leadership or fundamental choice), become functionless, honorific, decorative, and exploitative. Hence, quite reasonably, the highest positions in the most complex of public agencies (the post office, for example) were considered as plums to be passed out among the citizenry as rewards for political services entirely without relation to operating skill, organizational knowledge, managerial capacity, or any capability for performance whatsoever. That was how the agencies of government were run because, given the prevailing ideology, that was how they were expected to be run. But things are changing now, even down at the old post office!

INDEX

Transportation Act of 1920, 338
triple damages, under Sherman and Clayton Acts, 201
trusts, good, 121; steel, 93
tube trust, 93
TVA, see Tennessee Valley Authority
tying contracts, 114
Tyson v. *Banton*, 157

U

UHF wavelengths, 355
unfair trade practices, 113
United Shoe Machinery Corporation, Department of Justice attack on, 224
U.S. v. *Aluminum Company of America*, 215, 265; v. *American Can Company*, 122; v. *American Tobacco Company*, 120; v. *Bethlehem Steel Corporation*, 261; v. *Borden Company*, 199; v. *Butler*, 160; v. *Continental Can Company*, 263; v. *Darby Lumber Company*, 160; v. *Doremus*, 77; v. *E. C. Knight Company*, 96; v. *E. I. du Pont de Nemours and Co.*, 233; v. *E. I. du Pont de Nemours and Co., et al.*, 261; v. *El Paso Natural Gas Company*, 265; v. *General Electric Company*, 114, 205; v. *General Motors Corporation*, 276; v. *Griffith Amusement Company*, 212; v. *International Harvester*, 124; v. *Joint Traffic Association*, 104; v. *Lehigh Valley Railroad Co.*, 117, 125; v. *Line Material Company*, 204; v. *National Lead Company*, 205; v. *New York Great A&P Tea Co.*, 113; v. *Paramount Pictures, Inc.*, 212; v. *Penn-Olin Chemical Co., et al.*, 264; v. *Philadelphia National Bank*, 261; v. *Reading Company*, 117, 125; v. *Richfield Oil Corporation*, 209; v. *Rock Royal Cooperative*, 158; v. *Singer Manufacturing Co.*, 204; v. *Socony-Vacuum Oil Co.*, 104, 194; v. *Southern Pacific Company*, 125; v. *Steel Corporation*, 93; v. *Terminal Railroad Association*, 125; v. *Trans Missouri Freight Association*, 104; v. *Trenton Potteries Company*, 104; v. *Union Pacific Railroad Company*, 125; v. *United Shoe Machinery Company*, 224; v. *United States Gypsum Co.*, 204; v. *United States Steel Corporation*, 122; v. *Von's Grocery Company*, 262; v. *Western Electric Company*, 352; v. *Yellow Cab Company*, 276, 281

V

Valuation Act of 1913, 337
Van Camp v. *American Can Co.*, 118
vertical integration, 117; as market leverage, 212
vertical mergers, 269

W

Wabash, St. Louis and Pacific Railway Company v. *Illinois*, 336
wage-price control, 295, 397
wages, minimum, Supreme Court on, 79
Wallace, George, 357
war, and ideology, 165
War of Independence, 33; and American state, 38
Webb, James, 404
Wein, Harold, 327
Western Electric Company, 350
Wheeler-Lea Act, 99
Whitney, Simon N., 182, 213
Wickard v. *Filburn*, 152, 160
Wiesner, Jerome, 306
Wilcox, Clair, 183
Williams v. *Standard Oil Company*, 157
Wisconsin v. *FPC*, 236
Wolff Packing Company v. *Court of Industrial Relations*, 157
work week, maximum, Supreme Court rulings on, 78